SHULAMIT AND MARGARETE

STUDIES IN CENTRAL EUROPEAN HISTORIES

VOLUME 32

Editors

THOMAS A. BRADY, JR.
ROGER CHICKERING

SHULAMIT AND MARGARETE

Power, Gender, and Religion in a Rural Society

in Eighteenth-Century Europe

CLAUDIA ULBRICH

TRANSLATED BY

THOMAS DUNLAP

BRILL ACADEMIC PUBLISHERS, INC.

BOSTON • LEIDEN

2004

Library of Congress Cataloging-in-Publication Data

Ulbrich, Claudia.
   [Shulamit und Margarete. English]
   Shulamith and Margarete : power, gender, and religion in a rural society in
eighteenth-century Europe / by Claudia Ulbrich ; translated by Thomas Dunlap.
      p. cm. — (Studies in Central European histories)
   Includes bibliographical references and index.
      ISBN 0–391–04145–2
         1. Jewish women—Germany—Social conditions. 2. Jewish women—Germany—
History. 3. Jews—Germany—History—1096–1800. 4. Judaism—Relations—Christianity.
I. Title. II. Series.

DS135.G33U4313 2004
305.48'8924043'09033—dc22

                                                                        2003069595

This edition is an authorized translation of *Shulamit und Margarete: Macht, Geschlecht
und Religion in einer ländlichen Gesellschaft des 18. Jahrhunderts* (Aschkenas. Zeitschrift
für Kultur der Juden; Beihelft 4) © 1999 Böhlau Verlag, GmbH, Vienna, Cologne.

The publication of this work was subsidized by a grant from
GOETHE-INSTITUT INTER NATIONES, Bonn.

ISSN: 1547–1217
ISBN: 0–391–04145–2

CONTENTS

ILLUSTRATIONS

PREFACE TO THE ENGLISH EDITION

This book has a long history. When I began working on this topic in 1985, my scholarly interests were focused on the historical meaning of borders and boundaries. Since I believed it was not appropriate to limit the concept of borders merely to the sphere of politics or language and culture, my analysis came to include the question of the anthropological dimension of borders and boundaries. With this approach, boundaries between inside and outside, between purity and pollution came into view. This paved a way to women's and gender history as well as Jewish history. The interlinking of two scholarly disciplines for which the analysis of power relationships is a central theme opened up a fascinating field of research. What emerged along with the question about the meaning of hierarchy and inequality in an estate-based society was the question about spheres of agency and worlds of experience, about the drawing of inclusive and exclusionary boundaries and the relationships that cut across them.

An initial version of this text was submitted as a *Habilitation* thesis at the Ruhr University in Bochum in 1994. It was subsequently revised for the German edition, which was published in 1999. Although a number of studies on women's history, gender history, and Jewish history have appeared over the last few years, I resisted the temptation to revisit the sources, in the full understanding that historical scholarship has no finality but is an open-ended process. I therefore made only minor changes for the English edition. A footnote at the beginning of chapter 5 lists some recent works on the history of Jewish daily life. Some changes were made to the maps and illustrations. I was able to include the portraits of two of the protagonists of this book, Frommet Ausser Levy and Bernard Lipman, which Bernard Lyon-Caen, a descendant of the Lipmans, kindly made available to me.

The translation of the sources, especially of Abraham Jacob's will included in an appendix, was extraordinarily difficult. Thomas Dunlap tackled this challenge with considerable skill. I hope that the English version of the testament, its inherent difficulties notwithstanding, will stimulate further research on this important genre of sources. As for the many new studies on women's history and gender history, they have tended to confirm and expand my approach, rather than correct it. It is my hope that all these scholarly efforts will make it possible, in the near future, to replace the history of separate spheres of life with new narratives.

Although some reviewers raised critical questions about the title of the original German, *Shulamit und Margarete*, I have decided to retain it for the English translation. Ever since Paul Celan's poem "Death Fugue," which he wrote in response to the Holocaust, these two women's names stand for their respective cultures. Shulamit had already assumed that role at the beginning of the nineteenth century, at the latest. To the publishers of the journal of the same name, which first appeared in 1806, the German Shulamit [Hebrew "shalom," meaning "peace"] was the great woman of peace, embodying "more than usual female intelligence, more than common female courage, and yet only a woman." This male description is an apt image of the field of tension with which the present book deals. The names point to projections of femaleness and thus to those gender-constructing processes that contribute to the preservation of inequality. At the same time, the two women's names stand for the book's methodological approach: it starts from the richly preserved material of names, reconstructs women's lives and networks of relationships, and explores from this basis larger historical contexts.

This book is based on much prior work in many disciplines, only some of which could be listed in the references. But without my colleagues and friends, it would have hardly been possible to complete this project. I owe a special debt of gratitude to Andrea Griesebner, Michaela Hohkamp, Gertrud Hüwelmeier, Gabriele Jancke, Gertrude Langner-Ostrawsky, Martin Leutzsch, Veronica Springmann, and Gadi Algazi. Jacov Guggenheim encouraged me to undertake the chapter on Jewish history and read the initial draft with a critical eye. I am indebted to the staff of the libraries and archives I consulted, especially M. Gilbert Cahen. Lastly, I would like to thank Tom Brady, Roger Chickering, and Patrick Alexander of Brill for making this English edition possible.

Berlin, October 3, 2003

CHAPTER ONE

INTRODUCTION

This book tells the life stories of Christian and Jewish women who lived in the eighteenth century in Steinbiedersdorf, a small village southeast of Metz on the border between Germany and France.[1] The process of reconstructing these biographies moves women's lives from the margins of historical sources to the center, offering a new vantage point from which to discuss the interconnected issues of power, gender, and religion.[2] This investigation into the gender-order and its underlying symbolic systems within a rural society in early modern Europe was also motivated by a desire to deepen our understanding of what "gender" meant in an estate-based society. I view gender relations not as private or individual phenomena, but as socially and culturally constituted and endowed with the power to shape the structure of political domination, economic life, and culture.[3] The issue, therefore, is not whether, but how we can describe the relationship between gender and society and relate it to concepts of power and domination.[4]

Until recently there were no systematic studies on the nature of gender relations and their symbolic implications within estate-based society. Nearly two decades ago, Norbert Elias, reflecting on the "changing balance of power between

---

[1] Important impulses for my approach came from a study of Carola Lipp, "Überlegungen zur Methodendiskussion. Kulturanthropologische, sozial-wissenschaftliche und historische Ansätze zur Erforschung der Geschlechterbeziehung," in *Frauenforschung—Frauenalltag. Beiträge zur 2. Tagung der Kommission Frauenforschung in der deutschen Gesellschaft für Volkskunde. Freiburg, 22.–25. Mai 1986* (Frankfurt a. M., 1988), 29–46, and Gianna Pomata, "Partikulargeschichte und Universalgeschichte—Bemerkungen zu einigen Handbüchern der Frauengeschichte," *L'Homme. ZFG* 2, no. 1 (1991): 5–44.

[2] For the methodological approach see Lila Abu-Lughod, *Writing Women's Worlds. Bedouin Stories* (Berkeley, 1993), 1ff. In a critical engagement with the concept of culture, which "in anthropological discourse has the effect of giving force to demarcations that invariably entail a kind of hierarchy," she pleads for "ethnographies of the particular": "Gegen Kultur Schreiben," in Ilse Lenz and Andrea Germer, eds., *Wechselnde Blicke. Frauenforschung in internationaler Perspektive* (Opladen, 1996), 14–46; here, 15 and 29.

[3] Gisela Bock, "Geschichte, Geschlechtergeschichte, Frauengeschichte." *GG* 14, no. 3 (1988): 364–391; Joan W. Scott, "Gender. A Useful Category of Historical Analysis," *American Historical Review* 91 (1986): 1053–1075.

[4] For a conceptualization of gender, power, and lordship, see Michaela Hohkamp, "Macht, Herrschaft und Geschlecht. Ein Plädoyer zur Erforschung von Gewaltverhältnissen in der Frühen Neuzeit," *L'Homme. ZFG* 7, no. 2 (1996): 8–17.

men and women," pointed out that the history of gender relations is not a linear development.[5] More recently, Heide Wunder has argued that the category of gender "did not have the universal structuring force in estate-based society that it had in bourgeois society of the nineteenth century." But even if she is right, it still leaves the question what conceptions of gender existed and how they affected economic life, politics, and culture.[6] After all, individuals were categorized according to sex even in estate-based societies. Barbara Vogel and Ulrike Weckel have emphasized that "gender identity shaped the day-to-day experience of men and women as one factor among many determining a person's social place . . . that is to say, the differences between gender groups and within a given gender group were taken for granted."[7]

As we know from the work of historical sociologists like Max Weber and Norbert Elias, membership in a particular estate imposed the obligation to adopt specific ways of life. But such membership was not immutable. Upward and downward mobility was possible even within the order of estates, and substantial hierarchies and distinctions existed within the estates themselves. That is also true of the "estate of . . . men and women."[8] Neither estate nor gender was determined a priori by biology; rather, both were the result of complex processes of ascription. If one wishes to understand these very processes, it is essential not to accept sociocultural entities as a given, be they estates or binary gender groups, but to incorporate into one's analysis the reciprocal, interactive way in which these entities are constructed.[9]

Until now, the scope of women's agency and the world of women's experiences in Europe's preindustrial, rural society have been systematically studied

---

[5] Norbert Elias, "Wandlungen der Machtbalance zwischen den Geschlechtern. Eine prozeßsoziologische Untersuchung am Beispiel des antiken Römerstaats," *Kölner Zeitschrift für Soziologie und Sozialpsychologie* 38 (1986): 425–449.

[6] Heide Wunder, *"He is the Sun, She is the Moon." Women in Early Modern Germany,* trans. Thomas Dunlap (Cambridge, Mass., 1998), 205.

[7] Barbara Vogel and Ulrike Weckel, "Foreword" in their *Frauen in der Ständegesellschaft. Leben und Arbeiten in der Stadt vom spätem Mittelalter biz zur Neuzeit* (Hamburg, 1991), 7–26, here 9.

[8] "Stand" ("Estate"), in Johann Heinrich Zedler, *Universallexikon,* vol. 39 (Halle, Leipzig, 1744), cols. 1093–1103. In addition to the main estates of teaching, soldiery, and food production, Zedler distinguishes the nobility, burghers, peasants; the learned (clergy, lawyers, doctors) and the unlearned; soldiers, merchants, artisans; and young and old men and women.

[9] On the concept of "doing gender" see, especially, Candace West and Don H. Zimmermann, "Doing Gender," in Judith Lorber and Susan A. Farell, eds., *The Social Construction of Gender* (Newbury Park, Calif., 1991), 13–37, and Regine Gildemeister and Angelika Wetterer, "Wie Geschlechter gemacht werden. Die soziale Konstruktion der Zweigeschlechtlichkeit und ihre Reifizierung in der Frauenforschung," in Gudrun-Axeli Knapp and Angelika Wetterer, eds., *Traditionen Brüche. Entwicklungen feministischer Theorie* (Freiburg, 1992), 201–254. For the scholarly reception of this concept and criticism see Andrea Maihofer, *Geschlecht als Existenzweise. Macht, Moral, Recht und Geschlechterdifferenz* (Frankfurt a. M., 1995), 63ff.

primarily within the context of work, while other areas have been largely neglected.[10] There are a number of reasons for this. For a long time, the epistemological interests of historical social scientists (à la Hans-Ulrich Wehler) and their concepts of culture (à la Max Weber) steered the interest of historians in a different direction. The prevailing assumption that "individuals and groups everywhere are determined by supraindividual power structures"[11] seemed to justify the decision to focus not on individuals, but on structures and processes.[12] Scholars were looking for "dynamic centers of movement," which they hoped would provide the starting point for uncovering "other dimensions of society."[13] That hope soon turned out to have been misplaced.

After all, what precisely was a "dynamic center of movement"? What Hans Medick has called the "centrist perspective" decided what was relevant and historically meaningful, thereby predetermining some of the results of the historical inquiry.[14] Depending on the kind of knowledge that scholars were pursuing, certain thematic clusters were seen as fairly central, others as rather marginal.

---

[10] See especially Michael Mitterauer, "Geschlechtsspezifische Arbeitsteilung," in his *Familie und Arbeitsteilung. Historisch vergleichende Studien* (Vienna, 1992), 58–148; Heide Wunder, "'Jede Arbeit ist ihres Lohnes wert.' Zur geschlechtsspezifischen Teilung und Bewertung von Arbeit in der Frühen Neuzeit," in Karin Hausen, ed., *Geschlechterhierarchie und Arbeitsteilung. Zur Geschichte ungleicher Erwerbschancen von Männern und Frauen* (Göttingen, 1993), 19–39; Martine Segalen, "Aufgaben und Rollenverteilung bei Männern und Frauen im ländlichen Milieu des 19. und 20. Jahrhunderts: Frankreich und die Gesellschaften des Mittelmeerraums," in Jochen Martin and Renate Zoepffel, eds., *Aufgaben, Rollen und Räume von Frau und Mann* (Freiburg/Br., 1989), 915–936. On the relationship between work and property see David W. Sabean, "'Young bees in an empty hive: relations between brothers-in-law in a South German village around 1800," in Hans Medick and David W. Sabean, eds., *Interest and Emotion: Essays on the Study of Family and Kinship* (Cambridge, 1984), 171–186. By now the thematic spectrum has broadened. Alongside the "traditional" topic of witchcraft, increasing interest has been directed at honor, sexuality, mobility, and criminality. On these themes see, among others, the anthologies by Gisela Bock, ed., *Lebenswege von Frauen im Ancien Régime.* Geschichte und Gesellschaft 18, no. 4 (Göttingen, 1992); Otto Ulbricht, ed., *Von Huren und Rabenmüttern. Weibliche Kriminalität in der Frühen Neuzeit* (Cologne, 1995); Heide Wunder and Christina Vanja, eds., *Weiber, Menscher, Frauenzimmer. Frauen in der ländlichen Gesellschaft 1500–1800* (Göttingen, 1996).

[11] Hans-Ulrich Wehler, "Alltagsgeschichte: Königsweg zu neuen Ufern oder Irrgarten der Illusionen?," in his *Aus der Geschichte lernen?* (Munich, 1988), 130–151, here 142; "Was ist Gesellschaftsgeschichte?," ibid., 115–129, esp. 119.

[12] The subject has now returned to history through the roundabout way of the history of mentalities and the history of daily life. Carola Lipp, "Alltagskulturforschung im Grenzbereich von Volkskunde, Soziologie und Geschichte. Aufstieg und Niedergang eines interdisziplinären Forschungskonzepts," *Zeitschrift für Volkskunde* 89, no. 1 (1993): 1–33.

[13] Wehler, "Was ist Gesellschaftsgeschichte?," 120.

[14] Hans Medick, "Entlegene Geschichte? Sozialgeschichte und Mikro-Historie im Blickfeld der Kulturanthropologie," in Joachim Matthes, ed., *Zwischen den Kulturen? Die Sozialwissenschaften vor dem Problem des Kulturvergleichs.* Soziale Welt, Sonderband 8 (Göttingen, 1992), 167–178, here 167f.

This approach allowed Hans-Ulrich Wehler to exclude women's spaces from his social history,[15] even though he considered the structure of social inequality—defined as the "varied distribution of opportunities and risks"—a central axis in the system and called it "one of the basic experiences of social life."[16] To make his argument consistent, Wehler defined gender as an "anthropological universal of social hierarchies," which meant that one could exclude it from the historical synthesis without having to address the deficiencies of scholarship or open the door to further inquiries. Which brings us to another aspect that led to the neglect of the topic: the connection between personal experience, the specific kind of knowledge that was (or was not) being pursued, and the traditions of historical scholarship.

In the 1960s and 1970s, a time when women's roles were being profoundly transformed, historians' perception of the places that women occupied in society was rather static. Nonscholarly concerns and personal experiences undoubtedly played a role in this: after all, the crisis of the family has been one of the most intensely debated social transformations during the past few decades, one that few individuals have been able to escape. Critics have focused on the decline of family values and processes of disintegration and individualization—processes that, at least at first glance, appeared to be causally connected with the changes taking place in women's lives and their demands for self-realization.[17]

The yearnings and expectations that the contemporary family was less and less able to fulfill were—and still are—projected back into the preindustrial past. Surprisingly enough, women historians did not object vociferously to this projection. On the contrary: the debate over patriarchy, which was carried on with great intensity especially in the field of women's studies and was motivated by very different concerns, was apt to reinforce the notion of an ironclad gender order. As a result, the picture of the "good old family" was able to take root.

This picture was hardly painted on the basis of the historical realities of a given period; instead, it was constructed as a mirror image of contemporary fears and experiences of familial shortcomings.[18] It assigned women an unam-

---

[15] As early as 1984, at the annual meeting of historians, Karin Hausen raised the theme of "women's spaces" ("Frauenräume") and warned against hasty abstractions and mental templates that assign women specific spaces (patriarchy, private-public): "Frauenräume," in Karin Hausen and Heide Wunder, eds., *Frauengeschichte—Geschlechtergeschichte* (Frankfurt a. M., 1992), 21–24.

[16] Hans-Ulrich Wehler, *Deutsche Gesellschaftsgeschichte*, vol. 1: Vom Feudalismus des alten Reiches bis zur defensiven Modernisierung der Reformära: 1700–1815 (Munich, 1987), 125.

[17] Ulrich Beck and Elisabeth Beck-Gernsheim, *The Normal Chaos of Love*, transl. Mark Ritter and Jane Wiebel (Cambridge, UK, 1995).

[18] Jack Goody, *The Development of the Family and Marriage in Europe* (Cambridge, 1983), 2ff.; Martine Segalen, *Historical Anthropology of the Family*, transl. J. C. Whitehouse and Sarah Matthews (Cambridge, 1986), 260ff.; Michael Mitterauer and Reinhard Siedler,

biguous place. In the meantime, however, the concept of patriarchy has lost its central importance in the scholarly effort to unmask gender relationships.[19] Simultaneously, many presuppositions about the family have been exposed as clichés. Over the last twenty-five years, women sociologists, anthropologists, and historians have helped to deconstruct the notion of the traditional family that provided order, stability, and security. They have replaced the monolithic picture of the "good old family" with more differentiated constructs that reveal the variety of family models and their dependence on economic, social, and cultural conditions.[20] This scholarly effort has allowed us to focus on the worlds of women's experiences and the scope of women's agency. Yet the traditional images have shown remarkable staying power, especially since they seemed to be backed by a long scholarly tradition that saw the patriarchally organized family as an unchanging, natural, and fundamental building block of society.

Notions about the family as the natural place for women continue to shape our view of the past and the questions we ask about it. The assumption that being a mother, a wife, and a homemaker is a woman's natural vocation[21] has

---

The European Family. Patriarchy to Partnership from the Middle Ages to the Present, transl. Karla Oosterveen and Manfred Hörzinger (Chicago, 1982), esp. 24ff., 71ff.

[19] An overview of the discussion is offered by Gudrun-Axeli Knapp, "Macht und Geschlecht. Neurere Entwicklungen in der feministischen Macht- und Herrschaftsdiskussion," in Knapp and Wetterer, eds., *Traditionen Brüche*, 287–321.

[20] See especially André Burguière and François Lebrun, "The One Hundred and One Families of Europe," in André Burguière et al., eds., *A History of the Family*, transl. Sarah Hanbury Tenison, Rosemary Morris, and Andrew Wilson (Cambridge, 1996), 11–94; Jürgen Schlumbohm, *Lebensläufe, Familien, Höfe. Die Bauern und Heuerleute des Osnabrückischen Kirchspiels Belm in proto-industrieller Zeit, 1650–1860.* Veröffentlichungen des Max-Planck-Instituts für Geschichte 110 (Göttingen, 1994), 191ff.; Jürgen Schlumbohm, "The Land-Family Bond in Peasant Practice and in Middle-Class Ideology: Evidence from the North-West German Parish of Belm, 1650–1860," *Central European History* 27 (1994): 461–478; idem, "Familie, Verwandtschaft und soziale Ungleichheit: Der Wandel in einer ländlichen Gesellschaft vom 17. zum 19. Jahrhundert," in Rudolf Vierhaus et al., eds, *Frühe Neuzeit—frühe Moderne? Forschungen zur Vielschichtigkeit von Übergangsprozessen.* Veröffentlichungen des Max-Planck-Instituts für Geschichte 104 (Göttingen, 1992), 133–156, here 134f. A path through the vast amount of research is charted by, among others, Hans Medick and David W. Sabean, "Interest and Emotion in Family and Kinship Studies: A Critique of Social History and Anthropology," in Medick and Sabean, *Interest and Emotion*, 9–27; Karin Hausen, "Familie und Familiengeschichte," in Wolfgang Schieder and Volker Sellin, eds., *Sozialgeschichte in Deutschland.* vol. 2 (Göttingen, 1986), 64–89; Hartmann Tyrell, "Soziologische Anmerkungen zur historischen Familienforschung (Literaturbericht)," GG 12 (1986): 254–273; and Winfried Freitag, "Haushalt und Familie in traditionalen Gesellschaften. Konzepte, Probleme und Perspektiven der Forschung," GG 14 (1988): 5–37.

[21] Heide Wunder has repeatedly criticized the fact that this assumption fails to consider the possibilities that images of women and women's roles could be conditioned by society and thus by history; see, e.g., "Einleitung" in Heide Wunder and Christina Vanja, eds., *Wandel der Geschlechterbeziehungen zu Beginn der Neuzeit* (Frankfurt a. M., 1991), 7. See also the critique of Hausen by Brita Rang, "Zur Geschichte des dualistischen

led us to shift our focus to the house whenever we look at the conditions of women's lives in "pre-emancipatory" societies.[22] In doing so we enter a structure whose foundation walls were erected in the nineteenth century.[23]

The central concept in German scholarship has been that of the "integral household" (das ganze Haus), which was formulated in the nineteenth century by Wilhelm Heinrich Riehl. Confronted by the upheavals of his time, the conservative cultural historian Riehl was searching for "forces of continuity,"[24] and he found them in the nobility and the peasantry. Riehl constructed the picture of a self-sufficient, self-supporting household governed by a patriarchal-authoritarian housefather. The order of the house presupposed the inequality of the genders, which, in keeping with the thinking of Riehl's day, was understood as a law of nature.[25]

Nineteenth-century ideas about the order of the genders, characterized by a "pathetic excess of difference and hierarchy,"[26] were faithfully reflected in the "integral household." The obvious contradictions between house and association (Genossenschaft), between house law and manorial law, could be bridged only with the help of ingenious intellectual constructs.[27] Within the concept

---

Denkens über Mann und Frau. Kritische Anmerkungen zu den Thesen von Karin Hausen zur Herausbildung der Geschlechtscharaktere im 18. und 19. Jahrhundert," in Jutta Dalhoff, Uschi Frey, and Ingrid Schöll, eds., *Frauenmacht in der Geschichte. Beiträge des Historikerinnentreffens 1985 zur Frauengeschichtsforschung.* Geschichtsdidaktik—Studien, Materialien 41 (Düsseldorf, 1986), 194–205.

[22] A symptomatic example is Richard van Dülmen, *Kultur und Alltag in der Frühen Neuzeit,* 3 vols. (Munich 1990–1994), who essentially addresses women's lives only within the context of the house.

[23] For a critical assessment of the ideology of the house and of the most important, traditional theoretical lines—Riehl/Brunner, Le Play/Bourdieu, Bücher/Chayanov, Le Play/Laslett—we are indebted to Michael Mitterauer, "The Myth of the Large Preindustrial Family," in Michael Mitterauer and Reinhard Sieder, *The European Family,* 24–47, and to David W. Sabean, *Property, Production, and Family in Neckarhausen, 1700–1870.* Cambridge Studies in Social and Cultural Anthropology 73 (Cambridge, 1990), 88ff.; and Schlumbohm, "Familie, Verwandtschaft," 134ff.

[24] Wilhelm Heinrich Riehl, *Die bürgerliche Gesellschaft,* edited and with an introduction by Peter Steinbach (Frankfurt a. M., 1976). On the bourgeois conceptualizations of the peasantry in the nineteenth century see Regina Schulte, *The Village in Court. Arson, Infanticide, and Poaching in the Court Records of Upper Bavaria, 1848–1910,* transl. Barrie Selman (Cambridge, 1994).

[25] Karin Hausen has examined the process by which gender characteristics were placed on a new foundation through biology and nature during the transition from the "integral household" to the bourgeois family: "'Geschlechtscharaktere'—Eine Spiegelung der Dissoziation von Erwerbs- und Familienleben," in Werner Conze, ed., *Sozialgeschichte der Familie in der Neuzeit Europas* (Stuttgart, 1976), 363–393.

[26] Claudia Honegger, *Die Ordnung der Geschlechter. Die Wissenschaften vom Menschen und das Weib. 1750–1850* (Frankfurt a. M., 1991), X.

[27] On the connection between farmstead and the "house-authority (Hausherrschaft) of the independent man" see Otto Gierke, *Deutsches Privatrecht,* vol. 1, (Munich, 1895), 578. The Genossenschaft ("association") was thought of as a union of "free men." For

of the "integral household," discipline, authority, and father-rule, along with autarchy and self-sufficiency, were singled out as a priori socially stabilizing factors that were historically legitimated and endowed with positive connotations.[28] The result was the creation of a legend that has persisted in German historiography to this day, influencing the articulation of scholarly questions and scholarly approaches. The responsibility for this legend can be attributed less to Riehl's direct influence as to Otto Brunner, who adopted the concept of the integral household and developed it further.

Otto Brunner, a renowned proponent of the "political folk history" of the 1930s whose work found wide reception into the structural and social history of the postwar period,[29] saw in the house "the fundamental social construction of all peasant and peasant-noble cultures."[30] Brunner's concept of the integral household, which is fixated on a hierarchical, disciplined, and largely harmonious communal life, systematically excluded women as historical subjects from the process of history. For millennia—according to Brunner from the Neolithic period all the way to the nineteenth century!—women, along with children and servants, were firmly enclosed within walls that obeyed the never-changing laws of the housefather's authority.[31] Although the house (if we accept Brunner's concept), "as the nucleus of all lordship,"[32] represented an order of lordship

---

a critique of the older association theory from the perspective of legal history see Karl Siegfried Bader, *Dorfgemeinschaft und Dorfgemeinde. Studien zur Rechtsgeschichte des mittelalterlichen Dorfes*, vol. 2, (Weimar, 1962), 3ff. Following Bader's reflections, it would be worthwhile to examine the notion of association from the perspective of gender history, since the notion of the "associate" (Genosse) was neither hierarchical nor gender-specific prior to being forced into a theoretical concept.

[28] Wilhelm Heinrich Riehl, *Die Naturgeschichte des Volkes als Grundlage einer deutschen Socialpolitik*, vol. 3: Die Familie (Stuttgart, 1855). M. Frédéric Le Play played a similarly important role in France as Riehl did in Germany: *L'organisation de la famille selon le vrai modèle signalé par l'histoire de toutes les races et de tous les temps* (Paris, 1871).

[29] Winfried Schulze has brought out Otto Brunner's importance in reformulating social history and the roots of his conception of a "political history of the folk" in National Socialist ideology: "Der Neubeginn der deutschen Geschichtswissenschaft nach 1945: Einsichten und Absichtserklärungen der Historiker nach der Katastrophe," in Ernst Schulin, ed., *Deutsche Geschichtswissenschaft nach dem Zweiten Weltkrieg (1945–1965).* Schriften des Historischen Kollegs 14 (Munich, 1989), 1–38. We are indebted to Gadi Algazi for an ideological placement of Otto Brunner and an astute analysis of his language and his "concrete order thinking": "'Konkrete Ordnung' und Sprache der Zeit," in Peter Schöttler, ed., *Geschichtsschreibung als Legitimationswissenschaft, 1918–1945* (Frankfurt a. M., 1997), 166–203.

[30] Otto Brunner, "Das 'Ganze Haus' und die alteuropäische 'Ökonomik,'" in his *Neue Wege der Verfassungs- und Sozialgeschichte*, 2nd ed. (Göttingen, 1968) 103–127; here 107.

[31] Ibid., 107, we read: "The peasantry, from its formation in the Neolithic all the way to the nineteenth century, formed the foundation of the European social structure, and its substance was, during these millennia, hardly touched by the structural change in the political forms of the upper class."

[32] Otto Brunner, *Land and Lordship: Structures of Governance in Medieval Austria*, transl. Howard Kaminsky and James Van Horn Melton (Philadelphia, 1992), 211. For

and as such should be an object of historical study, it became an ahistorical category by virtue of its static structure, a category that—like the family— could be excluded from history.

The Brunnerian house owed its success less to its analytic validity than to the fact that it provided a convenient formula to describe the structural transformation from the old European economy to the political economy of modernity (or from the estate-based society to bourgeois society) as part of the history of ideas—it was, in other words, an intellectual creation.[33] If the use of this conception is limited strictly to the realm of intellectual history, there is little to object to—provided its reception is accompanied by a critical analysis of its underlying ideology.[34] In practice, however, this distinction has not been maintained. Medievalists and early modernists have used the integral household as a master key that unlocks the most diverse historical contexts, for it seems to offer adequate answers to questions pertaining to constitutional, structural, social, and family history, even to cultural history and the history of everyday life.[35]

The term *house* had and has a variety of meanings. In the early modern period it described not only the physical building, but also the corresponding social form. The house was a locus for work and life secured by social and legal norms, and at the same time an integral element of a structure of lordship that in some rural regions shaped human relationships far into the twentieth cen-

---

a critique see Gadi Algazi, *Herrengewalt und Gewalt der Herren im späten Mittelalter. Herrschaft, Gegenseitigkeit und Sprachgebrauch* (Frankfurt a. M., 1996).

[33] Ute Frevert used this image of the "Kopfgeburt" (lit. "mind-birth") in her critical engagement with the concepts, experiences, and visions underlying the model of the "bourgeois society:" Ute Frevert, "Bürgerliche Meisterdenker und das Geschlechterverhältnis. Konzepte, Erfahrungen, Visionen an der Wende vom 18. zum 19. Jahrhundert," in her *Bürgerinnen und Bürger. Geschlechterverhältnisse im 19. Jahrhundert*, Kritische Studien zur Geschichtswissenschaft 77 (Göttingen, 1988), 17–48.

[34] Brunner's approach in the history of ideas was initially used to bring out what was new in the bourgeois family. On this see above all the programmatic essay by Karin Hausen on the dissociation of working life and family life (Hausen, "Polarisierung"). However, approaches aimed at differentiating the patriarchal household according to estates (peasant, bourgeois, noble households) or the organization of labor (artisanal household, protoindustrial household, civil servant or clerical households), are reductionist. An internal differentiation of peasant households, which differ structurally, has barely been undertaken to date.

[35] On family history: Freitag, "Haushalt," 20f.; on cultural history and the history of daily life: van Dülmen, *Das Haus* (Kultur und Alltag, vol. 1). Despite some modification, Dülmen's house resembles a Brunnerian room. It is hierarchically structured, static across centuries, and described as a model of harmony: as an ordered unit of life, a life order, a community of protection, living, and solidarity. Conflicts are not excluded, but they remain embedded within a system of social control, traditional values, and unquestioned norms. Autonomous spheres of action are opened up for women by their work, which van Dülmen in a very concrete sense thinks of as restricted to the house: "The value and tasks of women are restricted to the domestic sphere" (43).

tury. Household authority was accorded great importance not only in the law, but also in the language of administration and in political theory. Only the person who exercised household authority and represented the house externally to other housefathers was a fully enfranchised citizen. The preindustrial norm of the integral household was widely disseminated through the so-called housefather literature, although scholars have yet to document just how far its influence extended into practice. For in the absence of other sources, historians consistently describe conditions within the house by invoking the normative sources that created the concept of the caring, responsible housefather always concerned about control, at whose side stood the housemother entrusted with numerous tasks of her own.[36] The scholarly rediscovery of the housefather literature was the work of Otto Brunner, who made use of it in his interpretation of social change.[37]

The attractiveness of the integral household, which comes very close to the above-mentioned ideas about the "good old family," has something to do with the fact that scholars of the medieval and early modern period find it difficult to get a conceptual grip on the objects they study. Cultural anthropologists have been very explicit about how different and strange modernity is from earlier eras. In the process, they have been very clear that the concepts and terminology they work with differ sharply from the way we understand them today. By contrast, historians, with their interest in developments that have given shape to the present, are continually confronted with the problem of devising an adequate terminology, the absence of which creates a lack of clarity and misunderstandings. Since the term *Familie* in German is of relatively recent date (reaching back to the seventeenth and eighteenth centuries), the house, according to Dieter Schwab, forms "the terminological casing of the scholarly concept of the individual family."[38]

Scholars used the word *house*, a term drawn from the sources, to describe the social form we would today call the family, although it differs in crucial points from the modern family. The real dilemma lies in the overlap of partly

---

[36] On the ideal of the house mother in the "house father literature," see Claudia Opitz, "Hausmutter und Landesfürstin," in Rosarion Villari, ed., *Der Mensch des Barock* (Frankfurt a. M., 1997), 344–394. Gabriele Jancke has shown that we can also find very different conceptions of household in the early modern sources: "Publizistin—Pfarrfrau—Prophetin. Die Straßburger 'Kirchenmutter' Katharina Zell," in Peter Freybe, ed., *Frauen mischen sich ein. Wittenberger Sonntagsvorlesungen* (Wittenberg, 1995), 55–80; and idem, "Die Kirche als Haushalt und die Leistungsrolle der Kirchenmutter. Katharina Zells reformatorisches Kirchenkonzept," in Heide Wunder and Gisela Engel, eds., *Geschlechterperspektiven. Forschungen zur Frühen Neuzeit* (Königstein, 1998), 145–155.

[37] Gotthardt Frühsorge, "Die Begründung der 'väterlichen Gesellschaft' in der europäischen oeconomia christiana. Zur Rolle des Vaters in der 'Hausväterliteratur' des 16. bis 18. Jahrhunderts in Deutschland," in Hubertus Tellenbach, ed., *Das Vaterbild im Abendland*, vol. 1 (Stuttgart, 1978), 110–123, here 113.

[38] Dieter Schwab, "Familie," in *Geschichtliche Grundbegriffe*, vol. 2 (Stuttgart, 1975), 253–301, here 261f.

competing, partly identical meanings. The terms house and family, both part of the modern vocabulary, call forth different connotations, which influence the way we think of family, house, and political domination. The house as family and the house as the political order point to different reference systems that do not necessarily share the same interests, to orders of kinship, neighborliness, state, and church. Depending on the strength of kinship bonds and control, the house becomes a place of competing claims to power, which become visible only when the house is dissected into its individual components. That such an approach is necessary especially with regard to the history of women becomes clear when we seek to determine precisely the place of women within estate-based society: Margaret L. King described the place of Renaissance women as located "at the intersection of two lineages . . . belonging to none."[39]

The house of Riehl and Brunner, which systematically blocked access to an understanding of structural differences and historical changes, has long since developed cracks. After Hans-Ulrich Wehler devoted a (short) chapter to the "legend of the economically self-sufficient 'integral household'" in the first volume of his social history of Germany,[40] Irmintraut Richarz raised questions about the issue of authority within the house, questions Wehler had ignored. She urged scholars to address not only the family's power of persistence but also its potential for change:

> Legends like that of the economically self-sufficient and hierarchical "integral household," as idealizing but also tendentious representations of historical processes, are problematic; not least because they keep us from realizing that human beings in history are constantly challenged by changing living conditions, and that the real achievement we should recognize is not the clinging to a static economy and its social structure, but the constructive responses and reactions to changing social conditions.[41]

Winfried Schulze, reflecting on the change of norms within estate-based society, has criticized the concept of the integral household for its rigidity and lack of dynamism and has modified and expanded it in a way that is exceedingly helpful for the study of female spheres of life. He shows that, as early as the sixteenth century, we find a thinking that was oriented towards needs; this thinking had to be balanced against the social value of a fitting subsistence as long

---

[39] Margaret L. King, *Women of the Renaissance* (Chicago, 1991), 48.

[40] Wehler, *Deutsche Gesellschaftsgeschichte*, 81–83, in reference to Irmintraut Richarz, *Herrschaftliche Haushalte in vorindustrieller Zeit im Weserraum* (Berlin, 1971). Wehler limited his critique to one aspect of the "integral household," the market economy based on a division of labor, and did not question the concept as such.

[41] Irmintraut Richarz, "Das ökonomisch autarke 'Ganze Haus'—eine Legende?" in Trude Ehlert, ed., *Haushalt und Familie in Mittelalter und früher Neuzeit* (Sigmaringen, 1991), 269–280, here 279. See also the critical remarks on Brunner's concept in Irmintraut Richarz, *Oikos, Haus und Haushalt. Ursprung und Geschichte der Haushaltsökonomik* (Göttingen, 1991), 156f.

as the basic economic conditions offered only a very small latitude for change. In articulating the orientation towards needs, Schulze confronts Brunner's static and harmonious concept with one that was dynamic and conflict-oriented; given the growing "discrepancy between accepted rules of behavior and real life," it is a concept that must have been very important.[42]

During the last years, criticism has been directed not only at the model of the integral household, but also at its continuing popularity in more recent sociohistorical research. The integral household, an incomplete and highly ideological model, has become obsolete because it maps poorly the social and economic realities of the premodern world, fails to draw a clear line of distinction between the Aristotelian *oikos* and the "Old European economy," and harmonizes complicated power relationships.[43] A fruitful approach would be to draw on Anglo-American and French social history, the history of mentalities, and historical anthropology.[44]

German scholarship is having a difficult time doing that. With the exception of the debate over protoindustrialization,[45] scholars continue to describe the transition from estate-based society to bourgeois society as a shift from familial to state power, as the loss of function of the integral household in favor

---

[42] Winfried Schulze, *Vom Gemeinnutz zum Eigennutz. Über den Normenwandel in der ständischen Gesellschaft der Frühen Neuzeit.* Schriften des Historischen Kollegs, Vorträge 13 (Munich, 1987), 29. On the importance of the notion of needs in the early modern period, see Renate Blickle, "Nahrung und Eigentum als Kategorien in der ständischen Gesellschaft," in Winfried Schulze and Helmut Gabel, eds., *Ständische Gesellschaft und soziale Mobilität.* Schriften des Historischen Kollegs, Kolloquien 12 (Munich, 1988), 73–93; and Renate Blickle, "From Subsistence to Property: Traces of a Fundamental Change in Early Modern Bavaria," *Central European History* 25 (1992): 377–386

[43] On the critique and reception of the house model see Renate Blickle, "Hausnotdurft. Ein Fundamentalrecht in der altständischen Ordnung Bayerns," in Günter Birtsch, ed., *Grund- und Freiheitsrechte von der ständischen zur spätbürgerlichen Gesellschaft.* Veröffentlichungen zur Geschichte der Grund- und Freiheitsrechte 2 (Göttingen, 1987), 42–64, here 62; Werner Troßbach, "Das 'ganze Haus'—Basiskategorie für das Verständnis der ländlichen Gesellschaft deutscher Territorien in der Frühen Neuzeit?" *Blätter für deutsche Landesgeschichte* 129 (1993): 277–314; Claudia Opitz, "Neue Wege der Sozialgeschichte?—Ein kritischer Blick auf Brunners Konzept des 'ganzen Hauses,'" GG 20, vol. 1 (1994): 88–98; Valentin Groebner, "Außer Haus. Otto Brunner und die alteuropäische Ökonomik," GWU 46 (1995): 69–80; Hans Derks, "Über die Faszination des 'Ganzen Hauses,'" GG 22, vol. 2 (1996): 221–242.

[44] For the discussion within ethnology see Janet Carsten and Stephen Hugh-Jones, "Introduction," in Carsten and Hugh-Jones, eds., *About the House: Levi Strauss and Beyond* (Cambridge, 1995), 1–46.

[45] Peter Kriedte, Hans Medick, Jürgen Schlumbohm, *Industrialisierung vor der Industrialisierung. Gewerbliche Warenproduktion auf dem Land in der Formationsperiode des Kapitalismus* (Göttingen, 1977); idem, "Sozialgeschichte in der Erweiterung—Proto-Industrialisierung in der Verengung? Demographie, Sozialstruktur, moderne Hausindustrie: eine Zwischenbilanz der Proto-Industrialisierungsforschung," Part 1, GG 18, vol. 1 (1992): 70–87; Part 2, GG 18, vol. 2 (1992): 231–255.

of the state's usurpation of functions,[46] paying little or no attention to the dynamic that emanated from rural social stratification,[47] from individualization processes, or from the triadic relationship of kinship group, family, and state. There are few studies on family and kinship that address the topics of conflicts and strategies, that move beyond the given social entities of house and family, and in doing so create, from a conceptual point of view, the possibility of gaining insight into relationships in the house. As early as 1984, Hans Medick and David Sabean lamented the fact that few historians had "systematically examined historical sources to ask about the nature of individual and family *strategies* in placing family members, in political activity, in economic enterprise, or in emotional support or to ask about the *use* of kin in pursuing such strategies."[48] Except for a handful of microhistorical studies based on elaborate family reconstructions, the state of scholarship has hardly changed for the better in the intervening years.[49]

The house model has been expanded, however, by research that has placed special emphasis on the role of the housemother.[50] Heide Wunder, with her reflections on spouses as a working couple (focused chiefly on the urban artisan couple), has brought out not only the economic but also the political dimension of the early modern "housewife existence." Wunder emphasizes that the wife, in her role as housemother, was part of the political public, a sphere from which she was excluded only when bourgeois society established the separation between the political and the private. More important than the wife's duty of obedience was the mutual interdependence of husband and wife in marriage, which alone made possible a life of social independence and responsibility.[51]

By expanding the perspective to incorporate work, Wunder takes in numerous spheres of women's activities that transcend domestic work in the narrower sense. By focusing on marriage she alters the integral household in a central point: it was not the discipline and authority of a housefather that created the harmony and stability of the house, but the relationship of the spouses to each

---

[46] Paul Münch, *Lebensformen in der Frühen Neuzeit. 1500 bis 1800* (Frankfurt a. M., 1996), 216f.

[47] On this dynamic see Josef Mooser, *Ländliche Klassengesellschaft 1770–1848. Bauern und Unterschichten, Landwirtschaft und Gewerbe im östlichen Westfalen* (Göttingen, 1984).

[48] Medick and Sabean, *Interest and Emotion*, 49.

[49] David W. Sabean, *Kinship in Neckarhausen, 1700–1870* (Cambridge, 1998); idem, *Property*; Schlumbohm, *Lebensläufe*; Hans Medick, *Weben und Überleben in Laichingen 1650–1900. Lokalgeschichte als Allgemeine Geschichte.* 2nd ed. (Göttingen, 1997).

[50] Gotthardt Frühsorge, "Die Einheit aller Geschäfte. Tradition und Veränderung des 'Hausmutter'-Bildes in der deutschen Ökonomieliteratur des 18. Jahrhunderts," *Wolfenbütteler Studien zur Aufklärung 3* (1976): 137–157, here 138.

[51] Wunder, *He Is the Sun*, 37ff. The concept of the working couple was first explored comprehensively by Wunder, "Zur Stellung der Frau im Arbeitsleben und in der Gesellschaft des 15.–18. Jahrhunderts. Eine Skizze," *Geschichtsdidaktik 3* (1981): 239–251.

other and to a higher authority.[52] Although Wunder indicates the possibility of conflictual relationships in various contexts, her approach, as well, is based on a model of harmony, a model that presupposes historical subjects who align their lives with the accepted norms of estate-based society.[53] As a result of her emphasis on togetherness and on the fact that individuals are embedded within social groups, the notion of hierarchy loses valence and a different notion of equality becomes visible, one that is more appropriate to the early modern period.[54]

Although Wunder does not elaborate this idea further, she does indicate a connection to the idea of the companionship of husband and wife derived from Protestant marital teachings, an idea that, in spite of its perceived ambivalence, appears as a countermodel to the hierarchy of husband and wife.[55] Perhaps it should be emphasized more strongly that companionship between husband and wife always remains embedded within a hierarchical relationship.[56] Companionship presupposes, to use Weberian terminology, "a willingness to obey" and a "submissiveness to ordered structures."[57] For that reason, there was

---

[52] Earlier, Marianne Weber had also emphasized the ideal of the equal responsibility of the spouses, which was more important than the aspect of economic dependence: *Ehefrau und Mutter in der Rechtsentwicklung. Eine Einführung* (Tübingen, 1907; reprint, Aalen, 1989). Heide Wunder goes beyond her approach, qualifying the notion of economic dependence by highlighting the shared labor. To be sure, she neglects the aspect of peasant notions of property, which in agrarian societies—depending on the legal framework—were surely at least as important as work and a women's right to property that she talks about (Sabean, "Young bees in an empty hive," 171; Wunder, *He is the Sun*, 185). For example, she deals hardly at all with dowries and Morgengabe, (donatio, a husband's gift to the wife). which were very important in securing women's property rights and their spheres of action.

[53] Her approach belongs with the group of studies that emphasize the complementarity of gender roles. Martine Segalen also works from the assumption that society tended to be conflict-free and had a balanced distribution of roles and tasks. Martine Segalen, *Love and Power in the Peasant Family. Rural France in the Nineteenth Century*, transl. Sarah Matthews (Chicago, 1983).

[54] Wunder, *He Is the Sun*, 206–207.

[55] Ibid., 52, 203. The thesis that Protestant marital teachings raised the profile of marriage has been argued vigorously by Steven Ozment, *When Father Ruled. Family Life in Reformation Europe* (Cambridge, Mass., 1983), 50ff.

[56] All theorists of natural law have seen in marriage a special institution that stabilizes social conditions. Although they conceive of marriage as an "equal society," they simultaneously establish the husband's supremacy through the marital contract, in which the wife submits voluntarily to the domestic authority of a single man: Ute Gerhard, *Gleichheit ohne Angleichung. Frauen im Recht* (Munich, 1990), esp. 30. Elisabeth Koch also emphasizes the hierarchical character of gender relations in a marriage: *Maior dignitas est in sexu virili. Das weibliche Geschlecht im Normensystem des 16. Jahrhunderts* (Frankfurt a. M., 1991), 233ff.

[57] On Max Weber's concept of lordship and power see Peter Baumann, *Macht und Motivation. Zu einer verdeckten Form sozialer Macht* (Opladen, 1993), 13–19; idem, "Die Motive des Gehorsams bei Max Weber: eine Rekonstruktion," *Zeitschrift für Soziologie* 22, no. 5 (1993): 355–370.

no such thing as a state of equal mutuality, as Luise Schorn-Schütte has postulated especially for the household of Protestant pastor.[58] More likely we can follow Axel Honneth in speaking of "domination backed by consensus."[59] Such an approach also makes it possible to articulate much more precisely the relationship between men and women within marriage: it is neither domination in the sense of the authoritarian housefather model nor companionship in the sense of equality, but "domination as social practice," embedded in a force field in which power was enforced.[60]

If we apply this model developed by Alf Lüdtke to marriage and household governance, the seemingly straightforward structure of "superior" and "inferior," which scholars have imagined as harmonious, dissolves, allowing us to perceive multifarious practices and forms of social intercourse that characterize the relationships among the ruled no less than the relationships between lords and their subjects. This kind of differentiation is necessary not least because early modern marriage was an existential union (Lebensgemeinschaft) in a sense very different from what it is today.[61]

The normative ideal of the monogamous form of marriage was expressed—given the imponderable risks to life and survival—in a common practice one might call "serial polygamy."[62] Second and third marriages tended to be the rule rather than the exception, at least during those periodically recurring times when wars, famines, or epidemics caused mortality rates to surge.[63] They differed from first marriages not only with respect to the potentially greater age difference between spouses, but also with respect to the disposition of the family's wealth.[64]

---

[58] Luise Schorn-Schütte, "'Gefährtin' und 'Mitregentin.' Zur Sozialgeschichte der evangelischen Pfarrfrau in der Frühen Neuzeit," in Wunder and Vanja, *Wandel der Geschlechterbeziehungen*, 109–153, esp. 145 and 153.

[59] Axel Honneth, *Kritik der Macht. Reflexionsstufen einer kritischen Gesellschaftstheorie* (Frankfurt a. M., 1985), 67.

[60] Alf Lüdtke, "Einleitung: Herrschaft als soziale Praxis," in Alf Lüdtke, ed., *Herrschaft also soziale Praxis. Historische und sozial-anthropologische Studien* (Göttingen, 1991), 9–63.

[61] Wunder, *He is the Sun*, 134ff.

[62] Burgière and Lebrun have aptly referred to this situation as the "splintered families" ("The One Hundred and One Families of Europe," 15).

[63] Mitterauer, "Myth," 40; Arthur E. Imhof, "Wiederverheiratung in Deutschland zwischen dem 16. und 20. Jahrhundert," in Rudolf Lenz, ed., *Studien zur deutschsprachigen Leichenpredigt der frühen Neuzeit* (Marburg, 1981), 185–211. According to Imhof's figures, the average duration of marriage rose between 1680 and 1974 from 31.1 years to 45.3 years: *Die gewonnenen Jahre. Von der Zunahme unserer Lebensspanne seit dreihundert Jahren oder von der Notwendigkeit einer neuen Einstellung zu Leben und Sterben* (Munich, 1981), 172. Freitag, "Haushalt," 28ff., has criticized the fact that family scholarship has paid too little attention to the strong fluctuation in the composition of families as a result of early death. He encapsulates the need to replenish or rearrange oneself or the stagnation in the situation of a remnant family under the term "Behelf" (makeshift), and demands that special attention be devoted to this aspect.

[64] Gerhard, *Gleichheit*, 27, emphasizes that the legal situation in this regard was confusing, unclear, and individual. If one is looking for broad surveys, scholars still point

Women who married a second time could bring wealth into a marriage that was qualitatively different from the dowry of a first marriage.[65] It is more than likely that this altered a woman's sphere of action and the possibility she had of asserting her interests. Because of the fear of a shift in marital power relationships, and because women who were economically independent of their husbands were less willing to subordinate themselves, marriage to an excessively rich woman was not regarded as advantageous.[66]

Second and third marriages gave rise to familial conflicts with greater frequency not only because of the changed economic circumstances, but also because of the altered in-law and step relationships.[67] The frequency with which remarriages, in particular, were denounced by charivaris may reveal the kind of explosive potential that could lie hidden in such relationships.[68] Maintaining order called for a continual balancing of interests—some accordant, some conflicting. Examining this balancing process is worthwhile for the simple reason that it opens a view onto the historical subjects involved, thereby creating the possibility of uncovering the interaction between social practice and social structure.

The advantages that a model of domination expanded by the perspective of the ruled offers to women's history and gender history is evident: it dissolves the rigid dichotomy between the rulers and the ruled; it allows us to uncover not only diverse forms of rule, but also diverse forms of what it meant to be ruled, which involves a good deal more than acts of cunning on the part of

---

to "classic" works like Robert Bartsch, *Die Rechtsstellung der Frau als Gattin und Mutter* (Leipzig, 1903); Weber, *Ehefrau und Mutter*; Hans Fehr, *Die Rechtsstellung der Frau und Kinder in den Weistümern* (Jena, 1912; reprint, Aalen, 1989); Antonic Kraut, *Die Stellung der Frau im württembergischen Privatrecht* (Stuttgart, 1934).

[65] In this context one should point especially to the importance of the "dotalium," the "donatio proper nuptias," "Widerlegung," "Wittum," "Morgengabe," and "Leibgeding." All these terms refer to something bestowed by the husband for the duration of the marriage as security for the wealth relinquished by the wife. In contrast to the "dowry" which the woman brings into the marriage, the law of the "dotalium" is hardly mentioned in the legal literature (Koch, *Maior dignitas*, 45). It would seem that skepticism is called for with respect to Weber's view that the dotal law was rather unimportant in Germany (*Ehefrau und Mutter*, 531). The fact that the dotalium was not discussed in the older legal history is more likely part of the strategy of rendering it invisible, and is an expression of a hierarchically conceived gender conception on the part of the writing elite, which determines the hierarchy of relevance.

[66] When it came to the low regard that jurists had for a marriage between a poorer man and a richer woman, it evidently did not matter that wives, apart from the freedom of testamentary disposition, had no rights they could exercise on their own (Koch, *Maior dignitas*, 50f.).

[67] Münch, *Lebensformen*, 227f., points to the importance of these conflicts, which were also reflected in fairy tales and witchcraft trials.

[68] See, among others, E. P. Thompson, "Rough Music," in E. P. Thompson, *Customs in Common*, (New York, 1991), 467–538, and Christian Desplat, *Charivaris en Gascogne. La "morale des peuples" du XVIe au XXe siècle* (Paris, 1982).

the powerless.[69] Analogously, the simplistic opposition between men and women can be replaced by multifarious constructions of gender.[70] In this way the dualistic interpretative approaches are forced open, which in turn opens the path for an examination of those intermediary zones "where the genders mix, where the boundaries between them blur or become indistinct."[71]

At the same time, a model that is subject-centered and focused on social practice sensitizes us to strategies of concealment and efforts at rendering certain aspects invisible—that is to say, to those forms of domination that appear to play an especially important role in the relationship between men and women. "It is part of the (persistent) power of patriarchal imprinting on the part of lordship," Alf Lüdtke has argued, "to conceal accomplishments by women in favor of the power, honor, and 'pleasure' of men."[72] If we examine domination as a form of practice, historical subjects cease to be victims of structures or passive participants in processes; instead, they become individuals who act and react, whose actions and experiences not only reproduce but also transform social structures.[73]

The focus on the subject employs one of the central methodological strategies of women's studies in order to "discover women as subjects behind the objects and to give them a voice."[74] One of the advantages of an approach that is subject-centered and focused on social practice lies in its multiple perspectives, which derive from the understanding that fields of power and domination follow their

---

[69] Claudia Honegger and Bettina Heintz, eds., *Listen der Ohnmacht. Zur Sozialgeschichte weiblicher Widerstandsformen* (Frankfurt a. M., 1984).

[70] The two-gender construct and the ontologization of sexual difference connected with it have been vigorously criticized by Andrea Griesebner in her dissertation "Interagierende Differenzen. 'Vergehen' und 'Verbrechen' in einem niederösterreichischen Landgericht im 18. Jahrhundert" (University of Vienna, 1998). On the meanings of gender see also Monika Mommertz's dissertation "Handeln, Bedeuten, Geschlecht. Konfliktaustragungspraktiken in der ländlichen Gesellschaft der Mark Brandenburg (2. Hälfte des 16. Jahrhunderts bis zum Dreißigjährigen Krieg)" (University of Florence, 1997).

[71] Michelle Perrot, Foreword, in Alain Corbin et al., eds., *Geschlecht und Geschichte. Ist eine weibliche Geschichtsschreibung möglich?* (Frankfurt a. M., 1989), 15–27, here 23.

[72] Lüdtke, "Herrschaft als soziale Praxis," 31.

[73] Marshall Sahlins, *Historical Metaphors and Mythical Realities* (Ann Arbor, 1981). Central to the concept of structure as I use it here is the cultural theory of Pierre Bourdieu: "Structures, *habitus*, practices," in P. Bourdieu, *The Logic of Practice*, transl. Richard Nice (Stanford, 1980), 52–65; with reference to the construction of gender: Bourdieu, "Die männliche Herrschaft," in Irene Dölling and Beate Krais, eds., *Ein alltägliches Spiel. Geschlechterkonstruktion in der sozialen Praxis* (Frankfurt a. M., 1997), 153–217, here 174ff.

[74] Lipp, "Überlegungen zur Methodendiskussion," 30, and Lipp, *Alltagskulturforschung*, 10f. An individualized perspective on the past has also been called for in recent household and family scholarship. See, for example, Richard L. Rudolph, "The European Family and Economy: Central Themes and Issues," *Journal of Family History* 17, no. 2 (1992): 119–138, who sees the special potential of family research especially in the linkage between individual and society.

own respective rhythms.[75] As soon as one respects the intrinsic value of the experiences and inner perspectives of historical subjects, the context becomes more important than the event.[76] In contextualization, which Gianna Pomata calls an "ecological" narrative method in contrast with the "chronological" method,[77] women appear as historical subjects even when scholarly interest is not focused explicitly on women's worlds.[78]

Reconstructing the worlds of experience and the intermediary and overlapping zones of male and female fields of action is possible only in a sociohistorical and ethnographic microstudy. That is why the present work is concerned with a single village. This approach makes Steinbiedersdorf not the object of an individualizing historiography, but the locus of contextual observations.[79] Only by limiting the geographical space is it possible to relinquish particularistic perspectives, to create through contextualization the necessary precondition for an interpretation of the dialogic structure of the sources, and to create a reciprocal relationship between macrohistorical insights and the results of microhistorical research.

The crucial factor behind the selection of Steinbiedersdorf was the unusually good availability of sources for the late seventeenth and eighteenth centuries. The surviving court records comprise forty volumes covering the years from 1719 to 1792.[80] In addition to numerous cases dealing with matters of debt, inheritance, and wardship, they also contain files of the criminal court. Depending on the extent of the record keeping, each volume provides detailed documentation of up to forty cases.

Apart from the court files, the protocols of thirty-eight annual court sessions (Jahrgeding) from the period 1722–1790 have survived, to some of which are still attached the awkwardly written reports from subordinate officials such as the police warden (Polizeischütz) and field warden (Feldschütz).[81] Since the Jahrgeding was the place where complaints and rebukes were presented and violations of the norms were punished, these protocols provide an important

---

[75] Lüdtke, "Herrschaft als soziale Praxis," 52.

[76] Schulte, *Village in Court,* 197–199.

[77] Pomata, "Partikulargeschichte," 40.

[78] Sabean, *Property,* 416ff.; Hans Medick, "Biedermänner und Biederfrauen im alten Laichingen. Lebensweisen in einem schwäbischen Ort an der Schwelle zur Moderne," *Journal Geschichte* 1 (1991): 46–61, here 56.

[79] Sabean, *Property,* 7ff.

[80] AD Mos. B 10041–10080: Actes judiciaires Pontpierre 1719–1792. At the time of my research, only twenty-seven volumes were available; the others, about one out of every three volumes, were inaccessible because of preservation work. In individual cases I supplemented these volumes with the available Actes judiciaires from other localities in the Imperial County.

[81] AD Mos. B 10081: Plaids annaux, Pontpierre, 1722–1790. These were supplemented by B 9931: Plaids annaux, Créhange 1744–1793; B 10012/10013: Plaids annaux de Niederwies, Denting, Momersdorf; B 10087: Plaids annaux Teting.

supplement to the court records. Additional information comes from the extensive records of so-called jurisdictio extrajudicialis (participation of courts and notaries in private legal acts, such as marriage contracts, last wills, and the like), which are found in the western regions of the empire that felt the administrative influence of France.[82]

Beginning in 1680, parish registers provide information about births, marriages, deaths, and godparents, and a number of visitation protocols record the complaints of the Catholic priests.[83] Over and above these local sources, excellent material is available on the economic, cultural, and social history of the Imperial County of Kriechingen.[84] Thanks to the fact that the county was supposed to be transferred to France in an exchange at the end of the eighteenth century, we possess detailed statistical data about house and farm ownership, household sizes, and occupational structure, while the resistance of the subjects produced a no less weighty documentary record at the imperial courts.[85]

The surviving material on the Jewish residents, who made up approximately one-sixth of the inhabitants of Steinbiedersdorf, is quite informative. One important source is marriage contracts (Tena), which settled the size of the dowry, the gifts, and the devolution of property upon death. Following the decree of Louis XIV in 1701 that Jewish marriage contracts had to be deposited with notaries,[86] these documents were increasingly registered in the entire Franco-

---

[82] Hans Stein has repeatedly noted that the availability of sources in the west of the Reich is particularly good when it comes to questions pertaining to social history: "Die Einwirkungen des französischen Notariats auf die freiwillige Gerichtsbarkeit im Westen des Reiches," in Peter Johannes Schuler, ed., *Tradition und Gegenwart. Festschrift zum 175 jährigen Bestehen des badischen Notarstandes* (Karlsruhe, 1981), 143–150; idem, "Die Archive des Départements Donnersberg. Eine Möglichkeit, die Methoden der französischen Sozialgeschichte für die deutsche Landesgeschichte nutzbar zu machen," in Alois Gerlich, ed., *Vom Alten Reich zu neuer Staatlichkeit. Alzeyer Kolloquium 1979. Kontinuität und Wandel im Gefolge der Französischen Revolution am Mittelrhein* (Wiesbaden, 1982), 152–177.

[83] AD Mos. 5E and 29 J 63, 66, 69, 70 (Fonds de l'évêché). The visitation protocols do not reveal the participation of jurors in the manner of the medieval Sendgericht.

[84] Gilbert Cahen, who compiled the Repertorium of the Sous Série 10 F, has emphasized, "Qu'il s'agisse de droits seigneuriaux ou de l'administration judiciaire ou financière ou de police, il est rare que l'histoire économique ou sociale ait à sa disposition des ensembles aussi complets de comptes, de registres d'audiences, de rapports de droits, de terriers de bans": Gilbert Cahen, *Archives départementales de la Moselle. Répertoire numérique de la série F* [Fonds divers antérieurs à 1790], *sous série 10 F* [Fonds de Créhange] (Metz, 1966), 6. I would like to take this opportunity to thank Monsieur Cahen for his help, especially his critical reading of the manuscript.

[85] LHA Koblenz 56/487–503, 505, 1801–1802, 2987.

[86] Registration (Insinuation, Contrôle des Actes) became generally obligatory in France at this time. A special decree for Alsatian Jews is mentioned by André Aaron Fraenckel, *Memoire juive in Alsace. Contrats de Mariage au XVIIIème siècle* (Strasbourg, 1998), XIII. In Alsace, many Jews deposited the originals written in Hebrew, with no translations made. They have been systematically listed in Fraenckel.

German border region.[87] In addition to the Hebrew originals, only some of which have survived, the notaries frequently prepared German or French translations or shortened versions, a large number of which are still extant.

The first notarized contract of a marriage performed in Steinbiedersdorf dates from 1739. By 1792, twenty-five Jewish couples or their parents or guardians had a notarized marriage contract drawn up here, which meant that these contracts were also valid in non-Jewish courts. For the period in question I was able to find a total of forty-one notarized marriage contracts in which at least one of the partners came from Steinbiedersdorf. These contracts are part of the inventory of more than two thousand Jewish marriage contracts in the area of the modern-day Département Moselle published by Jean Fleury in 1989.[88]

More difficult to access than the marriage documents are the Jewish wills that have survived in various court and notarial files.[89] In addition to these sources, a few scattered entries in the files of the rabbinical court offer insights into Jewish lives.[90] They are supplemented by the extensive written record from non-Jewish jurisdictions. This source exists because the Jewish residents in the villages of the county of Kriechingen made extensive use of the obligation and opportunity that had existed since the middle of the eighteenth century to settle their conflicts locally with the help of the sovereign's courts, to seek justice and defend their honor in a Christian forum.[91]

For reasons I shall explore, local Jewish women and men found committed advocates before the Kriechingen court, who gave them room to describe the circumstances of their lives.[92] In most instances the clerk kept a careful record

---

[87] The French notariate was introduced at the end of the seventeenth century in the newly won territories in the Franco-German border region. But even before that it had influenced the institutions of the Reich in this region: the notary or tabellion drafted documents for parties, prepared the finished papers, and filed the notarial deeds (Stein, "Einwirkungen," 145f.). Fonds de greffes et tabellionages (B and 3E) existed also in the Imperial County of Kriechingen. The Actes de Tabellionages contain numerous files of the Christian and Jewish population relating to matters of debt, marriage, and the division of inheritance (AD Mos. E Dépôt 553 Pontpierre, HH I).

[88] Jean Fleury, prompted by genealogical interests, surveyed the 8,500 items in the Metz archive and compiled 2,021 marriage contracts from the seventeenth and eighteenth centuries that were effected before the rabbinical authorities and deposited with a royal notary: Jean Fleury, *Contrats de Mariage juifs en Moselle avant 1792. Recensement à usage généalogique de 2021 contrats de mariage notariés* (n.p., 1989).

[89] Ad Mos. Actes judiciaires B 10062.: Testament von den wohlbestalt(ten) Oberbarnes Aberham Jacob in Steinbiedersdorff, 1775. See Appendix.

[90] On the rabbinical court see pp. 186–188.

[91] The situation was similar in Metz: in her memoirs, Glückel of Hameln notes that in the days when she first arrived in Metz, "no one heard of a man going out of the *Judengasse* to bring a case before a Gentile tribunal." *The Memoirs of Glückel of Hameln*, trans. Marvin Lowenthal (New York, 1977), 266–267. On the problems associated with resorting to non-Jewish courts, see Jacob Katz, *Tradition and Crisis. Jewish Society at the End of the Middle Ages* (New York, 1993).

[92] Susanna Burghartz has made a similar observation about the Zurich Council at the

of their statements. They teach us something about the village and lordship, living and working conditions, family and kin, inheritance and widowhood, love and marriage, honor and dishonor.[93]

Although some of the individual sources are quite detailed, each group of sources, looked at in isolation, provides only a partial insight into village life.[94] It is only with the help of data connected to individual persons that we can establish cross-links and work with a multiple perspective in an effort to break through the official imprint imposed on the sources.[95] At times we have only a few surviving fragments of spoken words and biographical data that we can pull together.[96] They provide insight into the fields of action and worlds of experience of men and women, make visible networks of relationships, and reveal a good deal about the unwritten rules that governed the daily lives of women and men.

Apart from the excellent sources, another reason for choosing Steinbiedersdorf for this kind of study is that it was a village of mixed religions.[97] I have already

---

end of the fourteenth century. The Jews of Zurich took their internal disputes, which, by Jewish law, were a matter for the Jewish courts, before the Council Court: Susanna Burghartz, *Leib, Ehre und Gut. Delinquenz in Zürich Ende des 14. Jahrhunderts* (Zurich, 1990), 198.

[93] While the sources on Steinbiedersdorf's Jewish history cannot be exhaustively examined within the framework of the present work, whose primary focus is on the spheres of women's actions and their experiential worlds, my hope is to pave the way for future research by framing the question so broadly.

[94] On the concept of what the Germans call "Lebenswelt" ("experiential world") see Rudolf Vierhaus, "Die Rekonstruktion historischer Lebenswelten. Probleme moderner Kulturgeschichtsschreibung," in Hartmut Lehmann, ed., *Wege zu einer neuen Kulturgeschichte* (Göttingen, 1995), 7–28.

[95] Michaela Hohkamp, "Vom Wirtshaus zum Amtshaus," *Werkstatt Geschichte* 16 (1997): 8–18, here 9.

[96] With regard to the biographical data, it should be noted that Christian and Jewish names appear in various spellings. Given names and family names vary depending on location, the writer, and the language chosen. The Jewish family name Cahen could also be written as Kahn, Cahn, Cain, or Caen. Biblical names were often given with very different equivalents in German and French. For example, the Hebrew name Benyamin is Louis or Oulif in French, Wolff in German. For the sake of clarity, the names for the same person are always written the same way, except in direct quotes from the sources. I have also standardized the writing of village names.

[97] Since the concept of "denomination" was developed only with respect to the Christian religion, I have largely avoided its use in the present book. I have retained the use of the word "religion" even in cases where religion should be understood in the sense of denomination. Heinz Schilling recently suggested that scholars studying confessionalization should turn their attention also to communities of faith that were not structured according to ecclesiastical denominations, especially Jewish minorities. However, the concept of confessionalization is unsuitable for the present study, for at least two reasons: First, it makes the development of the Christian denominations into the yardstick of development against which the Jewish minority is measured. This approach systematically obscures the potential for modernization emanating from that minority itself.

noted that about a sixth of the population was Jewish, the rest Catholic, while the territorial lord and his officials were Protestant. The coexistence of various religions provides a good setting to study the connection between religion and gender, which was so central to the early modern period.[98]

As we know from the work of Alice Rossi and Natalie Zemon Davis, the Reformation and the Counter-Reformation changed gender roles—and thus society—in different ways. While Protestantism sought to reduce the gap between opposites, Catholicism, with its female saints and convents, retained rather pluralistic structures.[99] What the two confessions shared, Davis believes, is that "women suffered for their powerlessness . . . in the late sixteenth to eighteenth centuries as changes in marriage laws restricted the freedoms of wives even further, as female guilds dwindled, as the female role in middle-level commerce and farm direction contracted, and as the differential between male and female wages increased."[100]

We do not know how this process unfolded in detail, and with what kinds of delays, since the influence of the religions on the rural worlds in the early modern period has been little studied so far. What is beyond dispute is the fact that, as late as the eighteenth century, there could still be "glaring differences" between Protestant and Catholic regions, differences that were reflected in the culture of daily life.[101]

And yet such observations had no discernible influence on the fields of research chosen by scholars.[102] To date, most studies that have looked at mar-

---

Second, the paradigm of confessionalization was derived from the theory of modernization, whose basic assumptions were drawn from the perspective of the nineteenth and twentieth centuries. This means that deviations can be discussed only as delays, costs, or regional variations. However, questioning a certain perspective on historical development, in this case a perspective derived from the theory of modernization, does not mean, as Schilling argues in his critical remarks about microhistory, that the latter "rejects every developmental historical perspective": Heinz Schilling, "Die Konfessionalisierung von Kirche, Staat, und Gesellschaft—Profil, Leistung, Defizite und Perspektiven eines geschichtswissenschaftlichen Paradigmas," in H. Schilling and Wolfgang Reinhard, eds., *Die katholische Konfessionalisierung: wissenschaftliches Symposium der Gesellschaft zur Herausgabe des Corpus Catholicorum und des Vereins für Reformationsgeschichte 1993* (Gütersloh, 1995), 1–49, here esp. 21 and 46.

[98] Merry E. Wiesner, *Women and Gender in Early Modern Europe* (Cambridge, 1993), esp. 179ff.; Olwen Hufton, *The Prospect Before Her. A History of Women in Western Europe. I: 1500–1800* (Oxford, 1994).

[99] Natalie Zemon Davis, "City Women and Religious Change," in her *Society and Culture in Early Modern France* (Stanford, 1965), 65–95, with reference to Alice Rossi, "Sex Equality: The Beginning of Ideology." Originally in *The Humanist*, September/October 1969, reprinted in E. Howe and F. Lauter, eds., *The Radical Teacher* (1969), 24–28.

[100] Davis, "City Women," 94.

[101] Peter Hersche, "Intendierte Rückständigkeit: Zur Charakteristik des geistlichen Staates im Alten Reich," in Georg Schmidt, ed., *Stände und Gesellschaft im Alten Reich* (Stuttgart, 1989), 133–149, esp. 143.

[102] The models of house and marriage employed by research into the early modern

riage, domestic rule, and the discipline of Christian morals in rural society, and thus touch on a central area of gender relations, have focused on Protestant territories, where—thanks to the protocols of church meetings—the available sources are far more extensive than in the Catholic regions.[103] Catholic areas come into view—if at all—under the aspect of popular religiosity.[104]

What has been barely studied, by contrast, is the Catholic culture that went beyond the narrow sphere of piety, a culture that was, according to Peter Hersche, "characterized in terms of social history and the history of mentalities by clerical dominance, agrarian thinking, a preference for leisure (feast days!), an absence of disciplining, an attitude of living for today, ostentatious wastefulness, a rejection of science, and the persistence of magical elements."[105]

Hans Medick, in his study of Laichingen, has shown that this culture, which one should by no means imagine as timeless or all-pervasive, was not necessarily and in all aspects sharply distinct from Protestant currents. Medick discovered a religious mentality he described as a "Protestant ethic" that lacked the "spirit of capitalism." "In the sense of a personal and awakened 'imitation of Christ,'" he writes, "which believers should strive for in this narrow and difficult

---

period were formulated in part through recourse to the "Protestant ethic," while an analogous development in the Catholic realm with reference to the Council of Trent was more or less presupposed. The selection of focal points of scholarly research is surely also connected with the fact that the debate over the process of social disciplining involves primarily the Protestant sphere: see Heinrich Richard Schmidt, *Konfessionelle Institutionalisierung im 16. Jahrhundert* (Munich, 1992), 100f. On the debate over Catholic confessionalization see Schilling and Reinhard, eds., *Die katholische Konfessionalisierung.*

[103] In southern Germany a favorite area of research is Württemberg, as we can see from the work of Hans Medick, David Sabean, Helga Schnabel-Schüle, Martin Scharfe, Wolfgang Kaschuba, Carola Lipp, and others. For Switzerland see Heinrich Richard Schmidt, *Dorf und Religion. Reformierte Sittenzucht in Berner Landgemeinden der Frühen Neuzeit* (Stuttgart, 1995). The area studied by Jürgen Schlumbohm (parish of Belm) was denominationally mixed (Lutheran and Catholic).

[104] There is, however, extensive research on the "classic" Catholic topics such as brotherhoods and pilgrimages. On this see the overview by Peter Hersche, "Devotion, Volksbrauch oder Massenprotest? Ein Literaturbericht aus sozialgeschichtlicher Sicht zum Thema Wallfahrt. Von der kirchlichen über die volkskundliche zur sozialgeschichtlichen Wallfahrtsforschung," in *Das achtzehnte Jahrhundert in Österreich* (Vienna, 1994), 7–34. P. Hersche, "Wider 'Müssiggang' und 'Ausschweifung.' Feiertage und ihre Reduktion im katholischen Europa, namentlich im deutschsprachigen Raum zwischen 1750 und 1800," *Innsbrucker Historische Studien* 12/13 (1990): 97–122. On "popular religiosity" (Volksfrömmigkeit) as a concept that is by no means free of controversy see Stefan Fassbinder, "Frömmigkeit. Entwicklung und Problemfelder eines Begriffs," *Saeculum* 47.1 (1996): 6–34, here 14; on the state of research see Hansgeorg Molitor and Heribert Smolinsky, eds., *Volksfrömmigkeit in der Frühen Neuzeit* (Münster, 1994).

[105] Peter Hersche, "Die protestantische Laus und der katholische Floh. Konfessionsspezifische Aspekte der Hygiene," in Benedikt Bietenhard et al., eds., *Ansichten von der rechten Ordnung. Bilder über Normen und Normverletzungen in der Geschichte* (Bern, 1991), 43–60.

path through life, this 'Protestant ethic' was primarily concerned not with economic success or earthly reward, but with the ability to 'endure' troubles and hardship, the burdens and exertions of work, sickness and death."[106] Especially when it came to the importance accorded to the magical, the people of Laichingen, whose "faith was shaped by the continual interlacing of coexistence and conflict with the Catholic world," do not appear to have been very different from their Catholic environment.[107]

As for Jewish history, Claudia Prestel has noted that an "intensive engagement with the history of rural Jews . . . is much needed in scholarship."[108] Although the last few years, in particular, have seen a large number of studies on Jewish village communities, our knowledge of the Jewish population's spheres of action within a Christian-dominated world at the time of emancipation, of the influence of religion on daily life and the attitudes of Jewish women and men toward house, work, and honor, is still marginal.[109]

A microhistorical study focused on a Catholic-Jewish village can elucidate the significance of the religions for the organization of life and uncover the web of relationships between the coexisting village communities. Needless to say, my concern is not with an analysis of religious practices for their own sake; rather, my aim is to understand religion as an interpretive culture that constitutes the entire reality of life and shapes the behavior of people, the horizon of their worlds and how they interpret them."[110]

This broad definition allows us to see the multifarious religious activities of women that would otherwise remain invisible in an institutional examination of the male church and of Judaism.[111] At the same time, it shifts our perception

---

[106] Medick, *Weben und Überleben*, 36.

[107] Ibid., 541 and 544ff.

[108] Claudia T. Prestel, "Geschichtsschreibung zur jüdischen Geschichte in Deutschland: Qualität oder Quantität?" *Archiv für Sozialgeschichte* 35 (1995). 457–494, here 468.

[109] On this see Monika Richarz, "Die Entdeckung der Landjuden. Stand und Probleme ihrer Erforschung am Beispiel Südwestdeutschlands," in *Landjudentum im Bodenseeraum. Wissenschaftliche Tagung zur Eröffnung des jüdischen Museums Hohenems vom 9. bis 11. April 1991* (Dornbirn, 1992), 11–21; M. Richarz, "Landjuden—Ein bürgerliches Element im Dorf?" in Wolfgang Jacobeit et al., eds., *Idylle oder Aufbruch? Das Dorf im bürgerlichen 19. Jahrhundert. Ein europäischer Vergleich* (Berlin, 1990), 181–190; M. Richarz, "In Familie, Handel und Salon. Jüdische Frauen vor und nach der Emanzipation der deutschen Juden," in Hausen and Wunder, eds., *Frauengeschichte—Geschlechtergeschichte*, 57–66.

[110] Thomas Nipperdey, *Religion im Umbruch. Deutschland 1870–1918* (Munich, 1988), 7. This definition encompasses only a small aspect of the concept of religion, though one that is central to the question pursued by the present study. Another important characteristic of Christian religion, especially in the eighteenth century, was "the distinction between a true inner religion as love for God, for authority, and for one's fellow human being, and an external, merely formal religion as the observation of prescriptions": U. Dierse, "Religion, 18. Jh.," in Joachim Ritter and Karlfried Gründer, eds., *Historisches Wörterbuch der Philosophie*, vol. 8 (Basel, 1992), 623–713, here 655.

[111] Susan Starr Sered, *Priestess, Mother, Sacred Sister. Religions Dominated by Women* (Oxford, 1994), 3ff.

to systems of religious symbols, which, as Edith Saurer has emphasized, "have profoundly influenced gender relations in discourse and practice."[112] That is especially true of ideas of purity, pollution, and taboo.[113] In the early modern period, purity, as "a metaphor of the sexual order,"[114] was central to the judicial discourse about premarital and extramarital sexuality.[115] This is also documented in many sources from Steinbiedersdorf, where, in the eighteenth century, not only Christian but also Jewish women and girls appeared in court. Their stories help us to decode the formative power of religious symbol systems and to clarify the interconnectedness of power, gender, and religion.

Another aspect that makes Steinbiedersdorf interesting as the setting of a history of women and gender is the tension between written and customary law. As late as the eighteenth century, many problems in Steinbiedersdorf were still settled in accordance with local custom. That custom was embedded within the common law (gemeines Recht), which had arisen from the reception of Roman law and stipulated that marriage "had no influence on the legal status and the property relationships of the spouses, which meant that it also did not impair a woman's legal capacity and ability to enter into contracts."[116]

Women appeared before the Kriechingen courts as plaintiffs and were often summoned in person as defendants and witnesses. Gender guardianship did occur, but it was not imperative.[117] The common law of Roman tradition that

---

[112] Edith Saurer, "Introduction" in E. Saurer, ed., *Die Religion der Geschlechter. Historische Aspekte religiöser Mentalitäten* (Vienna, 1995), 7–14, here 7, with reference to Alfred Lorenzer, *Das Konzil der Buchhalter. Die Zerstörung der Sinnlichkeit. Eine Religionskritik* (Frankfurt a. M., 1983), 11.

[113] Mary Douglas, *Purity and Danger: An Analysis of Concepts of Pollution and Taboo* (New York, 1966).

[114] Sabine Kienitz, *Sexualität, Macht und Moral. Prostitution und Geschlechterbeziehungen Anfang des 19. Jahrhunderts in Württemberg. Ein Beitrag zur Mentalitätsgeschichte* (Berlin, 1995), 285.

[115] On the significance of purity before Protestant courts see Susanna Burghartz, "Jungfräulichkeit oder Reinheit? Zur Änderung von Argumentationsmustern vor dem Basler Ehegericht im 16. und 17. Jahrhundert," in Richard van Dülmen, ed., *Dynamik der Tradition. Studien zur historischen Kulturforschung* (Frankfurt a. M., 1992), 13–40.

[116] Ute Gerhard, "Die Rechtsstellung der Frau in der bürgerlichen Gesellschaft des 19. Jahrhunderts. Frankreich und Deutschland im Vergleich," in Jürgen Kocka, ed., *Bürgertum im 19. Jahrhundert. Deutschland im europäischen Vergleich* (Munich, 1988), vol. 1, 439–468, here 450.

[117] On gender guardianship (Geschlechtsvormundschaft) see the essays by Gerhard Dilcher, Ernst Holthöfer, Susanne Weber-Will, David Warren Sabean, Regula Gerber Jenni, and Annemarie Ryter in Ute Gerhard, ed., *Frauen in der Geschichte des Rechts. Von der Frühen Neuzeit bis zur Gegenwart* (Munich, 1997), 55–72, 390–508. On the whole, conditions varied a great deal. For example, while the Sachsenspiegel did not permit women to take legal action without a guardian, Bavarian law largely accepted the capacity of women to sue in court: G. Werner, "Prozeßparteien," in *HRG*; vol. 4 (Berlin, 1990), cols. 62–66, here 64. In the Landgericht in Baar, women were admissible as parties to legal proceedings, though they were not allowed to bring a suit unless they were rep-

was favorable toward women appears to have still been widespread in the eighteenth century. It was used in the former imperial free cities (Lübeck, Bremen, Hamburg, Frankfurt), in the duchies of Oldenburg and Brunswick, as well as in Hannover, Hesse, and Württemberg.[118] Two facts may explain why the general notion of the legal incapacity of women has been able to persist until today in spite of the considerable local variations: first, the legal discourse beginning in the sixteenth century favored this development;[119] second, we can detect once again the lasting influence of nineteenth-century scholarship, which legitimized its conception of the gender order historically by positing the universal validity of the German legal tradition.[120]

Even if the women of Steinbiedersdorf did not leave behind any written testimony, they are present in the sources not least because of the legal framework.[121] Their presence also has to do with the fact that as unmarried women, wives, and widows they owned houses, shares of houses, properties, and gardens. This situation is attributable to favorable ownership rights. Only a small portion of the land in Steinbiedersdorf was held in manorial ownership. A mere 4.4 percent of the arable land was owned by the territorial lord, 78.2 percent belonged to the peasants themselves, the rest was held by outsiders; only a small portion was in the hand of the church.[122]

However, the almost complete absence of manorial ownership of the land should not be given too much weight in view of the fact that manorialism in southwestern Germany had been moribund since the sixteenth century. Even manorial regions were frequently characterized by good ownership rights and extensive powers of disposition on the part of the peasants farming the land.[123] Given the de facto powerlessness of manorial lords in many regions of southwestern Germany, the conditions in Steinbiedersdorf were not as exceptional

---

resented by a guardian. A wife, however, could represent her husband before the Landgericht. Gerd Leiber, *Das Landgericht der Baar. Verfassung und Verfahren zwischen Reichs- und Landrecht. 1232–1632* (Allensbach, 1964), 376. Michaela Hohkamp has shown that in the Austrian lordship of Triberg, women appeared in court as plaintiffs without male assistance: Michaela Hohkamp, "Frauen vor Gericht," in Mireille Othenin-Girard et al., eds., *Frauen und Öffentlichkeit. Beiträge der 6. Schweizerischen Historikerinnentagung* (Zurich, 1991), 115–124, here 118.

[118] Gerhard, *Gleichheit*, 146.

[119] The antiwomen tendency of that discourse has been retraced by Elisabeth Koch in *Maior dignitas*.

[120] Gerhard, *Gleichheit*, 148ff.

[121] For Ute Gerhard, "law is a trenchant expression of social reality; although legal practice is subject to cultural delays and contains a coarsening of social reality, it is still a yardstick for the power relationship—indeed, the violence relationship—between the genders": Gerhard, *Gleichheit*, 35.

[122] Pascal Flaus, *Comté et comtes de Créhange du XVIIe au XVIIIe siècle. Étude administrative, économique et sociale* (Metz, 1984), Appendix 2.

[123] Friedrich Lütge, *Geschichte der deutschen Agrarverfassung vom frühen Mittelalter bis zum 19. Jahrhundert* (Stuttgart, 1967), 159ff., 192ff.; Wolfgang von Hippel, *Die Bauernbefreiung im Königreich Württemberg*, vol. 1 (Boppard, 1977).

as it might appear at first glance. What mattered more than the legal form of peasant holdings were the forms and practices of property transfer.[124] These exerted a crucial influence on social relations within the village and on the character of gender relationships.[125]

We know from a number of studies that inheritance rules did not follow the precepts handed down by the higher authorities.[126] In practice, the difference between real division and the right of succession to an undivided farm estate was not clear-cut; rather, "these two principles were usually combined in some form or another."[127] In Steinbiedersdorf, too, we can observe a variety of ways in which property was transferred. The disputes that arose in connection with these transfers convey an impression of the complexity and multilayered nature of rural society.

If we shift our view into the village itself, matters do not get any simpler. The moment we depart from familiar paths and move from the institutional to the individual level, the homogeneous living arrangement we call "village" dissolves, and the amorphous mass of "peasants" turns into individual men and women seeking their place within society. Reconstructing their spheres of action and worlds of experience in the village is no simple undertaking. There are no sources that are specifically relevant to this task and no familiar ways of describing such a world. To be sure, historical demography and scholarship on the family, in particular, have developed approaches and methods that can guide us toward our topic, but these subdisciplines look for women chiefly in places where we would expect to find them anyway: the family and the house, where they are concerned with the work of giving birth and feeding their families. By contrast, the attempt to illuminate other spheres of human life, to probe into the presence and unruliness of women and inquire into the social meaning of their actions, takes us initially into a realm that is conceived of predominantly in male terms.

---

[124] On this point there is widespread consensus among scholars. Especially in Baden, numerous studies have described the futile efforts of territorial rulers to use prohibitions on partition to counteract the splitting up of holdings that accompanied the improvement in the ownership rights of peasants: Clemens Zimmermann, *Reformen in der bäuerlichen Gesellschaft. Studien zum aufgeklärten Absolutismus in der Markgrafschaft Baden 1750–1790* (Ostfildern, 1983).

[125] David W. Sabean, picking up on the theses of Goody, has brought out that it was not property—in view of the German conditions one should add: property-like conditions of ownership—but the reciprocal interconnection of claims and rights conveyed by property that shaped the relationships among people in crucial ways: Sabean, "Young bees in an empty hive," 171ff.

[126] Michael Hohkamp, "Wer will erben? Überlegungen zur Erbpraxis in geschlechtsspezifischer Perspektive in der Herrschaft Triberg von 1654–1806," in Jan Peters, ed., *Gutsherrschaft als soziales Modell. Vergleichende Betrachtungen zur Funktionsweise frühneuzeitlicher Agrargesellschaften* (Munich, 1995), 327–342.

[127] Albert Schnyder-Burghartz, *Alltag und Lebensform auf der Basler Landschaft um 1700. Vorindustrielle, ländliche Kultur und Gesellschaft aus mikrohistorischer Perspektive. Bretzwil und das obere Waldenburger Amt von 1690 bis 1750* (Liestal, 1992), 167.

When scholars talk about the village they usually mean the village community, in which women had no place—leaving aside the wives of village office-holders and the occasional participation by widows.[128] The two genders become visible and important only when one leaves the relatively well-researched institutional level of the village community. By looking at "women's gossip" one becomes aware of spheres of opinion-formation that are anything but marginal to the organization of daily life. Words of scolding and invective, "the usual weapon of women," point to gender-specific ways in which conflicts were carried out. And a look into the sphere of the church reveals that the purpose of attendance at Sunday mass was not only religious edification.

To penetrate into the complex and initially rather unstructured entity that is the village, which was not only an institution but also a way of life, which consisted not only of houses but also of people living in competing relationships, one must clear a path through the thicket of official documents to the human beings themselves, to ask how they shaped their lives and how they perceived and changed the world around them.[129]

The first part of the book (chapters 2–4) is devoted to the Christian community. It begins with a survey of the history of the village (chapter 2), which will provide the kind of orientation in space and time that historians need to find their way around a field of study. This will be followed by an attempt to reconstruct the lives of individual Christian women, to accompany them on their way to church, into the village, into court, or around the neighborhood (chapter 3). Using the "ecological narrative method" outlined above, I will uncover networks of relationships and power relationships, make visible spheres of action and experiential worlds, and analyze individual problem areas that become relevant through a focus on women.

None of this is possible without a thorough contextualization, to which the following chapter (chapter 4) is devoted. The socioeconomic, political, and cultural framework is analyzed with constant reference to the life stories previously introduced. What emerges in the process is the complexity of a world whose order is grounded in plurality and diversity.

The second part of the book (chapters 5–7) seeks to connect the various scholarly traditions of women's history, gender history, and Jewish history.[130]

---

[128] Heide Wunder provides a concise overview of life in the countryside and the meaning of women within the village community: *He Is the Sun*, 169–174; on women in rural society see Wunder and Vanja, eds., *Weiber, Menscher, Frauenzimmer*; on the village community see Werner Troßbach, "Bauern 1648–1806, in *Enzyklopädie deutscher Geschichte* 19 (Munich, 1993).

[129] On this see the reflections by Winfried Schulze, "Ego-Dokumente. Annäherungen an den Menschen in der Geschichte?" in Beal Lundt and Helma Reimöller, eds., *Von Aufbruch und Utopie. Perspektiven einer neuen Gesellschaftsgeschichte des Mittelalters. Für und mit Ferdinand Seibt aus Anlaß seines 65. Geburtstages* (Cologne, 1992), 417–450.

[130] On Jewish women's and gender history in the early modern period see Bernard Dov Cooperman, "Afterword: Tradition and Crisis and the Study of Early Modern Jewish

Following studies on Jewish women that have emphasized the need to analyze the lives and endeavors of Jewish women beyond the official religion, and to historicize gender conceptions, my primary aim will be to examine the life worlds of Jewish women within the concrete historical context.[131]

That is the reason why the history of the village will be written anew, this time, sources permitting, from the perspective of the Jewish population. This approach from multiple perspectives offers an opportunity to arrive at a deeper understanding of the complex power relationships within the village,[132] and to develop a critical stance toward notions of social difference and coherence that single out individual factors such as gender or religion in their explanatory models.[133]

Although it is unquestionably true that the living conditions of the Jewish population and the sphere within which it could develop were highly dependent on the possibilities allowed by its Christian environment,[134] I will begin by trying to sketch the Jewish community's own history to the extent that is possible given the state of scholarship (chapter 5). This is intended to create a framework in which to embed the individual life stories of Jewish women (chapter 6). These lives form the starting and end points for an analysis of the spheres of action, networks of relationships, and power relationships that demon-

---

History," in Jacob Katz, *Tradition and Crisis. Jewish Society at the End of the Middle Ages* (New York, 1993), 237–253, here 244f.

[131] Judith R. Baskin, for example, has emphasized "that the reality of women's lives and endeavors was often quite different from the rabbinical design": "Introduction," in her *Jewish Women in Historical Perspective* (Detroit, 1991), 15–24, here 16. Chava Weissler, after studying popular Yiddish religious literature (*tkhines*), which she compared to rabbinic literature, drew this conclusion, which we can undoubtedly generalize: "[T]he differences between the two genres are evidence of the multivocality of gender constructions in Ashkenazic culture." Chava Weissler, "Mitzvot Built into the Body: Thkines for Niddah, Pregnancy, and Childbirth," in Howard Eilberg-Schwartz, ed., *People of the Body. Jews and Judaism from an embodied perspective* (Albany, 1992), 101–115, here 111.

[132] The decision to take a multiple-perspective approach was influenced by the consideration that there is no social locus and no analytical position from which the "true" value of a text or a discourse can be determined: James C. Scott, *Domination and the Arts of Resistance: Hidden Transcripts* (Yale, 1990).

[133] On this see, for example, the discussion within Jewish history over the category of the other and the alien: Sigrid Weigel, "Frauen und Juden in Konstellationen der Modernisierung—Vorstellungen und Verkörperungen des 'internen Anderen.' Ein Forschungsprogramm," in Inge Stephan, Sabine Schilling, and Sigrid Weigel, *Jüdische Kulturen und Weiblichkeit in der Moderne* (Cologne, 1994), 333–351; Rainer Walz, "Der nahe Fremde. Die Beziehungen zwischen Christen und Juden in der frühen Neuzeit," in Paul Münch, ed., *Fremdsein—Historische Erfahrungen* (Essen, 1995), 54–63; Christina van Braun, "'Der Jude' und 'Das Weib': Zwei Stereotypen des 'Anderen' in der Moderne," *Metis* 2 (1992): 6–28.

[134] Jörg Deventer, *Das Abseits als sicherer Ort? Jüdische Minderheit und christliche Gesellschaft im Alten Reich am Beispiel der Fürstabtei Corvey (1550–1807)* (Paderborn, 1996), 9.

strate the variety and multiplicity in the experiences of women and their power to shape a given culture.

The final chapter is devoted to the marginal zones and border areas in which the relationships between Christian and Jewish men and women were situated (chapter 7).[135] In a critical engagement with the explanatory approaches that scholarship has so far offered, which are not free of contradictions and which move between the poles of harmony and discord, integration and segregation, emancipation and assimilation,[136] I will seek to redefine the importance of difference in early modern rural communities within the field circumscribed by power, gender, and religion.[137]

---

[135] Natalie Zemon Davis has used the term "margins" to describe the treatment of Christians in the memoirs of Glikl bas Judah Leib: "[T]he Christians are on the margins of her Jewish center, encircling the Jews with their institutions and worldly control." Natalie Zemon Davis: *Women on the Margins: Three Seventeenth-Century Lives* (Cambridge, 1995), 38. On Christian-Jewish relations see R. Po-chia Hsia and Hartmut Lehmann, eds., *In and Out of the Ghetto. Jewish-Gentile Relations in Late Medieval and Early Modern Germany* (Cambridge, 1995).

[136] See most recently J. Friedrich Battenberg, "Zwischen Integration und Segregation. Zu den Bedingungen jüdischen Lebens in der vormodernen christlichen Gesellschaft," *Aschkenas* 6 (1996): 421–454.

[137] On the discussion over the meaning of difference in women's and gender history see Griesebner, "Interagierende Differenzen." For Jewish history see Anne Zink, "L'indifférence à la différence: les forains dans la France du Sud-Ouest," *Annales* 43 (1988): 149–172.

Map 1. Les éstats due Duc de Lorraine, 1705.

CHAPTER TWO

APPROACHES: THE VILLAGE

Steinbiedersdorf was an enclave in the German part of Lorraine; until 1793 it was part of the Imperial County of Kriechingen.[1] Today, Steinbiedersdorf is called Pontpierre. The village, now French, is difficult to find on a map.

The name

Steinbiedersdorf makes its first documented appearance in 1026 as "Stegenbidersdorf."[2] The place name should be interpreted as "Biedersdorf on the path," and its creation seen in connection with the neighboring community of "Bambiedersdorf," whose name carries the distinguishing reference "Baum" (tree, here meaning forest).[3] The history of the name is as varied as the history of the village itself. "Stege" or "Stig"-Biedersdorf developed into Steinbiedersdorf and was in more recent times interpreted in popular etymology as "Stones near the village."[4] The name Pontpierre, the French name of the village attested since

---

[1] The history of the Imperial County of Kriechingen has been little studied to date. For the late Middle Ages see Victor Châtelain, "Histoire du comté de Créhange," *Annuaire de la Société d'histoire et d'archéologie lorraine* (1891): 175–231, (1892): 66–115, (1893): 92–138. For the period after the Thirty Years' War see Johann Matthias Sittel, *Sammlung der Provinzial und Particular-Gesetze und Verordnungen, welche für einzelne ganz oder nur teilweise an die Krone Preußens gefallene Territorien des linken Rheinufers erlassen worden*, vol. 2 (Trier, 1843), 517ff.; Jacques Touba, *Die vormals kriching'schen Dörfer Dentingen, Momersdorf und Niederwiesen* (Forbach, 1908). A more recent survey of the social and administrative history is provided by Pascal Flaus, *Comté et comtes de Créhange*.

[2] This earliest, though not necessarily reliable attestation, is mentioned in the article on Steinbiedersdorf in *Das Reichsland Elsaß-Lothringen. Landes- und Ortsbeschreibung*, publ. by the Statistische Bureau des Ministeriums für Elsaß-Lothringen, vol. 3 (Strasbourg, 1903), 1052.

[3] For help in interpreting the various place names I am indebted to Professor Wolfgang Haubrichs from the University of Saarbrücken. The name ending in -dorf (village) consists, according to Prof. Haubrichs, of a personal name (Germanic Bohari or Bidhari) and the addition of Stegen- or Stiegen.

[4] Individual attestations in, among other places, AD Mos. B, 10 F, E Dépot, in the article on Steinbiedersdorf in *Reichsland*, vol. 3, 1052, and in N. Dorvaux, *Les anciens pouillés du diocèse de Metz* (Nancy, 1902–1907). Specifically, we find the following: 1309 Stignenbudersdorf (*Reichsland*); 1360 Stenbenderstorf (Dorvaux, 16); 1392 Stegenbiderstorff (AD Mos. 10, F 3, fol. 38); 1412 Stegebidersdorf (AD Mos. 10, F 3); 1442 Bidersdorf (AD Mos. 10 F 3); 1465 Stegebiedersdorf (AD Mos. 10 F 3); 1594 Steinbidersdorf

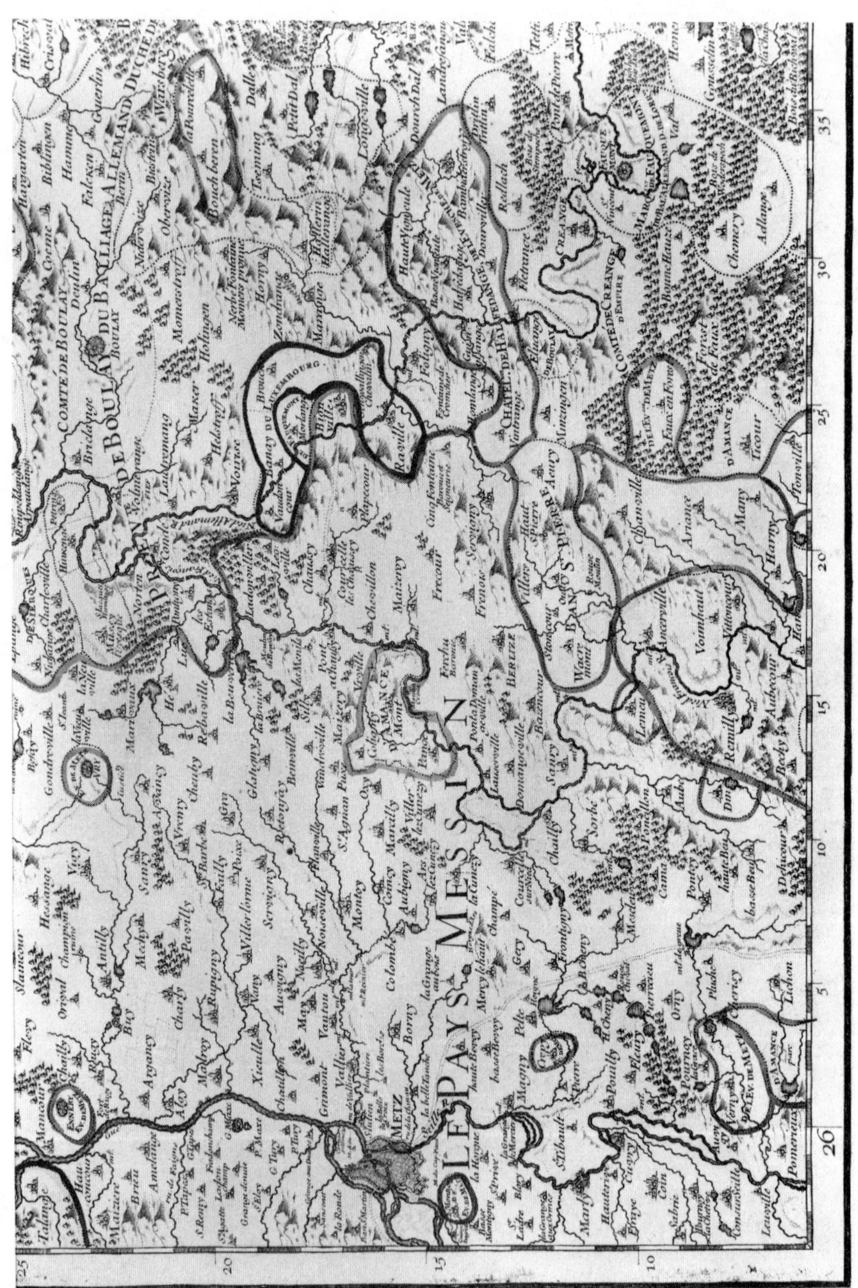

Map 2. Detail of Les éstates due Duc de Lorraine, 1705.

the beginning of the seventeenth century, also rests on a misunderstanding. Bilingual Francophones interpreted "Stegebiedersdorf" as "Peter's bridge" and translated it as "Pont de Pierre."[5]

Space and time

Steinbiedersdorf is located forty kilometers southeast of Metz in a fertile plain on the right bank of the Nied river. A path linking the settlement with the surrounding villages allowed for trade and communication beyond the borders of the village.[6] Larger roads ran to the east, west, and north: they led to Nancy and Saarlouis, Metz and Frankfurt, St. Avold and Dieuze. Of course the roads were frequented not only by travelers and traders, beggars and vagrants, but also by soldiers bringing in their wake hunger and pestilence, war and destruction. The quarrel over whether this scrap of land should belong to France or to the Holy Roman Empire, whether it should become Catholic or Protestant, was not decided until 1714 in the Peace of Rastatt. This, at long last, was the beginning of an extended period of peace, one that afforded the inhabitants some breathing space and an opportunity for a fresh start on the ruins of their collective memory.[7]

A brief history of the village

Steinbiedersdorf was originally a castle fief (Burglehen) belonging to the lords of Falkenberg and became part of the County of Kriechingen in the fourteenth century through marriage and inheritance, where it remained until the villagers opted for incorporation into France in 1793. Starting in the sixteenth century, half of the village was enfeoffed to the bailiwick of the landvogt of Hagenau, which meant it had close lordship ties to the Holy Roman Empire.[8]

In 1617, Emperor Matthias elevated Peter Ernst of Kriechingen to the rank of imperial count (Reichsgraf). He transferred the title to the entire family and to the localities that stood under imperial suzerainty, which were combined

---

(*Reichsland*); 1607 Steinbiderstorff (gallice Pont de Pierre) (Dorvaux, 159); 1688 Pontpierre (AD Mos. 10 F 51); 1699 Pontpier (AD Mos. 553 E Dépot FF 4, No. 21); 1716 Steinbiedersdorff (AD Mos. 10 F 120); 1725 Steinbiederstorff (AD Mos. 10 F 429); 1756 Pondepirre (AD Mos. B 10045); 1766 Steinbiederstroff (AD Mos. 10 F 520); 1774 Steinbetertorff (AD Mos. B 10059); 1793ff. Pontpierre. The popular etymological variant (Pierres prés du village), which supposedly indicates Gallo-Roman traces, is in Michel de La Torre, *Guide de l'art et de la nature: Moselle* (1985).

[5] According to Prof. Haubrichs's convincing and etymologically well-reasoned view.

[6] AD Mos. J 5818: Collection Richard.

[7] Original in the Staatsbibliothek, Berlin.

[8] "Steinbiedersdorf" in *Reichsland*, vol. 3, 1052. Supplemented by: AD Mos. 10 F 3: Chartulaire des Titres de la maison de Créhange, 1485. Steinbiedersdorf still had its own criminal court (Hochgericht) in the late Middle Ages. In the sixteenth century, half of the village was incorporated as a fief into the bailiwick of the landvogt of Hagenau. No traces of the rights of the landvogt can be found in the late seventeenth and the eighteenth centuries.

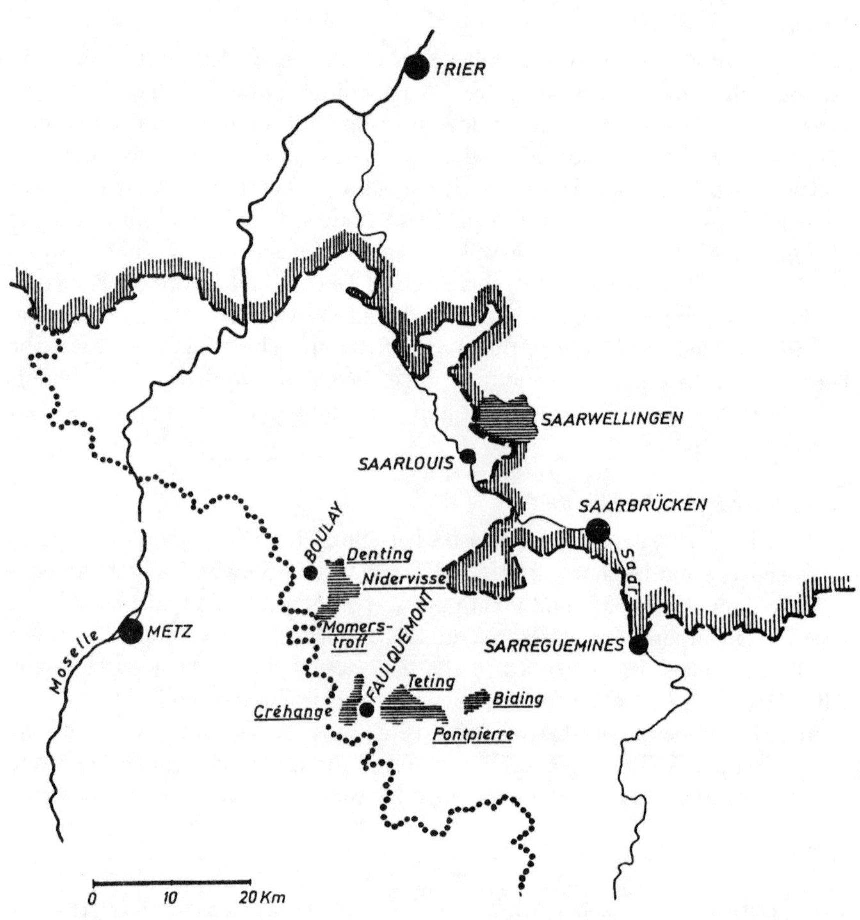

Kriechingische Orte (Créhange = Kriechingen, Pontpierre = Steinbiedersdorf)
Orientierungsorte (Major cities, included as geographic points of reference)
Sprachgrenze (Language border)
Reichsgrenze (boundary of the Italy Roman Empire)

Map drawn by Martin Wolff

Map 3. The County of Kriechingen before the French Revolution

into the Imperial County of Kriechingen. Henceforth, Kriechingen, Stein-biedersdorf, Dentingen, Momersdorf, Niedervisse, Büdingen, Tetingen, and the lordship of Saarwellingen made up "the land of the County of Kriechingen." This was an entity without territorial contiguity, defined by the shared subordination of its parts to the territorial lord, their assignment to the imperial district (Reichskreis) of the Upper Rhine, and the jurisdiction exercised by the imperial courts. These disparate parts had no contact with the villages of Kriechingen that stood under the suzerainty of France, Luxembourg, or Lorraine, but they did have contact with their French or Lorrainese surroundings.[9]

The region experienced hardly a single peaceful year during the seventeenth century: the Thirty Years' War, which ended in Lorraine only with the Peace of Vincennes in 1661, was followed during the Dutch war by French occupation, which extended right into the period of réunion.[10] The way for a political reorganization was paved with the establishment of the Chambre de Réunion in 1680. Count Ludwig of Kriechingen was asked to formally recognize the feudal dominion of the Bishopric of Metz over the County of Kriechingen. But when he was able to produce documentary evidence that the county was part of the Holy Roman Empire, Metz withdrew its original demand and laid claim to the county as a freehold (Franc-alleux). Shortly before his death, Count Johann Ludwig rendered an oath of homage to the King of France.[11]

With the death of Johann Ludwig in 1681, the older, Calvinist branch of the counts of Kriechingen (Kriechingen-Pittingen-Bacourt) died out in the male lineage. The succession quarrels that followed were settled by the parliament in Metz in 1688. Anna Dorothea—the sister of the last count and widow of Count Edgard Ferdinand Cirksema of East Frisia (who had died in 1668), who had spent at least some time living in Kriechingen—succeeded her brother in 1697.[12] She, too, paid homage to the French king. When she had to travel to

---

[9] In addition to the localities under imperial suzerainty, which included, in addition to the villages mentioned above, also Ahlingen and Falschweiler, the county of Kriechingen incorporated villages under French suzerainty (Laningen, Fremsdorf) and under Lorrainese suzerainty (Altrippen and Warsberg as Voué). Moreover, the county also included, alongside the lordship of Saarwellingen, the lordship of Püttlingen, which was under French suzerainty, and the lordship of Rollingen, which was under the suzerainty of Luxembourg: *Hochgräflich Wied-Runkel- und Crichingischer Staats- und Haus-Kalender* (Frankfurt a. M., 1767).

[10] We owe a detailed account of the events of the war and their catastrophic consequences to Johann Michael Moscherosch, who was the administrator (Amtmann) in Kriechingen at the time: Walter Ernst Schäfer, *Johann Michael Moscherosch: Staatsmann, Satiriker und Pädagoge im Barockzeitalter* (Munich, 1980), 89ff.

[11] HHSTA Vienna, Kleinere Reichsstände II, 12, Den. Rec. 1503 VV 65 (1), Reichshofrat, obere Registratur 1863: Wied-Runkel RC 2 (1–6); AD Mos. 10 F 77: Die Teutsche Reichsgrafschaft Kriechingen von Franzosen mishandelt. Ein historisches Bruchstück, 1793.

[12] Male succession prevailed in lordships that were part of the Bishopric of Metz and were located east of the Saar river, while a "patrimonial" law of inheritance existed west

East Frisia on family business, the county was confiscated and its revenues were leased out.[13] It was only after intense diplomatic efforts by the countess that the County of Kriechingen, minus a few villages, was returned to the house of Kriechingen in the Peace of Rjiswijk and once again placed under the over-lordship of the Holy Roman Empire.[14] In 1698, Anna Dorothea empowered an official (Oberamtmann) and a secretary to protect her interests and assured the utterly impoverished subjects that she would restore them to all their rights and privileges.[15] The officeholders were placed under oath to the emperor and the countess—"la dite excellence Madame comtesse d'Ostfriese et de Créhange."[16]

In 1702, the county once more fell to France for another twelve years. It was once again leased out and had to come up with high contribution payments. That same year, Anna Dorothea, by a testamentary disposition, appointed her younger son, Friedrich Ulrich of Kriechingen–East Frisia, to succeed her.[17] Friedrich Ulrich, whose tenure fell into the period of the War of the Spanish Succession (1701–1714), in turn made testamentary arrangements for his oldest son, and "in the absence of male descendants" for his eldest daughter and her issue, to inherit the county.[18] Following his death that same year, his widow, Marie Charlotte, was granted guardianship over their daughter Christine Louise.[19]

The Peace of Rastatt in November of 1714 paved the way for the return of the County of Kriechingen to the Holy Roman Empire. Marie Charlotte, who resided in East Frisia about a thousand kilometers away, charged her intendant with reclaiming the castle and lordship rights. The revenues from the county were leased out, much as they had been during the period of réunion and the preceding period of occupation. When the countess and her French officials interfered in the accustomed rights of the subjects, enshrined in an old, fourteenth-century Schöffenweistum (costumal), by blocking their access to resources

---

of the Saar: Gaston Zeller, "Note sur le rôle ancien de la Sarre comme frontière," *Bulletin de la société des amis de pays de la Sarre* (1928), 257–260. As the decision by the parliament shows, the County of Kriechingen, west of the Saar, was regarded as a region of apron-string tenure (feudum femineum) that passed to the female line upon the extinction of the male line. On the history of ownership see the article on Kriechingen in *Reichsland*, vol. 2, 539f.

[13] Flaus, *Comté*, 52.

[14] Ibid., 23ff.

[15] Ad Mos. 10 F 52: Acte de prise de possession du village de Pontpierre, confisqué sur la Comtesse de Créhange au profit du Roi, 1698.

[16] AD Mos. 10 F 14: Anna Dorothea to the officials in Kriechingen, April 29, 1698.

[17] Ad Mos. 10 F 14: Jus primo geniturae in der Grafschaft Kriechingen betr. Anna Dorothea had married Count Eduard Ferdinand of East Frisia in 1665. In the testament she excluded her eldest son, Edzard Eberhard Wilhelm, fom the succession.

[18] AD Mos. 10 F 14: Jus primo geniturae in der Grafschaft Kriechingen betr., 1710.

[19] In 1716 she was referred to as "Her Serene Highness, the widowed Princess of East Frisia as holder of said county" (AD Mos. 10 F 120). She had French officials and servants.

and raising dues and services, thus depriving them of the "fruits of peace," the result was unrest and lawsuits. The communities of Steinbiedersdorf and Büdingen retained a lawyer who was to procure a penal brief (Pönalmandat) against the "most serene (hochfürstliche) defendant."[20] Once the dispute had been settled, the subjects recognized Marie Charlotte as "overlord, *collator*, and half tithe lord" and held annual court sessions (Jahrgedinge) in her name.[21]

In 1726, daughter Christine Louise of Kriechingen–East Frisia, born in 1710, was given in marriage to Johann Ludwig Adolf of Wied, five years her senior. On the occasion of the marriage, Christine Louise had to renounce any and all hereditary claims to the Principality of East Frisia "for the special benefit of the male lineage of the Princes of East Frisia." She made a formal promise not to invoke the SC Velleianum to contest the declaration.[22]

Unlike her mother and grandmother, Christine Louise played no active part in politics. Into the marriage she brought the County of Kriechingen, including the lordships of Saarwellingen, Püttlingen, and Rollingen, which she had inherited from her father, thus providing an important source of income to her future husband, Count Johann Ludwig Adolf, who was locked in a legal struggle with his mother over the succession to the lordship of Wied.[23] Johann Ludwig Adolf was given governance over Wied in 1730. In 1732, after only six years of marriage, Christine Louise died a few hours after giving birth to their fourth child, Christian Ludwig, the designated heir of the County of Kriechingen.[24]

---

[20] AD Mos. 10 F 118, fol. 120: Bericht des Rates Schleiff an die Fürstin; Supplikation der Einwohner von Steinbiedersdorf und Büdingen beim Reichskammergericht, 1716; Bericht des Rates Schleiff über die Unruhen in Saarwellingen, 1718: reprinted in Gerd Weisgerber, "Widerspenstige Untertanen," *Quellen und Beiträge zur Geschichte des Dorfes und der Herrschaft Saarwellingen* 17 (1970): 1–4; 18 (1970): 1–4.

[21] AD Mos. 10 F 462. The Steinbiedersdorf Jahrgeding in 1722 was held in the name of "the Princess and Lady, Lady Marie Charlotte, née Princess in East Frisia, widowed Countess of Kriechingen": AD Mos. Actes judiciaires B 10081: Plaids annaux Pontpierre, 1722.

[22] STA Wiesbaden 3005–2188: Beweis des gräflich Wied- und Kriechingischen Sukzessionsrechts in Ostfriesland, 1746.

[23] On Johann Ludwig Adolf von Wied-Runkel see J. St. Reck, *Geschichte der gräflichen und fürstlichen Häuser Isenburg, Runkel, Wied, verbunden mit der Geschichte des Rheintals zwischen Koblenz und Andernach von Julius Cäsar bis auf die neueste Zeit* (Weimar, 1925), 259f. Johann Ludwig Adolf had legal quarrels with his mother, who, after a long regency, refused to hand the governance of Wied over to him. In 1730 he won his case in court, but a little later his mother sued him over her claims arising from her jointure: HHSTA Vienna, Kleinere Reichsstände II, 2, Den. rec. 1503, No. 65: Zu Wied-Runkel verwitwete Gräfin Sophie-Florentine gegen ihren älteren Sohn Graf Johann Ludwig Adolf zu Wied-Runkel, 1727–1746.

[24] HHSTA Vienna, Kleinere Reichsstände, II, 12; Den. rec. 1503 VV 65 (1); Reichshofrat, Obere Registratur 1863 Wied Runkel RC 2, 1–6.

Johann Ludwig Adolf assumed governance, although his mother-in-law, Marie Charlotte, retained rights and income from the county.[25] Evidently both the mother-in-law's and the son-in-law's interest in the lordship of Kriechingen continued to be chiefly fiscal in nature. Neither shied away from carrying on their disagreements at the expense of the subjects. Taxes were raised, and the court and the administration were handed over to officeholders with little qualification, some of whom purchased their offices and used the county to enrich themselves.[26] Innovations were constantly being introduced and the instruments of control were expanded.[27] To allow for greater oversight, the ruler demanded, at the Steinbiedersdorf Jahrgeding in 1748, that the community elect four wardens of public order (Polizeischützen) from its own ranks, who would be charged with supervising life in the village. Henceforth, premarital pregnancies and cases of immorality were to be reported to the authorities for punishment.[28]

The fact that the disciplinary interest of the officeholders focused on the bodies of the subjects and sought to penetrate into areas that had previously been supervised by families or the Catholic priest considerably intensified the conflicts.

---

[25] AD Mos. 10 F 429. The precise rights of Marie Charlotte, Countess of Kriechingen, need further clarification. After 1726 the Jahrgedinge were no longer held in her name, but in the name of Count Johann Ludwig Adolf, Count of Wied: AD Mos. Actes judiciaires B 10081: Plaids annaux Pontpierre, 1727; B 9931: Créhange, 1749. However, files from the Imperial Chamber Court (Reichskammergericht) suggest that she still retained lordship rights. For example, in 1743 "all the subjects of the lordship of Kriechingen brought suit against Marie Charlotte, widowed Countess of Kriechingen, née Princess of East Frisia, and her son-in-law, Johann Adolf, Count of Wied-Runkel and Kriechingen zu Dierdorf": LHA Koblenz 56/487; AD mos. E Dépôt 553 FF 4: Mandati im Prozeß der Untertanen gg. Marie Charlotte, 1742. As late as 1755, she drafted a power of attorney for a lawyer: HHSTA Vienna, RHR Ob. Reg. 1863, Wied-Runkel RC 2, 1–6.

[26] Ad Mos. 10 F 140 1742/43, Criechingische Bedientenansetzung und übeler Zustand der Grafschaft, 1742/43; and ibid.: Projekt besserer Administration der Grafschaft Kriechingen. It was charged that preference had been shown to the secretary Köppel "in that he is considered a good cameralist, because he has delivered to My Lord and Her Highness the Princess several hundred Reichstaler as prepayment for future lease revenues and has now also promised to take a lease of 100,000 fl on the Lordship of Kriechingen."

[27] As an example I give a Decree of Public Order attributed to Johann Ludwig Adolf. It was reprinted in Sittel, where it is incorrectly dated to 1710, since Johann Ludwig Adolf did not became territorial ruler of Krichingen until after his marriage in 1726. This decree contains a prohibition against the smoking of tobacco by young people and regulations pertaining to the weekly street cleaning. As an argument against the smoking of tobacco the decree points to the higher life-expectancy of previous generations: ". . . it being incontestable that our ancestors, before this vice arose, attained a far greater age than the tobacco smokers of today." Sittel, *Sammlung der Provinzial- und Particular-Gesetze*, 516–627. Since the dating of this frequently cited source is incorrect, the content, too, should be verified.

[28] AD Mos. E Dépôt 553 DD 3, No. 10: Anzeige des Fiskals, daß seit drei bis vier Jahren keine vorehelichen Schwangerschaften und Unzuchtsfälle gemeldet wurden, 1750. This was followed by a relevant order to the community.

The moral policies of the rulers, concerned less with moralizing than with exercising paramount authority, challenged the power of the housefathers. In the communal assembly the latter had an opportunity to shift their resistance to an institutional level. The members of the community who were empowered to do so decided to initiate legal proceedings against the officials. Sixty-nine men authorized the village court and seven delegates to represent the interests of all—that is to say, those members of the community who had political rights.[29]

To put a stop to this abusive administration and defend their rights, the community of Kriechingen also brought a suit against the chancery of Wied-Runkel in the Imperial Chamber Court (Reichskammergericht); it was settled in 1749.[30] The chief forestry officer, Köppel, in particular, was charged not only with "expensive, sumptuous, and ostentatious housekeeping and a lifestyle far in excess of his station and income," but also with venality, embezzlement, and wasteful exploitation.[31]

At least in the eyes of the lawyers who drafted the indictment, Köppel had violated the boundaries of his social place to a degree that was no longer tolerable. Moreover, he had threatened the entire social order, for by his excessive demands he deprived the subjects of the possibility of living in keeping with their own social rank. His daughter, too, violated the notions of an appropriate lifestyle through excessive luxury and transgressions against the rules of female honor. A later indictment claimed that she helped her father collect the seigneurial revenues and allegedly led a "disgraceful" and expensive life with soldiers, cavalrymen, and trumpeters. Within the legal argument laid out by the complaint, the reference to the "dissolute" life of the daughter appears not as a separate charge against the daughter, but as a device to underscore the accusations against Köppel, who was a failure not only as an official but also as a father. Such a man presented a danger to the lord, as well, seeing as he "has dreadfully harassed the subjects," and "the longer he exercised his office the more unrestrained and high-handed were his actions and depredations, as though the County of Kriechingen and its legitimate lord were to be

---

[29] Ibid., Vollmacht von 1748.

[30] LHA Koblenz 56/488: Gemeinde Kriechingen als Kläger gegen die Wied-Runkelsche Kanzlei daselbst; Verlgeich, 1749.

[31] STA Wiesbaden 3005–2244: Actenmäßige Geschichts-Erzählung und Deduction in Sachen des gewesenen Oberforstmeisters und Rechnungsführers Köppel contra den hochgebohrenen Grafen und Herrn, Herrn Christian Ludwig, regierenden Grafen zu Kriechingen, 3. Köppel hailed from a poor family. His father was a stable hand in the Lordship of Runkel, his mother came from a peasant family. He himself was first Heyduc, then page-attendant (Pagen-Aufwärter), and was eventually trained as a clerk by his predecessor in office. He occupied in succession the offices of Landschreiber, secretary, chamber councillor (Kammerrat), and chief forest warden, and he tried to become ennobled.

erased from the earth."[32] Christian Ludwig, finally, charged that he had conducted negotiations in Paris about the sale of the county.[33]

To prevent the "utter ruination" of the county, the twenty-one year-old heir
sent a petition to his father in 1753, asking that the government and administration of the lordship be handed over to him as governor. Preserving the land
and the people required, so he argued, the constant presence of a territorial
lord, one who made sure that "the officials of Kriechingen do not exceed the
limits of their offices, but carry them out in accordance with their oath and
duties."[34] In 1754, Johann Ludwig Adolf made his son coruler, and in 1757—
after the death of Marie Charlotte—sole ruler.[35] Between 1759 and 1760,
Christian Ludwig had a residence with secondary buildings and parks erected
in Kriechingen, but he usually spent only a few weeks each year in the remote
county. After all, Kriechingen was only one of many scattered lordships to
which the count laid claim. In spite of his mother's formal renunciation of any
inheritance claims, he fought for the succession in East Frisia after the house
of the counts died out.[36] In addition, he had his paternal inheritance in Wied
to look forward to. As early as March of 1761 he took over the administration of the upper county of Wied-Runkel. After the death of his father in May
1762, he succeeded to his office and established his residence at Runkel castle,
two hundred kilometers away.[37] In 1762 he married Charlotta Sophia Augusta,

---

[32] Ibid., 9.

[33] AD Paris, C. P. Allemagne, Petites Principautés, 18: Créhange (1737–1774): Letter
of protest from Christian Ludwig against any sale of the county. Since he had inherited
the county from his mother, his father could only administer it but not permit or carry
out any changes.

[34] AD Mos. 10 F 429: Gesuch von Christian Ludwig, Graf zu Wied-Runkel. On the
issue of the structure of the state at the lower levels see Michaela Hohkamp, *Herrschaft
in der Herrschaft. Die vorderösterreichische Obervogtei Triberg von 1737 bis 1780.* Veröffentlichungen des Max-Planck-Instituts für Geschichte, 142 (Göttingen, 1998).

[35] AD Mos. 10 F 116: Pleins Pouvoirs, accordés au comte le 7.8.1754. In 1757, the
Jahrgeding was held in his name for the first time. Since the Landeshuldigung had not
taken place, the new officials were sworn in with a handshake: AD Mos. Actes judiciaires B 10012: Plaids annaux de Niederwies, Denting, Momersdorf, 1757. The official
date of his entry into office was October 18, 1757 (Hochgräflich criechingischer Kalender).
That the assumption of sole rule occurred immediately after the death of his mother is
mentioned by Johann Ulrich Freiherr von Cramer, *Wetzlarische Nebenstunden* 98, 131:
Bericht über die Entstehung und den Verlauf der Auseinandersetzung zwischen Graf
Christian von Wied-Runkel als Besitzer der Grafschaft Kriechingen und den Untertanen
dieser Grafschaft bis zum Einsatz eines Exekutionskommandos im Juli 1758; newly edited
by Winfried Schulze, *Bäuerlicher Widerstand und feudale Herrschaft in der frühen Neuzeit*
(Stuttgart, 1980), 290–294.

[36] HHSTA Vienna, Obere Reistratur Num. 2, K. 1863: Christian Ludwig gg. den
König von Preußen pcto succ. Ostfriesland, 1758.

[37] Hochgräflich criechingischer Kalender, Kap. I: Hochgräflich Wied-Runkelische
Familie.

Countess of Sayn and Wittgenstein, eight years his junior, who played no discernible role in the governance of the County of Kriechingen.[38]

Dominion over the upper county came with a seat and vote in the Lower Rhenisch-Westphalian Imperial District (Reichskreis) and in the Wetterau Council of Counts (Grafenverein), while Kriechingen brought membership in the Imperial District of the Upper Rhine.[39] The apportionment of the district levies and Christian Ludwig's demand for the furnishing of soldiers was one of the central sources of conflict from the middle of the eighteenth century on.

Peasant resistance took on a new dimension under the rule of Christian Ludwig. At times all communities of the county fought the efforts of the territorial ruler to reorganize his dominion. It would appear that the conflicts triggered by the changes concerned far more the relations of the subjects amongst themselves, and thus the daily life of the village, than they did the institutional level.[40] Still, changes occurred even there. In the wake of the legal wrangling, the subjects who had not submitted began negotiations with the French king with the aim of placing themselves under his protection.[41] In so doing they triggered protracted exchange negotiations that had not concluded by the time the French Revolution broke out.

Christian Ludwig remained the territorial ruler of the Imperial County of Kriechingen. In July 1791, a few weeks before his death, he was elevated to the rank of imperial prince. His son, Karl Ludwig Friedrich Alexander, succeeded him in October 1791, but in spite of repeated offers of reconciliation, he was no longer able to assert himself in the county. As early as 1790, Steinbiedersdorf had seen the first joint actions in concert with the neighboring Lorrainese.[42] The common mill (Bannmühle) was stormed and nonlocal millers were allowed to ply their trade in the village.[43]

The situation heated up in the summer of 1792. In Teting, the bailiff was forced to kiss the liberty tree, to swear an oath on the French constitution, and to attend mass that was conducted by a communal priest who had sworn

---

[38] Ibid.

[39] The count maintained permanent envoys or agents in Regensburg, Frankfurt am Main, Cologne, Vienna, Wetzlar, Bonn, Paris, Metz, Lunéville, Luxembourg, and Boulay (ibid., IXf.).

[40] On the significance of communal differences within the context of peasant resistance see David Martin Luebke, *His Majesty's Rebels: Communities, Factions, and Rural Revolt in the Black Forest, 1725–1745* (Ithaca, 1997).

[41] François-Yves Le Moigne, "Versailles et Créhange au XVIIIᵉ siècle ou les aléas d'une politique frontalière," in *L'Europe, l'Alsace et la France. Étude réuni en l'honneur du Doyen Georges Livet* (Strasbourg, 1986), 307–316, here 311.

[42] A letter from Wetzlar dated November 5, 1790, concerning the uprising in the County of Kriechingen, in *Göttingisches Historisches Magazin* 8 (1791): 399–402.

[43] As early as the summer of 1789, large numbers of outside millers had been permitted in the village: AD Mos. 10 F 811: Mühlen.

the ecclesiastical oath required during the French Revolution.[44] Liberty trees
were erected in Steinbiedersdorf and Denting in October. Burgomasters and jus-
tices of the peace were elected and charged with setting up a municipalité.[45]
For Denting, at least, the evidence is incontrovertible that the carriers of this
first revolutionary movement were the former "rebels" against the lord.[46]

After France, on November 19, 1792, had pledged its support to all peoples
eager to regain their liberty, Merlin de Thionville was able to make the following announcement to the National Convention on December 15, 1792:

> I announce a new free people to the Assembly. The aforementioned prin-
> cipality of the Count of Créhange was an enclave in the département of
> Moselle; the inhabitants let it be known to their former prince that they
> were free, that they were following all the decrees of the National
> Convention, and that they were going to ask to be incorporated into the
> French Republic.[47]

Of course it would take several weeks for the incorporation to take effect, an
interval that further deepened the fissures within the community. In Steinbiedersdorf, the priest and the officials tried in vain to get the subjects to change their
minds. Faced with the National Convention's hesitation, the members of the
"société populaire" of Faulquemont described the difficult situation in the village, where the fissures reached into the families:

> The parish priest and the officials of the County of Créhange are taking
> advantage of the silence of the Convention to mislead their minds, throw
> dissension into their consciences, and split up families as they seek to
> convince them that the requested annexation will not take place.[48]

The legal proceedings that had been pursued at the Imperial Chamber Court
right up to this time, especially another quarrel over the use of the forest, the
admission of semi-outsiders, the law of the common mill, and the fact that the

---

[44] For a more detail account of the events in the summer of 1792 see Claudia Ulbrich,
"Die Bedeutung der Grenzen für die Rezeption der französischen Revolution an der
Saar," in Winfried Schulze, ed., *Aufklärung, Politisierung und Revolution* (Pfaffenweilter,
1991), 147–174, esp. 160ff.

[45] STA Wiesbaden 172–3381, Bericht, den Abfall der Grafschaft betr.

[46] Claudia Ulbrich, "Traditionale Bindung, revolutionäre Erfahrung und soziokultureller
Wandel. Denting 1790–1796," in Karl Otmar Frhr. Von Aretin and Karl Härter, eds.,
Revolution und konservatives Baharren. Das Alte Reich und die Französische Revolution
(Mainz, 1990), 113–130, esp. 124ff.

[47] Archives parlementaires 55, 66: decree of December 15, 1792; AN Paris, sect.
mod., F 7, 4401: protest by the count dated December 17, 1791, and referral to the
comité diplomatique on December 21, 1792. For a placement of these actions within
the context of the revolutionary events and a critical assessment of the sources see Claudia
Ulbrich, "L'impact de la Révolution française dans le comté de Créhange, pays enclavé
en Lorraine," in *Révolution Française 1988–1989. Actes des 113e et 114e congrès nationaux
des soc. sav.* (Paris, 1991), 425–435, here 431f.

[48] AN Paris, sect. mod., F 7, 4401: Letter of the Jacobin club of Faulquemont to the
National Convention, January 25 and February 2, 1793, respectively.

count had seized the monastic properties in the wake of the dissolution of the monasteries in France, as well as the fracturing of the community into mutually hostile groups who could take advantage of the new political situation—these circumstances did not create a favorable climate for persuading the villagers to change their minds.[49] The politically enfranchised members of the community, prorevolutionary in attitude and supported in their desire to join France by the Jacobine club in Faulquemont, persisted undeterred in their efforts to bring the administrative structures in line with revolutionary France. They replaced the office of the territorial clerk (Landschreiberei) with a "minispalit" (municipalité) and set up a militia.[50]

On February 14, 1793, after lengthy debates in the National Convention, Pont-de-Pierre, Teting-empire, and Püttlingen were incorporated into France and assigned to the Département Moselle.[51] Henceforth, French laws applied.[52] Jewish men and women acquired civic equality provided they were willing to swear the oath of citizenship.[53] In some places they were able to assume official posts within the communal administration.[54] The administrative and legislative transformation was followed by the adoption of the revolutionary calendar and of French as the language of administration. Profound changes occurred in the ecclesiastical constitution. A few days after the decree of réunion, the priest, who had refused to swear the ecclesiastical oath, was forced to leave the village, which he had described as a center of counterrevolution as late as Easter of 1792.[55] In the subsequent years, Steinbiedersdorf was officially ministered to

---

[49] AN Paris, sect. anc., Q 2, 193: detailed exposition of the course of action in a correspondence between the prince and the councillor (Regierungsrat) Lenz.

[50] AN Paris, sect. mod., F 7, 4401: Letter of the Jacobin club of Faulquemont to the National Convention, January 25 and February 2, 1793, respectively.

[51] On the reunions in the Saar-Mosel region see Ulbrich, "Bedeutung der Grenzen," here esp. 149. On Püttlingen (= Créhange-Puttelange) see Hans-Joachim Kühn, "Notizen zur Reunion der Gemeinde Püttlingen mit der Französischen Republik am 14. Februar 1793," in Johannes Schmitt, ed., *Revolutionäre Spuren . . . Beiträge der Saarluoiser Geschichtswerkstatt zur Französischen Revolution im Raum Saarlouis* (Saarbrücken, 1991), 237–246.

[52] On this point the incorporated communities differed from those that were taken through military conquest. The view of Cilli Kasper-Holtkotte that the Saar-Mosel area "was regarded as occupied enemy territory" down to 1798 (*Juden im Aufbruch. Zur Sozialgeschichte einer Minderheit im Saar-Mosel-Raum um 1800* [Hannover, 1996], 190) needs to be corrected for the simple reason that in 1793 thirty communities were incorporated and integrated into the Département Moselle. For the Jewish population, especially, this was an important distinction.

[53] On the emancipation of the Jews in eastern France (decree of September 27, 1791) see Patrick Girard, *La Révolution française et les juifs* (Paris, 1989), 148–189; Robert Badinter, *Libres et égaux. L'emancipation des Juifs sous la Révolution française (1789–1791)* (Paris, 1989), 213–218; Paula E. Hyman, *The Emancipation of the Jews of Alsace. Acculturation and Tradition in the Nineteenth Century* (London, 1991), 14f.

[54] For example, in Kriechingen, beginning in 1793, one Jew was a member of the communal council: Ulbrich, "L'impact de la révolution française," 433.

[55] AD Mos. 10 F 749.

by a priest who had taken the oath, but secretly by one who had not.[56] The division within the community caused by the unrest had survived the revolution, at least in the ecclesiastical sphere.

Karl Ludwig Friedrich Alexander lost his lordship and ownership rights to the County of Kriechingen once and for all in the Treaty of Lunéville. As compensation he received territories east of the Rhine.[57] Steinbiedersdorf became a French community with a varied political fate also in the nineteenth century. The incorporation into France marked the end of the decades-long process of the inner reorganization of the county.

The large-scale upheavals I have briefly sketched here, within which the transformation from an estate-based society to a class society began to take shape, also constitute one of the most interesting phases in the history of the village with respect to the gender order. It gave the men and women of the village time and space to find their own answers to the challenges of daily life. Analyzing these answers requires that I take a look at the spaces that were available to the men and women who lived in Steinbiedersdorf.

---

[56] AD Mos. 29 J 657: Affaires paroissiales des paroisses de l'actuel diocèse de Metz, Archiprêtre de Faulquemont: Pontpierre (An X-1893).

[57] Wilhelm von der Nahmer, *Entwicklung der rheinischen Territorial- und Verfassungsverhältnisse* (Frankfurt a. M., 1832), 586ff.

CHAPTER THREE

SEARCHING FOR CLUES: SPHERES OF FEMALE AGENCY IN THE MIRROR OF BIOGRAPHY

Anyone who sets out in search of the women of the village would do well to go to church on a Sunday morning, where the Christian community was gathered for mass. Here, all men and women, young and old, had their place, which they did not freely choose but assumed in accordance to fixed rules.[1] In most churches, men sat on the right, the better side, and women on the left. The underlying symbolic order of this seating arrangement was permanently enshrined in the spatial structure: since Christian churches were oriented toward the east, the right side faced south. While this side was associated with "light and life," the left side embodied "darkness and death." "This symbolic language, built upon the vocabulary of purity and impurity, represents," as Edith Saurer has emphasized, "order and the transgression of order, hierarchies and sin." Through this language, "the (woman's) body was endowed with a specific meaning that was based on the doctrine of the humors and was supposed to underscore women's susceptibility to evil."[2]

This notion found expression also in the practice of churching. Six weeks after the birth of a child, a Christian mother made her way to church. Accompanied by the midwife or other birth helpers, she waited at the church portal for the priest to come and get her. Where a separate door was provided for this ritual on the northern side of the church, its location reinforced the symbolism that connected women with death and the devil and was reflected in the seating arrangement. And even where no separate entrance existed, the rest of the ritual was structured accordingly.

---

[1] Quarrels over church seating were especially common in Germany after the Reformation. There was a profusion of local rules, whereby the subordination of women and their association with their husbands or the farmstead can be seen as two common principles. Additional literature: Jan Peters, "Der Platz in der Kirche. Über soziales Rangdenken im Spätfeudalismus," *Jahrbuch für Volkskunde und Kulturgeschichte* 28 (1985): 77–106; Claudia Ulbrich, "Zankapfel 'Weibergestühl,'" in Axel Lubinski, Thomas Rudert, and Martina Schattkowsky, eds., *Historie und Eigen-Sinn. Festschrift für Jan Peters zum 65. Geburtstag* (Weimar, 1997), 107–114.

[2] Saurer, "Einleitung," 9f.

As the priest was leading the woman into church, she had to hold the left end of the stole in her right hand. According to popular belief, this was the only way to exorcise the devil. The woman in childbed had to kneel before the priest, a man, and recite a prayer expressing humility and gratitude. In receiving the holy communion afterward, she was, as Susan C. Karant-Nunn has emphasized, reconnected in three ways to a patriarchal society: to her husband, to whom she once again owed the conjugal duties following her churching; to the Son of God, whom she received in the sacrament; and to the community, which resumed the place that had been taken by the women who looked after her during the pregnancy and birth. As a token of her gratitude and submission, the woman placed a gift on the altar.[3]

The inequality between the sexes that was expressed in such rituals and symbols was underpinned by the separation of men and women in the church. In this regard there was no difference between Christians and Jews.[4] In the synagogue, too, women had been segregated from men since the late Middle Ages, although the separation was stricter still in places that had a women's synagogue (Frauenschul or Weiberschul). As a space, the women's synagogue was self-contained; the connection to the men's synagogue was severed by the seating arrangement, which was focused toward the center.[5] A window allowed the woman leading the service to coordinate the prayers with what the men were doing.[6] Where no women's synagogue existed, the prayer space for women was separated from the men's with screens or cloths. As a place of ritual action, the men's synagogue had a higher degree of holiness than the women's shul, which was, "literally, an appendage of the synagogue."[7]

---

[3] Susan C. Karant-Nunn, to whom we are indebted for a persuasive interpretation of the churching rituals in the late Middle Ages, suggests that we should also see them as "rites de passage" in the way van Gennep understood the phrase: Karant-Nunn, *The Reformation of Ritual. An Interpretation of Early Modern Germany* (London, 1997), 82f.

[4] Edith Saurer has pointed out that while the Christian churches rejected the notions of pollution and taboo incorporated in the Jewish religion, they adopted these notions themselves in the practice of separating the sexes in the church and in the ritual of churching. Beginning in the seventeenth century, churching was once again prescribed for Catholic women in childbed. Comparable regulations existed also within the Anglican church: Saurer, "Einleitung," 9; Olwen Hufton, *The Prospect Before Her*, 189; and Siglinde Clementi's dissertation "Die Aussegnung und die Unreinheit der Wöchnerin: zur Geschichte eines Kirchenbrauchs und seiner Idee" (University of Vienna, 1994).

[5] Helmut Eschwege, *Die Synagoge in der deutschen Geschichte. Eine Dokumentation* (Dresden, 1980), 18. Rachel Monika Herweg, *Die jüdische Mutter. Das verborgene Matriarchat* (Darmstadt, 1995), 107, explains the separation of the genders with the "increasing elaboration—at that time of existential importance to the Jews—of their respective spheres of activities and the reciprocal gender roles that resulted from this."

[6] Freddy Raphaël and Robert Weyl, *Juifs en Alsace. Culture, société, histoire* (Toulouse, 1977), 79f.

[7] Eschwege, *Synagoge*, 18.

Even in a community as small as that of Steinbiedersdorf, where the place of prayer had been set up in the house of Abraham Jacob, the *parnas* (elected leader) of the Jewish community, the women's section and the men's section were separated. We learn this from a disposition in the testament of Abraham Jacob:

> From this day on and in the hour before my death, forever after, I make the shul in my house into an eternal sactuary. In return the protected Jews living here shall be obligated and bound to keep an eternal light burning for the sake of my soul from the hour of my death until our true and just redeemer shall come. To pay the expenses they may rent out and lease the places in the men's and women's shul, and my surviving heirs have no more claim to the shul than all the other resident protected Jews. However, I reserve for myself that the place in the shul where I now stand shall be assigned to the rabbi for free, and he need not pay anything for it.[8]

The revenue generated by renting out or auctioning off the places in the "men's and women's shul" was to be used to pay for the eternal light (*Ner Tamid*) that was to burn after Abraham Jacob's death.[9] Abraham Jacob stated explicitly that his heirs should not receive any preferential treatment over the other heads of Jewish households. Yet his instructions that his own place be reserved for the rabbi after his death reveals that differences in rank did exist in the allocation of places.

Social rank was also reflected in the Christian church space. Within the gender groups, individuals usually stood or sat in a hierarchical arrangement. Where seats or standing places had not been assigned permanently on the basis of the rank order of the farms (Höfeordnung), they were sold or auctioned off. Very few records of these proceedings have survived, though the few indications that are extant point to the special significance that women's places held in the thinking about social rank.[10] Women sometimes paid two to three times as much as men for the seats at the very front and along the center aisle.[11]

---

[8] Testament of Abraham Jacob: see Appendix (43b).

[9] The sentence should probably be understood to mean that Abraham Jacob intended the Ner Tamid as a memorial of his death in the synagogue, which may have something to do with the fact that his son had already died when he wrote his testament. On the Ner Tamid see Simon Ph. de Vries, *Jüdische Riten und Symbole* (Hamburg, 1990; original ed. published in the Netherlands, 1927 and 1932; reprint, Amsterdam, 1968), 39f. and 320ff.

[10] Peters, "Der Platz in der Kirche," 82f.; Richard van Dülmen, *Dorf und Stadt. 16.-18. Jahrhundert. Kultur und Alltag*, vol. 2 (Munich, 1992), 189f. The importance of the church space, however, goes beyond the fact that it mirrored the order of social rank; it also created that order, whereby a number of other factors (clothing, gestures) must surely be considered alongside a person's place. Many churches had on the women's or the men's side seats that could be freely chosen, which suggests that not all members of a parish were to equal degrees part of this thinking about social rank. This applies especially to the galleries and balconies.

[11] As was the case, for example, in the neighboring village of Denting, where a dispute

After all, the church was the sole and proper space where they could demonstrate the social place to which they laid claim. Here they had the opportunity to experience themselves as a group, if a subordinated one, and at the same time to draw lines of distinctions among each other.[12]

There are no sources about the seating arrangement in the church of Steinbiedersdorf. But for that very reason we may assume that the customary practice prevailed, since exceptions to the rule were generally mentioned. For example, a quarrel over the seating order erupted in 1772 in Mainvillers, because here, as in three other parishes of the region (Landroff, Lesse, and Flétrange), the men sat in front and the women in back. When the priest of Mainvillers, invoking the custom in Lorraine, tried to get the men to sit on the right and the women on the left, the result was a serious dispute with the parish. The latter lodged a complaint with the intendant of Lorraine, while the priest notified his ecclesiastical superiors, who advised him not to yield to the wishes of the parishioners. However, his superiors responded less favorably to his suggestion to reserve the front rows for the children who were preparing for the first holy communion, since these were the most expensive seats.[13]

A quarrel over the seating arrangement had also occurred in the neighboring community of Faulquemont. A few women, unhappy with the benches, had small, more comfortable seats made and set them up along the wall.[14] Here the need of the women for social distinction was more pronounced than in the smaller surrounding villages, where everybody knew each other. We can assume that those women of Steinbiedersdorf who had a high opinion of themselves also tried to get one of the better seats on the left side or along the center aisle. One who was undoubtedly willing to spend a good deal for her seat was Johannet Wahl, the wife of the seigneurial bailiff, who took an active part in her husband's affairs.

The bailiff's wife: Johannet Wahl

Johannet Wahl came to Steinbiedersdorf in 1737 following her marriage to the shoemaker Dominik Richard, and she lived in the village until her death in

---

over the auctioning of seats in 1792 came to blows: AD Mos. Actes judiciaires B 10011: 1792.

[12] Ulbrich, "Zankapfel 'Weibergestühl,'" 107ff. One episode related by Glikl bas Judah Leib in her memoirs indicates that the women's synagogue was also a place where women drew lines of distinction between one another. Glickl recounts a quarrel in the synagogue of Metz in 1714: "As customary on that occasion, all the holy Scrolls of the Law were taken from the holy Ark, and seven of them stood on a table. At that moment, a brawl broke out among the womenfolk, and they tore one from another the veils from their heads, so that they stood uncovered in the synagogue. Whereat the men joined in the fray, and set upon one another with blows." *The Memoirs of Glückl of Hameln*, trans. Marvin Lowenthal (New York, 1977), 276–277.

[13] AD Mos. 29 J 68 Mainvillers. We do not know how the conflict was resolved.

[14] AD Mos. 29 J 63 Archiprêtre de Morhange: États détaillés des paroisses, 1699–1700.

the summer of 1789. In 1739, at the age of twenty-three, she gave birth to their first and only child. The fact that the child's godparents were the priest, represented by the revenue collector of the county, and Anne Albert, the collector's wife, shows that Dominik Richard and Johannet Wahl had contacts to the better social circles of the county village.[15]

Soon after, Dominik Richard was appointed seigneurial bailiff and held that post until his death in 1773. His son, Peter, learned the baker's trade and occasionally worked as the village clerk (Dorfschreiber). Even after his marriage, Peter continued to live in his parents' house with his wife and child. The bailiff's house had thus been set up on the virilocal principle, which accorded the mother a strong position at least vis-à-vis her daughter-in-law. Officially the communal household was headed by the father, Dominik Richard.[16]

Rumor in the village had it, however, that the bailiff's house was ruled not by Dominik but by his wife and son. As one villager observed, the bailiff "can say or do nothing . . . if his wife and son don't want him to, in this way they have three bailiffs, namely, the mother, the father, and the son."[17] Since it had to be assumed that Johannet Wahl "as wife and mother helps her own," she should not be admitted as a witness in a family matter.

The comment about the three bailiffs in the village, which suggests associations with the Trinity, offers a clue about the vigor with which the bailiff's wife looked after the affairs of her husband's office. This also had to do with the fact that the bailiff did most of the business related to his official capacity at home. Since he was also running a farm, Dominik Richard was frequently outside the house, and in his absence his wife was an important contact person in official matters. We can see this not least from a complaint filed by Bartel Busendorfer, who had been involved in a brawl. Immediately after the incident he ran to the bailiff's house. Since the bailiff himself was not at home, he presented his petition to bring a criminal complaint to Richard's wife. In formal legal terms he had thus met his obligations and set further criminal proceedings in motion.[18]

There are no indications that the involvement of the bailiff's wife in her husband's affairs was based on a formal delegation of the office to both spouses. It is therefore unclear how far her authority extended, and whether she could have prevailed in a clash of interests if ever she did not represent the side of the lord.[19] In the case of the Wahl-Richard couple that was evidently not an

---

[15] AD Mos. I Mic. E.C. 553 Pontpierre, 1680–1793, GG 3: 1739.

[16] AD Mos. Actes judiciaires B 10079: Acta in Sachen der Gemeinde Steinbiedersdorf ca. Peter Richards Wittib von Longueville schuldige Gemeindegelder betr., 1788.

[17] LHA Koblenz 56/1301: In Sachen sämtlicher Untertanen und Dorfschaften der Grafschaft Kriechingen gegen Herrn Grafen von Wied-Runkel, Mandatis, fol. 137.

[18] AD Mos. Actes judiciaires B 10012: Niederwiesener, Dentinger, Momersdorfer Jahrgedingsprotokolle, 1754.

[19] On office-holding couples see Wunder, *He is the Sun*, 98f.; Wunder, "Herrschaft

issue, as Johannet Wahl looked after the affairs very much in the interests of the count. She knew what was going on in the village and was ready to pass the reports along reliably.

We are unable to tell from the sources whether Johannet Wahl ran a tavern or was simply very hospitable, but we do know that wine was consumed in the bailiff's house on numerous occasions. Michel Mangin, in any case, claimed that he did not go into the bailiff's house because one always had to drink there.[20] (From everything we know about how Michel Mangin lived his life, it was hardly the wine that bothered him.) If wine was served in the bailiff's house, the visitor was subject to its laws of hospitality. That altered the nature of the relationship between the bailiff and his wife and the member of the community. While all housefathers were equals within the community, the house was based on a hierarchical order: the host stood above the guest and was obligated to protect him. When it became customary to erect official buildings for office-holders, these structures were even more important than a bailiff's private residence: quarrels were now settled in the official building and no longer on location in the tavern. This changed the way in which conflicts were pursued and how we perceive them. As Michaela Hohkamp has shown for the lordship of Triberg, the shift of the process for settling disputes into an official space provided "the spatial and material conditions for methods of inquiry and questioning . . . that made possible an official interpretation of events and actions."[21]

Even if the bailiff's house was not yet an official place in this sense, it could fulfill that function in certain situations. Both Michel Mangin, who was reluctant to enter the bailiff's house, and Johannet Wahl, who displayed her hospitality, seem to have been aware of this. In 1763, when soldiers entered the village to seize the property of "rebellious" subjects, they went first to the bailiff's house for a bottle of wine. Johannet Wahl knew exactly who had come at what time into "her house, the house of the deponent (in ihr, der deponentin haus)." Since she later brought the guests a second bottle of wine, it is entirely possible that she was present during the conversation or at least heard a good deal of it. Apparently she took a keen interest in the entire affair. When the band of soldiers left to seize the property of the woman next door, Johannet Wahl went out into the street with them; eventually, as she could not see very well what was going on, she went to the upper chamber of her house. From there she watched as two men, among them her daughter-in-law's uncle, were shot. Later she obligingly related to the judge details about the incident that exonerated the soldiers:

---

und öffentliches Handeln von Frauen in der Gesellschaft der Frühen Neuzeit," in Gerhard, ed., *Frauen in der Geschichte des Rechts*, 27–54, here 52.

[20] LHA Koblenz 56/1301: In Sachen sämtlicher Untertanen und Dorfschaften der Grafschaft Kriechingen gegen Herrn Grafen von Wied-Runkel, Mandatis, fol. 45.

[21] Hohkamp, "Vom Wirtshaus zum Amtshaus," 9.

> As the chancery messenger (Kanzleibot) was opening the front door with
> an axe and also the locked kitchen door in the same manner, Nicolas
> Lorraine, who was shot to death, and his sons Peter and Hans Michel
> Lorraine called out "Avance, Alert, at them, at them," and . . . they picked
> up stones and threw them at the soldiers with such force that four of
> them had already been forced to withdraw to Court's threshing floor and
> they also thought that all of the soldiers would have to flee, which is
> something they also said to Dominik Barrell, that the soldiers would not
> be able to do it . . .[22]

After she had already placed her mark under her statement, she recalled that
she had seen three women outside her window who could testify as witnesses.
The women were summoned, but they tried to get out of testifying. One of
them, Anne Margarete Türk, made this statement: "When the soldiers were
shooting, she stood behind the wood and could not see it . . . she knew nothing else . . . and the witness absolutely did not want to sign her statement,
adding that she had nothing to sign.[23] Like Anne Margarete Türk, the other
two women also refused to affix their mark to a statement on the grounds that
they had been behind the woodpile and could not see anything. The attitude
of noncooperation is an indication that the women were lying. By claiming not
to have seen anything because their view was blocked by a pile of wood, they
were making use of a communicative strategy. That strategy points to collective patterns "with which the lower social strata sought to assert themselves
in court."[24]

Johannet Wahl was responsible for putting these three women into this
difficult situation in the first place. Her talkativeness in court reveals that she
stood unhesitatingly on the side of the lord and actively represented his interests. Since the bailiff exercised his office in his house (interestingly enough
referred to in one of the interrogations as "her, the deponent's house"), the
fact that living space and work space were still one and the same allowed
Johannet to participate extensively in her husband's affairs. And so the image
of the three bailiffs does seem to have been justified, and there is indeed witness testimony that the man who actually held the office was himself the most
personable of the three.[25]

---

[22] LHA Koblenz 56/491: Kommissionsbericht in Sachen der Gemeinde Steinbiedersdorf
gegen Herrn Grafen Christian von Wied-Runkel, Lit. JJ. o. As we can see, family interests did not always take precedence, at least not when it came to the family of her
daughter-in-law.

[23] Ibid.

[24] Silke Göttsch, "Zur Konstruktion schichtenspezifischer Wirklichkeit. Strategien und
Taktiken ländlicher Unterschichten vor Gericht," in Brigitte Bönisch-Brednich, Rolf W.
Brednich, and Helge Gerndt, eds., *Erinnern und Vergessen. Vorträge des 27. Deutschen
Volkskundekongresses* (Göttingen, 1989), 443–452, here 444; Silke Göttsch, "*Alle für einen
Mann . . .*" *Leibeigene und Widerständigkeit in Schleswig-Holstein im 18. Jahrhundert*. Studien
zur Volkskunde und Kulturgeschichte Schleswig-Holsteins 24 (Neumünster, 1991), 284ff.

[25] LHA Koblenz 56/491: Kommissionsbericht in Sachen der Gemeinde Steinbiedersdorf
gegen Herrn Grafen Christian von Wied-Runkel, fol. 217.

Despite the fact that Dominik Richard and Johannet Wahl took the side of the count, they were driven to financial ruin by the lawsuits the community brought against their lord. They were forced to go into debt and eventually had to mortgage their holdings, including their house and garden.[26]

Upon Dominik's death in 1773, his son inherited not only the holdings but also his father's debts. As he was not able to meet the demands of his creditors, he left in the middle of the night with his wife and child and went to Lorraine, where his creditors could not lay hands on his assets. In his wife's native village he found not only refuge, but also a living from the holdings his wife had inherited from her parents.[27]

Johannet Wahl remained in Steinbiedersdorf. To secure a livelihood she was able to fall back on her own landholdings, which could not be seized by the creditors.[28]

Testamentary control over her own property afforded her some possibility to make decisions in line with her wishes and interests. She took the liberty of treating the children of her son's first and second marriage differently. As a widow she supported the children of the first marriage, to whom she also sold pieces of land when she needed money in her old age. Contrary to regulations, she failed to obtain the consent of the ruler for these transactions. After her death this led to a lawsuit between the heirs, who were forced to accept an unfavorable ruling. Since the legal situation was not entirely clear, they had to auction off the land at candlelight: the land went to the bidder whose offer was on the table as the candle expired.[29] This legally enforced time limit was generally a disadvantage to the party putting the property up for auction, since there was no need to wait for the highest bid.[30] By neglecting to secure the lord's consent, Johannet Wahl had evidently crossed the boundary of what she could do.

The story of Johannet Wahl shows not only the degree to which Dominik Richard and his wife acted as an office-holding *couple* with respect to the husband's official functions. It also reveals that the bailiff's wife, as long as she displayed a commitment to the ruler's interest, had the opportunity to carve out a place of her own. The fact that she testified against her daughter-in-law's uncle indicates that her own interests were not shortchanged in the process. That she was able, as a woman, to have recourse to communicative structures

---

[26] AD Mos. Actes judiciaires B 10057: Gerichtliche Hypothek des herrschaftlichen Meiers Dominik Richard, 1771.

[27] AD Mos. Actes judiciaires B 10076: Acta in Sachen der Gemeinde Steinbiedersdorf ca. Peter Richards Wittib von Longeville schuldige Gemeindegelder betr., 1788.

[28] For the special protections for women's property see pp. 143–44.

[29] AD Mos. Actes judiciaires B 10080: Erbschaftsstreit der Erben Richard, 1790.

[30] On the use of the candle clock at auctions see Eugen Wohlhaupter, *Die Kerze im Recht. Forschungen zum deutschen Recht* 4.1 (Weimar, 1940), esp. 145ff.

not available to men is revealed by a look at Katharina Richard, the wife of the seigneurial clerk (Tabellion) Dominik Barell.[31]

Katharina Richard also had an important function in the village; above all, she was very well informed about village gossip.[32] When the house of a Jewish villager burned down and nobody knew whether it was an accident or criminal negligence, she was able to furnish important information. Her husband declared in court:

> The wife of the Jew Heim Neumark told his, the court clerk Dominik Barell's wife, that on the day before the fire, namely Sunday, Ahron Cain's people had twice baked there, namely cheese-cake and other such flatbread or tarts, and had poured the coals onto the stove in front of the oven and extinguished them with water, though they were not completely out . . . and this caused the fire.[33]

Barell's detailed statement left no doubt that the fire had been caused by negligence. It also shows the path that the gossip had taken: from Heym Neumark's wife to the clerk's wife to her husband, who put the report on paper and passed it along. Evidently Barell's wife also had access to what was being said within the group that was organizing the resistance to the lord. Like the Jew Jacques Levy, she caught wind of the rumor that the people of Steinbiedersdorf were planing an attack on the seigneurial prison to free the prisoners by force and had passed it on.[34]

Katharina Richard's competence lay in the field of oral communication. Allegedly she knew nothing about her husband's written records. And so, in 1764, when she found herself the target of efforts to hold her liable for debts that Dominik Barell had incurred during his lifetime, she sought outside help:

> There should be receipts among those papers, but as an uneducated woman she was not able to tell them apart. She therefore humbly asked to allow some time before deciding the main case, and to direct the territorial clerk (Landschreiber) on a certain day to search the existing records and other paper.[35]

---

[31] On the family situation see p. 77.

[32] On gossip: Regina Schulte, "Bevor das Gerede zum Tratsch wird," in Hausen and Wunder, eds., *Frauengeschichte—Geschlechtergeschichte*, 67–73; Pia Holenstein and Norbert Schindler, "Geschwätzgeschichte(n). Ein kulturhistorisches Plädoyer für die Rehabilitierung der unkontrollierten Rede," in van Dülmen, ed., *Dynamik der Tradition*, 41–148; Kienitz, *Sexualität, Macht und Moral*, 132ff.

[33] AD Mos. Actes judiciaires B 10047: Acta in Sachen fiscalis entgegen den Schutzjuden Ahron Cahen von Steinbiedersdorf, Beklagten, in pcto in des Behausung aufgekommenen Brands, 1759.

[34] LHA Koblenz 56/491, fol. 154: Kommissionsbericht in Sachen der Gemeinde Steinbiedersdorf gegen Herrn Grafen Christian von Wied-Runkel, Lit. C.: Extr. Protokoll v. 23.3.1763.

[35] AD Mos. Actes judiciaires B 10045: Acta in Sachen Johannes Hoen von Steinbiedersdorf gg. Greffier Barell hinterlassene Witwe, Beklagtin, pcto verkauften Holzes und dafür eingenommener Gelder, 1764.

With her petition she not only obtained an extension on the court date, but was also given the opportunity to bring in a third party, the clerk, who was on her side. Here, too, womanly ignorance appears part of a strategy, one that reveals an inferior though not hopeless position. Even if Katharina was not familiar with all the ins and outs of the office, she did participate actively in the affairs of her husband, the clerk Dominik Barell, whose house had a certain importance in the village. Years after his death, the village assembly was still being held in the house of the widow Barell.[36]

The example of the two wives of office-holding men brings out the existence of networks within rural society that interconnected the seemingly separate spheres of subjects and lords, men and women. The locus where the spheres mixed was the house, a domain that was largely shielded from outside gazes. From this perspective it makes sense that normative sources attached such importance to domestic order, asserting the authority of the housefather and the complementarity of the various spheres of tasks.

The rectory housekeeper: "Madmsell Lamber"

Although she appears to have performed her work largely hidden from sight, the rectory housekeeper was also part of village life.[37] The Catholic priests, who received a portion of their dues in kind and occasionally also worked parcels of land themselves and had breeding animals to look after, were dependent on her assistance. In the view of the ecclesiastical authorities, whenever possible the household of a priest should be run by a close relative, the mother or a sister. Although concubinage was far less common in the bishopric of Metz in the eighteenth century than it had been in the preceding centuries, the authorities felt once again compelled in 1772 to issue a reminder that priests should employ as housekeepers only relatives who were at least forty years of age and free of any suspicion of "disorderliness" (Unordnung).[38]

Jean Baptiste Lambert, who looked after the parish of Steinbiedersdorf from 1733 to 1775, followed this rule and brought his youngest sister, Anne Marie, into his house. Since they hailed from a family of rank, the social distance between them and the village was considerable to begin with. Still, Anne Marie, "Madmsell Lamber," as she is referred to in the sources,[39] was a popular godmother espe-

---

[36] LHA Koblenz 56/503: In Sachen sämtlicher Untertanen und Dorfschaften der Grafschaft Kriechingen gegen Herrn Grafen zu Wied-Runkel, 1784.

[37] On the role of the parsonage housekeeper see Claudia Ulrich, "Frauen und Kleriker," in Lundt and Reimöller, eds., *Von Aufbruch und Utopie*, 155–177; Wilhelm David Bowman, "Frauen und geweihte Männer: Priester und ihre Haushälterinnen in der Erzdiözese Wien, 1800–1850," in Edith Saurer, ed., *Religion der Geschlechter*, 245–259; Timothy Tackett, *Priest and Parish in Eighteenth-Century France. A Social and Political Study of the Curés in a Diocese of Dauphiné* (Princeton, 1977).

[38] Bernard Plongeron, *La vie quotidienne du clergé français* (Paris, 1979), 139. Tacket indicates a minimum age of fifty for France (Tackett, *Priest and Parish*, 191f.).

[39] AD Mos. Actes judiciaires B 10045: Fiscalis gegen Hanß Jörg Vogts Sohn, Peter Vogt, zu Steinbiedersdorf, 1745.

cially in the better social circles of the village. Other than that, however, she has left hardly any traces in the sources. Nor do we hear anything of the farmhand who worked for her.

To express his gratitude that Anne Marie "has now been with him for so many years and has shown him so much sisterly love and loyalty," Jean Baptiste Lambert in 1774 bequeathed to her the usufruct of his estate, though he strictly ruled out that she should have any power of disposal over it.[40] Even after the death of the priest, Anne Marie Lambert is not mentioned in any tax list. As housekeeper she—like her priest—was not part of the community in the narrower sense of the word.

It was not usual that the priest's housekeeper came from a higher social stratum, set herself apart socially from the villagers, as was the case with Madmsell Lambert, and had at least some of the work done by a farmhand. The wide range of tasks that had to be managed in a village priest's household made other criteria in choosing a housekeeper seem more important. Father Neumann, who looked after the parish of Steinbiedersdorf beginning in 1817, said as much: instead of a relative, he wanted to have a twenty-eight-year-old widow in his house, and he justified his selection by noting the difficulties "finding older service personnel who also have the other necessary skills required in our household and enough strength to work."[41] Even if this was not necessarily the true motivation behind the request for an exemption from the rules, it was an argument that one could present to the episcopal authorities.

In the early nineteenth century there were still numerous tasks in a village rectory that the priest's housekeeper had to take on by herself. That included not only farm work (looking after the animals, fields, and the garden), but also readiness to maintain contacts within the village and to gather information that the priest urgently needed to know about his parishioners. When Jean Baptiste Lambert's successor, the curé de Mondéville, was asked whether a shepherd boy in his parish had already received the first holy communion, he could rely neither on his church books, where such information was not recorded, nor on his memory. Instead, he sent his housekeeper to ask the boy's mother.[42]

Complaints from some parishes in the bishopric of Metz that the priestly housekeepers were quarrelsome women who were tyrannizing not only the priest but also the parish indicate that the "office" of priestly housekeeper could bestow some measure of power on those who held it.[43] That power was derived, first

---

[40] AD Mos. Actes judiciaires B 10061: Testament des Ehrenpastors Lambert, 1774. Evidently it was no exception that Catholic priests used the post of housekeeper to provide jobs for relatives: Tackett, *Priest and Parish*, 144.

[41] AD Mos. 29 J 657: Affaires paroissiales des paroisses de l'actuel diocèse de Metz, archiprêtre de Faulquemont: Pontpierre, An X–1893.

[42] AD Mos. Actes judiciaires B 10077: Acta in Sachen Oberjäger Beuters von hier, Denunzianten, ca. einige Steinbiedersdorfer Bauern an seinen Söhnen verübte Mißhandlung betr., 1788.

[43] Examples in Alois Hahn, *Die Rezeption des tridentinischen Pfarrideals im westtri-*

of all, from kinship bonds. As William David Bowman has emphasized, it is not hard to imagine that "female relatives working as housekeepers influenced their male family members in subtle and multifarious ways."[44] That was surely true more so for a mother or older sister than for younger siblings like Madmsell Lamber, who performed her job without attracting attention.

It is likely that a housekeeper's possibilities of exerting influence lay chiefly in the economic sphere: a priest was entitled to a portion of the fruits of his parishioners' labor. Since these dues were often products produced by the labor of women (Kleinzehnt), it is reasonable to assume that the housekeeper was involved in assessing, receiving, and collecting them. On the other hand, the influence of the priest's housekeeper, cook, or maid must surely be sought also in the sensitive public female realm of the village, which presumed to render judgment on the conduct of individual members of the community. However, the priest's housekeeper, like the priest himself, was always dependent to a special degree on this judgmental public. The goings-on in the rectory were followed with keen interest, and it was easy to discredit an unpopular priest through vicious slander. The Steinbiedersdorf records contain no indication that the priest or his cook led a "disorderly" life. Still, the priest's household, made up of the priest and his housekeeper who ran it and worked away from the public eye, could not attain a model character comparable to that of the household of a Protestant pastor.[45]

The structural difference between Catholic and Protestant parishes that emerges here is likely to have affected also the ways of life within the communities. Marriage was not the only desirable bond. Leaving aside the convents, which were probably not all that important to girls from the countryside, the ties that bound women to their families and village community remained significant. That was an especially important experience for older, widowed women, who made up a substantial portion of the village population.

The midwife: Anne-Marie Decker

Our search for the midwife takes us first into the church. For that is where Anne-Marie Decker, the wife of the sexton and teacher Pierre Martin, was elected by the women of the parish on a Sunday following mass and was subsequently put under oath by the priest.[46] The protocol about the election process has not

---

erischen Pfarrklerus des 16. und 17. Jahrhunderts. Untersuchungen zur Geschichte der katholischen Reform im Erzbistum Trier (Luxembourg, 1974), 367f.

[44] Bowman, "Frauen und geweihte Männer," 250. Bowman examined alleged and proven sexual relationships between priests and women in the archbishopric of Vienna, and has shown that the Catholic Church—which was so concerned about prestige and the preservation of its power—was quite fragile and vulnerable to attack.

[45] Love relationships in the rectory were not all that rare in the region in the eighteenth century: Ulbrich, "Frauen und Kleriker," 168f.

[46] For Steinbiedersdorf, the election of a midwife and the administration of the oath is mentioned only in the visitation protocol of 1699: AD Mos. 29 J 63 Archiprêtre de

survived, though it must have been similar to the record made by the priest of Pargny in 1765:

> On this day of March 25, 1765, Anne Masselot, wife of Jean Colon, a day-laborer, forty-eight years of age, was elected by the assembly of the women, by the majority of the votes, to hold the office of midwife, and she took the usual oath . . . in conformity with the ritual of this diocese.[47]

As long as women were selecting the midwives they gave preference to older women.[48] On this issue the interests of the wives overlapped with those of the church. A midwife should pose no "danger" to the husband, who had to remain abstinent during the days of the birth.[49] Like shabbes maids and the priest's housekeeper, midwives were supposed to be at least forty years of age. It would appear that this "canonical age" significantly reduced the attractiveness of the female sex in the eyes of those concerned, or at least the risks posed by their presence.

Anne-Marie Decker no doubt met the requirements. In 1723, the year she is first mentioned in the sources, she was fifty-three years old and had been married for over twenty years.[50] She seems to have done her work inconspicuously, performing her duties well as far as the women were concerned, and correctly as far as the authorities were concerned, for hardly a woman died in childbed while Anne-Marie Decker was midwife.[51] That record must have made

---

Morhange: États détaillés des paroisses, 1699–1700: Pontpierre. As Anne-Marie Decker was only thirty at the time, it is unlikely that this election refers to her. Since we have visitation protocols for only a few years, we cannot say anything definitive about the date of her election. The details of the election process in Lotharingia are described by Guy Cabourdin, *La vie quotidienne en Lorraine aux XVIIe et XVIIIe siècles* (Paris, 1984), 34ff. On conflicts surrounding the election of midwives see Eva Labouvie, "Selbstverwaltete Geburt. Landhebammen zwischen Macht und Reglementierung (17.–19. Jahrhundert)," GG 18, No. 4 (1992), 477–506, here 482.

[47] Quoted in Jean Vartier, *La vie quotidienne en Lorraine au XIXe siècle* (Paris, 1973), 29.

[48] Vartier, *La vie quotidienne*, 36. Among the 94 midwives who were trained in Neufchâtel in 1773 were 8 unmarried women with an average age of 33. The average age for the married women (80 percent of all candidates) was 43, for widows 48: Cabourdin, *La vie quotidienne*, 39. Other evidence for the age of midwives is in Labouvie, "Selbstverwaltete Geburt," 482.

[49] This is indicated by Adeline Gérardin, a midwife like her mother and grandmother. Her memoirs, which also incorporated the stories she heard from her grandmother, were written down by Docteur Alban Fournier, *Vieilles coutumes provenant des cultes antiques* (Saint Dié, 1900), and form the basis of Vartier's book. She also speaks about the customs that were meant to ensure that husbands practiced abstinence in the days surrounding the birth and while their wives were lying in.

[50] AD Mos. Mic. E.C. 553 Pontpierre 1680–1793. Entry for the year 1704: birth of her son Jean; 1724; she dies on October 8 at the age of fifty-four. As I have mentioned, it was not possible to determine the date when she started working as a midwife. An entry in the parish register in 1704 does not describe her as midwife.

[51] Anne-Marie Decker died in October 1724. In 1725, two women died in childbed, in 1727 one. All in all, deaths in childbed are seldom mentioned, and the mortality

an incidence in 1723 all the more heart-wrenching. We hear about it from an
entry in the parish register:

> Anne Marie Pierrard, the young wife of Jacob Floret, after having received
> Extreme Unction, being six months pregnant, expired. The midwife opened
> her side and pulled out the child alive, who was baptized and also died
> a short while later and was buried with the mother on the ninth.[52]

Anne Marie Pierrard was six months pregnant when she fell ill and her husband summoned the priest and the midwife. The priest administered extreme
unction and left the dying woman in the hands of the midwife and neighbors.
Immediately after Anne Marie's death, the midwife, Anne-Marie Decker, performed a Cesarean section to save the child.[53] Four days later she submitted a
report to the authorities about what had happened:

> Because of the need to protect the fruit of her womb, and in order that
> the child with which said Anna Maria was pregnant receive holy bap-
> tism, she therefore, as soon as Anne Marie Pierrard had expired, opened
> her right side, using the Cesarean cut, immediately removed the child
> halfway and baptized it . . . in the name of God. Afterwards she took it
> completely out of the body and saw that said child was a boy. However,
> fearful that said child had not been baptized properly, she baptized the
> child again at the urging of the women named below, provided it had
> not already been baptized. Said child also lived about a quarter of an hour,
> which she determined by feeling its heartbeat. Present were also Nicolas
> Decker, Ackermann, and Nicolas Albrechts, chief jurors [Meisterschöffen],
> who saw said child.[54]

---

rate for women of child-bearing age was low compared to that for men. Between 1694
and 1763, 330 people died in Steinbiedersdorf. In 74 percent of all cases we have information about the age of the deceased. Using those figures, of those who died between
the ages of 19 and 49, 16 were women (out of 103), and 45 were men (out of 140):
AD Mos. Mic. E.C. Registres paroissiales, Pontpierre 1694–1763. Within the parame-
ters of the present study it is not possible to make more detailed statements about mortality rates. Because of the possible underregistration and the lack of information about
causes of death, such statements would require very elaborate statistical methods. The
methodological difficulties have been noted by Schlumbohm, "Lebensläufe," 152ff.
According to his calculations, in the parish of Belm in the eighteenth century, on average 5 percent of all married women who had children died during or after giving birth.

[52] AD Mos. Mic. E.C. 553 Pontpierre 1680–1793: 1723.

[53] Wiesner, *Women and Gender*, 69, points out that midwives in Catholic areas were
still instructed as late as the middle of the eighteenth century to baptize the dead child
in case of a miscarriage, and to perform a Cesarean section on women who died trying to give birth in order to baptize the unborn child in the womb. The Cesarean section had to be performed immediately after the mother's death in order to save the
child. This placed a difficult and grave decision in the hands of the midwife or surgeon.
Around the same time a debate took shape, especially in France and Italy, about the
child in the womb, as a result of which Cesarean sections were also carried out on women
who were still alive, in spite of the extremely high mortality rate of the procedure: Nadia
Maria Filippini, *La nascita straordinaria. Tra madre e figlio la rivoluzione del taglio cesareo
[sec. XVIII–XIX].* Studie di ricerche storici 198 (Milan, 1995).

[54] AD Mos. Actes judiciaires B 10041: In Appellationssachen Jacob Floret von

Anne-Marie Decker was able to name three women and two men as witnesses
for her statement, which showed that her actions were in accordance with the
regulations of the midwife code. She placed special emphasis on the fact that
the child had been baptized immediately after the Caesarean section, and then
a second time shortly afterward on the advice of the attending women. Anne-
Marie Decker undoubtedly shared the view of the other women of the village
that there was nothing worse than letting a child die unbaptized, thereby con-
signing it to purgatory.[55]

But Anne-Marie Decker said nothing about this. It is quite clear that she
knew exactly how far her competence extended, and what she should reveal
to the authorities and what she would be better off concealing. Thus we find
no reference to forbidden practices she had used in an attempt to save the life
of mother and child. Given the environment in which she lived and in view
of what we know about the work of midwives at that time, it is rather unlikely
that she would have decided not to resort to these practices.[56]

It is not likely that a village in which weather processions were held and
herbs were blessed would have elected as midwife a woman who was not also
skilled in practices, blessings, and customs that were not tolerated by the
church.[57] That the priest of Steinbiedersdorf did not complain does not say very
much. After all, he tolerated a whole series of other "abuses."[58]

The priest in the neighboring village of Faulquemont was different when it
came to such matters. He did not dare administer the midwife's oath to a
woman who had violated the church's prescriptions. And that is why the women
in his parish had to make do with a midwife of whom he himself said that
while she was not superstitious, she was not very pleasant.[59] Since it was believed
that the qualities of the midwife were passed on to the newborn child, calling
upon the services of such a midwife was unacceptable not only to a mother,
but also to the child.[60] As a result, the women of the surrounding villages

---

Grißlingen ctra. die hochgräfliche Krichingische Cantzley pto. Mandato de exequendo
proprium judicatum in Betreff seiner Frau Verlassenschaft ctr. Louis Pierrard zu Steinbiedersdorf, 1735.

[55] In Catholic countries the effort was made to revive children who had died unbaptized in order to baptize them. Here, too, it all depended on the statement of the midwife as to whether—for example, upon looking at the Virgin Mary—she had recognized
a sign of life from the child: Hufton, *The Prospect Before Her*, 189f.; W. Stockums, *Das
Los der ohne die Taufe sterbenden Kinder* (Freiburg, 1923).

[56] On the significance of so-called Gauckeleyen (deceptions) see Labouvie, "Selbstverwaltete Geburt," 497.

[57] An overview of blessings common in the ecclesiastical sphere is provided by Adolph
Franz, *Die kirchlichen Benediktionen im Mittelalter*, 2 vols. (Freiburg i. Br., 1909; reprint,
Graz, 1960).

[58] See p. 148f.

[59] AD Mos. 29 J 63 Archiprêtre de Morhange: États détaillés des paroisses, 1699–1700.

[60] Vartier, *La vie quotidienne*, 29. Labouvie, on the other hand, regards the notion of

refused to summon the sworn midwife, asserting that there were plenty of skilled women among them who could hold the "office de sage-femme." The priest was well aware of that, and he would have been only too happy to dismiss the official midwife, who at least had passed an examination, if only one of the other women had been willing to take the oath. In Tenquin, as well, one of the two midwives to whom the priest wanted to administer the oath refused to take it.

The conflicts I have just described arose at a time when the church was trying to formulate the midwife's oath in more precise terms.[61] These conflicts reveal the connection between the choice of a midwife by the women, the administration of the oath by the priest, and the official obligation it placed upon the woman selected, who faced the threat of excommunication if she violated her oath. The instruments of control and punishment reduced the number of candidates in two ways: only those women could be chosen and put under oath who, first, seemed suitable to the resident village priest and, second, were willing to submit to the demands of the church and take the oath.[62]

Taking the oath entailed a renunciation of forbidden practices, which was important to the priest, integration into the seigneurial apparatus of supervision, which served the interests of the counts, and a readiness at all times to assist in births, which met the needs of the village women.[63] The oath posed a challenge to the peasant social order, which was built on mutual neighborly aid and asserted its own "right to knowledge."

---

character traits expected in a midwife as wishful thinking on the part of the authorities, emphasizing that "it was not infrequent for a village community to forgive a successful midwife human transgression extending all the way to criminal acts": Labouvie, "Selbstverwaltete Geburt," 483.

[61] Until 1700, the oaths in Lorraine varied from place to place, although the basic concern behind them, control over religious practices, was, as Cabourdin, *La vie quotidienne*, 34f., emphasized, much the same everywhere.

[62] To that extent it seems problematic that Labouvie speaks of an autonomous choice of the midwife in spite of the presence of representatives of the authorities. At least in the region I am examining, her positive assessment of the right of electing a midwife as the "sole public right of participation" (Labouvie, "Selbstverwaltete Geburt," 487) makes sense only in retrospect. It is only against the background of the later demands by the rulers or the state to appoint midwives that the duty to elect a midwife, which restricted earlier freedoms, became a right.

[63] The ecclesiastical and seigneurial interest in controlling the choice of a midwife is also reflected on the level of ordinances: around 1700, the formula of the oath was specified in greater detail and the ritual was fixed, in 1728 the High Court made the election of the midwife by the majority vote of the local women obligatory on the parish level. The close connection between the controlling authorities and the election by the women was made clear by the place where the election took place and how it was done. At least in Lorraine, the priest initiated the election process with a proclamation from the pulpit. In many cases, oftentimes together with the teacher, he chaired the election meeting: Cabourdin, *La vie quotidienne*, 36.

In rural society, death and birth were not "private matters."[64] Pregnancy and birth, as Regina Schulte has put it, were "social events shaped by gossip and concealment."[65] Knowledge of these things could impart power and was seen as threatening "as soon as it had to be perceived as gender-specific and exclusive."[66] The insistence by the authorities on controlled elections followed by the administering of the oath to the midwife makes sense for the simple reason that it created the possibility of tying the midwife into the seigneurial apparatus of supervision and transformed her knowledge into the ruler's knowledge.[67] It was especially through her role in the so-called Genießverhör, an inquiry to determine paternity, that she had to participate in the enforcement of "discipline and order."[68] Her knowledge of relationships in the village could be useful not only to the lord, but also to the subjects.

Jacob Floret, whose young wife Anne Marie Pierrard had died during childbirth, was dependent on the midwife's knowledge and on the women and men

[64] In the early modern period, the opposite of "public" was not "private" but "secret." While "private" and "public" were construed as complementary spheres, secretive behavior toward the authorities (clandestine marriages, clandestine practice of law, secret births) was not permitted. Merry E. Wiesner has emphasized that a nonpublic, "private" sphere began to emerge already before the nineteenth century in the realm surrounding birth and a midwife's work: Wiesner, "The midwives of south Germany and the public/private dichotomy," in Hilary Marland, ed., *The Art of Midwifery. Early Modern Midwives in Europe* (London, 1993), 77–94.

[65] Schulte, "Gerede," 69.

[66] Ibid., 73.

[67] I do not believe that the distinction between a seigneurial and a communal "version of the office" with respect to midwives that was drawn by Ulrike Gleixner gets us very far, since lordship was segmented as long as no state monopoly of power existed: Ulrike Gleixner, "Die 'Gute' und die 'Böse.' Hebammen als Amtsfrauen auf dem Land [Altmark/Brandenburg, 18. Jahrhundert]," in Wunder and Vanja, eds., *Weiber, Menscher, Frauenzimmer*, 96–122. Since even a communal office was a seigneurial office, we must apply different criteria. Possibilities for a differentiation could come, among other places, from an examination of access to the office, the administration of the oath, and means of control and punishment. Moreover, missing from the systematization offered by Gleixner is the church, whose influence on the activities of midwives in Brandenburg is not discussed.

[68] The so-called Genießverhör was usually carried out by the midwife in the presence of witnesses or officials. According to Hans Herold, who studied relevant ordinances in Switzerland, this procedure had "a certain similarity with medieval torture," since the midwife did not assist in the birth until the pregnant woman had made her statement: Hans Herold, "Das Hebammenamt in rechtsgeschichtlicher Betrachtung," in his *Rechtsgeschichte aus Neigung. Ausgewählte Schriften aus den Jahren 1934–1986*, ed. Karl Siegfried Bader and Claudio Soliva (Sigmaringen, 1988; first published in 1968), 367–376, here 375. I believe Christian Simon was right in emphasizing that the Genießverhör turned "a person who by her nature could have a helping function into an instrument of the ruler's supervision and use of force": *Untertanenverhalten und obrigkeitliche Moralpolitik. Studien zum Verhältnis zwischen Stadt und Land im ausgehenden 18. Jahrhundert am Beispiel Basels. Basler Beiträge zur Geschichtswissenschaft 145 (Basel, 1981), 105.

who had been present during the birth. Their testimony about the life and death of his child would determine whether or not he would inherit his wife's estate and thus be put in a position to live a comfortable life. As one who participated in the local gossip, who knew about life and death in the village, the midwife Anne-Marie Decker was well aware of the legal and economic import of her statement, even if she said not a word about the looming contest over the inheritance. She left no doubt that the child had "lived for about a quarter of an hour, which she determined by feeling its heartbeat." With these words she created the conditions for the property Anne Marie Pierrard had inherited from her mother to be passed on, via the child, to her husband, who was able to begin a new life. Actually it should have been the task of the barber-surgeon to testify about the child's life and death. At least in many other lordships, consulting a doctor was desirable in cases of difficult deliveries, especially if—as in this case—it was already apparent before the birth that it would be a difficult one.[69] Only in extreme emergencies and in a substitute function were women accorded such far-reaching decision-making power in economic and legal matters.[70]

The knowledge of the midwife and other women was also important when it came to supervising irregularities in matchmaking and controlling extramarital pregnancies.[71] It was especially to these areas, which provided access to the bodies of the subjects, that the ruling authorities had turned their attention in the eighteenth century.

Secular lordship explicitly staked its claim to knowledge by incorporating relevant provisions into the police regulations (Polizeiordnungen). The following proclamation was made in all communities of Kriechingen beginning with the Jahrgeding of 1754:

> Item, those women who have allowed themselves to get pregnant by illicit intercourse shall make the proper report of their pregnancy to the

---

[69] In general: Jacques Gélis, Mireille Laget, Marie-France Morel, *Der Weg ins Leben. Geburt und Kindheit in früherer Zeit* (Munich, 1980), 83 and 98ff.; Waltraud Pulz, "*Nicht alles nach der Gelahrten Sinn geschrieben*"—*Das Hebammenanleitungsbuch der Justina Siegemund. Zur Rekonstruktion geburtshilflichen Überlieferungswissens frühneuzeitlicher Hebammen und seiner Bedeutung bei der Herausbildung der modernen Geburtshilfe* (Munich, 1994), 126.

[70] The consequences of a birth and a mother's death on matters of inheritance law have not been studied to date in scholarship on midwifery. That this was surely a rare event is revealed by a finding by Schlumbohm, who has shown that 1 percent of all baptisms registered in the parish of Belm were emergency baptisms. Not every death of an infant had the sort of consequences in terms of inheritance I have described above (Schlumbohm, *Lebensläufe*, 165f.). However, what matters in my view is not how often a situation could occur in which a birth resulting in the death of the mother influenced succession, but that it could happen at all. See also note 247.

[71] In this context we should note especially the role of the midwife in the "Genies-" or "Genüsst" interrogation (see note 262). On the midwife's control function see also Gleixner, "Die 'Gute' und die 'Böse,'" 101ff.

count's government, in case of failure to do so and if the pregnancy is kept silent and concealed, they are to be regarded and punished as regular infanticides.[72]

Compared to the punishment laid down for infanticide in the Constitutio Criminalis Carolina, a small but revealing shift in meaning takes place here: not infanticide but pregnancy was at the center of the attention of authorities who were striving to make the female body into a "public place."[73] Since the reports had to be made at a time when women could not even be certain whether they were pregnant in the first place, pre- and extramarital sex became a special risk. If they obeyed the authorities and reported themselves they lost their honor even if it turned out subsequently that they were not pregnant at all. Moreover, the obligation of self-reporting made possible a targeted supervision of women pregnant out of wedlock. With this measure, as well, the ruler increased his influence on the structure of honor within the village.[74]

The new mechanisms of power combined with—or concealed themselves behind—new scientific insights about hygiene and with reformist-absolutist ideas about the connection between population growth and economic advancement.[75] And they did not stop at the boundaries of a village as remote as Steinbiedersdorf. Since the middle of the century, the midwife in Steinbiedersdorf had support or competition—it is hard to tell any longer—from the barber-surgeon Johannes Ladner, who was supposed to be consulted on difficult births. It is rather doubtful that this was of any advantage to the women, as Johannes Ladner was known throughout the village as a drunk. The village midwife's possibilities of pursuing her work were constrained not so much by him as by the increasing demands on the part of the state that midwives demonstrate specific qualifications.[76]

Midwifery in the countryside deteriorated considerably in the wake of the French Revolution. A law from Year XI stipulated that only recognized women

---

[72] AD Mos. Actes judiciaires B 10012: 1754, Niederwiesener, Dentinger, Momersdorfer Jahrgedingsprotokolle, 1754.

[73] Thus the programmatic title of Barbara Duden's book *Der Frauenleib als öffentlicher Ort. Vom Mißbrauch des Begriffs Leben* (Ulm, 1991) [English translation by Lee Hoinacki, *Disembodying Women: Perspectives on Pregnancy and the Unborn* (Cambridge, 1993)].

[74] Simon believes that the intention behind the obligation to report a pregnancy early on was, apart from control, the voluntary relinquishing of honor on the part of the pregnant women: Simon, "Untertanenverhalten," 104.

[75] See Michel Foucault, *Discipline and Punish: The Birth of the Prison*, transl. Alan Sheridan (New York, 1979), 197.

[76] See Calixte Hudemann-Simon, *L'État de la santé. La politique de la santé publique ou "police médicale" dans les quatre départements rhénans. 1794–1814* (Sigmaringen, 1995), esp. 289ff. The difficulties she describes in the implementation of the new criteria of training and testing, whereby the problem of language also came into play alongside the centralization of training, should also be applicable—at least in part—to the département Moselle.

with a diploma would be allowed to work as midwives. Disregard of this provision was punishable by a fine, and repeat violators were subject to imprisonment.[77] In this way, communities and women were supposed to be forced into making changes. But such change was impeded by technical difficulties as well as problems of mentality. On the one hand, the number of accredited midwives was exceedingly small, and on the other hand, women continued to be more interested in a midwife's character than her training.

Some of the communities sought a compromise: midwives were still chosen by the women under the supervision of the priest and the burgomaster, and after offering their pledge to the community, they were sent off for training.[78] However, the formal similarity with the earlier election of the midwife notwithstanding, the situation had changed fundamentally, since the office had been removed from the ecclesiastical-religious context.[79] At the same time the erstwhile qualifying traits of gentleness, intelligence, and probity became secondary virtues.[80]

The wife of the medicus: Margarete Finickel

Margarete Finickel was the daughter of Peter Finickel, who operated the oil mill in Steinbiedersdorf, and Anne Marie Richard.[81] In April 1743 she married Johannes Ladner of Mittelberg in Tyrol, who had come to Steinbiedersdorf the previous year. Almost exactly nine months after the wedding she gave birth to her first son, Pierre Silvester. He was given the name of both grandfathers, which was not the usual custom in Steinbiedersdorf.[82] At least in this regard Johannes Ladner had imported his own traditions into the marriage. When it came to the choice of domicile, however, he acted differently from the others: in most cases wives were the outsiders in a village, not husbands.

Johannes Ladner was also something of an outsider when it came to his profession: he worked in Steinbiedersdorf as a "medicus." His patients included men and women, Christians and Jews, and undoubtedly also children. Since

---

[77] AD Mos. E Dépôt I S I, Mainvillers, Déliberations du conseil municipal, 1790–1839: 1821.

[78] AD Mos. E Dépôt I D I, Mainvillers, Déliberations du conseil municipal, 1790–1839: 1821.

[79] Adeline Gérardin also pointed to the differences in comparing the work of her grandmother and her mother.

[80] At the election of the midwife of Mey, it was explicitly noted that the candidate distinguished herself by "douceur, probité et prudence": AD Mos. 5 E 11131–11132 (1758–1798): 8.12.1781. That matches the account by Gérardin, according to whom the most important criterion for the choice of her grandmother had been her character: douce, pieuse, honorable: Vartier, *La vie quotidienne*, 29.

[81] AD Mos. 10 F 429: Declaration oder Verzeichnis deren Unterthanen des Dorfs Steinbiedersdorf, unter die Grafschaft Crichingen gehorichen Orts, was Vermögen und Condition dieselbe anietzo sind, 1725.

[82] AD Mos. I Mic. E.C. 553 Pontpierre, 1680–1793, GG 3 on 1743.

he was summoned as an expert witness and doctor in quarrels and disputes, he had a certain influence in the village. For example, because of his testimony about the precarious state of health of a female Jewish villager, whose house had been attacked by young men, the leaders of the band were sentenced to a monetary fine and a shaming punishment.[83] After two Jewish men had beaten and severely injured the villager, Johannes Ladner was called in to bandage up her wounds. Partly on the basis of his testimony, the two perpetrators were banished from the territory for two years.[84] Occasionally we find indications that he was called to the bed of a pregnant woman or aided in a difficult delivery.[85]

The sources have far more to say about his weakness for alcohol than his work, a weakness that drove his family to financial ruin. Unbeknownst to his wife, who had brought substantial assets into the marriage, he made debts throughout the village and was soon unable to pay his tab in the tavern. His creditors included even Renelle Salomon, Abraham Jacob's maid.[86] In April 1769, Johannes Ladner was sued by a Jewish creditor. He made off to Tyrol, "his fatherland," and left his wife to handle the difficult situation on her own. That was undoubtedly a smart decision from the perspective of the family's finances, since Margarete Finickel was more likely than her husband to find mercy. It meant, however, that she would have to endure concrete disputes and countless appearances before the authorities. Margarete Finickel began with a small victory. She was able to obtain an extension on her credit, but four weeks later she was sued again, whereupon she filed for a separation of property.

Invoking the fact that she knew nothing of her husband's activities, she tried to escape liability with at least part of her assets. In court she acted at first quite self-assured as she declared: "As I know nothing of all these debts incurred by my husband, and as my husband wasted this money on dissolute living, I do not consider myself obligated to pay a single Heller, since I had no advantage from any of it".[87] The bailiff and the court agreed with her, confirming "that he does not head his household and is incapable of doing so, for whatever he earns he pours down his gullet, and if he happens to have anything, he has a separate wardrobe where he locks it up so his wife and children won't get any of it".[88]

---

[83] AD Mos. Actes judiciaires B 10047: 1760.

[84] AD Mos, B 10049: Heym Neumarks Ehefrau von Steinbiedersdorf gegen Isaak Israel und dessen Sohn, 1765.

[85] AD Mos. Actes judiciaires B 10059: Acta in Sachen Magdalena Wagner, Peter Richards Ehefrau, von Longeville ca. Feist Jacob von Steinbiedersdorf pcto an ihr verübten Exzesses auf der Straße, 1774.

[86] AD Mos. Actes judiciaires B 10051: In Sachen Renelle Salomon, des Abraham Jacob von Steinbiedersdorf Magd, gegen Johannes Ladner von da pco debiti, 1767.

[87] AD Mos. Actes judiciaires B 10053: Acta in Sachen verschiedene Creditorium ca. Johannes Ladner von Steinbiedersdorf pto. Debiti, 1769.

[88] Ibid.

It would appear that the bailiff and the court were defending one of their own against two very different outsiders. One, Johannes Ladner, had come into the village and failed to observe the rules; the other, a Jew, lived in the village and was advancing claims against the women for which, morally speaking, her husband should have been responsible. However, the sources do not allow us to substantiate this suspicion. It therefore seems much more likely that they simply did everything they could to help contain the damage and prevent the family from dropping below the poverty line. To pay off the debt for which she had signed, Margarete Finickel auctioned off her landholdings (with the possibility of buying them back). According to a statement from her lawyer in the famine year of 1771, what little she had left was auctioned off by a troop of soldiers "that cleaned out everything so thoroughly that the rocks in the walls were exposed."[89] But that statement is not entirely correct, since the landed property was not seized as a security. As a result the family of Johannes Ladner was at least much better off than those who had no landed property.

Despite the hard times on which the family had fallen as a result of Johannes Ladner's drunkenness, the marriage was maintained.[90] In 1772, both partners went to a notary together to transfer their real estate assets—the paternal and maternal inheritance—to the children. Michael, the oldest, was obligated "to keep his parents supplied with food and decent clothing for the duration of their lives, all in keeping with their social position, and in addition to always show them the proper paternal and maternal honor."[91]

Given Johannes Ladner's well-known lifestyle, which even his wife made no effort to conceal, the demand for proper honor could not have been more than an empty phrase geared toward the "normal case." After all, in the Ladner case it was common knowledge that "he was frequently out of the house for a month and, what he earned, he also consumed outside of the house;"[92] in other words, he was leading a "dissolute" life.

The family was supported by the labor of the eldest son, who worked his parents' holdings and had to defend them repeatedly against new demands from creditors. Through her work Margarete Finickel contributed to providing the daily livelihood. After her husband's death, faced by new demands from the creditors, she stated emphatically "that he had lived for the day, had been given to drink and had brought nothing into the house. On the contrary, I

---

[89] AD Mos. Actes judiciaires B 10069: Supplik von Ladners Witwe an die Regierung, 1778.

[90] We cannot say on the basis of the sources whether a divorce was considered. The absence of the officiality files places fundamental constraints on the possibility of examining the topics of marriage and sexuality intensively. However, the separation of property could point in the direction of an intended divorce.

[91] AD Mos. Actes judiciaires B 10053: Acta in Sachen verschiedene Creditorum ca. Johannes Ladner von Steinbiedersdorf pto. Debiti, 1769.

[92] Ibid., 17.9.1773.

had to provide him with the necessary sustenance from my own things. No sooner were a few ells of cloth on the weaving loom than they were sold."[93]

Margarete Finickel makes it very clear in her petition that she had secured the family's survival with her assets and her work. When it came to her husband's misconduct, she had never concealed it in public; after all, everyone knew about it.

Margarete Finickel was not a unique case. Suzanne Richard had married an outsider the same year as Margarete.[94] Her husband, Pierre Baumans from Brabant, also failed to settle down and make himself at home in Steinbiedersdorf. The family piled up substantial debts, as a result of which Suzanne's holdings had to be auctioned off after her death. As a widower, Pierre Baumans managed his household very poorly. Since he "went to the tavern every day, and not least maltreated his children very badly as he was drunk all the time," he was reported to the authorities.[95] Later he moved away and left his five children behind with no arrangements to care for them. They were placed with their uncle, Johannes Richard.[96]

In addition to Pierre Baumans there was at least one other problem case in the Richard family. Unlike Johannes Ladner and Pierre Baumans, Pierre Barell, the brother-in-law of Suzanne's sister Katharina, was not an outsider. His mother's complaint alleged that Pierre, the son of the count's collector and the younger brother of Dominik Barell, led a disorderly and profligate life. Because of this, and prompted by concern for his wife and children, she had him declared "pro prodiguo" and placed under the guardianship of another male member of the community.[97] This offered the mother, the widow of the count's collector, and the older brother, who had a very good reputation as a notary, an opportunity to publicly distance themselves from the "black sheep" of the family, and to stabilize their economic interests and the family's honor by taking the not very honorable step of having Pierre placed under guardianship.[98]

---

[93] AD Mos. Actes judiciaires B 10069: Supplik von Ladners Witwe an die Regierung, 1778.

[94] On the Richard family see p. 77.

[95] AD Mos. Actes judiciaires B 10048: Acta in Sachen Peter Baumans, 1755.

[96] AD Mos. Actes judiciaires B 10051: Handelsmann Baumans von Maxstadt gegen Johannes Richard von Steinbiedersdorf die Vergütung der im untersten Teil des Hauses gemachten Verbesserungen betr., 1767.

[97] AD Mos. Actes judiciaires B 10048: Acta in Sachen Fiscalis und Frau Rentmeisterin Anna Barell samt dem Sohn Dominik Barell gg. Ihren Sohn Peter wegen Verschwendung, 1756.

[98] Pierre Baumans had in fact been acting out in other ways. During an unrest aimed against the lord he was from the beginning on the side of the "rebels," while his mother, who as the widow of the count's collector played a special role in the village even after her husband's death, and his brother, as the count's clerk (Tabellion), were in the opposing camp. The action of having him declared incompetent restricted Pierre's ability to engage in legal contracts. Faced with the possibility of arrest during the rebellion, he was no longer able to provide bail for himself or his compatriots.

The situation was different for his wife: as early as 1756, in a letter to his son-in-law, Pierre Barell had blamed his wife for his drinking: he drank because "she was more fond of someone else than of him."[99] Prohibitions against serving him any alcohol were issued into the 1780s in both the Jewish and Christian communities, but to no avail.[100] Still, the couple stayed together. Divorce or separation was an option that women chose with great reluctance, even if they were financially secure. Another woman in the village, Anna Maria Finickel, stood by her husband even though he had "surrendered to drink." In 1764 she asked for permission to auction off a substantial portion of her holdings to pay off her husband's debts.[101] At the same time she petitioned that her assets be removed from the special protection they enjoyed under the SC Vellaeanum.[102]

That the consumption of alcohol could pose not only financial risks but a danger to the life and limb of family members is apparent from a charge brought against Michel Kremeter. A report in 1766 stated that one night he had been so "drunk and rowdy" that he "threw his wife out of bed and behind the door and trampled on her with his feet, shouting that a devil should come now and take him, and he had the bare knife in his hand and took old uncle by the throat, saying he still had to set fire to the house, and so she called for help."[103]

The scene inside Michel Kremeter's house sheds light on the inside of the home, where disturbances of the order could take place that exploded into violence against wives. It also points to the frustrations that men experienced at home or in the tavern, and which they took out on weaker individuals—the elderly, women, and children.[104] Apart from his inebriation, the threat that he would set the house on fire and his invocation of the devil as he was beating his wife make it very likely that Kremeter himself was in a personal crisis. It is not impossible that his wife or the uncle had triggered the crisis, but we have no evidence of that. What is clear, however, is that his act was embedded in a set of norms and values that tolerated violence on the part of husbands. Michel Kremeter beat his wife and threatened the uncle because as a husband and master of the house he was allowed to use physical force, and because he could assume that there would be no negative repercussions if he did so. Through physical force he reestablished his authority that had been challenged either inside or outside the home. Even if he had been repeatedly admonished in church to respect his wife, beating had never been explicitly prohibited.

---

[99] AD Mos. Actes judiciaires B 10054: Brief an Johannes Gaspard, 1756.

[100] AD Mos. E. Dépôt 553 FF 4 Archives communales: decrees from 1777, 1782, 1789.

[101] AD Mos. Actes judiciaires B 10048: Acta in Sachen Anna Maria, Hans Adam Oster von Steinbiedersdorf Ehefrau, um Erlaubnis, vor 1000 Pfd. von ihren Gütern an den Meistbietenden versteigern zu dürfen.

[102] Koch, *Maior dignitas*, 70.

[103] AD Mos. Actes judiciaires B 10049: Acta in Denunziationssachen gg. Michel Kremeter, 1766.

[104] That is suggested by the threat to set the house on fire; on this see the thoughts of Schulte, *The Village in Court*, 25–57.

Only when his violence exceeded the boundaries of what was acceptable could his wife hope for protection from the neighbors. But like the words from the authorities and the church, their involvement seems to have been aimed at reestablishing the "peace" (in the sense of order, not in the sense of reconciliation) and to persuade her to stick it out. Michel Kremeter's wife was sent back into her home the same night she had been beaten, and was compelled the next morning to seek protection from her husband once again. The situation must have been quite threatening, since she did not get dressed until after fleeing to her neighbor.

Evidently the neighbors misjudged the situation, otherwise they would not have put Kremeter's wife at risk once again. Surely they could have found a place for their neighbor to spend the night. There are some indications that this quarrel was not the first violent confrontation in the Kremeter household, but that the escalation, the repeat of the violence, had considerable significance for the way in which the case subsequently unfolded. The reluctance to take familial conflicts outside of the home and to prevail upon the authorities to get involved in family matters was quite strong, not only for the women who were affected but also for their neighbors. By bringing a charge they were compelled to acknowledge that they lacked the competence to settle such conflicts and had to accept interference in their own affairs by the authorities. Still, on the morning after the altercation, the neighbors of Michel Kremeter filed a report, which led to his being charged and subsequently admonished. Michel Kremeter did not appear in court in person. He had his uncle excuse his absence by claiming that "he still has a swollen head from the blows he received." The uncle pleaded for "merciful punishment" and asked that Kremeter's "wife, because of her malicious behavior, be punished by the authorities the very first time she gives cause for complaint."[105] Thereafter the court imposed a fine or, alternatively, a prison term.

The account by the uncle departs from that offered by the neighbors in that we are now told about blows that Kremeter received. The fact that Michel Kremeter did not even have to appear in person shows that the authorities had no interest in resolving the case or effecting a reconciliation between the spouses. It is clear from the protocol that the concern was much more to reestablish the "proper" order, which included the subordination of the wife. By issuing preventive rules of conduct concerning any future "malicious behavior" on the part of the wife, the court held her partly responsible for the "disturbance" that had occurred. She had been a cause of "vexation" and was to be punished if she became so again. By assessing blame in this way, the court in part justified Kremeter's behavior. The fact that he had clearly lost control under the influence of alcohol was reinterpreted in court into a posture that

---

[105] AD Mos. Actes judiciaires B 10055: Denunziation des Michel Kremeter von Steinbiedersdorf wegen in der Trunkenheit vorgefallener Schlägerei, 1769.

was in agreement with the normative behavior expected of a house father: if his wife had caused "vexation," he not only had a reason but a duty to correct her. She had gone beyond the limit, no more and no less. This reinterpretation of the events not only prevented the woman from becoming a "victim" in the eyes of the others; it also reestablished the honor of the house, at least in part. That was significant also for the accused wife, whose honor was tied in with that of the house. Not only did Michel Kremeter's wife have to take her husband's beating, for the sake of peace and order she also had to accept the blame.

To keep the punishment lenient, Michel Kremeter's uncle had to pay tribute to the lord. On the one hand he asked for "merciful punishment," thereby accommodating the interests of the authorities to "temper justice with mercy."[106] On the other hand, he suggested, on his own initiative, that the authorities henceforth become involved in regulating his nephew's domestic situation. In so doing he was abetting a tendency on the part of authorities that is discernible in many other measures: to meddle in family and village life.

Margarete Finickel did not let it get that far. The sources are silent on what happened inside her house when Johannes Ladner came home drunk. Perhaps Margarete fared better than other women, perhaps Johannes Ladner was less violent or the protection afforded by her sons or family of origin was better. Undoubtedly the situation was also eased by the fact that her husband was frequently away from home, sometimes for long periods, even though it also meant that Margarete Finickel and her children had to do all the work on their own. Still, the silence about the situation in the house indicates that there was a gray zone of violence that should not be taken outside because it was not honorable to do so, or simply because a wife had to resign herself to her lot.[107]

Margarete Finickel's story points to the problem of alcohol consumption and thus to the other side of a public drinking culture reserved for the male gender, a culture that became increasingly important beginning in the eighteenth century. At the same time it reveals the problems of men who were unable to live up to the behavioral expectations placed on them as husbands and housefathers because, among other reasons, their backgrounds or family constella-

---

[106] Into this context of mercy belongs also the importance of remorse, which Arlette Farge and Michel Foucault have noted in connection with marital conflicts: Arlette Farge and Michel Foucault, *Le Désordre des familles: lettres de cachet des Archives de la Bastille au XVIIIe siècle* (Paris, 1982), 42–46.

[107] Michaela Hohkamp, in a microhistorical study, has shown that women, because they were embedded in local networks of relationships, had difficulty asking for the court's help when they had been beaten, and that their interests in bringing a charge had to take a back seat to the economic interests of the shared household and consideration of the family's social position: Hohkamp, "Häusliche Gewalt. Beispiele einer ländlichen Region des mittleren Schwarzwaldes im 18. Jahrhundert," in Thomas Lindenberger and Alf Ludtke, eds., *Physische Gewalt. Historische Studien zu einer verschwiegenen Kontinuität* (Frankfurt a. M., 1995), 276–302.

tions made it difficult for them to integrate themselves into the structures of village life. The conflicts this triggered lead us into one of the realms in which the interests of the authorities and the experiences of women merged and opened up the way for changes.[108]

A widowed mother: Marie Morell

When her husband, the saddler Pierre Thomen, died after eighteen years of marriage, Marie Morell was left with two young children. A difficult time now began for Marie. She was still in her year of mourning when she became pregnant again. If we can believe her testimony, the unmarried Jacob Venner, a farmer's son, was the child's father. After an initial courtship in April, which she had rebuffed, he had visited her on several occasions in the late summer. He had dismissed her fears about a possible pregnancy by talking about their shared happiness: "She had often said to him what if something came of it and she got pregnant, and he had answered, what of it, it is for us."[109]

Although Marie had not set great store by a formal promise of marriage, she wanted Jacob Venner to marry her. In due course she made sure that her pregnancy became publicly known. Within the appointed period she had the bailiff and the court come to her house and declared her condition. She confirmed her statement under the pain of childbirth.[110] Jacob Venner refused to acknowledge paternity, accusing the no longer very young widow of loose living: "[He said that] the statement is false and deceitful. She is godless and unscrupulous. Such a person, who did not shy from committing such an immoral act and to violate the law, would have few qualms about breaking the law once again and lying about the father."[111]

His arguments—or, more precisely, those of the lawyer—reveal how futile the efforts of single mothers were to bring a successful suit of paternity in secular courts.[112] Women had already demonstrated their "immorality" by the mere fact

---

[108] Claudia Ulbrich, "Saufen und Raufen in Steinbiedersdorf. Ein Beitrag zur Erforschung häuslicher Gewalt in der ländlichen Gesellschaft des 18. Jahrhunderts," *HMRG* 8.1 (1995): 28–42.

[109] AD Mos. Actes judiciaires B 10048: Acta in Sachen des Jacob Venner, des Johannes Venner älteren Sohn, und der Witwe Morell pcto fornicationis et impregnationis, 1762.

[110] On the so-called Genießverhör see note 262.

[111] During the Kriechingen rebellion (see pp. 114–15), the peasants claimed that premarital conceptions had previously not been punished. Because of the high degree of mobility (marriage and thus entry into the parish register and the birth of the first child frequently did not occur at the same place) we cannot say anything definitive about how many premarital conceptions were legitimized after the fact by marriage.

[112] See Schnyder-Burghartz, *Alltag und Lebensformen*, 297ff., who sees in the unequal behavioral leeway for men and women with respect to sexuality an essential aspect of the asymmetry of the sexes. See also Peter Becker, "'Ich bin halt immer liederlich gewest und habe zu wenig gebetet.' Illegitimität und Herrschaft im Ancien Régime: St. Lambrecht 1600–1850," in Vierhaus, ed., *Frühe Neuzeit—Frühe Moderne*, 157–179. A comparison with findings from Catholic Bavaria shows that on this issue, in particular, there were

of being pregnant outside of marriage; they had lost their honor and with it
for the most part their chances of asserting their interests successfully. To be
sure, the government initially applied massive pressure to bring about a marriage, which alone could have resolved the scandal. But when it became clear
that Jacob Venner would not marry Marie, he was offered the opportunity to
take an oath of purgation. And in the second half of the eighteenth century,
that oath counted more in the eyes of the government than a declaration made
by a woman in the pangs of childbirth.[113]

After the birth of the child, Marie Morell had to leave the village for some
time, because of poverty, so we are told, and seek employ elsewhere. She
returned to Steinbiedersdorf after four years, at the latest: she had inherited a
house in the village, part of which she was able to rent out to a Jewish family.
In addition she now owned between eight and ten acres of arable land, a few
pieces of meadow and Etzeln [plot of common land given to individuals periodically or for life], and a quarter and a half of gardens.[114]

These things provided a livelihood. Even four years after the birth of the
child, she did not abandon her attempt to get Jacob Venner to accept responsibility. "In the public street" she accused him of being the father by "loudly"
telling her child whenever she saw him: "Look, there is your father."[115] Jacob
Venner must have felt quite beleaguered by her reproaches, for in 1762 he again
brought charges against her, accusing her of leading "a disorderly and lascivi-
ous life" and having "an evil mouth."[116] The court had no interest in over-

---

confessional differences: Stefan Breit, *'Leichtfertigkeit' und ländliche Gesellschaft. Voreheliche
Sexualität in der frühen Neuzeit.* Ancien Régime, Aufklärung und Revolution 23 (Munich,
1991).

[113] Of course, it must be emphasized that men who were accused of fathering a child
were rarely given the opportunity to take the so-called oath of purgation. But if the
man was granted the right to take this oath, it was superior to the women's declaration. Simon observed the same for the city and countryside of Basel: *Untertanenverhalten*,
105. In the Catholic duchy of Lorraine, great stock was placed on the woman's declaration, which had to be made both during the pregnancy under oath and in the pangs
of childbirth. The declaration brought with it the obligation to be careful about the
pregnancy and to raise the child Catholic: Aline Logette, "Naissances illégitimes en Lorraine
dans la première moitié du XVIIIe siècle d'après les déclarations de grossesses et la
jurisprudence," *Annales de l'Est* 35 (1984): 91–125.

[114] AD Mos. Actes judiciaires B 10070 and 10 F 429: Steinbiedersdorfer Deklaration,
1775. Her contribution to the district taxes was set at 10 pounds in 1775, which points
to a place in the middle of the income scale. The enforcement soldiers who came into
the village in 1771 had found only a kitchen cupboard and bed in her possession. I
have not been able to find any more information about the inheritance.

[115] AD Mos. Actes judiciaires B 10048: Acta in Sachen des Jacob Venner, des Johannes
Venner älteren Sohn, und der Witwe Morell pcto fornicationis et impregnationis, 1762.

[116] Men significantly improved their chances of avoiding child support by invoking
the loose living of women. We must assume that Jacob Venner was aware of this. For
a legal assessment of the "exceptio plurium concubentium" see Elisabeth Koch, "Pater
semper incertus," *Rechtshistorisches Journal* 9 (1990), 107–124, here 110f.

turning an earlier judgment and acquitted him once again. Marie Morell remained in the village and lived alone with her children.[117] The Jew Jacob Alexander also lived in her house.[118]

Marie Morell shows up in our documents one more time in 1774. At that time a quarrel had erupted between thirty young men from Steinbiedersdorf and a group of young people from the neighboring village. During the altercation a bottle had been thrown into the face of her son, Georg Thomen, inflicting "serious harm." Marie Morell came to his aid and threw herself between the combatants. "It is certain," one of the witnesses testified later, "that this Marie Morell had two young lads under her."[119] As this scene demonstrates, Marie Morell knew how to defend herself not only verbally but also physically. Since she had been running her household with the two minor sons on her own for a long time, she had to be able to put her shoulder to the wheel wherever it was necessary. She could hardly afford to pay any heed to considerations of gender-specific allocations of tasks, if they existed at all. In 1779, Marie Morell was one of three women who signed the pacification treaty between the lord and the subjects. She took care of her own affairs, without a guardian. Her widowhood and the birth of a child out of wedlock do not appear to have impaired in any significant way her two legitimate sons' chances of marriage. In 1770 and 1780, respectively, they married Anne and Catherine Stoffel, two sisters from a good family.

In many respects, Marie Morell seems to have fared better than other single mothers in the village. Unlike the unmarried, pregnant maids, she had a livelihood after she had come into her inheritance, and she had two sons who, as they got older, were able to help her with the work and take care of her. Unlike other women, she did not describe her sexual relationship with the father of her third child in terms that would have made her into the object of male desire. While others indicated in the charges they brought that a man had "used" them or had done violence to them, she mentioned Jacob Venner's statement "It is for us" in court. This sentence hints at notions of a relationship that two people sought to determine and define for themselves.

The difference to other women becomes fully apparent only when we take a closer look at the "circumstances" of Anne Marie Richard. In 1767, Anne Marie Richard lodged a complaint against Michel Mangin on the grounds that he "had had illicit relations with her," "moreover, after he had closed the

---

[117] In 1776 her youngest son earned a living in French military service: AD Paris, C.P. Allemagne, Petites Principautés, 18, fol. 56: Liste des sujets créhangeois actuellement au service de France.

[118] AD Mos. Actes judiciaires B 10055, 1769.

[119] AD Mos. Actes judiciaires B 10059: Acta in Denunziationssachen gegen verschiedene junge Purschen von Steinbiedersdorf und Falckenburg wegen vorgeworfener Schlägerey.

kitchen door, he had seduced her, a weak woman who is unable to defend her-self, and had promised to marry her."[120]

It sounds contradictory—at least from our perspective today—that Anne Marie Richard accused Michel Mangin of raping her and at the same time tried to enforce the promise of marriage. Help in interpreting this passage comes to us from Margherita Pelaja, who has intensively studied sexual violence and its depictions.[121] She has revealed the degree to which the institutional framework—in her case the papal courts—influenced the depiction of sexual relations.[122]

Towards representatives of the church, women had to stage a womanliness that was linked with weakness and made them into potential victims of sexual violence: "In the first decades of the seventeenth century, as soon as young girls who had 'bargained' their willingness to have sexual intercourse in return for a promise of marriage or other favors went to court because the promise had not been kept, they could not but depict their loss of virginity with images of male violence and female resistance."[123] For women who had consented to sexual contact and had lost their virginity, the only possibility of preserving their honor lay in establishing a connection between defloration and the use of force.[124] The fusion of two very different forms of extramarital sexual intercourse essentially deprived the complaining women of any possibility of verbalizing the violence they had suffered as such.[125]

In order to understand the link between marriage arrangements, defloration, and violence, we must realize that in Catholic regions—much as in Protestant ones—premarital intercourse in connection with a planned, subsequent mar-riage was a widespread practice, and that the doctrinal opinion of the Catholic church on matters concerning the establishment of a marriage were less clear-cut than in other Christian denominations.[126]

---

[120] AD Mos. Actes judiciaires B 10051: Acta in Sachen Michel Mangin und Anna Maria Richard von da, 1767.

[121] Margherita Pelaja, "Praxis und Darstellungsformen sexueller Gewalt im Rom des 19. Jahrhunderts," *L'Homme. ZFG* 7 (1996): 28–42; idem, *Matriomonio e sessualità a Roma nell'Ottocento* (Rome, 1994). As Ulinka Rublack has emphasized, the findings for Italy cannot be readily transposed to German territories. With regard to the latter she points to "the local interplay of socio-economic, administrative, institutional and confessional structures": *Magd, Metz' oder Mörderin. Frauen vor frühneuzeitlichen Gerichten* (Frankfurt a. M., 1998), 327f. See also Lyndal Roper, "'Wille' und 'Ehre': Sexualität, Sprache und Macht in Augsburger Kriminalprozessen," in Heide Wunder and Christina Vanja, eds., *Wandel der Geschlechterbeziehungen zu Beginn der Neuzeit* (Frankfurt, 1991), 180–197.

[122] Pelaja, "Praxis und Darstellungsformen," 33. On the processes of construction in court see Ulrike Gleixner, *'Das Mensch' und 'der Kerl.' Die Konstruktion von Geschlecht in Unzuchtsverfahren der frühen Neuzeit (1700–1760).* Geschichte und Geschlechter 8 (Frankfurt a. M., 1994).

[123] Pelaja, "Praxis und Darstellungsformen," 33.

[124] Ibid., 30.

[125] The perception and depiction of violence in the early modern period was anyhow closely linked with nonverbal signs: the suffering or presentation of visible wounds.

[126] There are some indications that premarital conception was more frequent among

In the eighteenth century, when Protestant authorities had long since adopted strict punishments for premarital pregnancies, many Catholic theologians were still advocating the position that "copula carnalis" established a marriage: "And that is why," Stefan Breit writes about Bavaria, "there also existed free marriage of young people, without consent of parents and without the blessings of the church or other formalities."[127]

The notion that sexual intercourse and not the church ceremony established marriage persisted in the countryside for a long time.[128] Even the fact that sexual intercourse outside of marriage was considered a mortal sin does not seem to have had much of an effect on this attitude.[129] Since the church was eager to "enforce the responsibility of the man toward the 'weak young woman,'"[130] Anne Marie Richard might have had a better chance for a sympathetic hearing before an ecclesiastical court. In the secular court of the Protestant territorial ruler the issue was neither the rape nor the failed marriage arrangement but the possible pregnancy. The court based its decision about the marriage complaint on the presence of a pregnancy, but not on the loss of virginity. The decision on the complaint would not be made until after the birth. When it turned out that Anne Marie Richard was not pregnant, the court imposed a whore's penalty on her for her false report. Although she emphasized once again in her petition that Michel Mangin had committed an "act of violence" against her, "a poor, broken person," the court upheld its decision "because of the scandal that had been caused." She was not afforded an opportunity to restore her respectability through marriage.[131]

The case of Marion Decker, who became pregnant by a soldier of a different confession, shows that the churches, or ways of thinking molded by the church, influenced the way in which marriage was contracted. The protocol noted: "Since he is committed to the Lutheran religion, while she is Catholic, she also understood that it would be difficult to get him into a marriage."[132]

The formulation "she also understood" indicates that it was not Marion Decker, but others—either the Protestant courts, the Catholic priest, or her Catholic parents—who believed that a marriage complaint was not appropriate

---

Catholics than Protestants. However, Schlumbohm, in his study of the mixed-confessional parish of Belm, found the differences between the two confessions fairly minor: *Lebensläufe*, 127.

[127] Breit, "Leichtfertigkeit," 76.

[128] Prior to the eighteenth century this definitely did not apply to the Jewish rural population; see p. 227.

[129] Breit, "Leichtfertigkeit," 76.

[130] Ibid., 161.

[131] Even for raped girls, marriage was the only possibility of recovering their respectability: Pelaja, "Praxis und Darstellungsformen," 30.

[132] AD Mos. Actes judiciaires B 10057, 1772: Acta in Sachen Marion Decker von Steinbiedersdorf ca. den Grenadier Samuel Hetzel pcto Impraegnationis et alimentationis partus.

in the first place given the difference in confessions. At the same time it reveals the influence of the church on the choice of a spouse. Other evidence for the effectiveness of Catholic marital and sexual ethics are the low rate of illegitimacy and the nearly complete absence of evidence about requests for divorce.[133]

It is possible that women, given the high risks of birth, saw Catholic marital and sexual morality as protective rather than restrictive, but the sources provide no indications to that effect. In principle we must note that the undeniably misogynistic attitude of the Catholic Church was countered by aspects of the Catholic religion that were favorable to women.[134] The latter could have included the disciplining of male sexuality as well as the emphasis on the importance of prayer and the saints. Moreover, by downplaying the meaning of earthly life, the Catholic religion could give comfort to those whose lives were not very happy. Through common prayer and song, women could give meaning to their suffering and strengthen the ability "to endure," a virtue called for by the Catholic faith.[135]

---

[133] Rainer Beck has looked at the possibility of divorce in the Catholic world by using Bavaria as an example. For his area of study he was able to analyze a whole host of actions for divorce or annulment: "Frauen in der Krise. Eheleben und Ehescheidung in der ländlichen Gesellschaft Bayerns während des Ancien régime," in van Dülmen, ed., *Dynamik der Tradition*, 137–212; see also Wolfgang Hans Stein, "Französisches Scheidungsrecht im katholischen Rheinland [1798–1803]: eine unbemerkte Revolution," *Palatia Historia. Festschrift für Ludwig Anton Doll zum 75. Geburtstag* (Mainz, 1994), 466–488.

[134] The tension between the Catholic Church and the Catholic religion indicated here belongs in the context of the discussion over popular religion. François-André Isambert has emphasized that it would be too narrow to think of popular religion as an "authentic cultural system" that stood in an antagonistic relationship to the prevailing religion: Isambert, "Empirische Vielfalt und ideologische Geschlossenheit: Populare Religion in Frankreich," in Michael N. Ebertz and Franz Schultheis, eds., *Volksfrömmigkeit in Europa. Beiträge zur Soziologie populärer Religiosität aus 14 Ländern* (Munich, 1985), 192–211, here 194.

[135] Hugh McLeod has brought out the importance of Catholicism for women within the framework of a "differentiated internal division of labor," which accorded women an active task in the life of the religious community through the duty of prayer. He has also spelled out the difference between Protestantism, with a male definition of the ideal of humaneness, and Catholicism, which had two ideals available in Jesus and Mary: McLeod, "Weibliche Frömmigkeit—männlicher Unglaube? Religion und Kirchen im bürgerlichen 19. Jh.," in Ute Frevert, ed., *Bürgerinnen und Bürger*, 134–156, 152f. At least in embryonic form, these developments probably played a role already in the eighteenth century. Medick (see p. 23) has emphasized that the ability to endure also played a role in Protestantism. In the religious history of the nineteenth century, the cult of Luise formed a Protestant counterpart to the Catholic Marian cult. See on this, for example, Wulf Wülfing, "Die heilige Luise von Preußen. Zur Mythisierung einer Figur der Geschichte in der deutschen Literatur des 19. Jahrhunderts," in Jürgen Link and Wulf Wülfing, eds., *Bewegung und Stillstand in Metaphern und Mythen. Fallstudien zum Verhältnis von elementarem Wissen und Literatur im 19. Jahrhundert*. Sprache und Geschichte 9 (Stuttgart, 1984), 233–275.

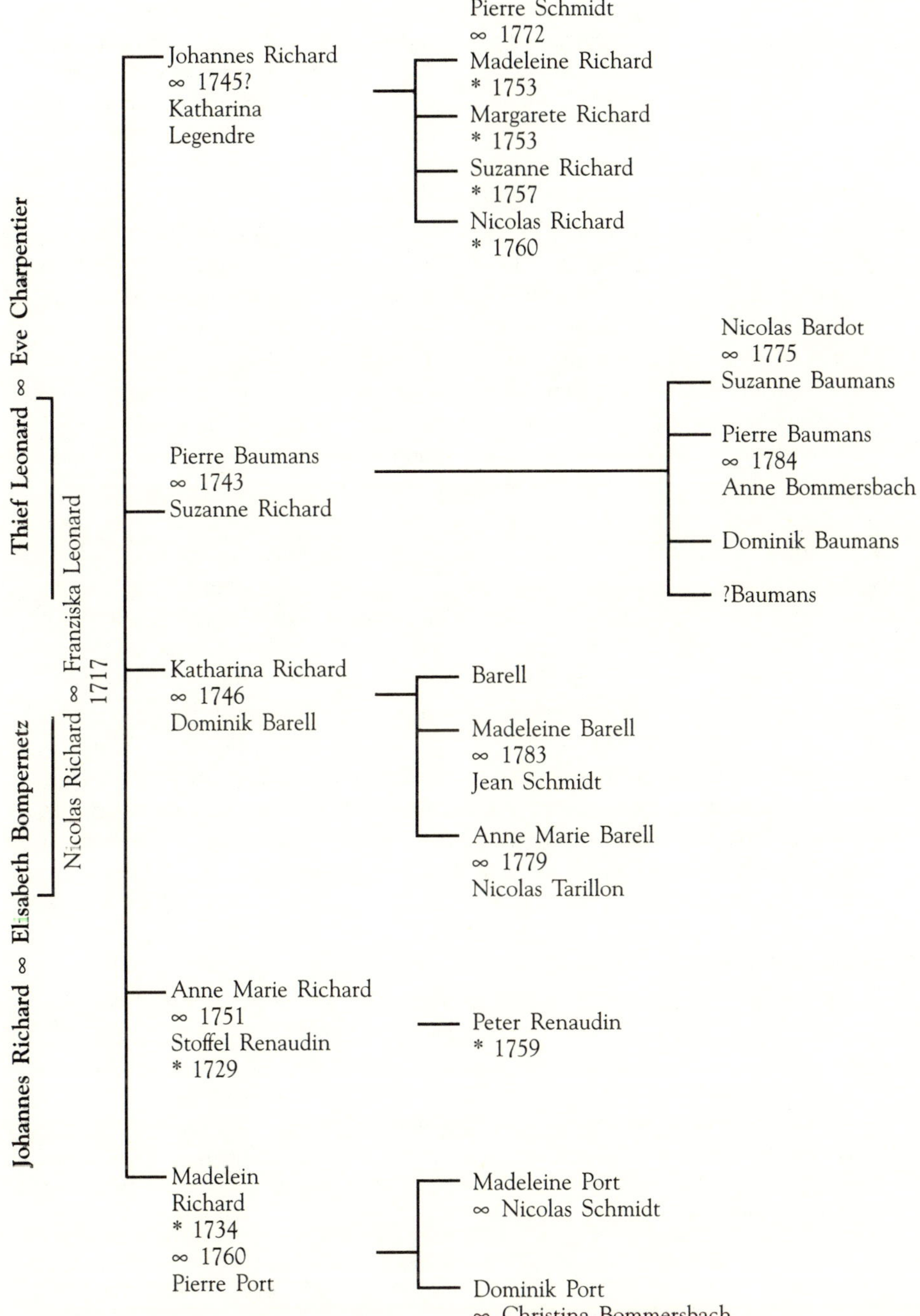

Table 1: The Richard Family

Jewish families dealt much more harshly than their Catholic counterparts with young women who became pregnant out of wedlock. With one exception, they were all expelled from the village. Only Perle Levy, a well-to-do widow, was able to successfully bring a suit of marriage. Her story, which takes us into the world of Jewish life, will be told later in a different context.

Humble widow or vicious woman: Katharina Legendre

Katharina Legendre was one of those women who moved outside the boundaries of what was expected of their gender. As a widow she pursued a suit through all the courts to enforce her claim to her daughter's estate against the sister and brother-in-law of her deceased son-in-law. Because of the tenacity with which she insisted on legal representation, and through the skill with which she was able to engage new lawyers time after time, she triggered a basic discussion not only about the prevailing law, but also about the count's jurisdictional rights.[136]

Her lawyers, meanwhile, argued over whether Katharina—who had troubled the courts not only on account of the disputed inheritance, but also over a cat, a Hungarian ox, and a puddle behind her house—should be seen as a "poor, abandoned, pitiful widow" or as a "vicious woman," who had poison hidden "between her old furrows and wrinkles."[137] They used their brief to draft extensive commentaries on the "just order," which had little to do with the ideas of their client and the world in which she lived.[138]

For Katharina, the question of who was allowed to wear the sky-blue dresses her son-in-law had made for his wife was much more important that the things the lawyers wanted to know about the arrangements in her house. The lawyers cared little about the dresses, because they did not, or did not wish to, understand their meaning, since their concern was with justice and ownership and not with the inner structure of a village to which they, as outsiders, had no access. Even if the sources do not talk about it, the story of Katharina brings us back to the church, where the sky-blue dresses could be worn and shown off.

Family circumstances

Katharina Legendre came from a well-off family that owned numerous holdings in Lauterfangen, Durchtal, Tetingen, and Lubeln. She was presumably

---

[136] AD Mos. B. Spire 10037: Acta in Sachen Johannes Richards Witwe wider Nicolas Thiel. Appellationes una cum restitutione in brevi manu. The count tried to bypass the imperial courts by asserting his own Kabinettsjustiz, the arbitrary exercise of justice by ministerial orders.

[137] AD Mos. B. Spire 11038: Acta in Sachen Nicolas Thiel gegen Katharina Legendre, die Verlassenschaft des verstorbenen Pierre Schmidt betr., 1781.

[138] Claudia Ulbrich, "Zeuginnen und Bittstellerinnen. Überlegungen zur Bedeutung von Ego-Dokumenten für die Erforschung weiblicher Selbstwahrnehmung in der ländlichen Gesellschaft des 18. Jahrhunderts," in Winfried Schulze, ed., *Ego-Dokumente. Annäherung an den Menschen in der Geschichte. Selbstzeugnisse der Neuzeit*, vol. 2 (Berlin, 1996), 207–225.

somewhere between twenty and thirty years of age when she had to leave her parents' home to begin a life with Johannes Richard in Steinbiedersdorf.[139] Her new role as a wife confronted her with the necessity of adjusting to unfamiliar surroundings. Unlike her husband, for whom the Legendre family does not seem to have held any special importance, Katharina Legendre had to familiarize herself with the anything but simple situation in the Richard house.

Katharina's husband, Johannes Richard, had been born in Steinbiedersdorf in 1718. He was the oldest son of Nicolas Richard and Franziska Leonard, who had married on April 27, 1717, in the first peaceful years following the endless wars and occupation of the seventeenth and early eighteenth centuries. At his baptism, Johannes Richard was given the name of his godfather, not coincidentally the same name as his grandfather. There were at least the beginnings of an effort to preserve a family tradition.

Johannes Richard did not grow up in poor circumstances. His father was a peasant who, according to the property list of 1725, had his own house and some wealth, which he and his wife Franziska Leonard administered and added to.[140]

Johannes Richard had four sisters, all of whom, unlike Katharina Legendre, were able to stay in their native village: as we have already seen, Suzanne, the oldest, married Pierre Baumans in 1743; after her death, when he treated his children badly and eventually left the village, the children were placed under the guardianship of their uncle, Johannes Richard. It was in their name that Johannes Richard filed suit against Pierre Baumans for his sister's inheritance.[141]

We learn from a property list of 1775 that the Baumans children in Steinbiedersdorf jointly owned a house and about fifteen acres of fields.[142] They were much poorer than their cousins. Still, two of them were able to find a spouse: in 1775 Suzanne Baumans married the village teacher Nicolas Bardot, and in 1784 Pierre Baumans married Anne Bommersbach. Dominik Baumans was taken in by Suzanne Richard's sister Madeleine. His guardian sent him to a tailor, where he learned the trade for a year or two. After that he returned to live and work in his aunt's house. A quarrel broke out in 1788, and Dominik Baumans sued the now widowed Madeleine Richard for overdue wages. The trail of the other two Baumans children disappears in the sources.

---

[139] According to the register of deaths she died in 1805 at the age of seventy-six. Her oldest daughter was born in 1750. If the entry is correct, Katharina was not even twenty at the time of her marriage.

[140] AD Mos. 3 E 6019, fol. 28: the tenant Nicolas Richard and his wife Franziska Leonard acquire property worth 34.5 talers, 1753. Ibid., fol. 99f.: in 1754, they purchase for 3,000 pounds of Lotharingian currency the holdings that Simon, Nicolas's unmarried brother, had inherited from his parents.

[141] AD Mos. Actes judiciaires B 10051: Handelsmann Baumans von Maxstadt gegen Johannes Richard von Steinbiedersdorf, die Vergütung der im untersten Teil des Hauses gemachten Verbesserungen betr., 1767.

[142] AD Mos. 10 F 429: Steinbiedersdorfer Deklaration, 1775.

Katharina, Johannes Richard's second-oldest sister, contracted the best marriage.[143] In 1746, she became the wife of Dominik Barell. Dominik was the son of Jean Barell and Anne Albert. Jean Barell was the collector of the county of Kriechingen, his oldest son, Dominik, was a tabellion, a kind of notary. Katharina, the future widow Barellin, acquired a prominent position not only economically but also socially. She owned one and a half houses in Steinbiedersdorf, forty-two Morgen (approximately thirteen hectares) of farmland, along with meadows and hemp plots (Hanfstücke).[144] Through her marriage she managed to rise into the social stratum of the seigneurial elite, and even after the death of her husband, whose parental house she inherited, she was able to benefit from his standing.[145]

Katharina Richard and Dominik Barell had two daughters and one son, born in 1750, 1752, and 1754. In 1779, Anne Marie Barell, the youngest, married the master locksmith Nicolas Tarillon of Faulquemont, who was involved in a smuggling affair in 1788. To prevent his imprisonment and to save "the honor and credit of the family," Anne Marie Barell vouched "for her husband by renouncing her benefits of the law" (that is, the legal protection of her property).[146] The end of the affair is not recorded.

Anne Marie Richard, the third sister of Johannes Richard, married Stoffel Renaudin, then twenty-two years of age, in 1751. Stoffel lived in modest circumstances.[147] The Renaudins had to get by with half a house and fourteen Morgen of arable land.[148] According to witness testimony from 1789, Stoffel Renaudin was a day laborer.[149] Their son Peter Renaudin was presumably born in 1759 and was still unmarried as late as 1789.

Madeleine Richard, the youngest sister, married Pierre Port of Val in 1760. Pierre Port was a farmer and lived with his family in the house of his in-laws. In Steinbiedersdorf, Pierre Port and Madeleine Richard owned a house, 17 Morgen of arable land, meadows, and Etzeln.[150] After the death of Nicolas

---

[143] On Katharina Richard (see pages 53 and 67).

[144] AD Mos. 10 F 429: Steinbiedersdorfer Deklaration, 1775.

[145] AD Mos. Actes judiciaires B 10073: Acta in Sachen der Witwe Barellin, ihr Erbe betr., 1784.

[146] AD Mos. Actes judiciaires B 11076: Acta in Sachen Heinrich Vogts von Steinbiedersdorf contra Nicolas Tarillon von da pcto Debiti, 1788.

[147] His share of the district taxes (Kreisgelder) was 12 Reichstalers. His brother-in-law Pierre Port and his father-in-law Johannes Richard, by comparison, each had to pay 30 Reichstalers: AD Mos. Actes judiciaires B 10070: Rolle zu den vom 9.2.1775 ausgeschriebenen Kreisgeldern, 1775.

[148] AD Mos. 10 F 429: Steinbiedersdorfer Deklaration, 1775.

[149] AD Mos. Actes judiciaires B 11076: Acta in Sachen Heinrich Vogts von Steinbiedersdorf contra Nicolas Tarillon von da pcto debiti, 1788. During the smuggling affair mentioned earlier, Tarillon had tried to warn his brother-in-law. He justified his actions by arguing that, as a relative, he was obligated to help.

[150] AD Mos. 10 F 429: Steinbiedersdorfer Deklaration, 1775.

Richard, Madeleine Richard's mother came to live with her, supported by all the children and grandchildren.

Madeleine Richard was widowed at a young age. Her three children were still not on their own when their father died. In 1787, shortly after her oldest son, Dominik Port, got married, she became embroiled in the above-mentioned suit with her nephew Dominik Baumans, who had lived and worked in her house for many years. Since the work relationship between relatives was not clearly defined, the two went through several courts disputing the question of whether and to what extent Dominik Baumans should be compensated for his work in the Port household. In the eyes of Dominik Baumans's lawyer, Madeleine Richard was nothing but a "plaintiff mired in a compulsion for denial and struck by blindness." She lost the suit in the original court and in the higher court.[151]

In 1762, when all five Richard children were married, Nicolas Richard and Franziska Leonard transferred their houses and landholding to their children because they were getting old. Lots were drawn to divide up the property: Pierre Port and Dominik Barell each ended up with a house, while the other two houses went to Pierre Baumans and Johannes Richard.[152] The parents kept three rooms in the large house and whatever they needed to live on.

After her husband's death, Franziska Leonard inherited not only his estate but also his debts. In connection with claims she had failed to pay within the stipulated time period, her creditors threatened to seize her belongings in 1768, during the Kriechingen rebellion. Franziska Leonard sought help from her son-in-law, Stoffel Renaudin, who came immediately accompanied by Peter Schmidt, one of the Kriechingen "rebels." Declaring "We—pardon the expression—shit on Weißenbruch's order and do not recognize him as our judge," they prevented anything from being carried out of the house.[153] When the "rebels" in the entire village had their possessions seized in 1771, Franziska Leonard was also among those who suffered.

This look at the Richard house makes clear how different the lives of the children of one family could be. In Steinbiedersdorf one can hardly speak of a closed society with self-contained social strata defined by family and wealth. The age that the father or mother attained, the number of children who had to share an inheritance, ability and success at earning one's livelihood, one's

---

[151] AD Mos. Actes judiciaires B 10077: Acta in Sachen Dominik Baumans von Steinbiedersdorf contra Madeleine Richard von da pcto debiti, 1788.

[152] AD Mos. Actes judiciaires B 10051: Handelsmann Baumans von Maxstadt gegen Johannes Richard von Steinbiedersdorf, die Vergütung der im untersten Teil des Hauses gemachten Verbesserungen betr., 1767.

[153] Jacques Touba, *Die Kriechinger Unruhen. Aufruhr von 1768* (Forbach, 1911), 22. For the expression s.v. (salva venia) or c.v. see David W. Sabean, "Soziale Distanzierungen. Ritualisierte Gestik in deutscher bürokratischer Prosa der Frühen Neuzeit," *Historische Anthropologie* 4, no. 2 (1996), 216–233.

place within the network of village life, and the choice of a spouse—all these factors had an importance one must not underestimate. Although all Richard children received the same share of their parents' inheritance, their economic and social standing in the village differed in many respects. Especially Suzanne lived in meager circumstances, while Katharina Richard, the youngest sister, shows clearly that marriage was one way for women to rise in the social hierarchy of the village. Our sources contain no information on how the marriages in the Richard household—the basis of this inequality—came about. Since the women, with the exception of Katharina Legendre, were all legally marriageable, a marriage without the consent of the parents would have been possible in formal legal terms. However, there is no indication of any conflicts between the Richards and their children over the choice of a spouse.

Katharina Legendre appears to have had active—though not always good—relations with her in-laws, sisters-in-law, and brothers-in-law, two of whom, the Ports and the Renaudins, were also her neighbors.[154] During the period of unrest, her husband was among the majority of those who had not submitted. Dominik Barell, the tabellion, had joined the side of the ruler early on. Katharina's other brothers-in-law were among the unsubmitted. Like her mother-in-law, she suffered the seizure of property and on several occasions heavy financial losses. Katharina Legendre's sisters-in-law had no other choice but to follow their husbands' decisions.

Years of marriage

Like all women in the village, Katharina Legendre retained her given name and family name during her marriage. Since she was an outsider, she was the only Legendre in the village for a long time. Only the imperial courts could not reconcile themselves to the naming practice in the village and referred to her as "Johann Richard's wife," occasionally adding the clarifying addendum "maiden name Legendre." These bureaucratic conventions embody different attitudes about the gender order. While the learned jurists situated women only in relationship to their husbands, within the village a woman retained her name, which was that of her father. The women of the village who knew about family connections assigned women to their paternal family, thus handing down a knowledge that was important for the concrete circumstances of life and for the transmission of property. For the female and the male inheritance each went their separate ways. That presupposed a detailed, generation-spanning knowledge about family circumstances.

Katharina Legendre and Johannes Richard had four children: Madeleine (born 1750), Margarete (born 1753), Suzanne (born 1757), and Nicolas (born

---

[154] See p. 176: site map of the house of Louise Keller, in which four or five households of Jewish community members were set up. The Keller house was presumably the former share of Suzanne, who was married to Pierre Baumans. The shared well lay behind Louis Keller's house.

1760). Only Madeleine and Margarete Richard reached adulthood. The family's financial foundation was secured by a dowry and inheritance. From her parents, Katharina Legendre had received landholdings in Lauterfangen, Durchtal, Tetingen, and Lubeln. Johannes Richard sold them with her consent in order to set himself up in the village. In 1762, he received his portion of the parental inheritance, in 1769 he and his wife purchased a house, and in 1773 they jointly bought their last piece of land. In 1775 they owned a house in Steinbiedersdorf, thirty Morgen of fields, Etzeln, and meadows.[155]

Widowhood

Katharina Legendre lived the last thirty years of her life as a widow. Since none of their children were married when her husband died, she was from the beginning faced with the responsibility for the farm and the children all alone. That would change only for a few years. In 1777, Katharina Legendre gave her oldest daughter, Madeleine, in marriage to the impoverished orphan Pierre Schmidt, who allegedly "brought nothing into the household except the clothes on his back and his shirts wrapped in a kerchief."

Dissension seems to have already broken out during the marriage arrangements. Since Pierre Schmidt "was a stranger and had no friend in the village who would have given him anything," Katharina Legendre arranged and paid for the wedding. Madeleine Richard and Pierre Schmidt shared a house with Madeleine's mother and sister and ran the household jointly. Although it was said that Pierre Schmidt paid for his own bread, all the other things that were part of a household, "meat, cheese, butter, milk, salt, fat, vegetables, seasonings, and other victuals," he received from his mother-in-law, who later demanded payment for board. The running of the farm remained in the hands of Katharina Legendre, who for the most part hired the day laborers and paid for the upkeep of the families and the workers. Her son-in-law Pierre Schmid also had to work for her as a day laborer.[156]

Pierre Schmidt slowly created a separate income for himself. With his mother-in-law's tools and implements he worked the land promised to him when he married Madeleine, using the proceeds to lease additional parcels of land. However, since he did not own any livestock, he was not able to run his own household. One outward sign of his emerging prosperity were the sky-blue dresses that Pierre Schmidt had made for his wife, and which would come to play a central role in the later dispute over the inheritance.[157] The good fortune

---

[155] AD Mos. 10 F 429: Steinbiedersdorfer Deklaration, 1775.

[156] See p. 99ff.

[157] On the importance of clothes in rural society see Medick, *Weben und Überleben*, 379ff. Medick noted in Laichingen in the second half of the eighteenth century an increase in the expenses lavished on dress among men and women: "The items of clothing that came to be increasingly valued were those that underscored feminity and emphasized the public display of the woman in the culture of renown" (ibid., 403f.).

in the home of Katharina Legendre was not destined to last very long. The first child of Madeleine Richard and Pierre Schmidt lived only fifteen months. Madeleine Richard died shortly after the birth of her second child, which followed its mother to the grave a few days later. Half a year later Pierre Schmidt, too, was dead. He had left the house of his mother-in-law and had gone back to his relatives to die.

We can reconstruct the misfortune that befell the family only from the register of deaths. The makeshift agreements when the marriage was concluded and the unclear arrangements in the house of Katharina Legendre, which led to a legal dispute between Katharina Legendre and her son-in-law's relatives, reveal that none of those involved had expected Madeleine and her husband to die such untimely deaths. When Pierre Schmidt fell ill, his relatives were aware of the uncertain legal situation. They had Katharina Legendre summoned to her son-in-law's deathbed on several occasions. If we are to believe her lawyer, they "tried to dupe her, a woman who was not on her guard."[158]

Suit against her

The question of whether the relatives of Pierre Schmidt had a claim to his and his wife's inheritance divided the two families. For more than a decade the parties pursued legal action against each other, exhausting every legal means in an effort to enforce or fend off the claims of Pierre Schmidt's relatives. While Nicolas Thiel, Pierre Schmidt's brother-in-law, sought to validate his claims with reference to territorial law (Landrecht), Katharina Legendre invoked local custom.

The legal proceedings reveal the possibilities and limitations that women encountered if they tried to enforce their interests through the courts.[159] Given the contradictory legal situation and the not always clear jurisdiction of various courts, working within the court system required extensive institutional knowledge.

Initially the dispute revolved around the fact that Nicolas Thiel wanted the clothes of his deceased sister-in-law and the holding that had been promised to Pierre when he married Madeleine. In addition, he claimed half of the paternal inheritance, a quarter of the paternal purchased property, and a quarter of the movable assets left behind. Since the marriage arrangements had been based on an amicable oral agreement without any legal safeguards, there were different opinions on various issues.

---

[158] AD Mos. B Spire 11038, fol. 335b: Acta in Sachen Nicolas Thiel gegen Katharina Legendre, die Verlassenschaft des verstorbenen Pierre Schmidt betr.

[159] AD Mos. B Spire 10037: Acta in Sachen Johannes Richards Witwe wider Nicolas Thiel. Appellationes una cum restitutione in integrum brevi manu, 1788; AD Mos. B Spire 11039, Fasc. II: Acta in Sachen Nicolas Thiel von Steinbiedersdorf, Kläger und Appellanten, contra Katharina Legendre, Beklagte und Appellatin, die Verlassenschaft des verstorbenen Pierre Schmidt betr.

Katharina Legendre countered the demands by Nicolas Thiel with claims for her son-in-law's rent and board. She also denied that the landed property was already part of the estate, since the grandmother, Franziska Leonard, was still alive and all holdings remained in her hands until her death. As for the dresses, she emphasized that her two daughters had taken turns wearing them and the younger one was now entitled to them.

Claiming that she wanted to see justice done, Katharina Legendre initiated legal proceedings. These proceedings took on a dynamic of their own, from which she could extract herself only with difficulty. As far as we can see, she brought the suit without any outside coercion. The passive acceptance of what she considered unjust demands would presumably have caused her less of a financial disadvantage than her active resistance and the legal dispute to which it gave rise, and which grew into a protracted and expensive case with suits and countersuits, appeals and counterappeals.

In the first instance the dispute was decided before the local court of arbitration, which was composed of two arbitrators and one presiding officer (Obmann). Nicolas Thiel appealed the decision that was issued in August 1781 to the government. In March of 1782, he received a legal order that affirmed the previous judgment only in part. Katharina Legendre's daughter, Margarete Richard, appealed this decision in her mother's name. Because of a procedural error, the appeal was not accepted, and Katharina Legendre was ordered to hand over a portion of her possession, including the black wedding dress, a golden cross, a ring, a silver cross, a sky-blue skirt, and another dress. When she refused to do so, the authorities, in the summer of 1782, ordered that the items be taken by force. It appears that Katharina Legendre and Margarete Richard put on the dresses to prevent them from being seized. At least that would explain her complaint about the cruel enforcement of the decision, in the course of which "the clothes were stripped off her body."

Katharina Legendre, who had had a falling out with her first lawyer, now hired the Privy Councillor Caroué from Trier, several hours away, to represent her interests. Caroué was familiar with village life, since he had represented the community in its suits against the territorial lordship.[160] To hear what he had to say, Katharina Legendre went to see him in Trier on a number of occasions. In November 1783, a decision by the territorial lord affirmed the judgment of the lower court in all essential points. Both parties appealed. Now the priest was charged with settling the dispute. As he was also unable to reach a settlement, the files were sent back to the chancery in Runkel, which, in May 1785, once more reaffirmed the earlier decision.

Katharina Legendre could now take advantage of the fact that the community was involved in yet another suit before the Imperial Chamber Court and had hired a lawyer, who was spending some time in the remote village. The

---

[160] LHA Koblenz 56/493a: Elisionsschrift und rechtliche Bitte vom 6.11.1786.

university-trained advocate took on her case and drafted a letter to the procu-
rator of the Imperial Chamber Court, a man by the name of von Sachs, who
was handling the Steinbiedersdorf case. Von Sachs looked after Katharina
Legendre's legal dispute in Wetzlar, a case that simultaneously furnished him
with important arguments for the community's suit. Using this case as an example, he was able to accuse the count of errors in legal procedure and the
unjustified use of so-called "Kabinettsjustiz."[161]

Von Sachs tried in vain to apply for legal aid (Armenrecht) for his client,
who was having increasingly greater difficulty paying for her legal expenses. In
spite of all her problems, Katharina Legendre refused to accept a settlement.[162]
In 1788, the two women, "the honorable Catharina Legendre, wife of the
deceased Johannes Richard, and her unmarried daughter, Margarete Richard,"
were able to borrow a larger sum of money, but Katharina Legendre had to
mortgage all her landed and moveable property in return. In the summer of
1792 she managed to avoid an auction of her assets. She had been able to get
her hands on assignats (interest-bearing bonds issued by the French government) and tried to use them to pay her debts, which had by now passed to a
merchant in Saarbrücken. When he refused to accept assignats, "she, in all stub-
bornness, the entire conversation having lasted less than a quarter of an hour,
opened the door and left. On the stairs, however, she said how she would now
no longer come here, but would have me advised to take possession of the offered
assignats in Criechingen."[163]

When her creditor objected and demanded additional interest, she protested
that he was holding her responsible "for something to which she had not put
her mark (Handzeichen)."[164] These final encounters with Katharina Legendre,
in particular, show the determination with which she acted and defended her
case.

Her involvement, knowledge, and nimbleness stand in marked contrast to
the picture that her own lawyers painted of her. In the documents drafted by
her legal counsel, Katharina Legendre is described for the most part as merely
a widow of limited mental capacity. In the very first petition that Caroué drew
up for her, he asked "that this utterly abandoned and so very dull-witted woman,
and the innocently robbed daughter of the same, be treated most kindly with

---

[161] In the second half of the eighteenth century, the counts claimed the right to
bring an appeal to the count's cabinet. By expanding the stages of appeal, they sought
to diminish the influence of the Imperial Chamber Court.

[162] Her suit was still not resolved by 1792, when the jurisdiction of the Imperial High
Court expired as a result of the political changes in the wake of the French Revolution.

[163] AD Mos. Actes judiciaires B 10086: Ein hochgräflich kreichingischer Regierung
auferlegte unterthänig gehorsamste Erklärung in Sachen des Regierungsadvokaten Braun
zu Saarbrücken gg. Katharina Legendre, Johannes Richards Witwe, und deren Tochter
Margarete Richard, 1792.

[164] Ibid.

the strongest sovereign understanding."[165] Like his predecessor, advocate Braun, Caroué based his arguments on stereotypes. Both described Katharina Legendre as "a poor woman of simple mind," an "abandoned wife" and "good-hearted mother." Evidently the use of this emotive language—which did not exactly match Katharina Legendre's behavior—was intended to improve their client's position before the court.

The letters to which Katharina Legendre affixed her mark were all written in the first person and are characterized by an extraordinarily deferential tone.[166] For example, we read this in a petition dated May 1783: "and so I submit to Your Grace, the Count, my most humble request that You will kindly deign to take me, an abandoned widow, into Your highest protection and will remedy the complaints I have indicated, submitted by me, who shall die in the most submissive respect, Your Grace's most humble servant, signed Johannes Richard's wife."[167]

The opposing lawyers for their part employed countervailing stereotypes. They devised the picture of the "vicious woman," who not only had "a disposition tending toward hatred and greediness," but also a "stubborn head," and poison hidden "between her old furrows and wrinkles." They interpreted her inability "to keep her affairs in order" as indicating that she "has a mind contrary to human nature."[168] Her adversary's lawyers did not limit themselves to countering the picture of the "poor widow" with that of the "malicious old woman;" to advance their client's cause they also fell back on the image of the stupid peasant who allows himself to be led and told what to do.

The words that were put into Nicolas Thiel's mouth, "I, as an inexperienced peasant, have until now had to let people guide me and tell me what to do as they wished," follow the same pattern of argumentation that was used to defend Katharina Legendre. From the perspective of the lawyers, the "inexperienced peasant" and the "stupid widow" were on the same level, one that blurred distinctions of gender. Nicolas Thiel's petitions, like those of Katharina Legendre, were written in the first person and reinforced with emotive words: he was turning to the ruling authorities "as a most submissive and obedient servant." Despite the similarity to the documents submitted by Katharina Legendre, the formulas of submission reveal the contours of subtle differences in gender-specific behavioral expectations: where Katharina has to be humble, Nicolas has to be obedient.

---

[165] AD Mos. B Spire 11038, Fasz. II: Acta in Sachen Katharina Legendre von Steinbiedersdorf, Beklagtin und Appellantin, ca. Nicolas Thiel daselbst, Kläger und Appellaten.

[166] Compare Monika Mommertz, "'Ich, Lisa Thielen.' Text als Handlung und als sprachliche Struktur—ein methodischer Vorschlag," *Historische Anthropologie* 4, vol. 3 (1996), 303–329.

[167] As note 165, fol. 99.

[168] Ibid., fol. 148.

Another counterimage to that of the "evil old woman" was that of the dili-
gent woman, whose work was worthy of special remuneration. Again and again,
pointed questions probed into the activities of the deceased daughter, who
could hardly "have been idle for four years without spinning and knitting":[169]
"So, what did the woman of the house do? Did she sit on a stool during her
marriage, or did she work for the mother, in which case she would have deserved
to be paid."[170]

For the opposing lawyer it was no question that a peasant's wife had to
work, as "was proper and befit her station": "The deceased woman, as the
daughter of a peasant, will hardly have been lying around on the sofa, but will
have lent a hand in keeping with custom and her station."[171] If his client had
not left behind anything at his death, the woman, the lawyer argued, "must
have been as lazy as stinking dung, or she must have lent a hand to coarser
and more difficult work."[172] Implicit in his statements are unspoken rules about
the proper behavior of housewives. These rules, precisely because they are not
spelled out in greater detail, indicate that women's contribution to a family's
livelihood was a matter of course.

In the lawyers' argumentation, characterized less by factual arguments than
an emotive or appellative use of language, gender stereotypes played a central
role. They reveal that the lawyers were treating their clients not as subjects,
but as "cases."

Katharina Legendre, on the other hand, was acting for herself and her remaining daughter. She had individual needs: to see justice done, to improve her
daughter's prospects for marriage, to preserve her status in the village. Although
she could neither read nor write, she found herself constantly confronted by
technical questions of legal procedure. She had to make sure she appeared at
hearings, had to hire lawyers, procure documents, and raise money. In the
process there occurred a whole series of conflicts that reveal how little the picture of the "stupid widow" and the "humble maid" was grounded in reality.

Already in 1779, Katharina Legendre had quarreled with and insulted one
of her creditors. Since he "placed importance on his honorable name," he sued
her, and Katharina Legendre was sentenced to a "public declaration of honor."[173]
The little scene documents not only the existence of a village or court public
transcending gender, but shows above all that women, through their ability to

---

[169] Ibid., fol. 53 b.

[170] Ibid., fol. 298.

[171] AD Mos. B Spire 11039 Fasc. II: Acta in Sachen Nicolas Thiel von Steinbiedersdorf,
Kläger und Appellaten, contra Katharina Legendre, Beklagtin und Appellantin, die
Verlassenschaft des verstorbenen Pierre Schmidt betr., fol. 46.

[172] Ibid.

[173] AD Mos. Actes judiciaires B 10071: Acta in Sachen des Handels um Kaspar
Braun von Kriechingen gegen Johannes Richards Wittib von Steinbiedersdorf pcto injuria
verbalia, 1780.

harm the honor of men, were integrated into the process of creating the social hierarchy within the village.

Another dispute, which appeared in the documents in 1787, reveals that Katharina Legendre pursued her conflicts not only in court, but also in church. In that year, Katharina Legendre was penalized for "highly punishable mischief committed in the public church." The charge against her stated that following vespers, she had bumped and shoved her adversary's wife, upon which, according to a female witness, his wife had said: "She is an old beast, she doesn't let up with the shoving." As she said this, according to another female witness who was kneeling in the back pew and heard tumult and laughter, she turned quite red.

Even before a complaint was brought to the authorities, the priest got involved in the quarrel. He summoned the church juror (Kirchenschöffe) and instructed him to ask Katharina Legendre whether she would agree to a fine of four pounds of candle wax. Katharina Legendre found a clever way to talk herself out of it, although she did not challenge the priest's authority and his right to impose a punishment. She told the church juror: "If she was guilty of the transgression, she would give the wax out of obedience to the ecclesiastical authority, if she was innocent, the wax should burn and be intended for her deceased family members."[174]

The following day she told the schoolmaster that, "though innocent, she would give the wax."[175] To the disciplinary measures of the ecclesiastical authorities she responded with a formal submission that contained a contradiction within itself. By emphasizing her innocence or at least the possibility of her innocence, and by earmarking the wax "for the comfort of her deceased," she reinterpreted the required obedience and directed it to her family's benefit, the salvation of the souls of her ancestors. In so doing she revealed quite a lot about her attitude toward (ecclesiastical) authority. She did not in any way question the priest's right or power to define whether or not she was guilty. However, in her own mind she arrived at a different, independent verdict.

The tension between independent action and submission or accommodation to the existing structure of authority is one of the most interesting aspects of the story of Katharina Legendre, who, with her "mischief" in the church, has brought us back to the very sphere were we began our search for clues.

These reconstructed lives have shown how inappropriate and uninstructive it is to restrict the sphere of female agency to the house, forgetting the church, the street, and the court, without which the order in the house would be unthinkable.

---

[174] AD Mos. Actes judiciaires B 10075: Acta in Denunziationssachen Nicolas Thiels Ehefrau von Steinbiedersdorf, Denunziantin, in Steinbiedersdorf ca. Katharina Legendre von da, Denunziantin in Betreff in der Kirche begangen sein sollenden Unfugs, 1787.
[175] Ibid.

That this order was exceedingly fragile, since the house not only offered protection but was to a special degree in need of protection, was revealed not only by the example of Michael Kremeter's wife, who had been beaten, but also by the unresolved work arrangements of Dominik Baumans, who had to sue for the wages he had earned in his aunt's household. The stories of Johannes Ladner, who drank away his wife's fortune, and of Johannet Wahl, who was running affairs, also shift our gaze from the house, as the embodiment of a normatively secured order, to those spheres where women and men were engaged in a "transgression of the norms," struggling with each other and with the authorities to define an order that would do justice to the needs and interests of individuals.

That sphere could be the church, where social rank was mirrored in the seating arrangements, it could be the clerk's office or the chancery, where they could lodge complaints or plead for mercy, it could be the street, where they restored their honor in brawls and publicized the injustice done to them, but it could also be the "wood pile" they hid behind to defend their own space with a wall of silence.

The attempt to illuminate these spheres leads us to the question about the structural framework that determined the lives of women and men in Steinbiedersdorf.

CHAPTER FOUR

Contexts:
Outlines of a Village Society

The socioeconomic framework

My examination of the socioeconomic framework will begin with an orientation in space. Starting with the boundaries of the village, I will ask about the soil and changes in its use in the course of the eighteenth century. This long-term analysis is combined with an examination of working conditions and ownership, population structure and mobility—that is to say, factors of fundamental significance in a society with essentially limited resources.

People, work, and property

The greater part of the district of Steinbiedersdorf, which encompassed an area of 845 hectares, was farmland. Good soil—shell limestone in the north, marl in the south—allowed the inhabitants to live from gardening and farming.[1]

In the fields the locals grew primarily wheat and oats, along with some rye and barley. They also cultivated plants for trade and manufacture (such as flax, hemp, and tobacco), legumes, and feed crops, especially vetch.[2] Cattle dominated animal husbandry.[3] Although cattle trading—pursued above all by the

---

[1] In the mid-nineteenth century, the chief crops were wheat and oats, alongside which rye, barley, vegetables, and potatoes were grown: AD Mos J 5818: Collection Richard. Tobacco cultivation also continued: E. H. Th. Huhn, *Deutsch-Lothringen. Landes-, Volks- und Ortskunde* (Stuttgart, 1875), 370.

[2] AD Mos. 10 F 70: Extract aus dem Bannbuch von 1732. Several field names point to the importance of the cultivation of plants for manufacturing: Hanffelden (hemp fields); Kurtze Flax Felder (short flax fields); Lang Flax Felder (long flax fields); Auf den langen Flaxfelder (on the long flax fields). They are listed as arable land in the nineteenth-century land register. Legumes (peas and lentils) were subject to the tithe, which means they were also grown in fields and not in gardens: AD Mos. 10 F 133: 1737.

[3] In 1786, 109 horses, 1 steer, 143 cows, 80 sheep, 38 pigs, and 1 goat were counted. Sixty percent of all houses had a barn: AD Mos. 10 F 70/2: Generaltabelle über sämtliche Population, den Viehstand und alle weitere Konsistenz der Reichsgrafschaft Kriechingen an Gebäuden, Gärten, andern Gründen, Wiesen, Wald u.a., 1786. The ratio of draft animals to other animals was 1:2.3. It is noticeably different from the regions mentioned by Abel: eastern Germany (1:0.7), northwest Germany (1:1.4); Hesse and Franconia (1:1.5): Wilhelm Abel, *Geschichte der deutschen Landwirtschaft vom frühen Mittelalter bis zum 19. Jahrhundert*. Deutsche Agrargeschichte 2, 3rd ed. (Stuttgart, 1978), 251.

Jewish villagers—had some importance, only a small percentage of the land was used for meadows and pastures. Meadows were cut several times, the yield (the rowen) being used for barn feeding.[4]

The land was cultivated by the owners of the farms or by day laborers, harvesting by sickle. We know from the work of Günter Wiegelmann that harvesting by sickle was a form of labor organization in which the work of women had special importance.[5] In Steinbiedersdorf, male and female cutters worked side by side. For example, in 1755, eighteen-year-old Peter Vogt made the following statement: "During the last grain harvest he helped Simon Richard in the cutting as a day laborer, and he truly did some cutting on a certain section along with his [i.e. Simon Richard's] wife, the weaver Franz, his wife, and Katharina Weiß."[6]

The harvesters caught a rabbit, which they intended to eat together in the house of their employer, for their contact was not limited to work in the narrower sense, and the shared meal in the evening was an integral part of their labor agreement.[7] One consequence of an organization of work that was based on day wages and that integrated women was far-ranging relationships between the women and men of the village, relationships that broke through the narrow boundaries of the house, on the one hand, and those of class or gender, on the other. Among the workers employed by Simon Richard it was not a farmhand or day laborer that occupied a special position but the employer's wife who was working alongside the hired help. That is also why she was later held criminally responsible for the prohibited rabbit hunt. Because of her "presumptuous incitement" she was to pay a fine of 30 Reichstaler as a warning and a "deterrent and example" to others.[8]

---

[4] See pp. 267–68.

[5] Günter Wiegelmann, "Bäuerliche Arbeitsteilung in Mittel- und Nordeuropa," *Ethnologia Scandinavica* 1 (1975), 5–22, esp. 20ff. See also Michael Roberts, "Sickles and Scythes: Women's Work and Men's Work at Harvest Time," *History Workshop* 7 (1979): 3–28; Harriet Bradley, *Men's Work, Women's Work. A Sociological History of the Sexual Division of Labour in Employment* (Cambridge, 1989), 85f.

[6] AD Mos. Actes Judiciaires B 10054: Acta in Sachen Simon Richards Ehefrau wegen eines gefangenen Hasens, 1755.

[7] Of interest in this case is a comparison with a similar situation described by Regina Schulte in the context of her reflections on poaching: *The Village in Court*, 124–127.

[8] It was alleged that with almost clairvoyant abilities she had foreseen the appearance of the rabbit and encouraged the others to the hunt. Even though Simon Richard's wife did not catch the rabbit herself, she was held criminally liable for this act of poaching. She was supposed to pay a fine of 30 Reichstaler, though half of it was forgiven later out of mercy. Still, between the fine and the court taxes, she had to come up with 42 livres de Lorraine. The fine was unusually high and was addressed in connection with other complaints in a suit before the Reich Chamber Court: LHA Koblenz 56/1801: In Sachen sämtlicher Untertanen und Dorfschaften der Grafschaft Kreichingen ctr. H. Grafen von Wied-Runkel, Mandatis, fol. 1023ff.: Gravamina Steinbiedersdorf betr.

The importance of day labor rose in the eighteenth century. At the same time, there were broad changes in the economic system that also touched on the gender-specific organization of work: in 1725, 41 percent of heads of households still indicated that they were peasants or villein farmers (Hofmänner);[9] sixty years later, the percentage of peasants had dropped to 14, while that of artisans had risen from 27 to 36 percent and that of day laborers from 30 to 50 percent.[10] If we include Jewish families—who were not part of the statistics—in this occupational survey from 1777, the picture shifts even more to the disadvantage of peasants: only 12 percent of households belonged to this group, while artisans made up 18 percent, day laborers 41 percent, and the Jews, who lived primarily from credit or pawn activities and from commerce, 17 percent.[11]

Since the peasants and artisans, once the majority in the village, claimed the sole right to the common pasture, conflicts were unavoidable. In 1749, invoking their contribution to the "common good" and their obligation of performing corvée labor, they challenged the pasturage rights of their Jewish fellow-villagers, who, because they were under the direct authority of the territorial lord, bore no share of the community's obligations. They also demanded that the Jewish villagers limit themselves to the rowen they acquired at auction.[12] The usufruct rights of day laborer households were also contested. Unlike Jewish families, they had to help pay the community's obligations, which were calculated by head, although they were disadvantaged vis-à-vis farmers and artisans when it came to rights of use. In 1757, an attempt was made to find a contractual settlement to the divergent interests of the various members of the community who were entitled to usage rights.[13] At least a portion of the common land was divided by lot and auctioned off and thus opened up to individual use.

When the soil had to feed an ever increasing number of people, locals began to grow potatoes, white cabbage, and yellow and white beets on the fallow land.[14] In addition, more and more hemp fields and gardens were marked off.[15] This

---

[9] AD Mos. 10 F 429: Declaration oder Verzeichnis denen Unterthanen des Dorffs Steinbiederstorff unter die Graffschafft Crichingen gehorichen Ort, was Vermögens und Condition dieselbe anietzo sind, 1725.

[10] AD Mos. 10 F 70: Generaltabellen über sämtliche Population, den Viehstand und alle weitere Konsistenz der Reichsgrafschaft Kriechingen, 1785.

[11] There was occupational data for only one hundred twenty-eight of the one hundred fifty-one Christian households. The missing information presumably concerned some of the widow households. We have no detailed data on the Jewish households.

[12] AD Mos. Actes judiciaires B 11058: Gravamina die Juden betr., 1750. Rowen was the grass from the second or third mowing. Rowen meadows were usually off limits to grazing: Abel, *Geschichte*, 240f.

[13] AD Mos. Actes judiciaires B 10046: Charles Wilbourg namens der Tagelöhner pcto Nutzungsrechte, 1757; AD Mos. E Dépot 553: Vergleich, 1757.

[14] The changed and more intensive use of fallow land resulted in numerous tithing suites.

[15] AD Mos. 10 F 429: Steinbiedersdorfer Deklaration, 1775; AD Mos. 10 F 70: Generaltabellen über sämtliche Population, den Viehstand und alle weitere Konsistenz,

removed them from communal control and liability for seigneurial dues, since gardens and garden fields, which were mostly worked by women, allowed for individual use and were exempt from dues.[16]

As the population of smallholders below the peasant class grew, the process of individualization progressed. During a stretch of eleven years, between 1775 and 1786, 30 houses with gardens, 152 Tagwerk of arable land, 38 Tagwerk of meadows, 12 hemp fields, and 29 gardens changed hands through purchase and sale (a Tagwerk is a measure of land varying between 27 and 47 acres).[17] The mobility of real estate, which concerned above all female spheres of work, and changes in land use are symptoms of a pauperization that had been accelerating since 1770, and in the wake of which the work of women continued to grow in importance.[18]

Table 2: Land use and mobility of real estate, 1775–1786[19]

	1775	1786	Total sales	1775–1786 share in %
Houses	104 1/2	120 1/2	30	28.7%
Gardens	68 M 3 V	155 M	29	42.6%
Hemp fields	32 M 3 V	125 M	12	37.5%
Etzeln	44 M 2 1/2 V		No data	
Fields	2182 M 31/2 V	1832 M	152	6.9%
Meadows	706 T 3 V	359 T	38	5.4%

1785. The district of Steinbiedersdorf accounted for 24 percent of the total area of the County of Kriechingen. Twenty-five per cent of the houses, 26.5 percent of the residents, 26.7 percent of all the gardens, 35.6 percent of all arable land, and 39.7 percent of the hemp fields in the County of Kriechingen were located in the district of Steinbiedersdorf.

[16] LHA Koblenz 56/1801: In Sachen sämtlicher Untertanen und Dorfschaften der Grafschaft Kriechingen ctr. H. Grafen von Wied-Runkel, Mandatis, 1764ff.: in the dispute over the potato tithe, it is emphatically stated that common land and gardens were exempt from dues. But as soon as potatoes were being grown in larger quantities on the fallow land, the lord tried to enforce a claim to the tithe.

[17] AD Mos. 10 F 69: Acta Austausch der Grafschaft Kriechingen mit Frankreich betreffend.

[18] What Mitterauer has said about the division of labor in agriculture ("Geschlechtsspezifische Arbeitsteilung," 93) is substantiated by the documentary material from Steinbiedersdorf.

[19] M = Morgen (0.6–0.9 acres), V = Viertel, T = Tagwerk. Sources: AD Mos. 10 F 429: Steinbiedersdorfer Deklaration, 1775. AD Mos. 10 F. 70: Generaltabellen über sämtliche Population, den Viehstand und alle weitere Konsistenz, 1785 and 1786. AD Mos. 10 F 69: Acta Austausch der Grafschaft Kriechingen mit Frankreich betreffend. Although the statistics are quite detailed, the data is not consistent: compare the differences between 1775 and 1786. The additions are almost always faulty. As a result, the numbers can only reveal trends. Kasper-Holtkotte, *Juden im Aufbruch*, 33f., on the

The land register of 1831 recorded 5,579 parcels. Seven hundred and twenty-five hectares, approximately 86 percent of the district, were listed as arable land. Forest accounted for 11 percent of the land. Many people in Steinbiedersdorf continued to work in agriculture, as day laborers, or as artisans. Others engaged in trade and commerce, lived off rent, or had a permanent job with the community. A new area of work opened up with the construction of the railroad. In 1875, brick making, beer brewing, and silk weaving offered additional opportunities to earn a livelihood.[20] Women's work is rarely mentioned in the statistical sources, which were shaped by administrative interests and based on the notion of the "normal family" with one male head of the household responsible for feeding the family: in the middle of the nineteenth century, one seamstress, two women teachers, and one midwife appear in the occupational statistics.[21]

The deficiencies of the statistical records affect not only women but also men working in occupations other than the "typical" rural ones. For example, the statistical table of 1785, which at first glance appears unusually detailed with its twenty-nine carefully filled-in headings, did not provide a column to record rentiers, merchants, or soldiers.[22] The statistics do no reveal that at least one out of every ten villagers earned a living for some time in French military service,[23] or give any indication that a whole series of iron dealers and tobacco manufacturers were found in Steinbiedersdorf or in other villages of the county.[24] Especially the mercantile professions were unusually important in this village, located so close to the border as it was. That importance was heightened further by the enormous demand for provisions, animals, and material by the French military stationed nearby, on the one hand, and by smuggling on the other.[25] Since some of the "merchants" were among the most influential and/or richest members of the village community, their activities have left many traces in the sources. These traces reveal that they referred to themselves as merchants

---

basis of a table from 1785 which she examined in the archive of the Leo Baeck Institute in New York (original in AD Mos.), arrives at conclusions very different from my own. For a critique of her views see chapter 5, notes 98 and 107.

[20] Huhn, *Deutsch-Lothringen*, 370.

[21] AD Mos. J 5818: Collection Richard.

[22] AD Mos. 10 F 70/2: Generaltabelle über sämtliche Population, den Viehstand und alle weiterer Konsistenz, 1786.

[23] AD Paris, C. P. Allemagne, Petites Principautés, 18 (1780–1825), fol. 56: Liste des sujets créhangeois actuellement au service de France.

[24] AD Mos. Actes judiciaires B 10073: Acta in Sachen des Handelsmanns Schmidts von Steinbiedersdorf ctr Johannes Richard und dessen Ehefrau von da pcto diversorum gravaminum, 1784.

[25] For the importance of the shadow economy see Edith Saurer, *Straße, Schmuggel, Lottospiel. Materielle Kultur und Staat in Niederösterreich, Böhmen und Lombardo-Venetien im frühen 19. Jahrhundert. Veröffentlichungen des Max-Planck-Instituts für Geschichte* 90 (Göttingen, 1989), 383ff.

and not as artisans or plowmen (Ackerer). As it is, the statistical data did not include plowmen as such, but differentiated between plows, artisans, and day laborers.

The number of plows was presumably identical with the number of those who called themselves peasants, but not with the number of people owning or working on the land, since some families shared a plow while others rented it out for pay. It is therefore difficult to estimate how many people pursued agriculture as a source of supplementary income.

Also not recorded in the detailed statistics of wealth is the income that some villagers derived from outside sources. Many men and women of Steinbiedersdorf owned land in France or Lorraine, for which they were even liable for corvée labor, depending on the precise legal status.[26] It is also unclear to which category work in the home was assigned, in particular spinning and weaving, an occupation that was, according to the inventories, frequently but not exclusively engaged in by women. Apparently the records subsumed under the heading of artisan a broad spectrum of occupations that differed considerably not only in terms of the actual work but also in terms of status and wealth.

From the neighboring village of Teting we have more precise occupational statistics from the year 1777, which give us an idea of the spectrum of activities and allows us to place them in some kind of social ranking. In Teting, the bailiff and—with one exception—the peasants belonged to the highest tax bracket, artisans (locksmiths, shoemakers, watchmakers, saddlers, coopers, potters, and cartwrights) were distributed among all three tax brackets, while day laborers, linen weavers, and wool spinners were occasionally assigned to the second bracket but mostly to the third. Widows, too, were assessed in the third bracket. Important activities, such as legal and illegal trade, soldiering, and the work of women also fail to appear in these statistics.[27]

Still, careful research uncovers numerous women who earned a living by gainful employment. In Steinbiedersdorf, Margaretha Becker, the wife of Johannes Hoß, washed the shirts of the dairyman (Schweizer) Johannes Roschy, in return for which she received about three pints of milk as payment.[28] Nanette Schilling,

---

[26] AD Mos. 10 F 429: Steinbiedersdorfer Deklaration, 1775. In Steinbiedersdorf, the number of "outlying holdings" was as follows: 3 houses (2.8 percent), 21 Morgen gardens (30.8 percent), 3 Morgen hemp fields (9 percent), 3 Morgen Etzeln (6.8 percent), 292 Morgen fields (13 percent), 148 Morgen meadows (20 percent). Given this intermixture of properties, it is not possible to obtain precise ideas about the residents' wealth, since the tax burdens evidently were based solely on the property within the specific village or county.

[27] AD Mos. 10 F 70: Consistenz der gantzen Grafschaft Crichingen an Untertanen, Ackerland, Wiesen, etc. Teting betr.

[28] AD Mos. Actes judiciaires B 10041: Acta Johannes Rochy, dahier gewesten Schweizers betr., Mai 1721. The word "Schweizer" (Swiss), outside of that country, is usually an occupational term for, among other things, work in animal husbandry or dairy production.

"a poor person," worked as a day laborer;[29] the daughter of a deceased shoe-maker fired nails in the oven, surely not only for her own use;[30] sixteen-year-old Bremel sought "a meager living with sewing, spinning, and work;"[31] and thirty-three-year-old Elisabeth Dimanche lived with her mother and had "food and bread to eat whenever they worked diligently."[32]

Since each house came with at least one vegetable garden or, in its absence, a plot of hemp, the basic conditions were in place for ensuring a person's subsistence at least on a modest level.[33] If they were lucky, older women found employ with Jewish families as a shabbes maid. In addition, important opportunities for gainful employment were available in the cultivation and processing of commercial plants, the importance of which can be seen from land use.

In the protocols of the Jahrgedinge we come across a very different form of women's work that was of some significance in providing the basic needs especially among the lower social strata.[34] We read about women, and occasionally men, who were reported to the authorities because they had pulled grass or onions, had gathered pears or other fruits and herbs, had cut grass and fruits with the sickle, or had moved fences. Other complaints concerned overgrazing and the illegal procurement of wood.[35] We must set the prohibitions and complaints about how extraordinarily widespread these offenses were against the backdrop of the pauperization described earlier. Not only do they reveal the variety of activities "close to home," they also show the extent to which women could come into conflict with the law in the attempt to obtain for themselves and their families the necessary foods and the no less vital wood. Of course it would be shortsighted to examine the economy of collecting and gathering only from the perspective of work and subsistence and to overlook the unique cultural meaning of these activities.

Gathering represented a gender-specific form of engaging in conflict, and it offered girls and women, beyond the immediate necessity of procuring food, the opportunity to acquire the capacity of "sustained industriousness" that was expected of them and to demonstrate their hard work to the outside world.[36]

---

[29] AD Mos. Actes judiciaires B 10047: Acta in Sachen Nannette Schilling gegen Louis Metzinger, Ackerman, pcto debiti, 1759.

[30] AD Mos. Actes judiciaires B 10081: Plaids annaux, 1760. A charge had been brought against her and her mother at the Jahrgeding because sparks had come from the chimney of their house.

[31] AD Mos. Actes judiciaires B 10073: Acta in Sachen der Jüdin Gelle, dermalen zu Steinbiedersdorf sich aufhaltend ctra Jacob Meyer Cahens Sohn von da, Gembel Cahen, pcto impregnationis ac satisfactionis, 1784.

[32] LHA Koblenz 56/491: Kommissionsbericht in Sachen der Gemeinde Steinbiedersdorf gegen Herrn Grafen Christian von Wied-Runkel.

[33] AD Mos. 10 F 429: Steinbiedersdorfer Declaration, 1775.

[34] On the Jahrgerichte see 136f.

[35] AD Mos. Actes judiciaires B 10081: Plaids annaux, Pontpierre, 1754, 1760, 1764, 1774.

[36] Johann Heinrich Campe, *Väterlicher Rat für meine Tochter* (1789), reprinted in Paul

It was an assertion of womanhood that was the functional equivalent of corresponding male models of socialization, though it followed a different pattern. Although the work had to be done clandestinely, it involved a presentable result. The male counterpart, poaching, plays a comparatively minor role in the Steinbiedersdorf sources.[37]

If the gathering activities in field, forest, and meadow were activities typically assigned to women, a glance into the house illuminates spheres of work that do not correspond to the conventional picture of socially standardized expectations regarding a division of labor according to gender. These spheres are causally connected with the law of inheritance and with the rules of transfer as practiced in Steinbiedersdorf.

The one hundred forty-three individuals or groups listed in the Steinbiedersdorf declaration as owners of more or less large landholdings included ninety-six married couples, nineteen widows, seven unmarried women, ten unmarried men, and a few communities of joint heirs.[38] Since a division of the estate was neither required nor commonly practiced when children married, it was not unusual for widows to hold on to their property during their lifetime. They hired farmhands or leased their holdings to their children or other interested parties. The high number of widow households in the eighteenth century (as much as 20 percent)[39] reveals that the organization of labor did not require remarriage and perhaps did not even make it seem desirable.

As in other areas in which the influence of manorial landlords was weak, farmhands could assume the role of overseers of the land.[40] Their status, however, was contested, since the women owners of holdings insisted that such individuals had merely performed the services of farmhands. It was not rare for work relationships to be part of the kinship network. For example, as we saw earlier, the widow Madeleine Richard took her nephew Dominik Baumans into her house and allowed him to work for her. Eight years later—presumably in connection with inheritance arrangements—a dispute arose, and Dominik sued his aunt for back wages. Madeleine Richard, who had three children of her

---

Münch, ed., *Ordnung, Fleiß und Sparsamkeit. Texte und Dokumente zur Entstehung der "bürgerlichen Tugenden"* (Munich, 1984), 260–270; Thorstein Veblen, *The Theory of the Leisure Class* (New York, 1899), spoke in this context more aptly of the "boring industriousness of women." The context is discussed in greater detail in Claudia Ulbrich, "Weibliche Delinquenz im 18. Jahrhundert. Eine dörfliche Fallstudie," in Ulbricht, ed., *Von Huren und Rabenmüttern*, 281–311.

[37] On the complex meaning of poaching see Schulte, *Village in Court*, 121–177.

[38] AD Mos. 10 F 429: Steinbiedersdorfer Deklaration, 1775.

[39] Since not all widowers or widows are likely to have run their own household, it is impossible to give precise figures.

[40] Michael Mitterauer, "Formen ländlicher Familienwirtschaft: Historische Ökotypen und familiale Arbeitsorganisation im österreichischen Raum," in Josef Ehmer and Michael Mitterauer, eds., *Familienstruktur und Arbeitsorganisation in ländlichen Gesellschaften* (Vienna, 1986), 185–323, here 242f.

own, claimed she had treated the defendant "like her own child." A child, however, could not ask to be remunerated for normal farm work. Dominik, she said, had lived, eaten, and drunk under her roof and had worked his land with her horses.

The plaintiff saw the matter differently. He claimed that as the chief farmhand, he had not only performed all the jobs of a farmhand, but had "also conducted most of the trade and business relating to the household."[41] The bailiff and the court confirmed that Dominik Baumans "had headed the household of Port's wife, had not only supervised the fieldwork as the chief farmhand, but had looked after the entire household with respect to buying and selling, the settling of accounts with artisans, receiving meadows, and other such relevant affairs as a careful housefather is wont to look after, and Port's widow had not paid attention to any such things."[42]

The criteria that the bailiff and the court applied to determine the position as head of the household were different in interesting ways from the widow's ideas: while she pointed to the spheres supervised by women (housing and food), to kinship relationships ("like her own child"), and to (her) ownership, the bailiff and the court emphasized the active role of the farmhand in the household, which corresponded to the normatively enshrined role of the housefather. While their statement appears to have conformed to gender roles, it would seem that it was not entirely correct. There were witnesses who confirmed that Madeleine Richard had looked after the farm on her own. In 1786, for example, she let Pierre Barell come into her house "to examine her French documents." On this occasion she also mentioned that she still owed Dominik Baumans a substantial amount.

What had begun as mutual help within the framework of kinship bonds ended after years in limbo in a fiercely contested legal case that both parties pursued through several courts. In court, the question of who was "the master in the house" was focused solely on the tasks that had to be performed inside and outside the house. Sex or ownership was of secondary importance. And the question of who had represented the house in communal matters also played no role in establishing the facts of the case.

Since there was no fixed, predetermined definition of what constituted the position of head of the household, it had to be confirmed in day-to-day actions. Everyday conduct become in court a retrospective indicator of the distribution of power within the house and determined the economic consequences that flowed from it. But for nearly a decade, Madeleine Richard and her nephew

---

[41] AD Mos. Actes judiciaires B 10079: Acta in Sachen Dominik Baumans ctr. Madeleine Richard, Peter Ports Wittib pcto schuldigem Canon, 1789.

[42] AD Mos. Actes judiciaires B 10078: Acta in Sachen Dominik Baumans von Steinbiedersdorf ctr. Madeleine Richard, Peter Ports Wittib pcto cond. Operam modo revisionis, 1789.

had gotten along without legally clarifying the farmhand's position in the house-hold. What was undisputed was the fact that both started from the assump-tion that there was a work relationship between them that resulted in a claim to wages. The long period of limbo and the ability to balance their shared and clashing interests indicate that these kinds of work relationships were by no means unusual. Women who owned landholdings could run and control them in person or in place of the housefather. And since work in the fields could not be accomplished by a single person, they had the choice of hiring a farm-hand or signing a contract of lease. The latter option was chosen by Madeleine Richard's sister-in-law, Katharina Legendre.

Katharina Legendre, too, had managed her farm alone for years. After her daughter got married, she had her son-in-law work for her. By declaring that she had maintained her daughter's husband in her house like a child, she tried to fend off inheritance claims advanced by his relatives.[43] Katharina Legendre argued, even more emphatically than did her sister-in-law, that her son-in-law had never occupied the role of a " housefather;" rather, she, as the owner of the farm, had been able to "make use of day laborers." The question of whether Katharina Legendre and her son-in-law each ran a separate household became important only when inheritance claims were asserted.[44] Until then, so it would seem from the many hearings, rather pragmatic considerations determined who would do whatever work needed to be done. After the death of her son-in-law, Katharina Legendre even maintained that she was working the farm all by herself. For example, in 1782 she requested a postponement of a court date with the following argument: "I, as a poor widow, do not have the time to con-duct a trial now, on account of the harvest, because I do not have a husband and must do the work by myself, nor do I have my lawyer present to advise me."[45]

As we have already seen, the dispute between Katharina Legendre and her son-in-law's heirs was also pursued through several courts all the way up to the Imperial Chamber Court, with Katharina Legendre able to take advantage of contacts to the court that had been established through the suits brought by the community.

While the two inheritance disputes in the Richard family show the fragility of work relationships in widow households, they also attest that women believed themselves capable of running a farm and successfully defended their position for many years. Thanks to an inheritance law that favored the surviving spouse, they were able to penetrate into spheres from which they were blocked under other legal circumstances. In this way they also acquired a fairly extensive financial freedom of action.

---

[43] See p. 84ff.

[44] On the meaning of house and household see Sabean, *Property*, esp. 101ff.

[45] AD Mos. B Spire 11038: Acta in Sachen des Nicolas Thiel gegen Katharina Legendre, die Verlassenschaft des verstorbenen Pierre Schmidt betr., 1781.

Since the death of a spouse did not entail the compulsory delivery of the farm, heirs did not necessarily wait for the death of one parent before getting married. Fifty-seven percent of all men and 71 percent of all women who got married in Steinbiedersdorf came from families where both parents where still alive. They had to try and build a livelihood with the help of the marriage portion that both partners brought into the marriage or by leasing land. According to "the custom in this area" it was usual that two individuals who got married were given a generous marriage portion and dowry by their parents and were thereafter responsible for earning their own keep.[46] However, in many cases the young couple had no choice but to turn to day labor. As long as the inheritance had not been paid out and their own assets were not enough to allow them to move into their own house, married children lived with their parents. In a transition phase that could also be the bride's family.[47]

All in all, if we apply a sufficiently crude matrix, Steinbiedersdorf in the eighteenth century can be assigned to an ecological type described by Michael Mitterauer as an agricultural economy of small farmers that was organized into small families and satisfied its need for labor chiefly by day labor.[48] The formation of smaller families, some of which were grouped together into household communities, was promoted by the right to divide landholdings, only a very small portion of which were tied into the seigneurial economy. This resulted in an extremely high mobility of land. The high need for credit that this entailed provided favorable conditions for the settlement of Jewish men and women, who, apart from financial transactions, engaged primarily in cattle trading. The required feed grain was grown in Steinbiedersdorf, which means that the respective economic interests complemented each other, especially so since the Jews

Table 3: Family situation at marriage (parish register 1680–1792)

First Marriage	Men	Women
Both parents alive	212	249
Father deceased	71	54
Mother deceased	23	26
Both parents deceased	1	5
Second/third marriage	58	36
No information	46	48
Total	414	414

[46] AD Mos. BSpire 10037: Acta in Sachen Johann Richards Witwe wider Nicolas Thiel. Appellationes.

[47] That was the case in the house of Louis Lahir, for example. AD Mos. Actes judiciaires B 10079: Acta in Sachen Jean Louis Lahir von Newingen ca. Elisabeth Müller und deren Aeltern zu Steinbiedersdorf pcto die Fortsetzung der angefangenen Ehe betr., 1789.

[48] Mitterauer, "Formen ländlicher Landwirtschaft," 185–323.

were also tied into the agricultural processes through their cattle trading, which involved the keeping of cattle to a certain extent.[49]

Women had extensive opportunities to become active within the form of labor organization I have described, opportunities that did not always correspond with the conventional picture of socially established expectations of a gender-specific division of labor. As I have already mentioned, special importance attached to the gathering economy.[50]

The divergent rights to the common land and the dependence on the increasingly scarce resource of land led to competition and conflicts, in which Christian peasants (men and women), artisans, male and female day laborers, as well as Jewish men and women advanced different claims. These resulted not only in legal disputes, which were closely connected with the simultaneous disagreements with the territorial lord, but also in an adjustment of the economic conditions: an expansion of the chiefly women-organized garden economy, on the one hand, and of the predominantly male handicraft and commercial occupations, on the other.

In view of the known demographic trends, it would seem reasonable to look for the primary cause behind the intensifying struggle over the distribution of resources in the second half of the eighteenth century in the growth of the population and in the agricultural economy linked to it.[51]

Population and household structures

Barely more than four hundred people lived in Steinbiedersdorf at the beginning of the eighteenth century. They were grouped into nearly fifty households, some Christian, some Jewish.[52] After the end of the war, life had become more tolerable and prospects for a long life had risen: 31 to 42 percent of the Catholic inhabitants (at least 45 women and 58 men) who died in the first half of the eighteenth century were older than 60 at the time of death.[53] Anne Paquotte

---

[49] The agricultural importance of animal husbandry lay not only in the potential use of the draft power of the animals, but also in the production of manure.

[50] See p. 97f.

[51] Abel, *Geschichte*, 285ff.

[52] AD Mos. 10 F 429: Declaration oder Verzeichnis deren Unterthanen des Dorfes Steinbiederstorff unter die Grafschaft Crichingen gehorichen Ort, was Vermögens und Conditio die ietzo sind, 1725.

[53] AD Mos. 5 E and Mic. E registres paroissiaux 1680–1792; J 5818: Collection Richard; I analyzed 346 deaths between 1694 and 1763, with indications of age available for only 243, and 374 deaths between 1800 and 1820. Since the parish registers were still quite inaccurate at the beginning of the eighteenth century—the indication of age is missing in 27 percent of all entries (54 F, 33 M)—it is not possible to determine the exact percentage of the elderly, but we do know from historical demography that "the biological shell of life" seems to have "expanded hardly at all over the course of time": Arthur E. Imhof, *Die Zunahme unserer Lebensspanne seit 300 Jahren und ihre Folgen*. Schriftenreihe des Bundesministeriums für Familie, Senioren, Frauen und Jugend 110 (Stuttgart, 1996), 95.

reached almost 100, Jeanne Isemer, who was married to her husband for 57 years, made it to 80, Mathias Martin, who was born in the middle of the Thirty Years' War, was 90 when he died. Catherine Vignon, the wealthy widow of Sr. Masson, is even said to have reached the age of 108.[54] Even if these were the exception, older people had substantial influence on village life.[55] Old age appears as a separate stage of life especially for women. That had at least something to do with the above-mentioned inheritance law favoring the surviving spouse.

By the end of the eighteenth century, the number of Christian inhabitants had risen from about 350 to 612, that of Jewish inhabitants from 69 to 135. The 747 residents of the village in 1785, who were grouped into 179 households, had 120 houses at their disposal, some of which were very small or subdivided into two or three sections. Sixty-one houses had barns, 72 had stables, and 17 had other auxiliary buildings.[56] As we have already seen, each house came with an herb garden or, in its absence, a plot of hemp. House and household were not always identical.[57]

The smallest house in the village in the 1780s belonged to Anton Bardot. It had no direct access to the garden, which meant that if he and his wife wanted to get some vegetables or fire wood, they allegedly had to climb out of the window. Although the parents granted the couple the formal right of passage, a quarrel broke out when his brother wanted to build a stable, and the dispute reveals how cramped living conditions had become in the course of the eighteenth century. If the brother had carried out his plan, Anton would have lost access to the courtyard and the garden and the daylight in his house, which he needed to work.[58]

In many houses, individual rooms were rented out or the houses were divided in such a way that, as the Steinbiedersdorf Declaration of 1775 put it, "2 or

---

[54] AD Mos. I Mic. E. C. 553 Pontpierre.

[55] The kind of statistical mean values that have been calculated by historical demographers mislead us into underestimating the importance of the elderly. Precisely because, as Imhof has calculated on the basis of data from Schwalm, only one in five reached the age of seventy as late as the nineteenth century, there is much to suggest that the smaller number of old people compared to today (more than half get to be seventy or older) meant that old people, because they were the exception, were valued and influential (Imhof, *Die gewonnenen Jahre*, 83). Van Dülmen undoubtedly conveys a false picture when he claims that "according to the information about life expectancy that has come down to us, hardly a farmer reached the age of 50" (*Haus*, 204). In purely quantitative terms, those over the age of seventy still made up a larger group in the village than the politically enfranchised members of the community, whose share of the total population, local fluctuations notwithstanding, is unlikely to have exceeded 20 percent.

[56] AD Mos. 10 F 70/2: Generaltabelle über sämtliche Population, den Viehstand und alle weitere Konsistenz, 1785. On this see note 19.

[57] AD Mos. 10 F 429: Steinbiedersdorfer Deklaration, 1775.

[58] AD Mos. Actes judiciaires B 10074: 1781.

more residents were grouped together."[59] The small size of households reflected
the living conditions. Apart from the priest's household, in which three people lived, the survey in 1785 counted 103 complete and 48 widow households
among the Christian population. Among the Jews in the same year, only 3 widows
but 25 married couples were running their own household.[60] One out of five
Christian households (22 percent) and one out of eight Jewish households (12
percent) was headed by a woman.

Statistically, a household had on average not much more than two children
and no additional personnel. Only one out of every six households employed
a farmhand or maid. The others used day laborers for seasonal work.[61]

In spite of the small household sizes, on occasion several families were combined into a single household. For example, the seigneurial bailiff Dominik
Richard, his wife Johannet Wahl, and his son Peter Richard and his wife
Margarete Bompernetz maintained a common household, which was headed by
Dominik Richard.[62] Such a pattern of residence, in which a married couple lived
with or near the husband's parents, gave the family of the husband a particularly strong position. It is conceivable that there was some connection between
the office of bailiff and the household structure, but we cannot prove it.

That shared households tended to be established in the family of the husband rather than that of the wife is revealed, apart from marriage rules, by disputes that arose in cases that deviated from the norm. For example, Jean Louis
Lahir of Newingen, who lived in the house of his in-laws during the first year
of his marriage, sued for the obligation of residency. In court he argued that
because the available living quarters in Steinbiedersdorf were scarce and expensive, he would have preferred to move in with his mother in Newingen. His
wife, however, refused to move, even though the house of her parents was very
small. Jean Louis Lahir, who sought to force the move to his mother's house
with a decision of the court, claimed that he did not even have a bed of his
own: "Moreover, my in-laws cannot even furnish me with a proper bed, and it
would be most unseemly if I had to spend the night in my father-in-law's bed
and my wife in her mother's bed."[63]

Although it is hardly conceivable, in view of the cramped living arrangements,
that Jean Louis Lahir had his own household, he did state as much in a submission to the government, although his account seems to have been a goal
to be pursued by legal action rather than a reflection of reality. Evidently the

---

[59] AD Most. 10 F 429: Steinbiedersdorfer Deklaration, 1775.
[60] AD Mos. 10 F 70: Extract aus dem Bannbuch, 1732.
[61] AD Mos. 10 F 70/2: Generaltabelle über sämtliche Population, den Viehstand und
alle weiteren Konsistenz, 1785.
[62] See p. 48.
[63] AD Mos. B 10079: Acta in Sachen Jean Louis Lahir von Newingen ca. Elisabeth
Müller und deren Aeltern zu Steinbiedersdorf pcto die Fortsetzung der angefangenen
Ehe betr., 1789.

mother-in-law had the say in the house, and "she even said that she would rather plunge a knife into her daughter's body than let her go with me to Newingen."[64]

The situation in the house of Katharina Legendre was unclear, though, initially. The courts had to deal with the question of whether she maintained a shared household with her two grown daughters Madeleine and Margarete Richard and with her son-in-law Pierre Schmidt from Viller.[65]

Jewish households were larger than their Christian counterparts: at the beginning of the eighteenth century, a Jewish household seems to have comprised nine or ten individuals, although later the number was closer to four or five.[66] We cannot be entirely sure whether these changes were merely formal phenomena—for example, a different administrative practice of recording households—or whether the changes affecting the household touched on the very sphere that was dominated by women. What does become clear, however, is that the household had neither a fixed size nor an invariable structure that would have corresponded to a normative thinking about the house that was unchanged for centuries.

Population growth slowed in the nineteenth century. After the Jews had been granted freedom of residency during the French Revolution, many, especially the wealthier and more educated ones, left the village to settle in larger cities. The share of Jews in the overall population declined from 18 percent to between 5 and 7 percent. A survey in 1866 counted 748 Catholic and 54 Jewish residents in Steinbiedersdorf. They were grouped into 181 households that were, statistically, a little larger than those in the eighteenth century. The number of houses had risen from 120 in 1785 to 171 by 1866 and was now almost identical with the number of households.

On the whole, we can detect for the nineteenth century a rise in illegitimacy, a decline in horizontal mobility, and a higher, crisis-related mortality rate. In the first two decades of the nineteenth century, 35 percent of villagers, 72 women and 59 men, were 60 or older when they died. The infant mortality rate, at 31 percent, was noticeably higher than it had been in the previous century.[67] Famines, which had left barely any traces in the parish registers in the eighteenth century, can now be read clearly from the death statistics, one indication that the population had become poorer, the food supply scarcer, and the options of leaving fewer.[68] The number of out-of-wedlock births surged. While

---

[64] Ibid.

[65] See p. 100f.

[66] For a more detailed discussion see p. 172f.

[67] On the difficulties that attach to these kinds of statements see note 51.

[68] The number of deaths exceeded the number of births in the years 1694, 1741–42 (war), 1772 (inflation), 1784 (inflation), 1788 (inflation), 1801, 1814 (famine), 1817 (famine), 1824, 1836 (cholera?), 1839, 1843, 1855–56, 1858, 1860, 1865, and 1869; source: parish register.

Table 4: Ratio of births and deaths, 1691–1840

	Births	Deaths	Ratio
1691–1740	723	190	3.8:1
1741–1790	1,117	509	2.1:1
1791–1840	1,467	993	1.5:1

only 14 out of 1,840 children in the hundred years between 1691 and 1790 were born illegitimate, which is less than 0.8 percent, in the following fifty years that was the case for 45 children out of a total of 1,467 births, a still low rate of 3 percent.[69] From 1831 to 1865, the illegitimacy rate fluctuated between 5 and 7.6 percent. A few of the children born after 1791 were legitimated by a subsequent marriage of their parents. The ratio of births to death was more balanced in the nineteenth century than it had been previously.

The statistically discernible changes between the eighteenth and nineteenth centuries point to the high importance of the factor of mobility, which merits a closer look since it had a decisive role in shaping the range of activities open to people and their world of experiences.

Horizontal mobility

Although the number of inhabitants all but doubled in the eighteenth century, the rise in the population was far below the excess of births. At times, births exceeded deaths by more than threefold. This finding seems important because it attests to an unusually high degree of mobility. Emigration eased the cramped conditions in the village, which would have contributed to causing some of the village population to fall below the poverty line. High mobility and a low illegitimacy rate right up to the time of the French Revolution suggest effective social control.

Many people seem to have left Steinbiedersdorf because they could not find a sufficient livelihood, as was the case with the children of Jeannine Malling or the widow of Johannes Caspar, who all moved to Hungary after the famine years of 1770–1771.[70] Others set out in search of adventure, like the son of Johann Hauser, who booked passage to East India.[71] Still others had difficulties fitting into the normative structure of the village, or they had run afoul of the

---

[69] For the region (pays mosellan), scholars have calculated an illegitimacy rate in the eighteenth century ranging from 1.1 percent in rural areas to 8.7 percent in urban areas: Marie-José Laperche-Fournel, "Le mariage en pays mosellan au XVIIIe siècle: formation et rupture du couple," *Les cahiers lorrains* 3/4 (1992): 398ff.

[70] AD Mos. Actes judiciaires B 10062: 1775. Ibid., B 10074: 1783.

[71] AD Mos. Actes judiciaires B 10074: Acta in Sachen Johanna Hauser gegen Nicolas Bommersbach.

law: Johannes Roschy, who had worked as a dairyman, and his lad Christoph took off after they had been seen stealing wine, flour, and whey.[72]

Isaak Israel and his son were banished from the territory for two years for beating a female cohabitant bloody.[73] The widow Marie Morell had to leave the village and seek employ elsewhere when she was expecting an illegitimate child, though she was able to return soon after and rent out her house.[74] The Jewish maid Madl also had to move away because she was pregnant out of wedlock, and because the fellow she was accusing of being the father had cleared himself through an oath.[75]

Poverty, dependent labor, marriage prohibitions, and conflicts with the law triggered by these circumstances were, apart from marriages outside the village, the most common reasons why girls and women left the village. Young lads and men were also enticed away by the military. Some sought foreign military service to escape family problems, bridge a shortage of money, or simply earn a living. Michel Mangin, for example, joined a regiment and disappeared for a few weeks when he was summoned to court over a debt matter.[76] Johannes Cury of Flittringen also decamped into military service after his wife had left him and moved in with her son-in-law in Steinbiedersdorf because her "husband had maltreated her so badly that she could no longer stand to be with him."[77] Two Kriechingen delegates (Deputierte) justified their outside military service by claiming that they were driven by dire necessity to take advantage of the favorable opportunities for foreign military service that existed in the border region, and "to seek at least a basic livelihood to fend off hunger."[78] A few Steinbiedersdorf housefathers alleged that they were allowing their sons to serve as a way of disciplining them.[79]

---

[72] AD Mos. Actes judiciaires B 10041: Acta Johannes Roschy, dahier gewesten Schweizers betr., Mai 1721 and see note 28.

[73] AD Mos. Actes judiciaires B 10049: Acta in Denunciationssachen Heym Neumarks Ehefrau gg. Isaak Israel und dessen Sohn, 1766.

[74] AD Mos. Actes judiciaires B 10048: Acta in Sachen des Jacob Venner, des Johannes Venner älteren Sohn, und der Witwe Morell pcto fornicationis et impregnationis, 1762.

[75] AD Mos. Actes judiciaires B 10073: Acta in Denunciationssachen der Madl Meyer von Steinbiedersdorf ca. Meuschel Levy von da, Beklagter, pcto impregnationis, 1784.

[76] AD Mos. Actes judiciaires B 10051: Acta in Sachen Michel Mangin und Anna Maria Richard von da, 1767.

[77] AD Mos. Actes judiciaires B 10070: Acta in Sachen Johannes Oury von Flittringen pcto injuria realia, 1779.

[78] AD Mos. 19 F 519: Criechingische Exekutionsakten de 1764–1772 vom Kreisgesandten de Neufville compiliert. Schreiben von zwei Kriechingischen Deputierten vom 9.7.1765.

[79] AD Mos. Actes judiciaires B 10074: Acta in Denunciationssachen ctr. verschiedene Soldaten vom Schweizer Regiment Salisamatte von Steinbiedersdorf und sonstige dasige Untertanen in Betreff an denen Employés auf lothringischem Territorium verübten Verwundung und sonstige Gewalttätigkeiten, 1785: the young lads were sent to the Swiss "dans l'esperance de les voir civilisés à leur retour."

In 1766, at least twenty-four men between the ages of nineteen and thirty-six were in service to the French king and thus intermittently away from the village.[80] Very few left their service in the military, an institution that inculcated male role models, as peaceful citizens, but military service did temporarily reduce the influence of the young men in the village. That in turn is likely to have had considerable influence on daily life, the distribution of work, and social interactions within the village.

How many Steinbiedersdorf women married outside the village can hardly be determined. The parish registers, however, leave no doubt that exogamous marriage was important. In 45 percent of all Christian marriages that were contracted in Steinbiedersdorf, the partner came from outside, from villages that were five to ten kilometers distant, and sometimes even fifteen kilometers or more.

Table 5: Place of origin of spouses (Catholic marriages)[81]

Both spouses from Steinbiedersdorf		226 marriages		54.6%
Place of origin of one spouse				
up to	5 km	71 marriages	17.2%	
up to	10 km	77 marriages	18.6%	45.5%
up to	15 km	19 marriages	4.5%	
up to	20 km	10 marriages	2.4%	
more than	20 km	11 marriages	2.7%	
Total		414 marriages		100%

As a rule, women who married someone from outside left the village to settle at their husband's place of residence.[82] There were a few exceptions, like the already mentioned Margarete Finickel: in 1743 she married Johannes Ladner from Tyrol, who ended up becoming a drunk. Perhaps as an outsider he had problems integrating into the village community, perhaps the reversal of the hierarchy that was visible in the choice of where the couple resided was difficult for him. Then there was Pierre Schmidt of Viller, who after his wife's death no longer felt comfortable in his mother-in-law's house and moved to the house of his uncle so he could die there.

---

[80] AD Paris, C. P. Allegmagne, Petites Principautés, 18 (1780–1825), fol. 56: Liste des sujets créhangeois actuellement en service de France.

[81] Registres paroissiales (AD Mos. Mic. E 553): four hundred fourteen marriages between 1680 and 1792.

[82] On the legal obligation of a shared place of residence see Koch, *Maior dignitas,* 33f.

Women were outsiders in the village much more frequently than men, and it was they who had to adjust and learn to fit in.[83] Girls who got married were expected to fulfill their "marital duties" by following their husbands. The lawyer of Jean Louis Lahir of Newingen wrote in 1789: "Nor is there a law anywhere that the man must comply with the woman, and establish his residence wherever it pleases her. Rather, the man is the head of the family, and since he must provide wife and children with all the necessities, the wife owes it to him to follow him to where he wants to go, and where he can best pursue his occupation."[84]

We can no longer determine whether Jean Louis Lahir was able to force his wife to leave her parents' home and move with him to Newingen to the house of her mother-in-law. The sources trail off in the eventful years of the revolution. However, it was not usual for girls to refuse to leave.

The Jewish community, as well, recruited its marriage partners to a large extent from outside the village. Of the 41 Jewish marriages that were notarized during the eighteenth century, only 3 were concluded between men and women from Steinbiedersdorf. In 23 cases the woman came from outside the village, in 14 cases it was the man. Steinbiedersdorf families chose the marriage partners for their children most frequently from Metz (8 times) or other villages and towns of the county (7 times). The others came from various villages in Alsace and Lorraine, or from other German-speaking regions (5 times).[85] Another indication of mobility is the large number of nonresidents (Ausbännige) who owned land in Steinbiedersdorf. A declaration of 1775 lists 29 nonresident owners. Almost without exception, they had leased their holdings, for the most part gardens and meadows, to locals.[86]

As these figures reveal, Steinbiedersdorf was an open village that was interconnected with the surrounding world through bonds of kinship and was characterized in the eighteenth century by a high degree of mobility. Women, and to a lesser extent men as well, were compelled, as a result of marriage, to leave not only the house of their parents but also their native village and to adjust to a foreign environment. This experience is likely to have reinforced an open-mindedness towards new things and a willingness to adapt to changing circumstances. The high degree of mobility is surprising, given the marginal political position of the village, and therefore calls for a special explanation.

---

[83] Schulte, *The Village in Court*, 38–41, has brought out the meaning of being an outsider and its connection with fear and ownership. On this issue, as well, Steinbiedersdorf displays differences with its different structure of work and ownership.

[84] AD Mos. Actes judiciaires B 10079: Acta in Sachen Jean Louis Lahir von Newingen ca. Elisabeth Müller und deren Aeltern zu Steinbiedersdorf pcto die Fortsetzung der angefangenen Ehe betr. 1789.

[85] Fleury, "Contrats de Mariage," 15ff.

[86] AD Mos. 10 F. 429: Steinbiedersdorfer Deklaration, 1775.

The political and administrative framework

Steinbiedersdorf's history was shaped by its location at a border that was for a long time one of the liveliest and most hotly contested in Europe.[87] This not only compelled the men and women of the village to constantly deal with the changing political landscape, it also offered an opportunity to take advantage of it. For the subjects the proximity to the border meant uncertainty and heightened control as well as a considerable expansion of their spheres of action, which we must examine if we wish to understand the lives of the men and women in the village.

A village on the border

Steinbiedersdorf was an enclave of the Holy Roman Empire within Lorraine.[88] That fact notwithstanding, the border that surrounded the village was neither a language border nor directly related to ecclesiastical organization. Despite the re-Catholicization policy of the French crown, it was not a confessional boundary, at least not for the Catholic inhabitants. Moreover, it was not identical with the currency boundary and did not even clearly correspond to a legal boundary, even in the eighteenth century. Customary law, which was still valid, did not pay much heed to political boundaries. In addition, the imperial border had no influence—or at least no obstructing influence—on marriages and kinship relations, on property and mobility.[89]

And yet, the border existed as a boundary between states, visible and important. It demarcated different spheres of sovereignty. For the people in Steinbiedersdorf, membership in the Holy Roman Empire meant above all that they were under the jurisdiction of the imperial courts and belonged to a Reichskreis (in this case the Imperial District of the Upper Rhine), were liable for contributions to imperial taxes, and had their laws adjudicated in the German language by a judge or an official experienced in imperial laws. The border that surrounded Steinbiedersdorf was thus complex but not convergent. It was, and this holds true in general for the border of the Holy Roman Empire in the eighteenth century, merely one of a vast number of borders that transected the society of the ancien régime and organized its spaces. This fact moderates the importance of the border, but at the same time it points to an element that shaped people's mental outlook.

---

[87] Fernand Braudel, *The Identity of France*, transl. Sîan Reynolds, vol. 1 (New York, 1988), 329–332.

[88] Steinbiedersdorf was "pays d'Empire," which meant that it belonged to the Imperial County of Kriechingen. The surrounding villages belonged in part to France (three évêchés), in part to the Duchy of Lorraine, in part to the County of Kriechingen under French suzerainty.

[89] This aspect is discussed in detail in Claudia Ulbrich, "Grenze als Chance? Bemerkungen zur Bedeutung der Reichsgrenze im Saar-Lor-Lux-Raum am Vorabend der Französischen Revolution," in Arno Pilgram, ed., *Grenzöffnung, Migration, Kriminalität* (Baden-Baden, 1993), 139–146.

In the ancien régime, political boundaries were not insurmountable barriers separating an "inside" from an "outside" and allowing unambiguous ascriptions. That was true at best from the perspective of the rulers, but even here it applied only to those seigneurial rights that were territorial. Borders were more of an obstacle for rulers seeking to control uniform, straightforward territorial spaces than for the subjects, for whom it was not the centripetal orientation towards a political center that was important, but the centrifugal movement toward the borders.

As long as the border was porous, it functioned as a hinge. It connected people on both sides and created a specific kind of economy. The border focused activities of the shadow economy in the region. In the east, it was predominantly the smuggling of salt and tobacco, commodities that had a special tax imposed on them in every single French province.[90] Since it was fairly easy for smugglers to withdraw into the enclaves, the French authorities considered the latter an "asylum for criminals and deserters and a home to contraband" (asile de criminels et de déserteurs et un foyer de contrebande).[91]

Like all enclaves, the village was surrounded by a chain of guards. Outwitting them required good border-crossing relations between buyers and traders, and a functioning network of information, warning, and surveillance. This system was organized chiefly through women and was based on a dense web of kinship connections and on reciprocal work relationships.[92] All attempts by the territorial ruler to put an end to outside and foreign marriages and to create an immobile village society failed, because such a plan could simply not be implemented, especially since it got no support from the Catholic priests.[93] There were good relations with the neighboring inhabitants of France and Lorraine, relations that were put to use not only in smuggling but also in the case of conflict.

Using the protective shield of the border, the subjects resisted their territorial lord throughout the eighteenth century and defended their traditional rights. They brought suits against the ruler, refused to hand over dues, and infringed upon seigneurial privileges of forest, water, and meadows. Such acts of insubordination, which were nothing other than legitimate self-help in the eyes of the subjects, were usually suppressed through military enforcement.[94] Such

---

[90] AD Paris C. P. Allemagne, Petites Principautés, Créhange, 19, fol. 342: Mémoire concernant la contrebande.

[91] Le Mogine, *Versailles et Créhange*, 311.

[92] On the role of women in smuggling see Bernard Briais, *Contrabandiers du sel. La vie des faux sauniers au temps de la gabelle* (Paris, 1984), 83ff.; and Saurer, *Straße, Schmuggel, Lottospiel*, 435ff.

[93] AD Paris C. P. Allemagne, Petites Principautés, Créhange, 18, fol. 13f.: complaint that the pastor of Denting was presiding at wedding ceremonies in spite of the prohibition, and that the communities were continuing to receive strangers and semistrangers, 1765.

[94] On the importance of military enforcements (distraints, enforcement by writ) as a

actions were difficult to carry out in an enclave, because the territorial lord, if he wanted to bring troops into the area, first had to obtain the right of passage for his soldiers from the French king. If troops did move in, the subjects could take themselves and their property to safety on the other side of the imperial border if they had received sufficient warning. In many cases, women and children remained behind to defend the house and the farm.[95]

Residents of the border region had another way of escaping the power of the overlord: placing themselves under the protection of a different lord. We are told that in 1660, the villages of the Imperial County of Kriechingen, including Steinbiedersdorf, for the first time subjected themselves voluntarily to the French king.[96] They were hoping that this decision would allow them to reduce the unbearable burden of debt that had accumulated during war. Beginning in the eighteenth century, they subsequently threatened on several occasions to switch lords. Half a century later the threat nearly became reality. In 1764, the subjects of the Kriechingen villages that were most threatened entered into talks with the intendant of Lorraine with the goal of having the country placed under French protection. In so doing they initiated lengthy negotiations about an exchange, but these had not concluded by the time the revolution broke out.[97]

The proximity to the border also determined the development of seigneurial rights and the practical exercise of seigneurial power, which stood in a peculiar relationship of tension between feudalism and modern statehood. The crucial changes occurred in the reign of Christian Ludwig (1754–1791).

Reform and rebellion

Life in the village had changed in the course of the eighteenth century, with a growing number of inhabitants forced to share dwindling resources. Interest groups and conflicts emerged, differences between individuals became more pronounced. Above all, the lord intervened to an ever increasing degree in village life. By assigning supervisory functions to various members of the community, he removed them from the existing network of relationships. Proximity to the ruler and the enhanced status it entailed became a new and increasingly important characteristic of the hierarchy within the village. That hierarchy could be

---

way of pacifying discontented subjects in the eighteenth century, which has found scant attention in scholarship and has certainly been underestimated, see Ulbrich, "Rheingrenze," 228f.

[95] LHA Koblenz 56/1802: Sämtliche Untertanen gegen de Grafen, Mandate, fol. 625: the official by name of Lex who was charged with carrying out the enforcement action complained in 1771 that the rebels were outside of the county. They were rarely in their homes, which they left to the care of "women and children."

[96] AD Mos. 10 F 77: Die Teutsche Reichsgrafschaft Krichingen von Franzosen mishandelt. Ein historisches Bruchstück, 1793, 10.

[97] Les Moigne, "Versailles et Créhange," 307–316.

read from the way in which people interacted in the street, how they greeted each other, and how they talked to and about each other.

The second half of the eighteenth century was the time of the peasant hat and the courtly wig, and it was no coincidence that these headcoverings were replaced in the French Revolution by the cap as the symbol of freedom and equality.[98]

Mathis Schmidt, who as the seigneurial bailiff posted a note outside the church that the villagers should raise their hats to him, was not the only one who placed extraordinary importance on the way in which others handled the male headcovering.[99] When the bailiff Dominik Richard made a report about the seizures carried at out the home of Nicolas Metzinger, he did not neglect to point out that the "rebels," when he forbade them in the name of the territorial lord to carry away the seized items, "did not even show enough respect to tip their hats until he had reminded them emphatically of their outrageous lack of respect."[100]

The overlord, even though he rarely came close to the subjects, was also aware of the significance of the hat, which could be used to establish a symbolic barrier to the outside world.[101] For example, the lawyer of Count von Wied-Runkel complained that the subjects in Kriechingen were acting like people "who didn't take orders from anyone and were their own masters." Since they were following "merely their wrong-headed and quite mad will," there was reason to fear "that they might get the idea that their territorial lord, if he insists that they take off their hats to him, must first cite a law to that effect."[102]

Raising one's hat was a simple, clear, and at the same time unambiguously masculine gesture by which one could express one's attitude towards the other person, towards lordship as such. Leaving the hat on one's head amounted to drawing a boundary between the individual and the lord, rebuffing his claim to rule the body and subject the soul. The significance that one accorded to the gesture of raising the hat reveals the extent to which power and domination,

---

[98] On the transformation of symbols in the French Revolution see Lynn Hunt, *Politics, Culture, and Class in the French Revolution* (Berkeley, 1984), 52–86. Wolfgang Hans Stein has noted the political transformations of the revolutionary period in the transition from the courtly wig to the revolutionary Jacobin cap to the bourgeois top hat: Stein, *Untertan—Citoyen—Staatsbürger. Die Auswirkungen der französischen Revolution auf den rheinisch-pfälzischen Raum* (Koblenz, 1981), 21ff.

[99] AD Mos. Actes judiciaires B 9924: Acta in Sachen Mathis Schmidt von Kriechingen ca. Johannes Schmidt von da, 1791.

[100] LHA Koblenz 56/1398: In Sachen sämtlicher Untertanen und Dorfschaften der Grafschaft Kriechingen ca. Herrn Grafen zu Wied-Runkel und Kriechingen. Mandati, fol. 802b.

[101] Robert Muchembled, "Pour une histoire des gestes (XVᵉ–XVIIIᵉ siècles)," *Revue d'histoire moderne et contemporaine* 34 (1987), 87–102.

[102] LHA Koblenz 56/489: Sämtliche Untertanen der Grafschaft Kriechingen gegen den Grafen, 1757–1800, fol. 26f.

but also subjection and resistance, were articulated with the help of symbols in a society in which a substantial part of communication took place through nonverbal signs.[103] But it also points to a focus on those spheres of life that were male-dominated. It is against this background that we must understand the reforms and the unrest during the second half of the eighteenth century.

Christian Ludwig, who had become coregent in 1754, had plans for reorganizing the county.[104] He began, we are told in a report about the unrest, "to organize the structure of his governance according to the latest regulations of the territorial lordship of the German imperial estates with respect to matters of forestry, politics, economics, and the military."[105] Access to the court was strictly regulated in terms of time. The promise by the territorial ruler to administer prompt and impartial justice had its counterpart in the obligation of the subjects to show obedience. Obedient subjects were told they could hope to find mercy; disobedient subjects, however, would meet with uncompromising severity.[106] A chancery messenger (Kanzleibote) was charged with the proper publication of the orders and prohibitions.[107] All of daily life, especially marriage and sexuality, was subject to stringent controls,[108] premarital and extramarital pregnancies were punished,[109] marriages with nonresidents were made subject to approval from the authorities, and the right of settlement was regulated.[110] The

---

[103] Penelope J. Corfield, drawing on examples from the seventeenth century, has pointed to the importance of raising the hat as a means of communication and to its political significance: "Ehrerbietung und Dissens in der Kleidung. Zum Wandel der Bedeutung des Hutes und des Hutziehens," *Aufklärung* 6, No. 2 (1991), 5–19. On the meaning of symbols see also the reflections by Edward P. Thompson, "The Patricians and the Plebs," in his *Customs in Common* (New York, 1991), 16–96.

[104] For the larger context see p. 33ff.

[105] Johann Ulrich Freiherr von Cramer, "Wetzlarische Nebenstunden 100" (Ulm, 1770), 131f., reprinted in *Quellen und Beiträge zur Geschichte Saarwellingens* (1971): 27–29. A first "project for an improved administration of the County of Crichingen" was drafted as early as 1742: AD Mos. 10 F 140: Crichingische Bedientenansetzung und übler Zustand der Grafschaft.

[106] Flaus, *Comté*, 60; AD Mos. 10 F 116: Pleins Pouvoirs accordés au comte le 7.8.1754; E. Dépôt 553, FF 4: Regierungsantritt Christian Ludwigs, 1754.

[107] Flaus, *Comté*, 60.

[108] This is attested by the newly introduced penal registers, which were presumably kept to control the revenues of the treasury (one-third of which came from fines). The extant register (AD Mos. 10 F 429) contains one hundred thirty-one entries for the period 1754–1761, among them many pertaining to money collected from Jews, as well as other entries that provide a collective record of the income from the Jahrgeding.

[109] AD Mos. E Dépôt 553 Pontpierre, No. 10: As early as 1750, the officials Köppel and Reusch issued an order that cases of illicit sexual relations and premarital pregnancies that had occurred within the previous four years must be reported for punishment. AD Mos. 10 F 172: Notariatsinstrument und Zeugenverhör wegen zu zahlen verbotener Fornicationsstrafe.

[110] AD Paris, C. P. Allemagne, Petites Principautés, 18: Créhange (1737–1774), fol. 11: prohibition for outsiders and foreigners to marry and set up a home in the Imperial County without permission from the territorial ruler.

target group of these disciplinary measures, which also included prohibitions against lingering in the tavern late, drinking, and card playing, was—as it had been in the time of Chief Forester Köppel—men much more so than women, for whom disciplining always also meant protection. For women, who were the subordinate sex to begin with, the intervention by the overlord in the communal and familial order was less consequential than it was for men, whose authority as housefathers was being curtailed.

The attempt to make the "strong sex" part of a structure created by the territorial ruler amounted to a limitation on a man's ability to act and violated a cultural ideal of manhood, an ideal in which the right to take action and the penchant for the just cause were intertwined: "A man, however, an honorable man, he thinks for himself and acts accordingly. He pays no attention whether he pleases this person or that, he overcomes all circumstances and does not allow anything in the world to disconcert him. He has no hidden agenda and no penchant for this or that but only for the just cause."[111]

This statement was formulated by one of the lawyers who were outraged that the people of Kriechingen were expected "to beg as a gracious gift what belongs to them by God and by right." It expresses not only a penchant for justice, but also an affirmation of the hierarchical relationship between the sexes. By no longer invoking the traditional image of the housefather, but that of men, the lawyer was advocating notions of gender differences that scholars have usually located within bourgeois society.[112]

The assertion to act autonomously culminated in Steinbiedersdorf in a dispute over the forest. A prohibition in 1754, which stated that the community could no longer chop wood in its own forests without permission from the forestry office, met with opposition.[113] The tenaciousness of the community's refusal to surrender the forest ax that was used to mark the trees to be cut down reveals that this dispute was about more than economic interests. The ax was the symbol of a legal title and more than that: as it embodied the ability to take action, it was an expression of communal and male independence.[114]

The question of whether in certain cases the community—at least on behalf of the territorial ruler—had a right to act on its own authority, or whether the rulers had "tutelary oversight" over all issues concerning the community, from which they could derive the right to introduce "salutary decrees aimed at the

---

[111] LHA Koblenz 56/493: Elisionsschrift mit rechtlicher Bitte des Anwalts der impetrantischen und sog. verglichenen Untertanen zu Dentingen, Momersdorf und Steinbiedersdorf Dr. Sachs an das Reichskammergericht, 1786ff.

[112] Ute Frevert, "*Mann und Weib*," 25ff.

[113] AD Mos. 10 F 462: Contentieux de la Communauté de Pontpierre: bois communaux du Bannbusch, 1716–1754.

[114] I examined this dispute and the importance of independent action in the eighteenth century: Ulbrich, "Rheingrenze, Revolten und Französische Revolution," in Volker Rödel, ed., *Die französische Revolution und die Oberrheinlande, 1789–198*, Oberrheinische Studien, vol. 9 (Sigmaringen, 1991), 223–244, 226ff.

best interest of the subjects themselves," played a central role in the dispute that followed.[115] Since the legal ideas about the nature of lordship were built upon the model of householder authority, this discussion also touched on domestic arrangements, which in no way corresponded to the normative thinking of the lordship, at least not to the claim that one person alone could define what was good for everyone else.

Christian Ludwig's reforms harmed the economic needs and interests of the villagers to no small degree. The obligation, first put into writing in 1755, that all monetary transactions be conducted henceforth in the presence of the lord's clerk (Tabellion) constituted a profound interference in the subjects' customs and usual manner of handling inheritances.[116] Henceforth the dues owed to the District of the Upper Rhine could no longer be paid in Frankfurt; instead, subjects were compelled to deliver the money in Kriechingen.[117]

In 1755, Christian Ludwig, partly to avoid the disputes arising from his reorganization, demanded for the first time the levying of a district contingent of troops in natura.[118] This change entailed substantial disadvantages for those Kriechingen subjects whose sons were earning a living in French military service. Another profound incursion into the economy of the subjects occurred in 1757, when the authorities, in the face of an impending shortage of grain, prohibited its export; the prohibition was especially onerous because there were no suitable markets within the enclave.[119] Additional decrees interfered in the freedom of trade, while others were aimed at raising taxes and dues.[120]

From the first days of Christian Ludwig's government, resistance formed to the innovations he introduced with regard to Imperial District dues, an increase in taxes, and the curtailment of collective rights, especially usufruct rights and communal autonomy.[121] The subjects refused to obey and initiated lawsuits

---

[115] AD Mos. 10 F 462: Contentieux de la Communauté de Pontpierre: bois communaux du Bannbusch, 1716–1754.

[116] Sittel, *Sammlung der Provinzial- und Particular-Gesetze*, 551f.; Jahrgedingsprotokoll von Kriechingen 1754, Art. 15: prohibition against drawing up documents on one's own initiative. This prohibition thus made it obligatory to use the services of a Tabellion, that is, to have recourse to jurisdictio extrajudicialis.

[117] Ibid., decrees of April 11 and August 9, 1755.

[118] STA Wiesbaden 3005–2247: Gruendlicher Beweiß, daß es dem Hochgeborenen Grafen und Herrn, Herrn Christian Grafen zu Wied, Isenburg und Criechingen nicht angemutet werden könne, aus alleiniger Versammlung der widerspenstigen Unterthanen der Grafschaft Kriechingen die Natural-Mannschaftsstellung aufzuheben, und dieselbe mit einem verhaltungsmäßigen Geldbeitrag zu vertreten.

[119] AD Mos. J 5818: Collection Richard.

[120] The subjects complained about these in several suits before the Imperial Chamber Court: Cramer, "Wetzlarische Nebenstunden" 100.

[121] On the signifcance of the efforts in rural societies to settle disputes in court see Schulze, *Bäuerlicher Widerstand*; Peter Blickle et al., eds., *Aufruhr und Empörung? Studien zum bäuerlichen Widerstand im Alten Reich* (Munich, 1980); Werner Troßbach, *Soziale Bewegung und politische Erfahrung. Bäuerlicher Protest in hessischen Territorien 1648–1806*

which, in spite of several settlements and final judgments, dragged on until the time of the French Revolution.[122]

The discontented subjects congregated, allied themselves, and deliberated their plans, at first secretly and at night on French soil, in the house of the pastor of Falkenburg.[123] The councilor Köppel, whom Christian Ludwig had dismissed from his services, allegedly took part in these meetings and "by his presence facilitated such rebellious gatherings and plans against the territorial lord and thus against the Holy Roman Empire."[124] Even if this accusation is not true, it is clear from numerous prohibitions that there were clandestine meetings where the enfranchised members of the community discussed their attitude toward resistance and the various steps that were to be taken.[125] At a very early stage in the conflict, the community elected deputies whom they endowed with far-reaching powers.[126] Women were excluded from these meetings and the decisions that were made there, and even the legal mandate was granted at best by widows or wives acting in their husband's stead.

The subsequent confrontational behavior by the men was also communal in nature. It was based on a formally adopted, ritually guaranteed resolution that called for joint action and excluded dissenters. Since in the community all were supposed to stand "as one man" (für einen Mann),[127] there was little possibility for an individual to make decisions based on his own needs and interests or those of his household.

(Weingarten, 1987); and most recently the survey by Peter Blickle, "Unruhen in der ständischen Gesellschaft. 1300–1800," *Enzyklopädie deutscher Geschichte 1* (Munich, 1988).

[122] On this see, "Bericht über die Entstehung und den Verlauf der Auseinandersetzung zwischen Graf Christian von Wied-Runkel als Besitzer der Grafschaft Kriechingen und den Untertanen dieser Grafschaft bis zum Einsatz eines Exekutionskommandos im Juli 1758," newly edited in Schulze, *Bäuerlicher Widerstand*, 290–294. A brief sketch of the course of the unrest is given in Touba, "Kriechinger Unruhen;" Flaus, *Comté*, 144ff.; Ulbrich, "Bindung," 117ff.

[123] Subjects who had a complaint against the count and his officeholders were supposed to approach the count as petitioners, not plaintiffs. Since they had no right of assembly on questions concerning the lord, their first meetings took place secretly. Andreas Suter has examined these issues in detail for his area of study, especially the significance of the oath as a way of "constituting the entity of rebellious action": Suter, *Der Schweizerische Bauernkrieg von 1653. Politische Sozialgeschichte—Sozialgeschichte eines politischen Ereignisses* (Tübingen, 1997), esp. 131ff.

[124] STA Wiesbaden 3005–2244: Actenmäßige Geschichts-Erzählung und Deduction in Sachen des gewesenen Oberforstmeisters und Rechnungsführers Köppel, 10.

[125] AD Mos. Actes judiciaires B 10012: Plaids annaux de Niederwies, Denting, Momersdorf, 1757: charge brought at the Jahrgeding in Momersdorf that Heimmeier and others were holding frequent secret meetings to consult on "communal matters."

[126] AD Mos. E supp. 553 Pontpierre: Élection des représentants de Créhange du 11 juin 1775.

[127] The phrase appears repeatedly in the Steinbiedersdorf sources, with additional references in Göttsch, "'Alle für einen Mann,'" 1ff.; Werner Troßbach, "'Rebellische Weiber'? Frauen in bäuerlichen Protesten des 18. Jahrhunderts," in Wunder and Vanja, eds., *Weiber, Menscher, Frauenzimmer*, 154–174, 156; and Heide Wunder, *He is the Sun*, 163ff.

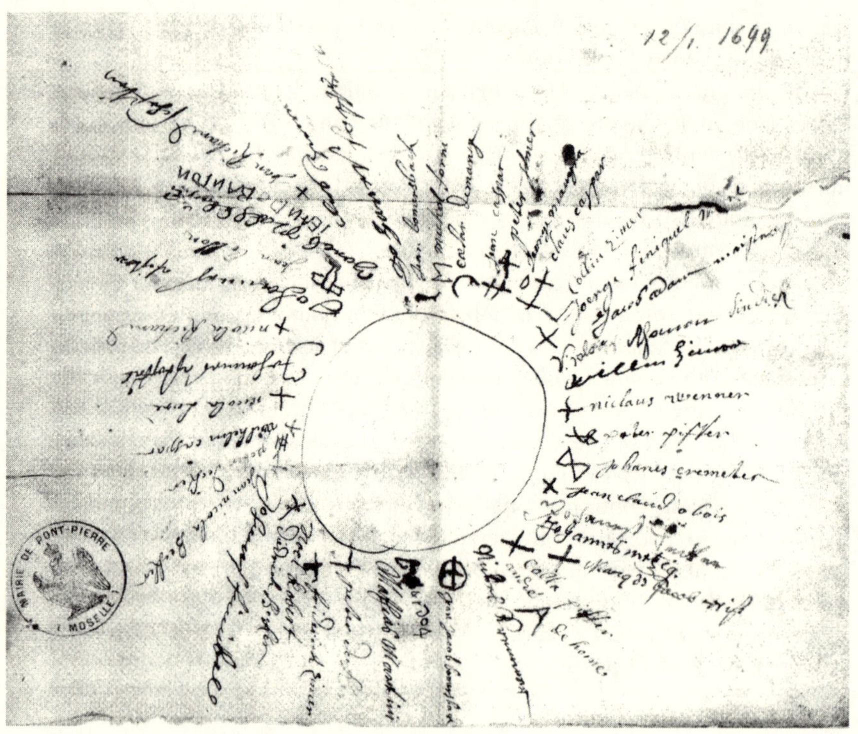

Illustration 1: Resistance resolution from Steinbiedersdorf, 1699[128]

The solidarity among the men was reinforced by gestures and symbols. The manner in which the men of Steinbiedersdorf signed a jointly adopted resolution of resistance in 1699 reveals what the phrase "as one man" meant: "rapping" (Einstupfen) the table inside the circle drawn on it created a mutual responsibility that superseded the needs of the individual household.

If the action began with a resolution adopted unanimously by all enfranchised men of the community, soon everyone, men and women, were drawn into the actions in one way or another. Of course, that becomes apparent only if one undertakes a careful analysis of the unrest, one that also incorporates the local traditions.[129]

---

[128] Copy from AD Mos. E. Dépôt 553 FF 4: AD Mos. 553 E. Dép. Pontpierre FF 4 No. 21. This "Einstupfen" is also mentioned in other actions: see, for example, Claudia Ulbrich, "La ribellione di Inzlingen (1600–1613). Un caso di resistenza contadina nella Germania sud-occidentale," *Conflitti locali e idiomi politici a cura di Lombardini, Osvaldo Raggio et Angelo Torre*, Quaderni storici 63 (1986), 759–776, 766.

[129] Conflicts usually appeared in the files of the Imperial Chamber Court only after

The residents of Steinbiedersdorf refused to obey any new prohibitions and seized every opportunity for a principled disagreement with the government. In 1755, an outsider was explicitly encouraged to sell brandy (Branntwein), thus violating the newly introduced seigneurial prohibition against its sale. A remark by Niclas Becker, who was later hauled into court as an "agitator and rebel" to answer a crimen laesae majestatis, reveals the self-confident manner in which the protest had been organized: "The lord could publish in front of the church whatever he wanted, brandy was merchant's ware and free, and the community would not allow itself to be deprived of any right, it would rather go to Wetzlar, and let him, the *comparent*, go to Kriechingen and tell this to the lord."[130]

The locals fought the dispute over the forest with the same determination and with firm confidence that they had the support of the Imperial Chamber Court. The Heimmeier refused to hand over the forest ax or to pay a fine imposed in response to his refusal.[131] When he and others resisted attempts to collect the fine by force and, in circumvention of the proper channels, engaged an imperial notary from Saarbrücken to represent their interests at the Imperial Chamber Court, their actions were regarded as tantamount to rebellion and punished by the seizure of property and prison sentences.

Undaunted, the Heimmeier and the "authorized officials" insisted on their position and threatened to oppose seigneurial force with "resistance." They prevented another seizure of goods by barring their houses. After several attempts to enforce the order or at least to divide the community had failed, the lord had the cattle on the common pasture impounded and driven to Kriechingen. Only a small group of individuals not involved in the rebellion—among them the pastor, the widow of the old revenue collector (Rentenmeister) Barell, her son, who held the office of court clerk, and the seigneurial bailiff—got their cattle back.

On the morning following the seizure, "nearly the entire community of Steinbiedersdorf came with large clubs in their hands" and got ready, with "horrible noise," to drive the animals home again by force. Faced with the "raging wrath of this mob," the lord's servants kept quiet. Prior to taking any action,

---

they had escalated to a certain point. The prior history, provided it was recounted at all, was usually confined to those areas that were relevant to the proceedings in question.

[130] AD Mos. 10 F 172: In Sachen Fiscalis ca. Niclas Becker zu Steinbiedersdorf pcto Branntweinverkaufens von Ausländischen, 1755. Niclas Becker was sentenced to a fine of 20 Reichstaler as an agitator and rebel who had done harm to the lord and the officeholders.

[131] The Heimmeier—called Pfleger, Keller, or Stabhalter in other regions—was charged with exercising supervisory functions within the community, especially with respect to the supervision and augmentation of the community's assets (Bader, *Dorfgenossenschaft und Dorfgemeinde*, 307ff.). During the Kriechingen unrest he represented the interests of the community. He was aided by deputies (authorized officials or so-called Gezogene) elected by the communal assembly and endowed with a power of attorney.

the deputized officials inquired formally into the reasons for the confiscation
and then withdrew to regroup. Witnesses reported that between four and five
in the morning, an even "larger group arrived, men and women . . . with staves
and clubs." One person who was in charge is supposed to have said to the
people of Kriechingen: "Folks, do not resist, otherwise you will fare badly,
whereupon the other men and women, tearing down by force a large piece of
the fence, broke in with much shouting and noise, drove out the animals and
took them away."[132]

Men and women together drove the animals home, with "two women"
allegedly threatening that if they met the sergeant, "he would get his share of
blows." The women left no doubt about their readiness to engage in violence;
after all, they had come to assist their men. Like the men they took part in
the forceful liberation of the animals, using peasant tools and implements to
do so. Their action had a concrete goal, the retrieval of their animals. In this
way they were defending the livelihood of their households and thus a sphere
that fell within what Heide Wunder has described as "the joint responsibility
and . . . mutual dependence" of husband and wife.[133] With respect to this limited action I agree with the interpretation of Heide Wunder, who is drawing
here on the scholarship of Werner Troßbach and Andreas Suter.[134]

The role assumed by the women of Steinbiedersdorf differed in one significant detail from the cases described by Troßbach and Suter. Although in
Steinbiedersdorf the women did not appear until the second morning and at
the instigation of the men, they carried out the action jointly with them. They
were not, as for example in Basel, sent ahead by the men, and the men were
not content to play a spectator role. The joint tearing down of the fences
points to a rather equal participation of women and men, one that found its
equivalence in the structure of work and in inheritance law. The threat of the
two women to beat up the sergeant, on the other hand, could be understood
against the background of gender-differentiated, asymmetrical concepts of honor.
It is possible that in Steinbiedersdorf, as well, much as in Basel, it was the role
of women to threaten the officials with blows and to dish them out, inflicting
additional dishonor through this assault on the honor of the male gender.[135]

---

[132] AD Mos. 10 F 462: Contentieux de la Communauté de Pontpierre: bois communaux
du Bannbusch, 1716–1754.

[133] Wunder, *He is the Sun, She is the Moon*, 177.

[134] Ibid., 174ff.; Troßbach, "Rebellische Weiber?," 154ff.; Andreas Suter, *"Troublen" im
Fürstbistum Basel (1726–1740). Eine Fallstudie zum bäuerlichen Widerstand im 18.
Jahrhundert.* Veröffentlichungen des Max-Planck-Instituts für Geschichte 79 (Göttingen,
1985), 349ff.

[135] Suter, *"Troublen,"* 352. An instructive example for the gender-specific meaning of
honor and the possibility of using this in conflictual actions is given by Barbara Krug-
Richter, "'Eß gehet die bauren ahn und nicht die herren.' Die Auseinandersetzung um
die Einführung neuer Dienste in der westfälischen Herrschaft Canstein 1710 bis 1719,"

But such an interpretation must remain speculative, at least as far as the Steinbiedersdorf sources are concerned. The threat by the two women should more likely be seen within the framework of their participation in the context of village life, their coresponsibility for maintaining order, and their right to stand up to the representatives of the authority to defend the interests of the family.[136]

Quarrels among women that came to blows contradicted the cultural model of femininity accepted by village society only in certain circumstances, not in principle. It would appear that women could use force regardless of their gender in defending their children or their household against outsiders. Here, too, they sometimes acted in concert with their men and sometimes alone.

For example, in 1788, the chief forester of Kriechingen, Beuter, who had dispatched his two sons to Steinbiedersdorf to check up on things, complained about "peasants of both sexes." The boys had shot ducks in the brook and had thereby aroused the ire of the villagers, men and women: "Whereupon a crowd of Steinbiedersdorf peasants men and women had charged his [i.e. Beuter's] sons and had chased them away with much scolding and cursing.[137]

Evidently it was important for Beuter to point out that the "abuse" of his sons had been perpetrated by men and women. Participation in violent actions was even more self-evident in cases that involved one's own children. Let us recall how Marie Morell had thrown herself at a group of young men to help her son involved in a fight.[138] Werner Troßbach has given many examples of women who resisted with force when officials or soldiers came to seize property or persons.[139]

Where the situation did not allow a physical attack, women were left with only their voice, "the customary weapon of women."[140] They could insult their enemies or call attention to their situation by raising a hue and cry. Nicolas Metzinger's wife tried to do both in 1757 when a detachment arrived in front

---

in Jan Peters, ed., *Konflikt und Kontrolle in Gutsherrschaftsgesellschaften. Über Resistenz und Herrschaftsverhalten in ländlichen Sozialgebilden der Frühen Neuzeit.* Veröffentlichungen des Max-Planck-Instituts für Geschichte 120 (Göttingen, 1995), 151–200, esp. 183ff.

[136] See p. 132ff.

[137] AD Mos. Actes judiciaires B 10077: Acta in Sachen Oberjäger Beuters von hier, Denunzianten, ca. einige Steinbiedersdorfer Bauern und seinen Söhnen verübte Mißhandlunge betr. 1788.

[138] See p. 73.

[139] Troßbach, note 127. These were not necessarily spectacular actions within the framework of collectively organized peasant resistance. Johannes Schäffer's wife from Lixing, for example, pushed the communal official (Gemeindebote) back into a kettle when he showed up to seize her because of corvée labor she had refused to perform. She justified her action by saying that she felt discriminated against compared to others: AD Mos. Actes judiciaires B 10088, fol. 57f.: 20.2.1725; Lixing.

[140] AD Mos. Actes judiciaires B 10007: Acta in Sachen Jacob Bouchy von Bolchen ca. Johannes Weißen Wittib von Dentingen pcto Injuriarum, 1778.

of her house to seize property.[141] Her husband, who at that time still belonged to the "rebels," along with two others had taken timber from the forest in 1756 and had been fined. Since they refused to pay, the group of men had come to collect the money by force.[142] When the detachment appeared, Nicolas Metzinger was not at home. Apart from his wife and a Jewish boy who was trying to buy some oil, only his mother-in-law was in the house. As the detachment approached, Nicolas Metzinger's wife bolted the windows and refused the order to open the door, whereupon the dechant and other servants of the lord broke into the house through the barn. The women hurled invectives at the intruders—among them the bailiff and the village jurors—"with the greatest and crudest insults," ran into the street, and screamed until the husband and a few representatives of the community hurried to the scene. Still, the wife was not able to prevent the men from carrying a pile of valuables, including tobacco, twine, hemp, and tow, out of the house. "During which action both the wife of the well-known Nicolas Metzinger and his mother cried profusely and reproached him, saying that he should have paid the lord long ago and should not have listened to the scoundrels, the deputies, who had advised him to resist the enforcement."[143]

Because the woman raised such a ruckus, the community was summoned, took on the matter, and tried to get the property returned. And thanks to her "uproar," the Heimmeier and the deputies (Deputierte) decided not to permit any more seizures henceforth.

The small scene that unfolded in 1757 in the house of the Metzingers shows what options women had to mobilize the community by causing a disturbance, but at the same time it also points to the limits of female participation in decision making.[144]

Metzinger's wife had no say in the decision whether her husband paid the fine or risked the forceful seizure of his property. Men discussed these kinds of issues among themselves when they gathered at the communal assembly or in the tavern. Household interests had to take a back seat. In the tavern, as a sphere of male sociability, and in the community, as the institutionalized form of housefatherly rule, "patriarchal-authoritarian social structures," to which Andreas Suter has rightly called attention,[145] asserted themselves and formed

---

[141] LHA Koblenz 56/2987: In Sachen sämtlicher Unterthanen und Dorfschaften der Grafschaft Crichingen ca. Herrn Grafen zu Wied-Runkel und Crichingen, Mandati, 1757, fol. 801ff.

[142] AD Mos., 10 F 462: Contentieux de la Communauté de Pontpierre, 1716–1754.

[143] LHA Koblenz 56/1398: In Sachen sämtlicher Untertanen und Dorfschaften der Grafschaft Kriechingen gegen den Grafen von Wied-Runkel, Mandati, 1757.

[144] Rudolf Dekker has noted the importance of women in the mobilization of resistance: "Women in Revolt. Popular Protest and its Social Basis in Holland in the seventeenth and eighteenth Centuries," *Theory and Society* 16 (1987), 337–362.

[145] Suter, *"Troublen,"* 351.

a structural background to peasant resistance. This insight casts a different light on the shared household responsibility of which I spoke earlier: that responsibility determined individual actions but not fundamental decisions.[146] A man "disregards all circumstances" was the view of the lawyer we met earlier, who defended the peasants for many years, sat with them in the tavern, and undoubtedly had more contact with them than the priest in the chancel. His notion applies only in part to a peasant society, which placed joint actions above the interests of the individual. Even men had to yield to the pressure of the majority.

One of the first to discover that in Steinbiedersdorf in 1757 was Nicolas Bommersbach, a twenty-eight-year-old day laborer. He had not married Barbara Decker until she was well advanced in her pregnancy, and he was supposed to pay a fine for doing so. Since the communal deputies regarded the fine as excessive, they forbade its payment. According to the statement by Nicolas Bommersbach, "the authorized leaders of the community" declared the following: "Since the legal proceedings in Wetzlar were already under way and the innovations introduced by the lord were contested, while this act here, the punishment of his transgression, was an innovation, he should wait a while longer."[147]

Given various forms of economic dependence, the "rebels," as long as they were the majority in the village and were potential employers, had an easy time controlling the day laborers. As was the case with their own wives and those who lived in their homes, they could force them to adhere to the orders of the community. It becomes clear especially with respect to legal proceedings to what extent women, in particular, were structurally disadvantaged vis-à-vis men. They were not allowed to participate in the decision making, yet they were liable in their persons and property for the consequences. Engaging in conflict, which entailed considerable financial risks, was a communal matter and thus an affair reserved for men. That became clear also in the subsequent course of the Kriechingen unrest.

In 1757, after individual communities had initially submitted single complaints, all subjects and villages of the imperial county joined forces. The Kriechingen subjects, experienced in these matters since they had already brought several cases against the territorial lord before the Imperial Chamber Court during the preceding decades, organized the resistance on the territorial level.[148] They hired lawyers to draft their complaints and initiate court proceedings.

---

[146] Claudia Ulbrich, "Frauen im Aufstand. Möglichkeiten und Grenzen ihrer Partizipation in frühneuzeitlichen Bauernbewegungen," in Ursula Fuhrich-Grubert and Angelus H. Johansen, eds., *Schlaglichter Preußen-Westeuropa. Festschrift für Ilja Mieck zum 65. Geburtstag* (Berlin, 1997), 335–348.

[147] AD Mos. 10 F. 172: Notariatsinstrument und Zeugenverhör wegen zu zahlen verbotener Fornicationsstrafe des Nicolas Bommersbach.

[148] Earlier cases: Steinbiedersdorf regarding the procuring of salt, Saarwellingen against the rights claimed by the countess; 1716: Büdingen and Steinbiedersdorf; 1730: Saarwellingen on account of the use of water, forest and meadow; 1736: on account of wood

Deputies (Deputierte) were dispatched to Vienna and Wetzlar. Confidence in the ability of the Imperial Chamber Court and the Imperial Court Council (Reichshofrat) to resolve conflicts was very high, though certainly higher than it deserved to be. While it is true that the imperial courts listened to the complaints of the subjects, they sent out into the county not only expensive commissions, but also cruel enforcement troops that threatened the life and limb of the subjects. After all, the Kriechingen unrest affected not only the interests of the lords, but—owing to the district taxes—those of the Holy Roman Empire, as well.

As early as 1755, the District of Upper Rhine had already carried out a military enforcement because of the refusal to hand over district taxes. The subjects had refused to be intimidated by this action. When the demand for monetary payments was replaced by the requirement to furnish payments in kind, the subjects resisted again. In 1758, troops moved in on no fewer than three occasions. The first time, only twelve soldiers were sent into the county to carry out a seizure. The entire community, women and men, blocked their way and prevented the action.[149] Only a group of nine men, most of them functionaries (bailiff, clerk [Greffe], head juror, dechant), had submitted to the demands of the lord.[150]

The villagers turned back a second enforcement detachment, now sixty men strong, by locking the houses and posting the women as guards, while the men fled to neighboring villages belonging to Lorraine or France. Eventually, toward the end of the year, the rebels were forced to yield to a superior military force of two hundred footsoldiers and fifty hussars from the Electorate of the Palatinate. To pay the costs of the enforcement action, the communities, chief among them Steinbiedersdorf and Kriechingen, had to take out a loan of 17,600 gulden from ritmaster Otto Lacapelle and his wife in Saarbrücken.[151] The debenture had to be signed by each debtor in person. Among the signatories were also six women villagers from Steinbiedersdorf: four widows and two wives acting on behalf of their husbands placed their marks under the contract. But according to debt law, all wives, even those who had not signed in person, were liable with all their assets. From this moment, at the latest, the legal proceedings had also become their affair.

The repayment of the loan was an enormous burden for the communities and triggered intense internal conflicts. Henceforth the community was split

---

use; 1740: on account of corvée services; 1740ff.: all subjects on account of the incorrect collection of imperial and district taxes; 1747ff.: Community of Kriechingen on account of wood; 1754ff.: Community of Steinbiedersdorf on account of the forest ax.

[149] LHA Koblenz 56/2987: In Sachen sämtlicher Unterthanen und Dorfschaften der Grafschaft Crichingen ca. Herrn Grafen zur Wied-Runkel und Crichingen. Mandati, 1757, fol. 1092ff.

[150] Ibid., fol. 1306.

[151] Touba, "Kriechinger Unruhen," 6ff.

into three factions: the submitted, who had yielded to all demands by the lord and been richly rewarded in return; the nonsubmitted, who clung to the legal proceedings; and the neutrals, who had moved into the area later and who wanted nothing to do with the legal cases and the repayment of the debts. Without the approval of their husbands, wives had practically no possibility of staying out of or becoming involved in a case brought by the community. They had to go along with their husbands' decisions simply because of the asymmetrical legal property relationship within the marriage.

By contrast, widows and unmarried women were to some extent able to decide for themselves which of the two parties in the conflict they would support. Widows who had entered upon their husbands' inheritance also had to take over their share of the trial costs. They could not avoid that obligation even by a formal submission to the lord. In a few instances a widow would follow in her husband's footsteps. Shortly before his death, the oil miller Johannes Baur from Denting admonished his wife, Anna Clement, to stick with the nonsubmitted.[152] She joined the community in carrying on the cases her husband had supported as one of the (financially) strongest "troublemakers," authorizing her son to raise money for the community. Even during her husband's lifetime, Anna Clement had always been on the side of the rebels and had seen to it that the brutality of the soldiers was brought up in court.[153]

In spite of the efforts at mediation by the imperial courts and several settlements, military enforcement continued to play a large role during the subsequent course of the conflicts. Women were involved in all of the actions. Their most important contribution to the way in which the conflicts played out was "enforcement resistance," or, in positive terms, the defense of home and farm against soldiers who were carrying out seizures or arrests. Once the confrontation had been set in motion and their men at the communal assembly had voted for or against legal proceedings and individual actions, the women had no choice but to back up the decisions and to defend themselves and their families. No matter what side they were on, they were drawn into the conflicts they had not initiated themselves, though they had not prevented them, either. Let me illustrate this with a few examples:

The community of Steinbiedersdorf was supposed to defray the expenses for the military interventions directed against it. To raise money, wood was chopped in the communal forest in 1762 and distributed for a fee to every household, including those of widows and the unmarried. Since the group of the submitted, who at the time still formed a small minority,[154] refused to purchase this wood, they were subjected to forced collection by a group of eight or nine rebels.

---

[152] AD Mos. Actes judiciaires, B 10743: Erbstreit des Georg Baur, 1785.

[153] LHA Koblenz 56/492d, fol. 54.

[154] By 1763 only thirteen men and one woman had submitted. That compares with eighty-two nonsubmitted (men and widows).

In the course of this action, "the wife of Johannes Arnoud, who resisted, was very badly manhandled." The sergeant Nicolas Arnoud and his wife, Catherine Mangin, suffered a similar fate.[155] In a report to the bailiff and the court, Nicolas Arnoud declared he had resisted the enforcement, "whereupon he and his wife had been so badly maltreated and beaten that he surely would have died if Peter Richard had not come to his aid."[156] What Nicolas Arnoud neglected to mention was that Michel Mangin, one of the leaders of the gang, was his brother-in-law.[157]

The actions described had repercussions. Since the rebels refused to return the items they had seized, soldiers were called in. Immediately a hue and cry was raised in the village and "young and old, men and women" assembled to drive them away.[158] In the aftermath, five of those involved in the seizure were summoned before the authorities. They were accused of having carried out the action on their own authority, "propria auctoritate," had refused to honor a summons to the chancery, and had instead "taken off" to a tavern in Faulquemont.[159] They were incarcerated without a trial, first for two weeks, a little later for an additional fifteen weeks. Rupp, the lawyer for the subjects, described the conditions of their incarceration in the tower of Kriechingen with some concern:

> To lie at the bottom of the tower for fourteen days, without a piece of straw for a bed, to suffocate in one's own excrement and filth, to be eaten by vermin, to lie on the ground day and night without cover like a worm, exposed to the cold in the frigid spring nights, fed barely enough bread and water to satisfy one's hunger, to allow no one to see the captives who might offer some consolation, to constantly hear the threat "submit or your house will be razed, a gallows will be built upon which you will be hanged," all this is unknown among civilized peoples, and even criminals condemned to death are not treated with such unheard-of cruelty.[160]

Elsewhere the lawyer stated that the imperial courts had rarely encountered such "barbarous treatment," which attested to a "cannibalistic frame of mind."[161]

In the spring of 1763, the wives of the imprisoned men not only had to run their households and farms entirely on their own, but also were supposed to

---

[155] LHA Koblenz 56/1301: In Sachen sämtlicher Unertanen und Dorfschaften der Grafschaft Kriechingen gegen Herrn Grafen von Wied-Runkel, Mandatis, Lit. R., fol. 180.

[156] Ibid., fol. 193f.

[157] According to the parish register, Michel and Catherine Mangin were siblings. The conduct of Johannet Wahl (see p. 51) likewise shows that the uprising was also used to engage in familial conflicts.

[158] As note 523, Lit. Q, 175f.

[159] Michel Mangin justified their action by declaring: "We have the order from our heads and need no other": LHA Koblenz 56/1301, fol. 154.

[160] Ibid., fol. 89f.

[161] Ibid., fol. 997f.

defray the costs of feeding their husbands.[162] On June 25 they were asked to pay 100 livres de France within a period of seventy-two hours. Since the women were unable or unwilling to pay, they were threatened with a "real enforcement" (Realexekution) on account of their "malice and refractoriness." They refused to be intimidated, locked their houses, and removed their household effects to safe places.

Soldiers moved in on July 1. Among them were sons of Steinbiedersdorf families who did not even know why they had been sent. It was only in the bailiff's house that they sat down to a "bottle of wine" and were filled in on their mission. Peter Richard, the bailiff's son and one of the submitted, had run into his brother-in-law, who was part of the detachment, and had informed him that his own mother (the soldier's mother-in-law), Marguerite Hoen, was targeted for seizure. Marguerite Hoen, now married to Michel Mangin, one of the incarcerated rebels, sided with the rebels and joined the other women in refusing to pay the cost of the prisoners' food. Her son and daughter were among those who had submitted. They persuaded her to pay voluntarily and she was spared.

To prevent the seizure, everyone, men and women, had gone out into the street. But they were helpless against the soldiers, who shot and killed two men and seriously injured a third. The women, too, were chased off the street with threats and were in danger of their lives. They barely knew how to put their terror and fear into words: "She was like a dead person," one of them said later under questioning. "Like others, they did not know whether they were still of this world," is how three other women described the situation. The sergeant had threatened them by saying: "If you three damn scoundrels don't leave the room, I will put a bullet in your head!"[163]

In view of the escalation of violence, any special consideration for the honor or reduced legal status of the female sex that might have prevailed during more controlled actions was suspended. Still, women were sent to the fore. Frank Lillig, for instance, readily admitted that he did not dare go into the street again after one of the men had been shot. And since the schoolmaster, too, lacked the courage to do so, "a woman" was sent to see what had happened. Her chances of getting through were better than the men's, but even she could not be sure how the soldiers would react.[164]

One woman who watched the events with interest and described them dispassionately was Johannet Wahl, the bailiff's wife, who openly took the side of

---

[162] The community had set up a fund that was used not only to supply the men who had organized the resistance with food, but also to "support their wives at home": LHA Koblenz 56/491: Kommissionsbericht in Sachen der Gemeinde Steinbiedersdorf gegen Herrn Grafen Christian von Wied-Runkel, fol. 22.

[163] Ibid., Li. Z, fol. 283, witness testimony.

[164] Ibid., Lit. JJ, fol. 524, witness testimony.

the soldiers.[165] Her decision to side with the interests of the lord, which meant that she also sided with the submitted in the village, is easier to understand against the backdrop of the formation of factions in the village and the deep divisions within families. At the same time, however, it also becomes clear in what a difficult a situation she had placed the three women she had named as witnesses. Through their testimony they would have betrayed the rebels' community of solidarity and lost their own protection within this group. The refusal to testify and place their mark under the protocol appears as an important "action" within the context of the entire act of resistance on the part of the community. Not signing meant rejecting the court and the lord, resisting their claim to assert themselves over the individual.

In the course of the following years the conflicts throughout the entire county intensified into the Kriechingen rebellion.[166] There were more disputes over the delivery of district taxes. The submitted followed the orders of the lord and wanted to pay in Kriechingen. The nonsubmitted, on the other hand, suspicious of the officials against whom legal proceedings were still ongoing in Wetzlar, insisted that the money be collected by them and delivered directly to Frankfurt. They were supported in this demand by a notary from a neighboring community. The rebels throughout the county united to carry out property seizures against the submitted. In Steinbiedersdorf the action targeted Peter and Heinrich Vogt, Anton and Nicolas Metzinger, Anton Sitzmann, Claude Lorraine, Carl Spitz, and Johannes Bernard. Anton Sitzmann was not at home. His wife, who begged in vain for mercy "for the sake of her poor innocent children," lost among other things her bedding. Heinrich Vogt's wife suffered worse: she had to watch as her husband and son were beaten and "thrown against the stove, such that he thought he would leave behind on it life and limb." That, in any case, is how Heinrich Vogt himself described the attack later, pointing out that his wife was in an advanced stage of pregnancy and did not know whether the imminent birth would occur without harm to the child, given the fright she had suffered.[167] In the other villages, as well, the women were not spared. In Denting, for example, "the bailiff's wife . . . was beaten such that she is still feeling terrible pains."[168]

The rebellion was followed in 1771 by a military enforcement action in the course of which eighty-three men and fourteen women had their property seized in Steinbiedersdorf alone. George Court, one of the alleged instigators and leaders, painted the following scene of the action, which is given here in place of lengthier descriptions: "Around midnight the execution invaded Steinbiderstorff with 70 men, beat down doors and windows, seized men and women, beat, pushed, and dragged them around, tortured them and thus treated them so

---

[165] See p. 51.
[166] On the course of the events see Touba, "Kriechinger Unruhen," 11ff.
[167] AD Mos. 10 F 522: 1768.
[168] LHA Kobl. 56/492d., fol. 227.

tyrannically you'd have thought the stones in the street would take pity on them."[169]

The soldiers attacked the villages even during vespers and laid hands "on the men and women with cruel fury." They threatened that "those women who refused to serve the soldiers food would be struck in the stocks, and that this would make them submit."[170] This punishment was supposedly inflicted on one woman and three men to make an example of them. Afterward the woman was released again, but the men were thrown into the dungeon. Unlike the Imperial Chamber Court, which made acceptance of a case dependent on the consent of two-thirds of the community members who enjoyed full rights (house-fathers), which in some instances amounted to no more than 10 percent of the inhabitants, the soldiers made no distinctions between the sexes. Women were also held responsible for what their men had decided. Wherever possible, the women tried to minimize the damage: for example, they clandestinely pulled out hemp and flax that was slated for the auction block and took it to other villages.[171]

If the troops failed to catch the entire community by surprise under cover of darkness or during church services, the men were the first to take flight, leaving the women to confront the detachments. The Oberamtmann of Saar-brücken, a man by the name of Lex who was supposed to carry out a seizure in May of 1771, complained, for example, that the rebels were rarely ever at home: "Instead, they leave the houses in the hands of women and children, and they themselves stay outside of this county."[172] If the troops were approaching, it was up to the women to swiftly lock doors and windows and to try and chase the soldiers away by hurling invectives at them. The fact that this kind of "division of labor"—which seems strange at first glance—between women and men was practiced indicates that it made sense from the perspective of those involved.[173] Although the enforcement actions put the women who had remained behind in the homes into an extremely precarious situation—espe cially since the soldiers' threshold had been additionally lowered by prior con-sumption of alcohol—the risk they were taking was still lower than it would have been for their men. As the example mentioned above has shown, they could at least hope to be spared incarceration.[174]

---

[169] LHA Koblenz 56/1802: In Sachen sämtlicher Unterthanen und Dorfschaften der Grafschaft Crichingen ca. II. Grafen zu Wied und Kriechingen, Mandati, 1–698, fol. 595.

[170] Ibid., fol. 572.

[171] LHA Koblenz 56/498: 1771.

[172] LHA Koblenz 1802: Sämtliche Untertanen gegen der Grafen zu Wied-Runkel, Mandatis.

[173] Various explanations have been offered by Suter (an expression of a legally infe-rior position and capacity of insulting someone's honor), Troßbach (defense of one's own spheres of work), and Wunder (shared responsibility and mutual dependence).

[174] This has also been explicitly emphasized by Wolfgang Schmale, who noted in the

From a legal point of view the women were not part of a legal case and therefore innocent. At least that was the position advocated by the lawyer who defended the men of Steinbiedersdorf and their women after the enforcement action of 1771. He argued that the official Lex had had no right to "auction off the property belonging to the wives of his clients" and demanded that it be returned.[175]

Even though he was not able to enforce this demand, it points to the legal understanding on which it was based: if the women, as nonparticipants, are not subject to punishment, it is possible to exploit the tension between individual rights and responsibilities and the rights that relate to the house or the couple. From this perspective it was expedient to send the women ahead (or, more precisely, leave them behind) in an effort to prevent or at least control a seizure of property, and to keep the damage to a minimum. By remaining inside the house, the women made the shared home into their own realm and demonstrated to the outside world the injustice perpetrated by the forced entry into the house.[176]

The defense of the houses, in particular, makes clear that the differing conceptions of masculinity and femininity, and the different legal status of men and women, could be used to expand—if only to a moderate degree—the spheres of action open to both spouses.[177] In the extreme situation when property was about to be seized, the protection of the house, and with it the safeguarding of the means of subsistence, was entrusted to those especially in need of protection themselves, "innocent women," as they were often called. In other words, it was entrusted to those whom one did not believe capable of courage, but who had the possibility of pleading for mercy or at least mobilizing the public if the limits of what was acceptable had been crossed. And so when subjects testified in court, they were usually not content to note that a woman was in the house. One is struck by the frequency with which women in advanced stages of pregnancy are mentioned, even though it would presumably have been possible in most cases to send them away and have someone else take

---

area he studied that among the women it was widows who had to reckon most with the likelihood of punishment: Schmale, "Vergleichende Analyse der Seigneurie in Burgund und der Grundherrschaft in Kursachsen," in Jan Peters, ed., *Gutsherrschaft als soziales Modell*, 101–125, here 122.

[175] LHA Koblenz 56/493 (unpaginated).

[176] Troßbach has pointed to the special responsibility of women for animals and household goods: *Bauern*, 105. In my view this explanation, which is based on the notion of complementary worlds, does not go far enough. In defending the house, women were defending not only their own sphere of life and work, but also that of their men.

[177] The question of whether the authorities, judges, and rural subjects did in fact have different ideas about gender roles at the end of the eighteenth century requires further study.

their place. At least in court, one could strengthen one's case by invoking children, old people, and pregnant women.[178]

Since most cases of unrest in Steinbiedersdorf were not decided in trials but in accelerated procedures called Mandatsverfahren, none of the settlements issued in 1763, 1778, and 1786 were able to restore calm once and for all. Nor was it possible to force the opposition to its knees through enforcement soldiers. On the contrary: with every such action the chasm between the submitted and the nonsubmitted became deeper.

The question of who had to pay which percentage of the "pacification levies" was the cause of new trials in the 1780s that the submitted and nonsubmitted pursued against each other and against the lord. When the submitted eventually agreed to a settlement and declared their willingness to contribute something to the expenses of the rebels, they explained their decision by pointing to the "daily complaining by their wives and children." Since giving in was not what a man did—"a real man . . . pays no heed whether he pleases this person or that"—this step required an elaborate justification. In addition to pointing to their wives and children, the men invoked conscience and reason. Responsibility for the nonsubmitted, who were "exposing their wives and children to the plunder of the most bitter poverty," was also part of an argument based on paternalistic thinking.[179]

The settlement did not create peace. The profound political changes engendered by the French Revolution did put an end to the resistance against the lord, but not to the tensions within the village, which now shifted into the ecclesiastical-religious realm.[180]

The decades of unrest had transformed life in the village. Villagers had found themselves confronted with the necessity of classifying their neighbors and relatives as friends or foes. New bonds of solidarity became important and demanded from the men—as the preferred objects of a new mechanism of domination—decisions that were oriented more toward communal interests, relationships of power and dependence within the community, or personal relationships than they were toward the needs of the individual house or household, which were all too often neglected. And even though women were excluded from the important decision-making processes, because of the way in which they were tied into the life of the village, they did not stand on the sidelines during the revolt. We can observe a special kind of involvement during various phases of the rebellion: in the phase of mobilization as well as in collective actions when wives and widows, in particular, were defending the position in their homes and had to demonstrate strength. The inequality under the law, the fact that

---

[178] This aspect must be kept in mind when reading all the examples given here in which cruelty against women was highlighted.

[179] LHA Koblenz 56/493 (no folio numbering).

[180] See below, 153ff.

women were subject to less severe punishment, and the special protection of women's property could prove an advantage in these situations—but they were no guarantee of safety, as we learn from the many incidents in which women were the victims of violence.

As a consequence of the organization of the resistance and the trials that went on for years, the spheres for which only men were responsible grew in importance, while the care for daily life was pushed into the background, with the result that no small number of families became impoverished.

Even if it made strategic sense for women to defend the house while the men fled and hid in the forests beyond the borders of the county or assembled in taverns, we see the symbolic beginnings of a division of spheres of life and authority into a female "inside" sphere and a male "outside" sphere, a division that did not (yet) correspond to normal life. In a geographic sense the radius of the sphere in which they were active expanded considerably, at least for some villagers. Numerous trips had taken the deputies (Deputierte) to Wetzlar, Vienna, Frankfurt, and Nancy. But now and then we also encounter women on the road. For example, we find Katharina Legendre in Metz, where she procured assignats, in Trier, where she found a lawyer, and in Saarbrücken, where she paid debts.

For these women, as well, the frequent presence of lawyers provided an opportunity to try out new ways of engaging in conflicts, and to acquire a deeper knowledge of legal contexts and of patterns of judicial argumentation. Katharina Legendre took her quarrel with her adversary to the Imperial Chamber Court. She was able to make the necessary contacts when the advocates and commissioners were in her village. And if no lawyer was at hand, Philipp Laguerre, one of the rebels, took care of her correspondence.

Court and administration

Because of the great distance to the lord's residence, the seigneurial officials in the County of Kriechingen had an especially important role during the entire period under discussion. Kriechingen was home to a councilor (Regierungsrat), an advocate and a secretary, a chancery servant (Kanzleidiener) and several messengers (Landboten), a chamber councilor (Kammerrat) and chamber clerk (Kammerschreiber), a Gegenschreiber and chamber messenger (Kammerbote), a forestry councilor (Forstrat), forest secretary (Forstsekretär), chief forester (Oberförster), and forester (Förster). The office of the territorial clerk (Land-schreiberei) included a Landschreiber (territorial clerk), four village and court clerks, as well as a territorial physician (Landphysikus).[181] On the communal level, the Jahrgedinge formed an institutional hinge between lord and subjects, while the bailiff (Meier) along with the clerk (Schreiber) and chancery servant (Kanzleidiener) constituted such a hinge in terms of personnel. The bailiffs, as

---

[181] Hochgräflich Crichingischer Kalender.

the representatives of the territorial lord, were elected in each of the county's villages from the ranks of the common men and confirmed by the territorial lord. On numerous occasions the lord tried to circumvent the election rights of the community and install a bailiff "on his own authority."[182]

This kind of measure not only represented a meddling in intercommunal affairs; it also unsettled the social hierarchy, especially if day laborers were appointed as bailiffs. For proximity to the lord and the gain in status such an appointment entailed exerted considerable influence on the position of the individual within the community. The question over the distribution of political offices and the need for representation on the part of the local elites shows the degree to which lordship touched not only the relationship between the ruler and the ruled, but also, and much more fundamentally, the relationships among the ruled themselves. And as we shall see, this applies also to the relationship between the Christian and the Jewish communities.[183]

Since domination was not readily recognized as such or institutionalized locally, it had to continuously prove itself in practice.[184] The insistence on deference, reflected in the formulas of greeting, the excessive zeal in the exercise of the office of judge, manifested in the willingness to vigorously defend also members of marginal groups, and the active efforts to assert seigneurial interests: all these actions were also—and perhaps primarily—intended to secure a person's own status. The bailiff and the local court of Momersdorf, another Kriechingen community, expressed this notion explicitly in 1743 when they demanded a seigneurial penalty against Peter Mück and the widow of Dominique Mück, who was resisting a chancery order and had scolded the officials as "Weidenbuben" (the lowliest kind of servant, young boys who take animals out to pasture). In the protocol the bailiff and the local court noted: "If, then, the seigneurial commands are not respected, how will the commands coming from the bailiff and the courts be respected? If every person is his own master, we can no longer maintain any rules."[185]

This interwoven way of thinking, which established a connection between the notions of order on various political levels, also permits indirect inferences about the order in the house. Whoever wanted to assert power had to acknowledge power himself, had to bind himself into a solidifying hierarchical order. The earlier examples of Johannet Wahl and Katharina Richard have shown that wives were also involved in the assertion of this order, which secured them a favored status within the village community. Membership by marriage in the

---

[182] The first complaints about this were voiced in 1716: AD Mos. 10 F 120: Supplikation der Einwohner von Steinbiedersdorf und Büdingen beim Reichskammergericht, 1716.

[183] See 266ff.

[184] Hohkamp, *Herrschaft in der Herrschaft*, and "Vom Wirtshaus zum Amtshaus," 8ff.

[185] AD Mos. Actes judiciaires B 10012: Niederwiesener, Dentinger, Momersdorfer Jahrgedingsprotokolle.

household of a seigneurial official opened up spheres of agency which these women developed and expanded on their own.

At the level above the village, the connection between lord and subjects was established by the court. The highest jurisdiction lay in the hands of the counts of Wied-Runkel in their capacity as lords of Kriechingen. It encompassed high, middle, and lower jurisdiction. Since the count was rarely present, the jurisdiction for civil and criminal matters was transferred to a councilor (Regierungsrat) as the lord's representative. He presided over the high court and conducted the proceedings. In civil cases, his decision could be appealed to the Imperial Chamber Court.[186] In criminal matters his decision was not open to appeal.[187] The basis for bringing an action was either a charge by a member of the village community or a report from one of the lord's officials.

Beginning in the middle of the eighteenth century, the proceedings took place only on fixed dates. Twice a week, between eight and twelve in the morning, individuals could present complaints and disputes and submit petitions and trial documents (Prozeßschriften). One morning was reserved for financial matters (Kameralsachen), another for forestry matters.

Since there were no locally effective institutions of social control, penal practice depended on many coincidences. To a certain extent it lay within the discretion of local officeholders to expose transgressions and file a report about them.

The village officeholders were under oath and enjoyed a high degree of protection from the lord. They were particularly willing to rebuke others when their interests were affected or their authority or special status were challenged. Charges of slandering a village functionary were fairly common and were interpreted as though the territorial lord himself had been insulted.[188] Those who uttered the slanderous words were not infrequently women.

When the warden (Schütze) wanted to report the plowman Johannes Kremeter because he had transported the body of the deceased schoolmaster of the Jewish community to Kriechingen on a Sunday morning, Johannes Kremeter's wife asked him "what business it was of his, he had such a big mouth."[189] That same

---

[186] In the second half of the eighteenth century, the counts claimed the right to bring an appeal to the count's cabinet. By expanding the stages of appeal, they sought to diminish the influence of the Imperial Chamber Court: Jürgen Weitzel, *Der Kampf um die Appellation am Reichskammergericht. Zur politischen Geschichte der Rechtsmittel in Deutschland* (Cologne, 1976), 310ff. On the structure of the court system and the administration of justice see also Sittel, *Sammlung der Provinzial- und Particular-Gesetze*, 521ff.

[187] AD Mos. B 978: Aveux et dénombrements de la comtesse d'Ostriese du 17.6.1688. Partially reprinted in Touba, *Dörfer*, 3.

[188] See, for example, AD Mos. B 10049: 1766: Klage gegen Nicolas Bommersbach injuria real. Charges were brought against Nicolas Bommersbach, one of the wealthiest villagers, because he had called the Dechant a rogue (Spitzbube), thus "having most grievously injured a man who was in the services of the lord."

[189] AD Mos. Actes judiciaires Pontpierre B 10081: Plaids annaux 1722–1791; 1755.

day he was verbally assaulted by Jacob Levy's wife, who was engaged in butchering with her husband behind closed doors.[190] Both women were defending their spheres against outside interference. Magdalene Stoffel did something similar when she claimed that she had not noticed the pregnancy of the maid Zarle, which was the talk of the village, because "she had not paid attention."[191]

The conflicts between these women and the warden make clear that the institutionalization of an apparatus of control within the village marginalized the responsibility that married women had for maintaining order in the village. Only the midwives retained their supervisory functions. However, they were bound into the seigneurial apparatus of control through the strict implementation of the obligation to swear an oath, while the role of the other women was restricted to the choice of a midwife. The verbal attacks should therefore be seen not merely as a way of taking advantage of the inferior legal status of women; they were also, and primarily, an attempt to defend an order that was upheld by both women and men.[192] To give just one example: it was "two frightened women" who sounded the alarm when a fight had broken out.[193] By making noise they were able to summon witnesses and prevent the violence from getting out of hand.

The task of supervising order in the village was assigned to local officials (wardens) who were bound to the lord by an oath, much the same way in which midwives supervised births and had to swear an oath to the lord. Both were part of an effort by political powers from the top to penetrate into spheres previously controlled by women. The connection between court and power also becomes clear in penal practice: punishments were employed at every level of the system to show mercy and create gratitude. As a rule the authorities did not insist on exacting the full measure of a punishment or fine.[194]

Women had essentially the same possibility as men to lodge a charge with the clerk of the village court, the bailiff, or, in his absence, his wife, thus setting legal proceedings in motion. They were also regularly summoned to

---

[190] Ibid.: she had asked the Schütze (warden) "why they were not opening up, they had butchered a wolf."

[191] See p. 222.

[192] One example of the responsibility of the village women for maintaining order in the village is the "assault of the women in Wellingen," which I have discussed in detail elsewhere. In this case the women had stormed the rectory to "pay a visit" to the priest's housekeeper, who was suspected of infanticide along with the priest: Ulbrich, "Frauen und Kleriker," 162f. Schmale has also noted the responsibility of the women for upholding the order in the village in the context of the supervision and denunciation of illegitimacy and infanticide: "Vergleichende Analyse," 122. This defense of order in the village can also explain the involvement of women in some actions of peasant resistance.

[193] AD Mos. Actes judiciaires B 10080: 1792 Acta in Denunciationssachen Jean Louis Lahir.

[194] AD Mos. 10 F 429 Strafregister, 10 F 166: Suppliken um Strafmilderung.

Kriechingen as witnesses or defendants. As we have seen, gender guardianship did occur, but it was not obligatory. Wives could appear in court in place of their husbands and defend themselves or their spouses against an accusation. In 1755, for example, Louis Becker, who had been accused of theft, sent his wife to Kriechingen. She excused her husband's absence, explained the situation, and obtained an acquittal. The costs of the proceedings had to be borne by her or her husband.[195] Substitute court representation was also possible in parent-child and sibling relationships. Peter Finickel sent his daughter to Kriechingen to negotiate on his behalf in a criminal matter.[196] Nicolas Bommersbach had himself represented by his sister.[197]

Because the world of village life was so transparent, making contact with the village functionaries or their wives did not present a problem to the villagers. A trip to the authorities in Kriechingen, however, was much more anxiety-laden, especially if women had been summoned as defendants or witnesses. The wife of Bernard Lipman, the parnas of the Jewish community, who was supposed to testify in a marriage complaint brought by her maid, excused her failure to appear on the grounds of inclement weather and her inability to procure a "chaise." Her maid, who had also been summoned, sent a message that she had no shoes, whereupon the authorities issued an order that she should be given shoes or put on a horse.[198]

However, the fact that the points of contact in Kriechingen were men had not only disadvantages: the seigneurial advocate (Regierungsadvokat) accorded at least some of the women protection out of a sense of paternal obligation and defended them vigorously. As I noted in a different context, this was also an opportunity for him to solidify his position within the apparatus of the county.

Since women were admitted before the seigneurial court as a party or were summoned in person for questioning or as witnesses, they had certain possibilities of influencing their cases.

The situation was different at the Jahrgedinge. It appears that women were not present at these regularly held judicial assemblies. They were represented by their fathers, husbands, or employers, who also had to deposit money for any of their fines. The Jews, too, did not participate in the Jahrgedinge, even though the protocols record several cases in which judgment was rendered against them. The Jahrgedinge were held once a year in each village in the name of the territorial ruler and presided over by the Oberamtmann and his

---

[195] AD Mos. Actes judiciaires B 10045: Fisc. gg. Luis Becker wegen eines aufgehalten und verschwiegenen Lammes, 1755.

[196] Ibid., Fisc. Amtskläger gegen Peter Finickel wegen eines von ihm dem Louis May geschlagenen Pferds, 1755.

[197] AD Mos. Actes judiciaires B 10080: Johannes Bompernetz gg. Nicolas Bommersbach pto debiti, 1790.

[198] See p. 230.

councilors. In addition to the representatives of the lord, the meeting was occasionally attended by the priest and functionaries of the community, as well as by all the male heads of households and the nonresident owners of landed property. At the Jahrgeding, the laws of the lord were read, offices were filled, and the oath was administered to the functionaries (bailiff, Meisterschöffe [master juror], Gerichtsschöffe [court juror], Bannschütz [field warden], Polizeischütz [police warden], Waldknecht [forest warden], and so on). All those in attendance were called upon to report breaches of the rules and to bring charges.

Women were not formally exempted from the Rügepflicht (obligation to report misdemeanors), but because the only place they occupied within the seigneurial conceptions of social order was inside the home, they were simply overlooked. In Steinbiedersdorf it was noted for the first time in 1764 that "at this year's Jahrgeding, as in previous ones, the widows of this community had neither appeared nor been noted in the list, although they should also be regarded as members of the community (Gemeinsleute)."[199] The clerk was instructed, on threat of a fine, to include them in the list, and the dechant was ordered to summon them. And in the following years the widows did in fact participate in the Jahrgeding; after 1777 they stayed away again and thus also escaped the Rügepflicht. Since one out of every five households in Steinbiedersdorf was headed by a widow, the gaps in seigneurial record keeping and in the supervisory and penal system were substantial. This "defect" was further heightened by the fact that wives were tied into the system of seigneurial supervision only indirectly via their husbands. The exclusion of women from the institutionalized public space of the Jahrgeding accorded them unencumbered spheres of agency that were not available to men and which they certainly could use to their advantage.

At the Jahrgeding, as well, most transgressions came up for trial as a result of the reports from the field and police wardens who were obligated to go on regular tours of inspection. The willingness to file reports differed among individuals and presumably depended far more on the attitude of a respective official toward the lord and the community, or toward the transgressors, than on the transgression itself.

As early as 1748, the community of Steinbiedersdorf decided to resist the seigneurial order to provide police wardens.[200] Resistance was also offered in the other communities of the county. In 1750, the police warden of Kriechingen

---

[199] Since attendance at the annual court assembly involved a Rügepflicht, the obligation of appearing was by no means one of the desirable forms of political participation. On the organization of the Jahrgeding: AD Mos. B 9993, B 10012/10013, B 10081, B 10087. On the organization of the Jahrgedinge, the Frevelgerichte, and the Ruggerichte see the study by Rudolf Hinsberger, *Die Weistümer des Klosters St. Matthias in Trier* (Stuttgart, 1989), 164ff., and André Holenstein, "'Local-Untersuchung' und 'Augenschein.' Reflexionen auf die Lokalität im Verwaltungsdenken und- handeln des Ancien Régime," *Werkstatt Geschichte* 16 (1997): 19–31.

[200] AD Mos. E Dépôt 553 DD 3: 1748.

was accused of failing to make a report even though it was clear that garden
and orchard thefts had occurred, fences had been moved, and many persons
were spending too much time in the tavern.[201] In 1761, the field wardens of
Steinbiedersdorf were fined because "they had failed to submit reports, in violation of their oath and possibly out of pure malice toward the gracious territorial lord."[202] In 1773 it was ordered that they would be personally liable for
damages if they did not report the culprits. In Saarwellingen, another community
of Kriechingen, the seigneurial officials tried to compel the wardens to present
at least a few reports against the subjects at the Jahrgeding, whereupon the
subjects complained to the Imperial Chamber Court that the wardens were
being induced by the ruler's practices to denounce the innocent.[203]

Since the charges brought by the sworn wardens were accorded "complete
credibility," the potential for abuse was considerable.[204] In Momersdorf the
atmosphere was so poisoned that the subjects, who were locked in a dispute
with their lord, appointed wardens on their own authority and prevented the
sworn officials from exercising their office.[205]

Under these conditions, the wardens did not exercise effective control, which
meant that the goal of disciplining the subjects with the help of the Rüge
courts (inferior courts of justice) could be achieved only on a very limited
basis. It also means that the protocols of the Rüge courts, in spite of their considerable richness compared to other sources, in and of themselves are not a
reliable source for "delinquency." Especially the spheres controlled by women
were not systematically dealt with in the Rüge court. We have already seen
that in connection with the gathering activities of women, with field, forest,
and pasture thefts.[206] The matters that were to be adjudicated at the Jahrgeding
were stipulated by the costumal (Weistum) and the police regulations, which
were continuously expanded.[207] The only paragraph of the police regulations

---

[201] AD Mos. Actes judiciaires B 9931: Plaids annaux, Créhange, 1750.

[202] AD Mos. Actes judiciaires B 10081: Jahrgedingsprotokoll von 1761.

[203] LHA Koblenz 56/1801: In Sachen sämtlicher Untertanen und Dorfschaften der
Grafschaft Kriechingen ctr. H. Grafen von Wied-Runkel, Mandatis, fol. 1063.

[204] AD Mos. Actes judiciaires B 10045: Fiscal gegen Jacques Levy and Lazar Ulrich
wegen verbotenen Durchfahrens mit einer Kuh durch die Wiese, 1756: when the
Bannschütz tried to seize the property of the accused, they allegedly set the dogs on
him, grabbed him by the throat, and took his hat away. The accused Jews denied the
charges, but they were not granted the right of proof since the accusation was being
brought by a sworn official.

[205] Ad Mos. B 10013: Plaids annaux Momersdorf, 1771.

[206] See p. 97.

[207] The costumal of 1392 was still being invoked in the eighteenth century. It regulated the trial procedures for felons: "Würde ein diep begriffen, es were man oder wip,
das den lip vermacht hette, welcherleige wiß das were, . . . den sol man lieberen dem
vorgenannten Hern Bannmeier zu Bidersdorff . . ." (If a thief was caught, be it a man
or a woman, who was to be punished with death, the thief was to be handed over to
the Bannmeier in Bidersdorff): AD Mos. 10 F 198.

that concerned women unequivocally obligated those who were pregnant out of wedlock to report their condition to the officials within a specific period of time.[208] However, complaints concerning the honoring of promises of marriage on the grounds of illicit sexual relations or premarital pregnancy were settled not at the Jahrgeding but brought before the government. In any case, we cannot discern a clear material separation of the jurisdictions of the two courts. What we can say, though, is that the Jahrgedinge were increasingly marginalized.

Alongside the seigneurial jurisdiction and the Jahrgeding, there originally existed village courts that assembled as needed to adjudicate minor transgressions and supervise commercial transactions. As early as 1698 their authority was restricted by obliging them to consult the government on any decisions they rendered.[209] A decree in 1727 stipulated that all contracts entered into before a court had to be incorporated into the protocols of the chancery. This transferred control over the economic life of the village into the seigneurial realm. As a result, the village court lost not only certain powers but also revenue.[210] In spite of the increasing seigneurial control and supervision, various forms of control and conflict regulation within the village survived for a long time. They included also an arbitral jurisdiction within the village, though its existence can be demonstrated only in concrete cases.[211]

Another authority that punished quarrels and violations of the norms without involving seigneurial jurisdiction was the priest. However, not least because of the confessional differences, he cannot be seen merely as an extension of the lord, even though the latter, very much in the Protestant spirit, tried repeatedly to incorporate the priest into the seigneurial system of control and supervision.[212] It would appear that the priest's response to these demands left something to be desired. He rarely participated in the Jahrgeding and rarely brought a complaint, even though he was explicitly questioned. In 1757 he complained about card playing and in 1763 about lax attendance at instruction in the Christian faith and at school, about drinking, gluttony, and once again card playing.[213] If he reported his problems with parishioners at all, he did so within

---

[208] See p. 63.

[209] AD Mos. 10 F 51: Acte de prise de possession du village de Pontpierre, confisqué sur la Comtesse de Créhange au profit du Roi, 1698.

[210] Ad Mos. E Dépôt 553, FF 4: Supplik von Meier und Gericht, 17. Juni 1727.

[211] For example, a court of arbitration is mentioned in the quarrel between Nicolas Thiel and Katharina Legendre (see p. 85).

[212] Because of the biconfessional nature of the village, the problem was more acute in Steinbiedersdorf than in other areas. However, the tension in the role of the priest between demands from above and community expectations has been observed also in areas with a single confession: see Simon,"Untertanenverhalten," 210ff.; Rainer Beck, "Der Pfarrer und das Dorf. Konformismus und Eigensinn im katholischen Bayern des 17./18. Jahrhunderts," in Richard van Dülmen, ed., Armut, Liebe, Ehre. Studien zur historischen Kulturforschung (Frankfurt a. M., 1988), 107–143.

[213] AD Mos. B 100081: Plaids annaux 1722–1791: protocols of 1757 and 1763.

the channels of ecclesiastical jurisdiction.[214] It would appear that he punished minor transgressions with the instruments of penance available to him, although the sources on this are only haphazard.

The Jewish villagers also had their own jurisdiction, at least until the middle of the eighteenth century. In addition they made use of the option of taking their conflicts to the count's court.[215]

Alongside the courts mentioned above there was also a jurisdictio extraterritorialis (involvement of the courts and notaries in private legal affairs), which was important especially in inheritance and marriage matters, and, as already indicated, the option of appeal to the Imperial Chamber Court. Several civil suits by women and men from Steinbiedersdorf were pending at that court, as well as communal and territorial suits. The people of Steinbiedersdorf made ample use of the possibility to register complaints in Wetzlar about the introduction of new dues and services, violations of the old law, and transgressions against the common good.[216]

Despite the extensive institutional possibilities of settling differences by involving third parties, the formal complaint took a back seat to attempts at settling a conflict on one's own, either through force or kind words. This is revealed by the brawls that men engaged in as well as by the gossip, shoving in church, and garden thefts that women engaged in, all of which point to nonjudicial, gender-specific forms of pursuing conflict. On the whole the circumstances of village life were difficult to grasp, at least for outsiders. Even the reforms by Christian Ludwig did little to change that. As late as 1763, an imperial commissioner who had been sent to Steinbiedersdorf to investigate the deaths that occurred during the forced seizure of property by soldiers complained about the dismal state of the county: "No one has thought of matters of government and public order, no institution of policing (Policeyanstallt), no registry, no proper judicial system have been introduced."[217] Surely conditions were not as disorderly as this lawyer believed. But the poor fit between everyday village life and the seigneurial organization on the communal level did not exactly simplify matters. The complex and confusing web of various courts, which in part corresponded also to differing notions of the law, created for women and men possibilities that no longer exist in a modern administrative state.

---

[214] Ad Mos. 29 J 63 and 29 J 63: Archiprêtre de Morhange, visitation protocol.

[215] The Jewish jurisdiction and changes in its powers in the eighteenth century are described in detail in chapter 5.

[216] They also used the opportunity to appeal several criminal judgments that had been rendered by the count's court, against whose decisions there was, in theory, no appeal. See, for example, LHA Koblenz 56/2987: In Sachen sämtlicher Unterthanen und Dorfschaften der Grafschaft Crichingen ca. Herrn Grafen zu Wied-Runkel und Crichingen. Mandati, 1757 fol. 1023ff. (Particularklagen aus Steinbiedersdorf).

[217] AD Mos. 10 F 117: Berichte von Kanzleidirektor Mülmann nebst darauf erlaßnen Rescripten 1763, Sept.-Nov. in Regierungssachen. Beilage: Canzlei-Directoris Mülmann Diarium 1763.

The cultural framework

The following discussion of the cultural framework is based on a narrow conception of culture. Law and tradition, religion and piety, as well as language and the ability to read and write are analyzed chiefly with a view to Christian society and probed for their significance to the organization of life. Beyond this, culture also points to patterns of thought and action that are involved in shaping and managing everyday life.[218] Culture, as Lila Abu-Lughod has emphasized, entails the drawing of boundaries that "invariably bring with them a kind of hierarchy."[219] This cannot be adequately grasped with dichotomous concepts such as culture and society, the people and the elite.[220] That is why the goal of this chapter is to describe the multilayered nature of the cultural framework in its historical context.

Law and tradition

The basis for the administration of justice in Steinbiedersdorf in the eighteenth century was chiefly seigneurial statutes,[221] along with the territorial code (Landesordnung) of Nassau-Katzenellenbogen[222] and imperial law. On the other side, local custom still played a decisive role in civil law. This custom was the result of a lengthy and conflictual adjustment of common law to local conditions. As far as we can make out, the framework had been established in the "Coutumes de Metz."[223] One of the principles of this customary law was an egalitarian

---

[218] In connection with this one should recall Pierre Bourdieu's concept of habit, which he defined as "the principle of practical understanding and acts of recognition of the magical boundary line that creates the distinction between the rulers and the ruled, that is, their social identity, which is completely contained within this relationship": Bourdieu, "Die männliche Herrschaft," 170, and his chapter entitled "Structures, *Habitus*, Practices," in his *The Logic of Practice*, trans. Richard Nice (Stanford, 1990), 52–65.

[219] Abu-Lughod, "Gegen Kultur Schreiben," 15.

[220] A sound critique of the dichotomous concept of culture and the myth of popular culture can be found in Lipp, "Alltagskulturforschung," 19ff. She opposes especially those conceptions of popular culture that suggest a closed world of the "life of the people" (illiterate, magical, stubborn) which resisted the prevailing culture and/or was destroyed by it: "In its simplifying contrasting technique, the concept of popular culture becomes a deductive conceptual system that is committed to a monolinear perspective of historical development. In the final analysis we are dealing with a negative modernization theory, which classifies social phenomena with the label popular culture before they have even been studied within contexts" (ibid., 20).

[221] In addition to the already mentioned police regulations, these included very detailed forestry, forest, and Rüge codes and many individual statutes. Most have been collected in Sittel, *Sammlung der Provinzial- und Particulargesetze*, 117ff.; statutes concerning Saarwellingen applied also to Steinbiedersdorf.

[222] Wilhelm von der Nahmer, *Die Land-Rechte des Ober- und Mittelrheins*, vol. 1 (Frankfurt a. M., 1831), 115ff.

[223] *Coutumes de l'évêché de Metz* (Nancy, 1761). On the significance of the coutumes in the eighteenth century see Anne Zink, *L'Héritier de la maison. Géographie coutumière du Sud-Ouest de la France sous l'Ancien Régime*. Civilisations et Sociétés 87 (Paris, 1993).

inheritance law,[224] another was "local freedom," that is, the absence of serfdom in the territory of the bishopric of Metz: "In the bishopric of Metz, which since ancient times has been called the Free Bishopric, individuals are deemed to be in a condition of freedom until there is evidence to the contrary."[225] In positive terms this meant freedom of movement and freedom of marriage within the bishopric.[226] The fact that this regulation dating back to the Middle Ages was still valid in the eighteenth century and had not yet lost its distinctive force, and that it had not yet been smothered by the new political structures exemplifies the difficulties the territorial ruler faced in trying to forbid marriages to outsiders and stop a mobility that negated the political boundaries.[227] Within the county of Kriechingen, serfdom existed only in Saarwellingen, the only village that belonged, in ecclesiastical terms, to the bishopric of Trier.[228] The survival of older structures that becomes visible here is by no means the only, but certainly a clear, indication of the importance of older legal traditions.[229]

When it comes to gender relations, the Coutumes de Metz contain unambiguous statements. Married men, widows, and unmarried sons and daughters age twenty or older were—in legal terms—responsible for themselves. Wives stood under the guardianship of their husbands, children under that of their parents, "wastrels" and the "feebleminded" under guardians appointed for them. All those who were not legally responsible for themselves could have recourse to a court only if they wished to bring charges of slander or violence committed against them. They were not allowed to conduct monetary transactions without permission from their husband, father, or guardian.

As for wives, the right of disposing over all property rested solely with the husband: "However, during their marriage, the husband alone is its [i.e. the property's] master and lord, and can dispose over it as he sees fit, without the consent of his wife."[230] The circumstance that men could dispose over the

---

[224] We read the following on inheritance: "En directes, fils ou filles, sans distinction, succèdent également, sans que l'un puisse prétendre avantage sur l'autre": "Recueil des Coutumes générales de l'évêché de Metz, Fait en l'an 1601 par Messieurs à ce deputez de Monseigneur & les Etats de l'évêché de Metz," in *Coutumes*, 40.

[225] Ibid., 3, art. 1.

[226] An area of free movement pertaining to the territory of the bishopric of Metz is mentioned in the (late) medieval costumals: Irmtraut Eder, *Die saarländischen Weistümer— Dokumente der Territorialpolitik*. Veröffentlichungen des Kommission für saarländische Landesgeschichte und Volksforschung 8 (Saarbrücken, 1978), 73ff.

[227] AD Paris, C.P. Allemagne, Petites Principautés, 18: Créhange (1737–1774), fol. 11: prohibition for outsiders and foreigners to marry or settle in the imperial county without seigneurial permission. The prohibition was unenforceable.

[228] Philipp de Lorenzi, *Beiträge zur Geschichte sämtlicher Pfarreien der Diöcese Trier* (Trier, 1887).

[229] The overlap of various kinds and notions of law and its importance with regard to inheritance law was also noted by Schlumbohm in his study of the parish of Belm, where impartible inheritance was practiced: *Lebensläufe*, 381.

[230] *Coutumes de Metz*, sect. II, art. III.

joint assets without their wives' knowledge could endanger the family's livelihood. The coutumes provided no protection against the structural disadvantage of wives that is apparent in this law. Although the territorial code imposed considerable restrictions on the husband's right of disposal, this did not resolve the problem but only shifted it. Chapter I, Section XII of the code stipulated the following: "Moreover, a husband may not sell what his wife brought as marriage good, including land. If he does, such a contract can be completely retracted and overturned."[231] Women's assets enjoyed a special protection that was laid down in the "exceptio Velleiani." Because the coutumes were based on the notion that women needed special help and protection, which was once again justified with reference to the "imbecillitas et infirmitas" of the female sex, women were not allowed to assume obligations for the benefit of a third party.[232]

If women wanted to expand their legal sphere of action, they had to make a formal renunciation and simultaneously relinquish the claim to the protection of their property. The Steinbiedersdorf debt cases reflect, on page after page, that this was not merely legal hairsplitting but harsh reality.[233]

The fact that men, upon entering into a marriage contract, settled their assets upon their wives in return for the dowry they brought into the marriage did represent an additional security for women's property, but in case of heavy indebtedness, these assets were, at least de facto, not protected against third-party claims.[234] This was something not only those women had to discover whose husbands had pledged their participation in the lawsuit against the lord with their signature, and who had seen all their property seized but for the bare necessities (pot and bed); even women who, like Anna Maria Finickel, were married to a "drunkard" learned this the hard way. As we have seen, to pay off her husband's debts, Anna Maria Finickel was forced to auction off a

---

[231] Nahmer, *Land-Rechte*, 128.

[232] Koch, *Maior dignitas*, 69ff. In this regard the regulations in the neighboring electorate of Trier were similar. Maria Dirks has emphasized "that on the one hand the C. Vellaeanum is introduced, and on the other hand, in a departure from the common law, women are given the option of forgoing this benefit, which imposed a binding obligation." She believes this supports "the assumption of a mixture of principles from common law and German law." Dirks, *Das Landrecht des Kurfürstentums Trier. Seine Geschichte und seine Stellung in der Rechtsgeschichte* (Cologne, 1965), 53f.

[233] For example, the marriage contract between Jean Claude Etien and Catharina Richard, which was concluded on July 2, 1792, formally recorded that the bride was renouncing the protections of the SC Vellaeanum: AD Mos. E Dépôt 553 II,1. In this context we should also recall the renunciation that Countess Christine Louise was compelled to make at her marriage (see p. 37) and the problems of indebted women (see p. 64).

[234] This was stipulated in many marriage contracts: AD Mos. E Dépôt 553 II, 1: Eheabredungen. On the legal meaning of dos (marriage goods, dowry) and dotalium (wedding gift) see Koch, *Maior dignitas*, 44ff.

large portion of her own property. Unlike her husband, who was constantly running up debts without telling his wife, she had no right to dispose of her property on her own. Moreover, from her petition it becomes clear that it was oftentimes not the debts, but the court costs connected with the forced collection of money owed that were seen as a peril.[235] Evidently both spouses were liable with their property for these costs. The number of complaints about the court fees that were generated by inheritance and debt cases reveals the importance that attached to what was perceived to be unjust exactions.

One possible way for women to protect themselves against financial ruin caused by reckless behavior was to have their men publicly declared spendthrifts. As we have seen, some Steinbiedersdorf women decided to take this difficult step, which brought little honor to their family.[236]

A woman who wished to enter upon an inheritance after the death of her husband also had to assume his debts, the extent of which were not always known in advance. She had only a brief period of time to make up her mind. The coutumes stipulated the following: "Nevertheless, the woman may, within twenty-four hours after learning of her husband's death, renounce the said property by throwing the keys onto the grave."[237] That this provision was at least known is revealed by the above-mentioned disputes over the payment of the debts of Johannes Ladner. His creditors demanded the money from his widow, Margaret Finickel, on the grounds that in order to escape this liability she would have had to renounce the inheritance and draw up an inventory of the remaining property, "or as is generally described, she should have placed the key upon the grave." The unmistakable conclusion of the lawyers was that whoever takes a single soup spoon must also assume the debts.[238]

Regardless of the possibility of moderating the inequality of men and women through contractual agreements, the ability to engage in economic activities reveals a clear asymmetry, which, as the few examples given here demonstrate, was not merely theoretical. We are dealing with a structural disadvantage of wives, one that could erupt in any financial crisis and which to a considerable degree leveled out the equality of men and women in inheritance law.[239]

---

[235] AD Mos. Actes judiciaires B 10048: Acta in Sachen Anna Maria, Hans Adam Oster v. Steinbiedersdorf, Ehefrau um Erlaubnis vor 1000 Pfd. an ihren Gütern an den Meistbietenden versteigern zu dürfen.

[236] See p. 67.

[237] *Coutumes de Metz*, Section II, Art. VIII.

[238] See chapter 3, note 87.

[239] Since parents could also give preference to individual children, it would require a quantifying analysis of inheritance practices to determine what kind of familial, gender, and class-specific differences and changes existed in inheritance practice. That was not possible within the framework of the present book. M. Hohkamp, in her study of Triberg, has shown that one cannot infer inheritance practices from inheritance laws and regulations. She was able to argue persuasively that there was probably a connection

Unlike wives, who in any case did not have legal majority, widows were allowed to dispose over their own property and that of their deceased husbands. Even if they transferred assets to their children during their lifetime, they usually retained the usufruct for the remainder of their lives. A complaint by Simon Kindel reveals that people did not always take a close look at the legal status of property when widows made purchases or sales: Simon Kindel alleged that his mother had sold parts of her movable property and land even though it had already been transferred to her children. She protested vigorously and successfully against a decree that placed the eighty-five-year-old woman under the guardianship of her son, who was to "look after and support her" in a manner befitting "a well-meaning child": "However, since the mother in no way agreed with this, nor wished to accept or ask for food from him, and absolutely opposed such an order, it is decreed through the seigneurial bailiff that the mother will be assigned a guardian from among her other close relatives."[240] Given the difficulties in settling the property affairs of a widow, the clerk simply remarked "that the assembly in Paris does not have so much trouble governing France in accordance with the wishes of all the people." That says it all.[241]

The favorable legal status of widows and widowers had to do with the inheritance law as practiced in Steinbiedersdorf, which took its cues alternately from the coutumes and the territorial code. While the latter stipulated that half of the property should pass to the married children upon the death of a spouse, in Steinbiedersdorf the surviving spouse often retained control over all of it.[242] This practice involved not only a postponement of the transfer, which gave greater influence and security to the elderly, but a procedure that influenced very broadly the way in which property was passed down and was the source of numerous quarrels. It came into play not only if the widowed spouse remarried, but also if children predeceased their parents and a quarrel broke out between the two families related through the marriage of their children. In the legal battle that Katharina Legendre fought with the heirs of her deceased son-in-law, she invoked local custom. According to this custom she should have retained or received back all property after the death of her daughter, grandchildren, and son-in-law. That would have allowed her not only to secure her livelihood, but to improve the dowry for her second daughter. The opposing party, invoking

---

between the changes in inheritance practice in favor of women and the economic conditions: "Wer will erben?," 339. If we compare the Steinbiedersdorf land registers from the seventeenth and eighteenth centuries, there are signs that the ownership of houses and land by women increased rather than decreased. However, given the tremendous parcellation of land, the high mobility, and the situation of landholdings within the territory and outside, it would require very elaborate methods to prove this.

[240] Ad Mos. E Dépôt 553 FF 4: Untertänigste Vorstellung und Bitte von Seiten Simon Kindels von Steinbiedersdorf die Unterhaltung siner Mutter betr.

[241] Ad Mos. Actes judiciaires B 10080: 10.4.1791.

[242] Ad Mos. 10 F 133.

territorial law, argued that part of the inheritance of the daughter had passed through her child to the father and from him to his relatives.[243] It would appear that the parties invoked one law or the other depending on what best served their interests. The inheritance regulations called for in the territorial law, and practiced elsewhere, through which the assets of the mother passed through the children to the father's family, could imperil a woman's very livelihood.[244]

Not all women and men put off the transfer of property until after their death. Many decided to hand it over during their lifetimes. The division was carried out in front of the notary and depended on the number of children. The movable and landed property was divided into equal parts and distributed by casting lots. Since it was not always possible to divide the house, the youngest child was sometimes granted a right of choice, or it was agreed that the son or daughter who inherited the house by lot would pay monetary compensation to the other siblings.[245] Even when the house was transferred in an undivided state, it could never assume an importance resembling that of the undivided transfer of a property.[246] Allocating women to a house or a farm was here possible on a much smaller scale than in regions where farmsteads were transferred whole.

The late transfer of property and the favorable usufruct rights placed the elderly under a special protection and strengthened kinship bonds. The division of the house regularly created a situation where related individuals continued to live under one roof. Katharina Legendre, about whom we know the most, had her house, farm, and stable directly next to her sister-in-law Madeleine Richard; another two houses down lived her brother-in-law Christoph Renaudin. Three of the five children of the Richard family, two daughters and one son, thus lived in immediate proximity throughout their lives.[247] This example also makes clear that for women it was not only the marriage into which they brought their assets that was important, but also the paternal family, from which they could both take over the house and look forward to an inheritance even after entering into a marriage.

As already mentioned, the continuing bond to the paternal family is also revealed by the practice of naming. Within the context of village life, married Christian and Jewish women kept their (paternal) name throughout their lives.[248]

---

[243] See p. 84.

[244] Compare on this the considerations during the Caesarean section carried out on Anne Marie Pierrard, p. 58.

[245] AD Mos. E Dépôt 553 Pontpierre II, 1: Protocole des actes reçus par le tabellion Bomans du comté de Créhange, résidant à Pontpierre 1791–1794. The protocols on a voluntary division of inheritance date mostly from the end of the eighteenth century.

[246] For the connection between the importance of the house and its transfer see the work of Zink, *L'Héritier de la maison*.

[247] See p. 176, ill. 2.

[248] Davis, *Women on the Margins*, emphasizes that in the Jewish community it was

The allocation of husband and wife to different families that is expressed in this practice is likely to have had a significant influence on the way women perceived themselves and were perceived by outsiders. However, this custom did not allow them to establish a family tradition that rested on the female line, since children were given their father's name. Practices such as the determination of freedom or serfdom, which in the late Middle Ages followed the closest "womb" (mutermagen), that is, the female kinship line, apparently did not survive.[249]

The decline of the ordering element represented by the house and the existence of competing systems of allocation limited the authority of the housefather, who could not "govern" a clearly defined, self-contained entity, but had to take outside rights into account in his household. Since the paternal inheritance did not pass to the children upon the death of the father but to the wife, in practice these "outside rights" often belonged to women, who as widows were able to dispose over their own property and that of their deceased husbands. Therein lay a crucial difference to those practices—stipulated in the territorial law—that provided for the transfer of at least a portion of the assets to the children upon the death of a spouse, thereby considerably restraining women's power of disposition.

The principle of equal inheritance rights and the late transfer of property were an expression of and starting point for a notion of equality that took on a programmatic character during the Kriechingen rebellion. In the years leading up to the French Revolution, the lawyers representing the subjects demanded

---

usual for daughters to bear the name of their father, which was occasionally expanded by the name of origin (for example, Glikl bas Judah Leib). If a Jewish woman signed her name in non-Hebrew script, she "added one of the surnames her father had assumed for Christian recordkeepers and Jewish tax collectors." Whether the system described by Davis applied also in Kriechingen would have to resolved by a separate study. In the sources I chiefly consulted, which are of Christian provenance, the practice of naming is quite diverse. On occasion the name of the father is handled like a surname (for example, Perle Levy) or both of the fathers' names are used (for example, Fromet Oster Levy: Fromet was the sister of Perle Levy and the daughter of Oster or Ausser Levy), although occasionally "daughter" was added by analogy to the Hebrew. I have largely adopted the naming of the sources, but have standardized the different ways of writing the name of the same person (Perle, Besle, Pesle).

[249] On the establishment of serfdom through the closest female relatives see Claudia Ulbrich, *Leibherrschaft am Oberrhein im Spätmittelalter.* Veröffentlichungen des Max-Planck-Instituts für Geschichte 58 (Göttingen, 1979), 154f. Gertrud Hüwelmeier has shown that a tradition founded on women could be established not only through kinship but also through the names given to houses: Hüwelmeier, "Kinship, Class and Identity in a German Village," in Victoria Goddard, ed., *Gender, Agency, and Change: Anthropological Perspectives* (London, 2000). The Steinbiedersdorf material also contains scattered indications that houses were recorded with the names of women, but not—as was the case in the area studied by Hüwelmeier—that this was continued after the death of these women.

equality for all before the seigneurial courts, elevated equal treatment in the allocation of wood, bean poles, and pea sticks (Erbsenreisern) into a basic principle, and sued to enforce the principle that all those entitled to usufruct rights bear an equal share of the communal burdens. It would appear that behind these demands lay very concrete notions of how life could be arranged at the village level.[250]

While the form of property transfer that was practiced in Steinbiedersdorf bore the danger of constant conflicts, it also promoted the need to develop rules to resolve and settle such conflicts. In this context one should mention especially the importance of drawing lots, a practice that was employed not only in the division of inheritances, but also in the allocation of common land, and, as the protocol of the election of a midwife in another village reveals, in case of a deadlocked vote.[251] It points to legal notions that were rooted in tradition and are an expression of the ability of early modern rural societies to engage in conflict.

As we discovered in the life stories of the women we met in chapter 3, the egalitarian principles in inheritance law could, in certain familial circumstances, create for women spheres of agency that constituted a countermodel to the authoritarian social structures that undoubtedly existed. Needless to say, this possibility was open only to a small village elite that set itself apart from the other village women. As the example of the Richard family showed us, it was not sufficient to be born into this elite; rather, one's social position had to be continuously created and recreated. That was done not only in the house or within the context of kin relationships, but also in the public sphere. In this context, as well, great importance attaches to the church and the practices of piety.

Church and piety

In ecclesiastical terms, Steinbiedersdorf was part of the Deanery of Mörchingen/ Morhange in the bishopric of Metz, until 1808, when it was assigned to the Canton Faulquemont. Patronage and collation lay with the Counts of Kriechingen as the territorial lords, who split the tithe with the priest.[252] The church in Steinbiedersdorf, first attested in a document in 1308, was dedicated to the pope and to the martyr St. Calixtus. It was rebuilt at the end of the seventeenth

---

[250] On the demands for equality before the revolution see Ulbrich, "L'impact de la Révolution française," 429. The fact that bean poles and pea sticks that is, the kind of wood that was needed in the garden to cultivate beans and peas—were mentioned alongside fire wood—is interesting for the simple reason that gardens were not subject to any seigneurial control.

[251] Ad Mos. 5 E 11131–11132, Régistres paroissiales 1781: "Les voix étaient égales pour deux. Nous avons jugés de tirer un sort."

[252] Dorvaux, *Pouillés*, 402. The potato tithe led to protracted disputes, which were fought out before the Imperial Chamber Court. In 1763, the counts were granted the right to the potato tithe.

century and enlarged between 1739 and 1742.[253] Near the village stood a chapel that was home to a hermit.[254] As early as 1700, Steinbiedersdorf had a Brotherhood of the Blessed Sacrament, which was administered by a master brother and was open to women and men.[255] It would be reinvigorated in 1822. That same year, a foundation in honor of saints Erasmus, Rochus, and Sebastian, established in 1744–1745 and prohibited during the French Revolution, was brought back to life.[256]

The church included the presbytery and the walled cemetery with an ossuary. Neither the church nor the cemetery served exclusively religious purposes. As we have seen, the church space was also an important place where the social hierarchy within the community was created and affirmed,[257] and the cemetery was a place of refuge, a place to commemorate the departed and to cultivate tradition and family.[258] The galleries of the church, at least according to the complaints of Jean Baptiste Lambert, were for some a place to engage in illicit sexual conduct and for others a welcome place to sleep. To prevent this misuse ("usage très abusif"), which was widespread in rural churches, he recommended doing away with galleries during the renovation of the church, thus literally abolishing niches that offered spaces free of control.[259] The complaints by the priest about the "libertins" cast doubt on a causal connection that is often assumed to exist between the low rates of illegitimacy and sexual repression. Rather, the seclusion of the gallery indicates that the inside of the church—

---

[253] AD Mos. E Dépôt 553 FF 4: the necessary enlargement of the church led to disagreements over the question of whether the parish was obligated to perform corvée labor, and if so, how much.

[254] On the hermits see Ch. François, "Les ermites en Lorraine," *La revue populaire* 18 (1977): 224f.

[255] The Brotherhood of the Sacrament was among the brotherhoods that accepted women: Annick et Louis Châtellier, "Les premières catéchistes des temps modernes. Confrères et consoeurs de la Doctrine chrétienne aux XVIe–XVIIIe siècles," in Jean Delumeau, ed., *La religion de ma mère. Le rôle des femmes dans la transmission de la foi* (Paris, 1992), 287–299, here 287. There does not appear to be any other documentation for Steinbiedersdorf.

[256] The impulse behind the foundation was a cattle plague in the village: Registres paroissiales 1744/45. The system of foundations was substantially expanded in the nineteenth century. In 1873, sixty-one endowed masses were celebrated each year in the church of Steinbiedersdorf, most of which (fifty) dated from the period after the revolution. Masses were endowed by women and men: AD Mos. 553 E. Dépôt II, I: Protocole des actes reçus par le tabellion Bomans du comté de Créhange, résidant à Pontpierre v. 21.5.1791–9.1.1794; AD Mos. 29 J 657: Affaires paroissiales, paroisses de l'actuel diocèse de Metz, archiprêtre de Faulquemont, an X–1893.

[257] See p. 47.

[258] Akiko Mori has pointed to the importance of the cemetery, noting that care of the graves was women's activity in a "public" sphere, one that was "directly connected with the 'domestic' household": Mori, "Familiengrabpflege in ethnologischer Sicht: Eine Dorfforschung in Südostkärnten, *L'Homme. ZFG* 6 (1995): no. 2, 86–97, here 97.

[259] AD Mos. 29 J 66: Archiprêtre de Morhange, visite canonique à Pontpierre, 1740.

though presumably outside of services—offered spaces removed from the controlling gaze of the public.

The church itself was also a place of entertainment, at least occasionally. Young
people were drinking, smoking, and playing in the church during vigils, of all
times. The belief that one had to ring the bells all night to help the deceased
find peace was still widespread.[260] The situation was not much better with the
cemetery. A comital ordinance from the year 1701 not only called for a stricter
church piety, it also forbade the continued use of the cemetery as a meeting
place, for dancing, and for the transacting of business.[261]

If we can believe the visitation protocols, the Sunday morning service, which
lasted from nine to eleven, was regularly attended. The kind of "abuses" that
occurred in neighboring Teting, where women and girls in the summer attended
service scantily clad, or in Faulquemont, where women and maids left the
church en masse at the beginning of the sermon, are not documented in
Steinbiedersdorf.

Between Easter and Ascension Day, mass was regularly preceded by a procession to the cemetery, during which the dead were commemorated with a
communal song (De profundis).[262] Other processions led around the village
or—as on the Feast of St. Martin[263] or the Rogation Days immediately preceding Ascension—to other parishes, sometimes more than an hour away.

As long as everything went off in an "orderly" fashion, every parishioner
fulfilling the duty of participating and taking his or her assigned place in the
line, processions met the needs of both laity and clergy. Through joint prayers
and songs, and through their direct relationship to the space they circumscribed, they contributed to creating a group consciousness grounded in church
and religion and transcending relationships of family and work. The processions could strengthen the community of believers internally and externally, and
give a public demonstration of the influence of the church.[264] Discord arose as
soon as members of the community sought to put the processions to exces-

---

[260] AD Mos. 29 J 63: États détaillés des paroisses de l'archiprêtre de Morhange,
Pontpierre en 1699.

[261] AD Mos. 10 F 116: Réorganisation de la police en 1701, according to Flaus,
Comté, 74.

[262] In the Toulois region, since the end of the seventeenth century, these processions,
firmly tied to the weekly mass and embedded in ritual life, stood under the sign of the
battle against heresy: Philippe Martin, *Les chemins du sacré. Paroisses, processions, pélerinages en Lorraine du XVIe au XIXe siècle* (Metz, 1995), 153.

[263] Since the end of the eighteenth century, the procession on the Feast of St. Markus
included a blessing of the animals and the troughs (ibid., 164).

[264] Processions are a good example for the above-mentioned critique of dichotomous
concepts of culture. They cannot be unambiguously assigned to either clerical or lay
piety, nor can they be understood solely as an element of popular religiosity. For the
ecclesiastical and social meaning of processions, see Martin's comprehensive study on
western Lorraine: *Les chemins du sacré*, 119ff.

sively worldly uses—for example, if the village elites insisted on special routes, stopping points, or altars in front of their houses.[265]

Another aspect that was evidently not welcome was an excessive spatial expansion of the processions. In Steinbiedersdorf, at any rate, complaints were voiced at a visitation about processions around the village and into other parishes. The question of whether processions in this area lost their popularity during the second half of the eighteenth century in favor of a more internalized piety, as was the case in western Lorraine, is not something we can answer on the basis of the available sources.[266]

The processions to the cemetery, around the village, to the village boundaries, and to neighboring parishes within and beyond the borders of the territory are hardly reflected in the sources. Still, the few surviving clues not only reveal the beliefs of clerics and laity and their need for order, they also point to a local network of parishes that was supraordinated to the political organization. This network held great significance in connection with marriage arrangements and the observable preference for exogamous marriages.

Matchmaking was embedded in local customs and permitted, to a certain degree, free choice of a partner. A not insignificant role was played by the feasts of patron saints and annual festivals celebrating the dedications of churches, where young girls and boys from various villages came together to dance. These feasts were a thorn in the side of Father Richard, the priest of Steinbiedersdorf, for they violated his sense of the proper order of things. As early as 1699 he proposed that the dedication feasts throughout the diocese be held on the same Sunday.[267] In so doing he became a protagonist in the discussion over the reduction of feasts and holidays, which became a central theme within the Catholic Church in the eighteenth century.[268] That his suggestion did not meet with much approval is something we learn in 1761, when in Steinbiedersdorf once again "several dances took place to screeching music" at the feast of the dedication. Johannes Bernard, who got married shortly thereafter, had auctioned off the dances as the "leader of the unmarried lads" and "had held a kirmess dance on his own authority."[269] The priests were no less scandalized by the nighttime gatherings of women and young girls[270] and the so-called "lenten marriages."[271]

---

[265] Ibid., 140.

[266] Ibid., 125. The agents of this interiorized piety were the brotherhoods, which did exist also in Steinbiedersdorf, but once again the source material is not sufficient for further investigation.

[267] As note 628. The authorities also considered excluding those who engaged in public dancing from acting as godparents.

[268] Hersche, "Wider 'Müssiggang,'" 97ff.

[269] AD Mos. Actes judiciaires, B 10047: 1761.

[270] The "veillées" where women and girls got together are mentioned in many visitation records of the region, though not for Steinbiedersdorf.

[271] Lenten marriages were a matchmaking custom that should be seen as a preliminary

On the eve of the first Sunday of Lent, young men went from house to house and, outside the door of every young man and girl, called out the "valentine" that had to be bought back at mid-Lent by presenting gifts to the valentine. After the exchange of gifts the courtship was confirmed in a procession on horseback. The names of the couples were determined by drawing lots, or at least that is the description we have for Metz.[272]

The only trace of the "fachenottes" in the Steinbiedersdorf sources refers to a failed attempt at matchmaking. Johannes Roschy, a dairyman, had come to the house of the parents of Elisabeth Stoffel on the first Sunday of Lent and had eaten dinner with the family. The next visit occurred on Easter Monday. Two girls and two boys were present in addition to Johannes Roschy and Elisabeth Stoffel. They summoned musicians, danced, and drank wine. We know about these events because Johannes Roschy was later accused of having stolen from the family.[273]

There is other evidence as well that girls and young men met at social gatherings at home. Like matchmaking, this type of entertainment, which, along with familial feasts, especially weddings, broke the monotony of everyday life, was linked to the ecclesiastical calendar. It points to the importance that religious practices played in the way people organized life and coped with existence.[274]

Efforts by bishops and local clergy to embed practices of which the church tended to be critical in ritual or abolish them altogether could be implemented only slowly, if at all. The priest of Steinbiedersdorf, Richard, encountered opposition in 1719 when he tried to prevent a weather procession and issued a prohibition against the "banner" and the general ringing of bells. Three men threatened to retrieve the banner from the church by force to allow the supplicatory procession—"to ask for rain"—to go ahead. The men insulted the priest as a "seducer of the people and a thief."

Threats of draconian punishment—incarceration, public apology, and seizure of property—were used to force Nicolas Krämer, the chief instigator, to relent. He threatened to sue the priest in the Imperial Chamber Court for introducing an innovation, but he does not seem to have made good on his threat. We cannot determine whether Nicolas Krämer's real motivation was to go ahead with a procession the church did not approve, or whether he merely wanted

---

step to an engagement. In Lorraine they were also called Fehhenates and Valentins, among other things, in the Saarland region Lehenausrufen: R. de Westphalen, *Petit Dictionnaire des traditions populaires messines* (Metz, 1934), cols. 263ff., and Nikolaus Fox, *Saarländische Volkskunde* (Bonn, 1927).

[272] Cabourdin, *La vie quotidienne,* 242f. R. de Westphalen places the custom more strongly into the context of matchmaking: *Petit Dictionnaire,* cols. 263ff.

[273] AD Mos. Actes judiciaires, B 10041: 1721.

[274] On the significance of religion in the day-to-day life of rural, precapitalist societies see also Ellen Badone, ed., *Religious Orthodoxy and Popular Faith in European Society* (Princeton, 1990).

to test the strength of his position—as a subject of a Protestant territorial ruler—vis-à-vis the Catholic clergy. But the quarrel shows that within the relationship between priests and parishioners, as well, there were spaces for action that had to be measured out time and again.[275]

Apart from the different confession of the territorial ruler, the still existing pluralistic forms of Catholicism might also have influenced the attitudes of the parishioners to their local clergyman. A seemingly casual remark in the visitation records about collections reminds us of the extent to which the rural population in Lorraine was influenced by regular clergy. Their number is said to have vastly exceeded that of the parish clergy. These rural missions took on special importance especially in the regions bordering Protestant territories.

While missionaries in the time of the Counter-Reformation had focused their activities on re-Catholicization, in the eighteenth century they made the internalization of Christian life and the teachings of the church their primary task.[276] With the goal of educating the individual into a conscientious and responsible Christian, they promoted Catholic culture, the Catholic faith, and ties to the Catholic Church, but at the same time they weakened the disciplinary control of the local priest.

A central role in this conflict was played by confession: as "an institutional confession, a place for the forced admission of wrongdoing, an effective instrument for disciplining and controlling impulses," it provided access to a person's inner life.[277] At times one could escape the reach of the clerical authorities and the compulsory confession they imposed by choosing a confessor outside the village or by engaging in other—collective—forms of penance. Although the church strenuously opposed such behavior especially in the eighteenth century, its response shows that these things were actually done.[278] These practices are attested especially for the period of the French Revolution. For example, the priest of Steinbiedersdorf complained in 1792 about the large number of people from neighboring parishes who asked to take Easter confession from him:

---

[275] Beck, "Pfarrer," 107ff., has also pointed out how fragile the relationship was between priest and village community.

[276] Louis Châtellier, "De 'la crise de la conscience européenne' aux missions rurales: Changement religieux dans les campagnes au début du XVIIIe siècle," *Historie. Économie. Société* 8 (1989): 237–248, and "Les missions et le changement religieux des campagnes aux XVIIe–XVIIIe siècles au pays de Sarrebourg," in Hans-Walter Herrmann, ed., *Die alte Diözese Metz L'ancien diocèse de Metz. Referate eines Kolloquiums in Waldfischbach-Burgalben vom 21.–23. März 1990.* Veröffentlichugnen der Kommission für Saarländische Landesgeschichte und Volksforschung 19 (Saarbrücken, 1993), 211–224.

[277] Edith Saurer, "Frauen und Priester. Beichtgespräche im frühen 19. Jahrhundert," in van Dülmen, ed., *Arbeit, Frömmigkeit und Eigensinn,* 141–170, here 141.

[278] On confession and obligatory confession in the Catholic realm see Jean Delumeau, *Sin and Fear,* trans. Eric Nicholson (New York, 1990), and *L'aveu et le pardon. Les difficultés de la confession XIIIe–XVIIIe siècle* (Paris, 1992). It would appear that gender-specific behavior toward confession, especially its rejection by men as Delumeau describes for the nineteenth century, is not yet visible in the eighteenth century.

"I nearly lost my life from the enormous crowd from all the villages of France and Lorraine who were seeking the Easter confession."[279]

Even though the situation in 1792 was profoundly different as a result of the anti-papal legislation issued by revolutionary France, what becomes visible here is the significance of the interlocal network we encountered in connection with processions and church feasts. In conjunction with the pluralistic tendencies of Catholicism, reflected in the missionary activity of the orders, and with coping mechanism that were not tied to the church, it was possible for individuals to subvert local control.

It would seem that even the long-term relationships between priests and parishioners did not fundamentally change this situation. Before the revolution, no priest relinquished his post in Steinbiedersdorf early or transferred. Father Jean Richard, who took the position after the death of his predecessor Alexandre Adam in 1694, ministered to the faithful entrusted to his care for thirty-nine years. At his death in 1733 he was succeeded by Jean Baptiste Lambert, who ran the parish longer still, forty-two years. His successor, Jean Baptiste Boucier de Mondéville, was driven from his post in February of 1793 after nineteen years: in 1792 he had heard the Easter confession of many faithful from the surrounding French lands and had refused, following Steinbiedersdorf's incorporation into France, to swear the oath to the revolutionary constitution.[280] The demand that priests take the oath carried the revolutionary tensions into a community and overshadowed or heightened the older conflicts that existed there. Each faction now looked for its own priest. While some of the faithful attended the mass conducted in the parish church by a priest who had taken the oath, others met secretly in private homes to hear the mass of a priest who had not taken it. This split in the church destroyed the unity of the community of the faithful, which gathered each Sunday not only for prayer, but also to create a visual demonstration of the social order within the community.

As the church space was more important to women than men, this loss was particularly painful for them, especially since all the outward-directed expressions of piety were also abolished. Many practices of piety, which were an essential component of the world of women's experiences, were shifted into the inside of the church or the house. At the same time, the role of the church as the most important agent of the prerevolutionary policy of disciplining the faithful was challenged, and the door was once again opened to traditional forms of piety within the official church.

In order to assert itself against the new state, the church had to open itself up to the "unofficial" culture of the "non-elites." It began to tolerate religious practices it had been fighting since the beginning of the Enlightenment.[281]

---

[279] AD Mos. 10 F 429: Curé de Mondéville an den Rat von Kriechingen, 19.4.1792.
[280] See 43f.
[281] In the late stages of the Enlightenment, the church had tried to "purify" piety, to lead it back to the "pure faith": Fassbinder, "Frömmigkeit," 15.

Weather processions and local pilgrimages experienced a renaissance, and the belief in miracles, suppressed by the church in the eighteenth century, also revived.[282] This meant that increasing importance attached to forms of piety that were in the nineteenth century ascribed, with increasing exclusivity, to women. In this way the developments on the local level became part of the widely observed process of the feminization of religion.[283]

The religious divisions in Steinbiedersdorf were not healed by the signing of the concordat. The attempt to restore the unity of the community by appointing a new priest was frustrated by differences that reached back into the revolutionary period. Only Father Neumann, appointed in 1817, seems to have been accepted by all.[284]

The quarrel over the priests and the struggle to retain or regain popular expressions of piety, which also opened up spheres of action for women, reveals the limits of the church's power, which was contested throughout the eighteenth century. Behavior that negated ecclesiastical authority was a tradition not only in Steinbiedersdorf: in German-speaking Lorraine, a region characterized by deep religiosity and exposed to the influence of diverse ecclesiastical-religious currents, the official church long fought a losing battle in its efforts to reduce the feast days and abolish "superstitious" practices as well as "pagan" customs.[285] Visitation records from the end of the seventeenth century complain about the many pilgrimages and feast days, about the lust for pleasure, the women's feast (Weiberkilt), and the excesses that occurred in the "scandalous" matchmaking customs during carnival and Lent.[286]

As we have seen, a concrete quarrel erupted in Steinbiedersdorf in 1719 when the local priest, on instructions from the bishop, sought to prevent a weather

---

[282] Claudia Ulbrich, "Die Jungfrau in der Flasche. Ländlicher Traditionalismus in Deutschlothringen während der Französischen Revolution," *Historische Anthropologie* 3/1 (1995): 125–143.

[283] McLeod, "Weibliche Frömmigkeit—männlicher Unglaube," 134–156; Geneviève Gabbois, "'Vous êtes presque la seule consolation de l'église.' La foi des femmes face à la déchristianisation de 1789 à1880," in Jean Delumeau, ed., *La religion*, 301–325; Ralph Gibson, "Le catholicisme et les femmes en France au XIXe siècle," *Revue d'histoire de l'église de France* 79 (1993): 63–93. Saurer, "Einleitung," 13, emphasizes that one cannot infer from the presence of women in Catholic and Protestant churches in the nineteenth century that they had stronger religious ties, rightly pointing out that the discussion of such a thesis requires a social and sociostructural differentiation.

[284] AD Mos. 29 J 657: Affaires paroissiales, paroisses de l'actuel diocèse de Metz, archiprêtre de Faulquemont, (an X–1893).

[285] On the opposition of the Catholic population of Lorraine against Enlightenment trends within the church see Cabourdin, "La vie quotidienne," 254ff.

[286] AD Mos. 29 J 69: 1699. "Scandale" or "scandaliser" appear frequently in the visitation records. It belongs into the context of the teachings on "offense" that Beat Hodler has examined in relationship to the political ethics of the reformation: *Das "Ärgernis" der Reformation. Begriffsgeschichtlier Zugang zu einer biblisch legitimierten politischen Ethik.* Veröffentlichungen des Instituts für Europäische Geschichte 158 (Mainz, 1995).

procession.[287] A statement by the curé de Mondéville makes clear that the authority of the priest did not go unchallenged also in the second half of the eighteenth century: the curé admitted that the hermit who lived at the outskirts of the village was held in greater esteem by the peasants than he himself was.[288] In Faulquemont, women used their domestic affairs to escape the sermon: claiming they had to look after their children or kitchen, they returned to church only after the priest had finished his sermon.[289] In this way they fulfilled their ecclesiastical-religious duties. We already know that in 1772 in the parish of Mainvillers, the Amtmann, the mayor, the lay judges, the residents, and the parishioners complained to the ecclesiastical and secular authorities that the priest had attempted to change the seating arrangements in the church.[290] Two years later harmony had been restored, and the priests supported the institution of a yearly procession in honor of the Visitation of Mary. The parishioners wanted it as a reminder that in 1735 and 1760 they had been saved from a serious epidemic after making a pledge to the Virgin Mary. As they saw it, Mary had helped while medicine, (pharmacie) had failed.[291]

In Steinbiedersdorf, as well, the villagers solicited the help of the saints in times of crisis, at least in addition to other measures. Saint Margaret, who was invoked by mothers-to-be at the hour of birth, enjoyed great popularity. Many parents named their daughters after this great helper of peasants in need.[292]

This concluding reference to the veneration of saints is intended as another reminder of how many expressions of piety could be practiced and asserted by the faithful in the eighteenth century within the framework of or at the margins of Catholicism, expressions that were not always closely tied to mediation by the church and were open to men and women from all social strata.[293] The

---

[287] AD Mos. Actes judiciaires B 10041: Fiscalis ctra. Nicolas Krämer und Cons., 1719.

[288] AD Mos. 10 F 751. Even after the revolution, German-speaking Lorraine remained the site of "scandalous scenes." For example, in Faulquemont in 1814, a priest complained that the faithful were approaching the sacrament "like pigs at the trough": Henry Contamine, "Les plaintes contre le clergé rural en Moselle sous le consulat et l'empire" *Annuaire de la fédération historique lorraine* 3 (1930): 110.

[289] AD Mos. 29 J 63: États détaillés des paroissses de l'archiprêtre de Morhange, Pontpierre en 1699.

[290] See p. 48.

[291] AD Mos. 29 J 68. The veneration of the Notre-Dame-de-la-Visitation in Mainvillers was still strong far into the twentieth century (Chapel 1955). See La Torre, *Guide de l'art*.

[292] On the cult of Saint Margaret at birth see Franz, *Benediktionen*, vol. 2, 193f. Margarete was the most common baptismal name for girls in Steinbiedersdorf: 68 instances among 411 baptisms and 36 different names.

[293] Hersche, who has summarized the existing research on the topic of pilgrimages also from the perspective of gender ratios, notes that women participated in pilgrimages at "slightly disproportional rates." That means that for several days each year women were on the road and tied into contexts others than the domestic one: Hersche, "Devotion," esp. 21f.

broad spectrum of religious practices around birth and death, suffering and healing, work and feasts that is hinted at in these conflicts with the official church opened for women religious spheres of action which they largely shaped themselves in conjunction with or in opposition to the official male church. As Susan Starr Sered has emphasized, these practices come into view only if one analyzes rituals instead of theology.[294] As the references to the consecrations show, these rituals are closely linked with rites of passage that mark important stages in the life of the family.[295] At the same time they point to the importance of the house for the cultural and social order of the rural world.

While expressions of piety such as pilgrimages and the belief in miracles, which I have mentioned here only in passing, could support visions of equality,[296] others could be used to establish coherence, hierarchy, and difference within the family and the community. That applies especially to the weekly mass and the procession, which solidified both the dominance of the clergy over the laity and the hierarchy within the community of the faithful and between it and the outside world that held a different faith.[297]

School, language, literacy

Among the 802 residents who were counted in Steinbiedersdorf/Pontpierre in 1866, there were at least 58 illiterates. While 197 individuals could only read, 391 could read and write. The level of education of the other residents could not be determined at the time.[298] Even if we could add them to those who knew how to read and write, the numbers point to a modest level of education and fit with the common notion of the "uneducated peasant" that was propagated by contemporaries.[299] Studies undertaken in the 1960s and 1970s, which were closely based on the premises of modernization theory, contributed

---

[294] Sered, *Priestess, Mother, Sacred Sister*, 6.

[295] Isambert, "Empirische Vielfalt," 195.

[296] Rebekka Habermas has noted ideas of freedom and equality in the belief in pilgrimages and miracles: *Wallfahrt und Aufruhr. Zur Geschichte des Wunderglaubens in der Frühen Neuzeit*. Historische Studien 5 (Frankfurt a. M., 1991), 73.

[297] I have not been able to find any indication of conflicts between Jews and non-Jews in Steinbiedersdorf over processions. Deventer mentions such conflicts in Corvey, *Das Abseits als sicherer Ort?*, 140f. Jews had to keep their windows and doors closed during the processions and were not allowed to live along the processional routes. Such regulations indicate that the procession was less an immediate demonstration vis-à-vis people of other faiths than an expression of a claim to spaces and paths articulated by the church.

[298] AD Mos. J 5818: Collection Richard. François Xavier Richard from Steinbiedersdorf was the archivist beginning in 1858 and has left behind in his notes extensive information about the conditions in Steinbiedersdorf in the second half of the nineteenth century.

[299] In this context one should recall the images of "good peasants" and "degenerate peasants" which long shaped the picture of the peasant in historical scholarship: Riehl, *Bürgerliche Gesellschaft*, 571ff.

to solidifying this image. They regarded the ability to read and write as an "indicator of the process of modernization and secularization that took hold of European society in the modern period and transformed it."[300] Scholars judged the ability to read and write in the eighteenth century from this retrospective and imputed a gradient between town and countryside without considering geographic, temporal, and social differentiations. Ever since the work of Hans Medick on book ownership in Laichingen, at the latest, we have known that this picture needs to be revised—that is to say, it is possible "that the nineteenth century compared to the eighteenth can be described as a time of limited literacy."[301] His notion "that this socially diffused 'literacy' of the eighteenth century owed its existence primarily to specifically religious impulses, and much less so or hardly at all to contemporaneous enlightenment endeavors,"[302] applies in Steinbiedersdorf in all likelihood especially to the upper strata of the Jewish community, among whom learning was held in high regard. Abraham Jacob, the *parnas* of the Jewish community, expressed this by setting aside, in his last will, a considerable portion of his estate to allow a rabbi and his family to live, study, and teach in his house. The rabbi and Baruch Levy were to study the Five Books of Moses, the prophets, the psalms of David, and the Talmud for an hour a day at a set time.[303]

A look at the inventory of Lion Pfalzburg, who left behind a small library of sixty-eight books, shows that other Jewish villagers were also very well read.[304] We know nothing about the titles or contents of these books, or of the two volumes which the Jewish maid Perle called her own, but it is likely that many of them—as was the case elsewhere—fell into the category of practical religious literature, many examples of which have been found in the *genizot* of rural synagogues (Landsynagogen).[305] Without specific and targeted research, we can say even less about book ownership among the Catholic villagers. The Catholic schoolmaster Anton Bardot, for example, left two books upon his death, one of which was "the most sacred book" (das Buch Allerheiligen).[306]

---

[300] Medick, *Weben und Überleben*, 447.

[301] Ibid., 450, and idem, "Buchkultur und lutherischer Pietismus. Buchbesitz, erbauliche Lektüre und religiöse Mentalität in einer ländlichen Gemeinde Württembergs am Ende der frühen Neuzeit. Laichingen 1748–1820," in Vierhaus et al., eds., *Frühe Neuzeit—Frühe Moderne*, 297–326.

[302] Medick, *Weben und Überleben*, 450.

[303] Testament of Abraham Jacob (33b).

[304] See chapter 5, n. 69.

[305] *Genizah—Hidden Legacies of the German Village Jews. Genisa—Verborgenes Erbe der deutschen Landjuden.* Exhibition catalogue edited by Falk Wiesemann (Munich, 1992), esp. 108.

[306] AD Mos. Actes judiciaires B 10049: 1763. In the inventories for Laichingen examined by Medick (1748–1829), 7.3 percent of households had fewer than five books, 0.9 percent had thirty-one or more: Medick, *Weben und Überleben*, 465.

Compared to the rest of France, the literacy rate in the Département Moselle, to which Steinbiedersdorf belonged after 1793, was unusually high on the eve of the French Revolution.[307] Eighty-nine percent of all men and 60 percent of all women were able to sign their own names in the parish register.[308] Although we do not know whether these figures apply also to the enclaves, they do reveal that there was not always a connection between a marginal location and a low rate of literacy. On the contrary: thanks to the development of schooling for girls, which was the work of school sisters, literacy among girls had made especially large strides.[309]

Even before the spread of the school orders it could happen that parents preferred to have their sons taught by a woman rather than place their education into the hands of a not very trustworthy male teacher. A pertinent remark in a visitation protocol from Racrange may reflect local peculiarities, but it does show that there were no fundamental reservations about the intellectual capacity of the "other" sex: "The schoolmaster does not keep school because his lodgings are too cramped. There is a woman who has a school, who has better lodgings than said schoolmaster, and the convention has arisen that she has the girls and he has the boys, yet the mothers and fathers of said children would rather send their sons to said woman than to the schoolmaster, saying that they would learn more from her."[310]

It would appear that in Steinbiedersdorf at least the Catholics did not place great stock in a school education. Unlike the Jewish families, who, if they were wealthy enough, even hired tutors for their sons and daughters, Catholic parents did not regularly send their children to school.[311] At the end of the seventeenth century they were still content to have their children taught for only half a year between All Saints' Day and the Feast of St. George (November 1–April 23),

---

[307] In France, the average literacy rate of men and women was 47 percent: Cabourdin, *La vie quotidienne*, 290. On literacy, especially the ability to sign one's name, to which great attention is paid in French scholarship, see the overview by Etienne François, "Alphabetisierung und Lesefähigkeit in Frankreich und Deutschland um 1800," in Helmut Berding, Etienne François, and Hans-Peter Ullmann, eds., *Deutschland und Frankreich im Zeitalter der Französischen Revolution* (Frankfurt a. M., 1989), 407–425.

[308] Alix de Rohan-Chabot, *Les écoles de campagne au XVIIIe siècle* (Nancy, 1985), 159.

[309] Within a period of a hundred years (1686–1786), it had risen in the Département Moselle from 17.92 percent to 59.71 percent: Rohan-Chabot, *Les Écoles*, 159.

[310] AD Mos., 29 J 63 and 29 J 64: Archiprêtre de Morhange. Visitation protocols.

[311] Whether these schoolmasters taught more than a basic knowledge of reading and writing is questionable, however. See Deventer, *Das Abseits als sicherer Ort?*, 108. Comparative studies on literacy show that the ability to read is usually more widespread in a society than the ability to write, and that literacy is a continuum stretching from the ability to write one's own name to the composition of long, complicated texts. In many societies, the ability of artisans and traders to write is higher than the average for their society as a whole: see the lierature surveyed by William V. Harris, *Ancient Literacy* (Cambridge, Mass. and London, 1989).

in order to have them available during the rest of the time for agricultural work. The community did not purchase a school house until 1770.[312]

The scant availability of schooling should not obscure the fact, however, that in Steinbiedersdorf there were men—and a very small number of women, as well—who knew how to write. For example, several letters have survived from the hand of Georg Court, one of the instigators of the rebellion. Pierre Barell not only corresponded in personal matters with his brother-in-law, but was also able to read through "French writings." Pierre Barell's brother Dominik Barell was the seigneurial clerk and notary; like the clerk (Greffier) Richard, he had no problems writing, in any case. The same was true for the apothecary Schaupp, who drafted a complaint for the widow Perle Levy.[313]

Almost all the men were able to write their name, but that alone says little about the significance of written culture and even less about the ability to get along in such a culture. After all, most women and men who lived in the village in the eighteenth century wrote virtually nothing. If contact with the written culture was desired or unavoidable, they had others read or write for them. In a world with a semi-oral culture, they could count on finding someone who would read written information to them or put their concerns on paper.[314] A note signed by Katharina Legendre may reveal how women and sometimes also men dealt with written messages.[315] Katharina had someone write the following for her: "When I came home my window was open. I found a small slip of paper lying there, which I had read to me, and nobody could determine from it why I was supposed to appear here."[316] It was only because she was able to have others read and write for her that Katharina Legendre was able to pursue her legal cases at the Imperial Chamber Court; there was no need for her to write anything herself.

Her regular communication with cultural mediators may have been much more important to what sort of opinion she formed on the issues, to how she saw

---

[312] AD Mos. E Dépot 553, FF 5: Gemeinderechnung.

[313] See p. 207.

[314] On semi-orality see Jean Quéniart, "Alphabetisierung und Leseverhalten der Unterschichten in Frankreich im 18. Jahrhundert," in Hans Ulrich Gumbrecht, Rolf Reichardt, and Thomas Schleich, eds., *Sozialgeschichte der Aufklärung in Frankreich*, part II: Ancien Régime, Aufklärung und Revolution 4 (Munich, 1981), 113–146, here 113; Brigitte Schlieben-Lange, *Traditionen des Sprechens. Elemente einer pragmatischen Sprachgeschichtsschreibung* (Stuttgart, 1983); and "Schriftlichkeit und Mündlichkeit in der Französischen Revolution," in Aleida Assmann, Jan Assmann, and Christof Hardmeier, eds., *Schrift und Gedächtnis. Archäologie der literarischen Kommunikation*, vol. 1 (Munich, 1983), 194–212.

[315] Hans Jacob Krämer from Denting also had a demand for payment read to him, even though he was able to write his name and was thus evidently able to read, as well: Ulbrich, "Bindung," 115.

[316] AD Mos. B Spire 11038: Acta in Sachen Nicolaus Thiel gegen Katharina Legendre, die Verlassenschaft des verstorbenenen Peter Schmidt betr., 1781.

herself and was seen by others. These cultural mediators not only read the seigneurial orders to her, they also formulated texts and put them into the "proper" language. Their work, which gave them influence and provided maneuvering room to the men and women who used them, resembled more that of a translator from the spoken into the written language than that of a clerk.[317]

We can get a sense of how texts were created from Margarete Finickel, the widow of the Steinbiedersdorf barber-surgeon, who was supposed to pay her husband's debts after his death: "I can believe that this specification is not drafted as correctly as it would have been by someone learned in the law, and the plaintiffs cannot fault me for it, since they know that I am inexperienced in reading and writing. I told the writer of this specification the content of the sentences, but I was not able to read whether everything was written down properly and in the number indicated by me."[318] Margarete Finickel, from whom several writings in the first person have survived, claims that she dictated this statement to a scribe. By noting that her ability to control what was written down was limited, she was able to use her ignorance to protect herself in a situation that was critical for her.

When it comes to their voluntary or imposed distance from written culture, women differed from men not in kind but in degree. The men of the village were for the most part also inexperienced in writing and were skeptical towards the written nature of many legal proceedings.[319] The fear of the "rebels" that "there are snares on the paper to once again catch unlearned people like themselves" could be so profound that it delayed or prevented agreements and settlements.[320]

Of course, even oral communication with the learned jurists was not easy for the peasants. For example, they complained about the lower Saxon dialect of the jurists, who "didn't quite understand the German of Lorraine."[321] These kinds of communication problems were of little consequence in daily life.[322] How else could one explain the commercial and work relationships of Christians and Jews with French business partners, or the willingness of young men from

---

[317] A brief introduction to the social history of language can be found in Peter Burke, *Küchenlatein. Sprache und Umgangssprache in der frühen Neuzeit* (Berlin, 1990), 7ff. See also Peter Burke and Roy Porter, eds., *The Social History of Language*. Cambridge Studies in Oral and Literate Culture 12 (Cambridge, 1987).

[318] AD Mos. Actes judiciaires B 10053: Acta in Sachen verschiedene Creditorum ca. Johannes Ladeners Wittib von Steinbiedersdorf pcto debiti, 1769.

[319] On the relationship of rural subjects to language and literacy see Götsch, "*Alle für einen Mann*" 284ff.

[320] LHA Koblenz 56/492, fol. 20: Pazifikationsverhandlungen in der Reichsgrafschaft Kriechingen, Bericht des Untertanenanwalts von Sachs vom 20.4.1786.

[321] LHA Koblenz 56/493, fol. 301.

[322] On communication along the linguistic border see Ulbrich, "Bedeutung der Grenzen," 147–174.

Steinbiedersdorf to enter French military service?[323] Nor would it appear that the communication with the Jewish villagers presented any problems. As we shall see, such problems were to a considerable extent limited to business dealings that were conducted in writing.

Amongst themselves, the Jews of the village spoke West Yiddish with influences from the local language.[324] Evidently it was possible to speak Yiddish or German at the rabbinical court in Metz, which was for a time responsible for the Jewish community in Steinbiedersdorf. At least Samuel Kerner notes that in the Hebrew court files, everyday circumstances were recorded in these two languages, while the French terms were adopted and transcribed into Hebrew when it came to legal or administrative language.[325] A comment by Glikl bas Judah Leib reveals that the French language was widely spoken at least within the Jewish population of Metz; Glikl noted with regret that she had no command of French, which meant that her husband had to speak for her.[326] The writing and reading of most of the legal and religious texts presupposed a knowledge of Hebrew, a language to which women had no access. When it came to the exclusion from learned discourses, the experiences of Christian and Jewish women were identical.[327] However, all of this was less important for the daily life in the village, the establishment of commercial relations, and contacts with the lord.

---

[323] That trade and commerce demanded knowledge of the language of the region is something that Pierre Mendel has also emphasized for Bionville, which was not far away and lay within the French language sphere. He notes that in a contract in 1769, a few Jews wrote their names in French (which probably means in Latin letters): Pierre Mendel, *Les juifs de Bionville en pays messin du 17ᵉ siècle à nos jours* (Metz, no year), 21.

[324] On the whole, the Steinbiedersdorf sources I studied provided little insight into the linguistic practices of the Jewish population (see, for example, p. 230). On West Yiddish see Israela Klaymann-Cohen, *Die hebräische Komponente im Westjiddischen am Beispiel der Memoiren der Glückel von Hameln.* Jiddische schtudies, vol. 4 (Hamburg, 1994). For an example of the mixing of Hebrew and German words in West Yiddish texts from the eighteenth century in a neighboring linguistic region see Hermann Arnold, *Juden in der Pfalz. Vom Leben pfälzischer Juden*, 2nd ed. (Landau, 1988), 148ff.

[325] Samuel Kerner, "Les registres inédits des tribunaux rabbiniques de Metz (1771–1779) et de Niedernai (1755–1777)," *Revue des études juives* 138 (1979): 495–497, here 496.

[326] *The Memoirs of Glückel of Hameln*, 243. However, Pierre-André Meyer writes that the language of the Jewish residents of Metz was Yiddish: *La communauté juive de Metz au XVIIIe siècle: histoire et démographie* (Nancy, 1993), 71. Gilbert Cahen suspects that only a small minority wealthy enough to hire tutors spoke French: "Les juifs dans la région lorraine des origines à nos jours," *Le pays lorraine* 53 (1972): 55–82, here 72. The question arises whether French was spoken in the Jewish upper class or whether Glikl's comment was referring to her communication with non-Jews. The inclination of young Jews to learn the French language gave the rabbi of Metz, Jonathan Eybeschütz, cause for complaint, because he believed that the study of Torah was being neglected: Samuel Kerner, *La vie quotidienne de la communauté juive de Metz au dix-huitième siècle. Thèse de doctorat de 3eme Cycle* (Paris, 1979), 215.

[327] On Yiddish as a sign of a gender-specific asymmetry of language see Gabriele

In a predominantly oral culture, a significant portion of communication takes place through nonverbal signs. Especially in the eighteenth century, with its theatrical display of power, language was highly ritualized and incorporated nonverbal forms of communication.[328] The nature of a greeting, the act of threatening someone with an agricultural implement, or the locking of houses were all unmistakable messages.[329] Of course, not everything could be expressed in the language of gestures. Given the increasing bureaucratization and the importance of a legal culture that was largely based on written texts, neither women nor men could dispense entirely with writing. The essential difference to other periods lies not only in the number of things that were put down in writing, but also in the manner in which the texts were created.

Writing was a profession, and literacy was embedded within a functioning system—based on a division of labor—for the production of texts and communication. Not only agents of the lord, paid legal experts, and wandering notaries and clerics, but also individual villagers, male and female, who were not necessarily of high social status, were able to read and draft last wills or marriage contracts, accounts, and notes of indebtedness, petitions, or complaints.

Much was also dealt with orally. Let us recall that the priest sent his housekeeper to a mother to find out if her child had already taken communion. We learn from a witness in 1790 that women could also be informed about matters of debts: "But after his return he always heard his mother and sister say that the plaintiff's mother-in-law had lent a lot of money to the community and at times had suffered losses."[330] The role of women as witnesses and plaintiffs becomes visible in the reconstruction of women's lives. Once again it is Katharina Legendre, with her tireless battle in various courts, who shows us that it makes little sense to draw clear boundaries between an oral and a written culture. Jean Quéniart has observed that "in a society composed largely of

Jancke, "Die Sichronot (Memoiren) der jüdischen Kauffrau Glückel von Hameln zwischen Autobiographie, Geschichtsschreibung und religiösem Lehrtext. Geschlecht, Religion und Ich in der Frühen Neuzeit," in Magdalene Heuser, ed., *Autobiographien von Frauen. Beiträge zu ihrer Geschichte.* Untersuchungen zur deutschen Literaturgeschichte 85 (Tübingen, 1996), 92–134, here 95f.

[328] Wolfgang Kaschuba, *Volkskultur zwischen feudaler und bürgerlicher Gesellschaft. Zur Geschichte eines Begriffs und seiner gesellschaftlichen Wirklichkeit* (Frankfurt a. M., 1988), esp. 41ff. For the meaning of the theatrical style of rule in the eighteenth century and the theatrical symbolism in popular unrests see E. P. Thompson, "Patrician Society, Plebeian Culture," *Journal of Social History* 7 (1973/74): 385–405.

[329] For example, Silke Göttsch, in her work on the rebelliousness of serfs in Schleswig-Holstein, was able to show the extent to which peasant tools such as pitchforks, sticks, and axes were media of communication with the lord: "Zur Konstruktion schichtenspezifischer Wirklichkeit," 443–452.

[330] AD Mos. Actes judiciaires B 10080: Johannes Bompernetz ca Nicolas Bommersbach pcto debiti, 1790.

illiterates," a few individuals are sufficient "to pass on orally information that was for the most part written down, information remembered all the better because one knew that one had only one's memory to rely on."[331] The inability to write therefore did not mean that a person was excluded from written culture.

This becomes especially clear if one considers the frequent recourse to the court, where—as the first-person documents show—oral forms of communication and writing were very closely interrelated.

The right to bring a complaint and the knowledge that there was someone who could do the writing was probably a crucial element in the individual integration of women into the political-legal framework. This experience was not reserved exclusively for the well off, as we learn from the example of Nanette Schilling, who filed a complaint against her employer because he had failed to pay his debts and "had called her a whore in anger and slapped and kicked her." Nanette Schilling first presented her case to Dominik Barell, "on oath and in tears." Barell wrote a report for her and thus set in motion a complaint by the public prosecutor (Fiskal). The Fiskal firmly rebuffed the attempt by her employer to block her complaint to the court because she was poor, arguing that equal rights existed for servant and master. In the records, these thoughts are even placed into the maid's mouth: "The plaintiff responded to this that she was a subject just like the defendant, and that she was therefore not obligated to furnish a guarantor for the complaint she has rightfully brought."[332] Even though the defendant's wife, who was summoned as a witness, was supposedly more on the side of her husband than on the side of truth, Nannette Schilling won a favorable verdict, and with it the feeling that justice was possible even for a poor day laborer, at least in cases where her interests coincided with those of the lord. As long as this system for the production of texts and communication functioned, the possibility of participating in legal and economic life was not necessarily tied to formal knowledge; rather, what mattered was the ability to mobilize supporters.

This microhistorical examination of the structural conditions confirms and expands upon the findings from the biographical excursus into the lives of the village women. The multiplicity of individual worlds that became apparent in these life stories corresponds to the complexity of the regulatory systems that structured daily life and determined gender roles and gender attributions, which in turn influenced daily life. We have found these regulatory systems in the law as well as in economic life, religion, and communication.

The existence side by side of partly complementary, partly contradictory principles points to an ordering system grounded in plurality. It allowed individuals to be flexible in responding to changes, but it also demanded from them a

---

[331] Quéniart, "Alphabetisierung," esp. 133ff.
[332] AD Mos. Actes judiciaires B 10074: Fisc. in Sachen Nannette Schilling ca. Louis Metzinger, 1759.

high capacity to engage in conflict. Once we accept this notion of a pluralistic construction of reality,[333] it also becomes possible to examine Christian-Jewish relations in a way that goes beyond the usual alternatives of integration or segregation.[334]

---

[333] On this concept, which is borrowed from the postmodernism discussion, see, for example, Wolfgang Welsch, *Unsere postmoderne Moderne*, 3rd ed. (Weinheim, 1991), esp. 36ff.

[334] Battenberg, *Zwischen Integration und Segregation*, esp. 428ff., creates the impression, however, that the demonstration of Christian-Jewish relations is conceivable only in a—Christian-hegemonial—integration model.

CHAPTER FIVE

A SHIFT IN PERSPECTIVE: THE HISTORY OF THE JEWISH COMMUNITY*

Steinbiedersdorf was the most important Jewish village in the Imperial County of Kriechingen.[1] The census in 1786 counted one hundred thirty-five Jewish residents: they made up 42 percent of all Jews in the County of

---

* Since the original publication of this book in German, a series of important studies on the history of the Jews in Germany and eastern France have appeared. Here I would like to mention the following: Sabine Ullmann, *Nachbarschaft und Konkurrenz. Juden und Christen in den Dörfern der Markgrafschaft Burgau 1650–1750* (Göttingen, 1999); idem, "Poor jewish families in early modern rural Swabia," in Laurence Fontaine and Jürgen Schlumbohm, eds., *Household strategies for survival, 1600–2000* (Cambridge, 2000), 93–113; and Robert Liberles, "An der Schwelle zur Moderne: 1618–1780," trans. Alice Jakubeit, in Marion Kaplan, ed., *Geschichte des jüdischen Alltags in Deutschland. Vom 17. Jahrhundert bis 1945* (München, 2003), 20–122. Of particular importance for the interpretation of the history of the Jewish community in Steinbiedersdorf were the findings of a project on court Jews carried out by Friedrich Battenberg and Rotraud Ries. Their work reveals how important also the court Jews of the small and microterritories were, most of whom functioned as court suppliers. See Rotraud Ries, "Status und Lebensstil—Jüdische Familien der sozialen Oberschicht zur Zeit Glikls," in Monika Richarz, ed., *Die Hamburger Kauffrau Glikl. Jüdische Existenz in der Frühen Neuzeit* (Hamburg, 2001), 208–306; and Rotraud Ries and Friedrich Battenberg, eds., *Hofjuden, Ökonomie und Interkulturalität. Die Wirtschaftselite im 18. Jahrhundert* (Hamburg, 2002). Stimulated by these studies, I have been able to work out additional aspects of the history of the Jewish families of Steinbiedersdorf, especially the formation of networks and the connections to the Alsace. On this see my essay "Eheschließung und Netzwerkbildung am Beispiel der jüdischen Gesellschaft im deutsch-französischen Grenzgebiet (18. Jahrhundert)," in Christophe Duhamelle and Jürgen Schlumbohm, *Eheschließungen im Europa des 18. Jahrhunderts. Muster und Strategien* (Göttingen, 2003), 315–340. Particularly helpful to my effort at providing further contextualization were Bernard Lyon-Caen, Pierre André Meyer, Jacques Blamont, and other members of the Cercle Généalogie Juive, descendants of Steinbiedersdorf Jews who made their genealogical data and numerous copies of sources available to me, none of which I was able to consult during my work on the original German edition of this book.

[1] The phrase "Jewish village" (*Judendorf*) is used here in the way Utz Jeggle uses it, as a technical term for villages with a synagogue community: Jeggle, *Judendörfer in Württemberg* (Tübingen, 1967), 7.

Kriechingen and 18 percent of the village population.[2] Most were poor and made a living through trading or small-scale money-lending; others, like sixteen-year-old Bremel, sought "to earn a meager livelihood by sewing, spinning, and working," or, like eighteen-year-old Oury, "ran errands" for others to get some money.[3] A few wealthy individuals had also chosen to live in Steinbiedersdorf, among them "the rich Jew Abraham," who had loaned substantial amounts of money to the count and his many officials.[4]

During his fifty-seven years in office, Abraham Jacob held the post of *parnas* (head) of the Jewish community in Steinbiedersdorf until his appointment as chief *parnas*[5] of all Jewish communities in the County of Kriechingen. Abraham Jacob's second wife was Sara Isaak Goldschmied, the widow of Raphael Lipman of Bouxviller[6] and the daughter of Isaak Kassel of Frankfurt.[7] This wealthy city woman had brought a lot of money, pearls, and diamonds into the remote village, along with Torah ornaments (*kele kodesch*) such as a hanging curtain (*parokhet*) and horizontal top piece (*kapporet*) for the ark, and a Torah mantle. All three pieces were embroidered in gold and silver.[8] These items were to remain in the synagogue as long as Sara Isaak Goldschmied lived in Steinbiedersdorf.[9]

---

[2] In all, 2,818 residents were counted in 1,786 in the villages of the County of Kriechingen that were enclaves in France, among them 318 Jewish men and women: AD Mos. 10 F 69: Tableau général de la population de la constitution du comté de Créhange, 1786.

[3] AD Mos. Actes judiciaires B 10073: Acta in Sachen der Jüdin Gelle, dermalen zu Steinbiedersdorf sich aufhaltend, ctra. Jacob Meyer Cahens Sohn von da, Gembel Cahen, pcto impregnationis ac satisfactionis, 1784.

[4] LHA Koblenz 56/1801: In Sachen sämtlicher Untertanen und Dorfschaften der Grafschaft Kriechingen gegen Herrn Grafen von Wied-Runkel, 1763, fol. 208.

[5] On the office of the *parnas* see p. 183.

[6] LA Saarbrücken Mi 35/36 Collection Steinthal des Bestandes des Leo Baeck-Instituts: 3 E 6019, 111–113. Ehekontrakt zwischen Bernhard Liebmann, ehelichem Sohn des verstorbenen Raphaël und der noch lebenden Mutter Sara Isaak Goldschmied, der zweiten Ehefrau des Judenvorstehers Abraham Jacob, und Fromet Oster Levy von Kriechingen, der Tochter des verstorbenenen Judenvorstehers.

[7] Ibid.; on the Goldschmied-Kassel family see Alexander Dietz, *Stammbuch der Frankfurter Juden. Geschichtliche Mitteilungen über die Frankfurter jüdischen Familien von 1349–1849* (Frankfurt a. M., 1907), 115–121. Dietz unfortunately limited himself to recording the male family members. The married daughters of Glikl bas Judah Leib also used the name Goldschmied when they signed documents for Christian notaries in France (Davis, *Women on the Margins*, 8). The names varied, though, depending on whether they were written in Hebrew or Latin characters (ibid., 222, note 6).

[8] LA Saarbrücken Mi 35/36 Collection Steinthal des Bestandes des Leo Baeck-Instituts: 3 E 6019, 111–113: Ehekontrakt.

[9] The Torah scroll is the most important Jewish religious object. The parchment sheets containing the text of the Torah (Five Books of Moses) were and are sewn into a scroll, wound around two wooden rods, tied with a binder, and covered and protected with a mantle: Wiesemann, ed., *Genizah*, 80ff. On the custom of presenting the synagogue with gifts of Torah mantles and decorations see de Vries, *Jüdische Riten*, 20, and Gilbert Cahen, ed., *Catalogues: Les Juifs Lorrains: Du Ghetto à la Nation 1721–1871*

This dowry of Sara Isaak Goldschmied, consisting of money and jewelry as well as religious objects, was not only a symbol of the wealth and standing of a Jewish family living in the countryside, it is also a reminder that marriage and family were the central focal points for the opportunities and risks in the lives of women.

Unlike Sara Isaak Goldschmied, the best Bremel could hope for was a marriage in very modest circumstances. As an unmarried, poor Jewish woman living in the countryside she stood in virtually every respect at the lower end of the social hierarchy: as a poor woman vis-à-vis the rich, as an unmarried woman vis-à-vis the married, as a country girl vis-à-vis the city dwellers, but also as a Jew vis-à-vis the Christians, and as a woman vis-à-vis men.

Within Bremel's immediate world, Abraham Jacob stood on the uppermost rung of the social ladder: he was by far the richest man in the village; he held a political office that brought him power, honor, and a certain proximity to the ruler; and he had a wife, children, servants and maids over whom he could command, and money to fund an endowment intended to last for all eternity. And yet in spite of his wealth and power, Abraham Jacob had one experience in common with Bremel: his presence in the village was not based on law but on an act of seigneurial favor, which meant that he could be expelled any day. In this regard he stood even below the Christian village poor, to whom he left charitable bequests in his last will.[10] Like many of his coreligionists, Abraham Jacob had transmuted this experience into religious terms.[11] In his pious foundation he also remembered poor Jewish girls like Bremel: their chances for marriage were to be improved through the grant of a small sum of money, however modest.[12]

The feeling of insecurity shared by Abraham and Bremel may have reinforced the cohesion within the Jewish community of the village, though it did not level out social differences. When S. J. Cohen—who stands for many similar voices—emphasized in the first issue of the magazine *Sulamith* that the calling of women was "to be wives to their husband, mothers to their children, heads of their households," it takes only a little sociobiographical data to show that this allocation of roles meant very different things to Sara Isaak Goldschmied and to Bremel.[13] What is more, is such a description of social roles even adequate to delineate the spheres within which Jewish women were active?

(Metz, 1990), 18ff. For a general overview see "Torah ornaments" in *Encyclopaedia Judaica*, vol. 15 (Jerusalem, 1972), 1255–1258.

[10] Testament of Abraham Jacob: see Appendix (43). Appended to the last will is a list of the poor in the parish of Kriechingen, which contains the names of eighteen men and twenty-four women.

[11] Ibid., (27). Katz, *Tradition and Crisis*, 14, has pointed to the interaction between the temporary right of residence in a Christian community and religious self-understanding.

[12] Testament of Abraham Jacob: see Appendix XXIII Q (45).

[13] S. J. Cohen, "Über die religiöse Bildung der Frauenzimmer jüdischen Glaubens," *Sulamith* 1 (1806), 473–490.

A look at the memoirs of Glikl bas Judah Leib teaches us something different: Glikl was not only a wife and mother but also an unusually capable businesswoman who was involved in trade and credit operations and set up a shop in Hamburg for the manufacture of stockings.[14] And she was not the only Jewish woman who earned money and was active outside of the house.[15] Her memoirs leave no doubt that one cannot adequately explain the world of Jewish women by invoking the religious law and the patriarchal Jewish tradition, which called for a strict separation of gender roles and restricted the circle of a woman's activities to home, children, and family.[16] Although the Jewish women of Steinbiedersdorf have not left behind any written records, it is possible to reconstruct sections of their life stories. Even if this is done chiefly on the basis of protocols written during legal proceedings in non-Jewish courts, these stories are part of the still largely unexplored context of the Jewish community. In an effort to make at least the contours of this community visible, I will retrace the history of Steinbiedersdorf, this time from the perspective of the Jewish members of the community.

Settlement conditions and demographic trends

Steinbiedersdorf is only a few hours from Metz, where a respected Jewish community had evolved under the protection of the French kings.[17] That this city in eastern France possessed a certain attraction for members of the Ashkenazic Jewish upper class is revealed by the list of its rabbis, who came from well-known families in Prague, Vienna, or Cracow.[18] The immigrants in Metz included

---

[14] Davis, *Women on the Margins*, 13.

[15] One could list many other examples beside those mentioned by Davis. An incident mentioned by Deventer, *Das Abseits als sicherer Ort?*, 66, makes clear that these activities outside the home concerned not only work and business: when Jewish men were incarcerated in Höxter in 1648, the wives delegated two women who, in the name of "all Jewish wives," lodged a complaint with the Vogt in Corvey.

[16] For some time, Jewish women's studies has been calling upon scholars to examine precisely this fact and to uncover the multilayered nature of gender constructions (see Introduction, notes 130–137), but as of now only a few empirical studies exist. Many studies that deal with women, marriage, and sexuality are ahistorical. For the most part they orient themselves toward the Bible, the Talmud, and rabbinic norms, and emphasize the high esteem in which women were held in the Jewish religion and the special religious significance of marriage as a relationship of partners with a distribution of complementary roles: see, for example, Herweg, *Die jüdische Mutter*; Mendell Lewittes, *Jewish Marriage. Rabbinic Law, Legend, and Custom* (Northvale, 1994); Seymour J. Cohen, *The Holy Letter. A Study in Jewish Sexual Morality* (Northvale, 1976). Judith Frishman has pointed to misogynistic aspects of the Jewish tradition: "Als Mann und Frau erschuf sie sie. Feminismus und Tradition," in Andreas Nachama, Julius H. Schoeps, and Edward van Voolen, eds., *Jüdische Lebenswelten. Essays* (Berlin, 1991), 86–107.

[17] Meyer, *La communauté juive de Metz*, 30ff.

[18] Roger Berg, *Histoire du rabbinat français (XVIe–XXe siècle)* (Paris, 1992), 20f.; Meyer, *La communauté juive de Metz*, 67.

Glikl bas Judah Leib, whose memoirs remind us of how insecure the foundation was on which the Jews of Metz had built their renown and wealth.[19] Glikl had taken the advice of her son-in-law who lived in Metz and had married the widower Reb Herz Levy, who had been presented to her as an honorable Jew and a learned and wealthy man. Her decision was motivated by the hope that she might spend her "last years in a pious community, for Metz had the name of such in those days . . . and do somewhat too for the good of my soul."[20]

That there had been anti-Semitic excesses in the area of Metz in the second half of the seventeenth century,[21] that the parlement of Metz had sentenced a Jew from Boulay to death at the stake in 1760 on a charge of ritual murder,[22] and that her son-in-law's grandfather had been accused of blasphemy—none of this could dissuade Glikl bas Judah Leib from her plan to move to Metz.[23] After all, Metz was a Jewish community that stood under the special protection of the French king.[24] Following the exodus of the Huguenots after the revocation of the Edict of Nantes, greater tolerance was extended to the Jews in Metz than had previously been the case.[25] Those who had grown rich cultivated a luxurious lifestyle, to the extent that was possible in the constrained conditions of the Jewish quarter, though they also saw to the expansion of the community's religious and cultural life. In 1704, for example, Abraham Schwab and his wife bequeathed to the Jewish community their house and a larger sum of money to establish a Talmud school.[26]

---

[19] Glikl's husband had been ruined by creditors and in the process also lost a large portion of his wife's dowry, as a result of which Glikl was for a time in straitened financial circumstances. She suffered especially as a widow, as long as she was unwilling to move in with one of her children: *Memoirs*, 264ff. On Glikl's time in Metz see Davis, *Women on the Margins*, 15ff.

[20] *Memoirs*, 226. Metz was the city of the Torah: it was called Ha-maqom, the city of the divine residence: Berg, *Histoire du rabbinat*, 20.

[21] Cahen, ed., *Catalogue: Les Juifs Lorrains*, 28ff.

[22] Patricia Behre, "Raphael Levy—'A Criminal in the Mouth of the People,'" *Religion* 23 (1993): 19–44.

[23] Davis, *Women at the Margins*, 17, points out that Glikl would have known about these events for the simple reason that when she came to Metz, the Jews of the town were still fasting on the twenty-fifth of Tevet to commemorate the death of their innocent martyr.

[24] The man who was condemned to die at the stake, Raphael Levy, came from Boulay, which was part of the Duchy of Lorraine. That is probably the reason why the Jews of Metz referred to him as an outsider. Evidently they did not support Levy very vigorously. It was only when their own situation deteriorated following the execution of Levy that the Jews of Metz turned to the French king with a supplication that mentioned this incident. I believe that the interpretation by Behre, "Raphael Levy," should take greater cognizance of the political background, which was significant also for the Jewish population.

[25] Two-thirds of the money-changers and bankers in Metz were Huguenots: Meyer, *La communauté juive de Metz*, 31.

[26] Ibid., 53. This occurrence reminds us of Abraham Jacob's donation for the establishment of a Talmud school nearly seventy years later.

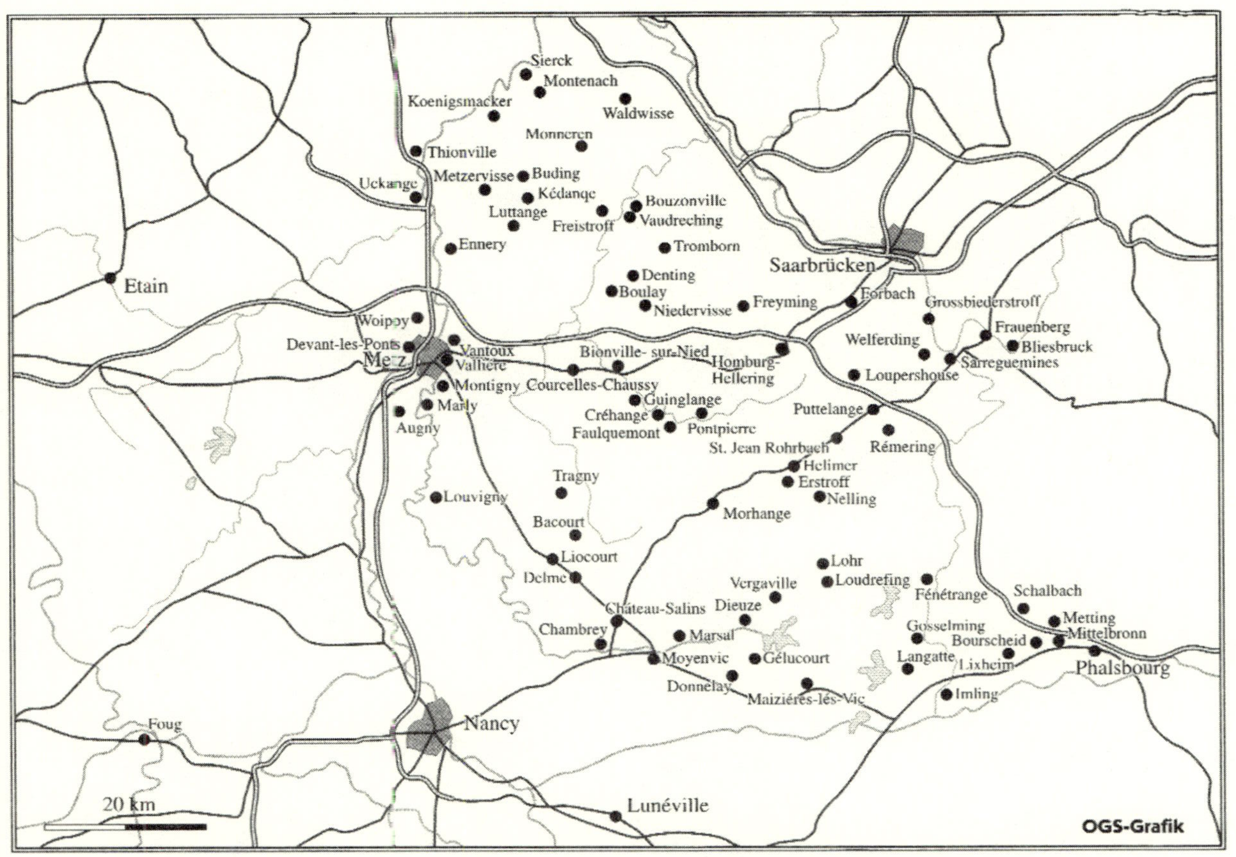

Map 4. Jewish Communities in the territory surrounding Steinbiedersdorf

The connections and skills of the Jewish traders and moneylenders were in demand not only in the garrison city of Metz, but also in the immediate neighboring border region.[27] After the wars of the seventeenth century, immigration was promoted in German Lorraine, in the enclaves of the empire, and along the route de France by the financial and commercial needs of the military, the smaller local and territorial lords, and the small farmers and rural population.[28] The number of Jewish immigrants living in the border region grew slowly in the seventeenth century and then surged at the beginning of the eighteenth.[29] In Metz, the Jewish population more than tripled between 1650 and 1717, primarily through immigration from the Rhineland and the surrounding villages.[30] After that the community grew more slowly. As Pierre-André Meyer was able to show in his careful demographic analysis of Metz, the size of the Jewish population at the end of the eighteenth century was only 17 percent larger than it had been at the beginning, while the size of the Christian population had grown by 36 percent in the same period. This finding banishes into the realm of myth the claim, circulated at the end of the eighteenth century, that the Jewish population was growing especially rapidly compared to its Christian counterpart.[31]

The findings with respect to the rural population are similar. Not only Jewish men and women, but Christians of both confessions also, came from far away to build a new life for themselves in the region devastated by wars.[32] In the Imperial County of Kriechingen, the growth in the Jewish population was comparable to that in the Christian population: at the end of the seventeenth cen-

---

[27] However, the political background conditions in the regions belonging to France, in the Duchy of Lorraine, and in the principalities of the Holy Roman Empire remained very different for a long time yet. Reservations about the Jews existed especially in the Duchy of Lorraine. In 1721, all Jews of Lorraine who had immigrated in 1689 were forced to leave the land. Seventy-three families were left, four-fifths of which lived in the northeastern part of the duchy, chiefly in its German-speaking part. They were allowed to practice their religion to a certain extent: Guy Cabourdin, *Les temps modernes: de la paix de Westphalie à la fin de l'Ancien régime.* Encyclopédie illustrée de la Lorraine. Histoire de la Lorraine 3.2 (Nancy, 1990), 116.

[28] Robert Anchel, *Les juifs de France* (Paris, 1946), 176; Gilbert Cahen, "La région lorraine," in Bernhard Blumenkranz, ed., *Histoire des Juifs en France* (Toulouse, 1971), 77–136, here 83f.

[29] However, there were significant local differences. Many Jews lived in lesser German states such as territories of the immediate nobility of the empire. We have hardly any information on the period before the Thirty Years' War. Jews are attested in the County of Kriechingen in the late sixteenth and at the beginning of the seventeenth century: AD Mos. 10 F 80: Beschwerde der Juden, die keine bürgerlichen Lasten tragen wollen; 1563, Streit wegen Wucher, 1620.

[30] Cahen, "Les juifs dans le région lorraine," 64.

[31] For details see the work of Meyer, *La communauté juive de Metz*, esp. 27ff.

[32] The immigration is partly documented in the parish registers, which also record Protestants, to the extent that they converted. On Steinbiedersdorf: AD Mos. I Mic. E.C. 553 Pontpierre: 1680–1793.

tury, 41 Jewish families were counted here,[33] but by 1775 the number had risen to 92.[34] We can provide more detailed information for Steinbiedersdorf: between the middle of the seventeenth and the end of the eighteenth century, the Jewish population more than doubled, from more than 30 to 69 residents.[35] In 1708, 7 Jewish families lived there. At that time the Jews, accounting for 69 residents, already made up one-sixth of the population. The number of Jewish households rose to 10 in 1724,[36] 17 in 1737,[37] 19 in 1739,[38] 30 in 1763,[39] and 32 in 1775. In the years that followed, the number of Jewish households stabilized between 28 and 32.[40] Because, as was already mentioned, new criteria for recording the population in administrative and fiscal terms were presumably devised in the eighteenth century, the increase in households in no way reflects the real population increase: while the number of households increased four-fold, the number of registered residents barely doubled.[41] The 135 Jewish men, women, and children who lived in Steinbiedersdorf in 1786 were grouped into 28 households, which now longer contained 8 or 9 members on average as they had at the beginning of the century, but only 4 or 5.[42] At 18 percent, their share of the village population was marginally higher than it had been at the beginning of the century.[43]

Surely not all Jewish women and men remained in the village. While marriage was the reason for some to move away, others, unable to find housing or

---

[33] LA Saarbrücken M 35 Collection Steinthal des Bestandes des Leo Baeck-Instituts.

[34] Cahen, "La region lorraine," 95ff. There were five villages with Jewish minorities in the Imperial County of Kriechingen: in 1775, 26 households were counted in Kriechingen, 32 in Steinbiedersdorf, 20 in Saarwellingen, 8 in Denting, and 6 in Niederwies: AD Mos. 10 F 373: 1775.

[35] LA Saarbrücken M 35 Collection Steinthal des Bestandes des Leo Baeck-Instituts.

[36] AD Mos. F 428: Droit de protection des juifs. Affaire relative à la commune de Pontpierre.

[37] AD Mos. F 428: Droit de protection des juifs. Livre des comptes concernant Pontpierre, Denting et Niedervisse, 1737–1739. At that time the territorial lord received 96 pounds in protection money.

[38] Ibid., 1739.

[39] LHA Koblenz 56/1301: In Sachen sämtlicher Untertanen und Dorfschaften der Grafschaft Kriechingen gegen Herrn Grafen von Wied-Runkel, Mandatis.

[40] AD Mos. 10 F 69: Statistiques générales concernant la comté de Créhange, 1785.

[41] As Meyer was able to show for Metz, the simple question of whether widows should be counted as separate households already altered the statistics considerably: Meyer, *La communauté juive de Metz*, 29.

[42] In Lorraine at the time of the rule of Stanislas (that is, in the first half of the eighteenth century), the housefather, his children, and all male offspring were counted, provided they lived under a single roof: Cahen, "Les juifs dans la région lorraine," 70. It would appear that in the County of Kriechingen the separate household was a criterion when counting the Jews, although one must always take into consideration the specific purpose of the statistical recording.

[43] In 1786, one hundred thirty-five of seven hundred forty-five residents were Jewish: AD Mos. 10 F 69.

a livelihood, would have looked for work elsewhere or joined the vagrant army of Jewish beggars.[44] Only the well off would have been able to settle in Metz, the French capital of Askhenazic Jewry.[45] The others had to remain in the country and try to create there an environment that also served their religious needs. Once the Jewish population had been given freedom to settle anywhere after the French Revolution, a large-scale rural exodus took place.[46] As early as 1791, the *parnas* Bernard Lipman, Abraham Jacob's stepson and successor in office, left Steinbiedersdorf with his wife, Frommet Oster Levy, to take up residence in Metz.[47] Others followed his example. Henceforth economic and sociocultural opportunities determined the place of residence, not social and political acceptance.[48] In the middle of the nineteenth century, only one out of fifteen residents of Steinbiedersdorf was still Jewish (previously, one out of five).[49]

Living conditions, age at marriage, household structure

Jewish families who sought to settle in the German-French border region at the beginning of the eighteenth century seem to have found favorable conditions in some villages and towns of the Imperial County of Kriechingen. At least that is how one could interpret the complaint by Gaspard de la Croix,

---

[44] On Jewish beggars and vagrants see Rudolf Glanz, *Geschichte des niederen jüdischen Volkes in Deutschland. Ein Studie über historisches Gaunertum, Bettelwesen und Vagantentum* (New York, 1968).

[45] Immigration into Metz was limited more strongly by the Jewish community than by the French king. As Meyer, *La communauté juive de Metz*, 174f., was able to show, the leaders of the community, in particular, were concerned to admit only individuals with a certain degree of wealth, who could pay a share of the rising taxes. In 1780 the head of the Jewish community complained about the growing number of "Vagabonds escrocs." Individuals who gave shelter to vagabonds were to be punished, a measure that was difficult to enforce given the duty of charity.

[46] In the département Moselle, 6,506 Jews were counted in 1808, which indicates that initially many remained in the cities of the region: Gildas Bernard et al., *Les familles juives en France. XVIe siècle–1815* (Paris, 1990), 57.

[47] Cahen, ed., *Catalogue: Les Juifs Lorrains*, nos. 349–350. One of the grandsons of Bernard Lipman was chief rabbi of Metz and later of Lille.

[48] Utz Jeggle made a similar observation about economic opportunities in Württemberg, where legal equality for the Jews was followed by a strong rural exodus: Jeggle, *Judendörfer in Württemberg*, 7. At look at the community of Niederweis, which was also part of the County of Kriechingen, suggests that sociocultural reasons—the presence of a sufficiently large Jewish community, a synagogue, and a cemetery—might have played a role in the choice of a new place to live: here the percentage of Jews rose continuously in the nineteenth century to as high as 38 percent: Jean Daltroff, *Les Juifs de Niedervisse. Naissance, épanouissement et déclin d'une communauté* (Sarreguemines, 1992).

[49] In 1840, 81 of 900 residents (9 percent) were still Jewish; in 1846 it was 84 of 929 (9 percent), and by 1866 it had declined to 54 of 802 (6.7 percent): AD Mos. J 5818, 17 J 44, No. 15: Etat nominatif de tous les individus israélites domiciliés dans la commune de Pontpierre, 1840; 17 J 45: Etat nominatif de la population israélite de la commune de Pontpierre, 1846.

the priest of Kriechingen, who wrote in 1716: "The intercourse (la conversation) with the Jews is so extensive that the Christians . . . rent to them not only houses, but also rooms within their houses . . . One Jew bought a house of his own, which he renovated."[50]

A document from 1719 suggests that the situation in Steinbiedersdorf could have been similar to Kriechingen. At that time, Nikolaus Krämer had leased his house together with his hemp garden to a Jewish family and was living with his father-in-law.[51] A few years later each of the ten Jewish families in Steinbiedersdorf is said to have occupied a house in Steinbiedersdorf.[52] Over the next decades, the living situation deteriorated for many. Only the wealthier among the Jewish families of Steinbiedersdorf could acquire houses of their own, which they occupied themselves or leased to others.[53] Last wills and inventories convey an impression of the size and furnishings of these houses. Although things were not quite as luxurious as in the houses of banking families in Metz described by Glikl,[54] these homes do attest to the existence of a rural upper-class culture that set itself apart from the lifestyle of the Jewish lower class and the majority of the Christian rural population.[55]

Those who did not own their own house did not necessarily live in straitened circumstances. At least some of them had the opportunity to rent or lease houses and sometimes even land, occasionally making use of business contacts to do so. For example, in 1772 Bernard Lipman bought the house of Georg Becker in Borg when the latter moved away to settle in Dorrweiler, his wife's birthplace.[56] By 1775, Bernard Lipman was already among the few Jewish homeowners.

An overview of house ownership is provided by the Steinbiedersdorf Declaration of 1775, which recorded the real estate holdings as well as the owners of the

---

[50] AD Mos. 29 J 69: Fond de l'évêché: Visitation 1699, Créhange.

[51] AD Mos. Actes judiciaires B 10041: Fiscalis entgegen Nicolas Bernard und Consorten, 1719.

[52] AD Mos. 10 F 428: Droits de protection des juifs, 1724. At that time the protection money had been auctioned to an administrator, who tried to maximize his profit. Among other things he came into Steinbiedersdorf and had the Jewish houses seized: Supplik v. 19.5.1724.

[53] A complaint that the members of the community had to muzzle their dogs, while the Jews were not required to, shows that Jewish houses, like Christian ones, were guarded by dogs. AD Mos. Actes judiciaires B 10081: Plaids annaux, 1767. The Jews were subsequently ordered in the synagogue to keep their dogs at home during the day and to muzzle them at night.

[54] See, for example, *Memoirs*, 240f.

[55] Deventer, *Das Abseits als sicherer Ort?*, 134, has also noted for Corvey that there were favorable conditions in the eighteenth century for the emergence of a wealthy Jewish upper class in the countryside. Kasper-Holtkotte, *Juden im Aufbruch*, 33, however, has argued that "in principle we can say that the Jewish population was poorer than the non-Jewish population."

[56] AD Mos. Actes judiciaires B 10057: 1772.

104.5 houses of the village.[57] Eleven houses belonged to Jewish residents, 86.5 to the Christian residents. The remaining 7 houses were owned by the lordship, the church, and nonresidents. The Jewish residents thus owned 10.5 percent of the houses, which was below their population ratio of 18 percent. The Christians owned 83 percent of the real estate, which corresponded almost precisely to their ratio of the village population.

Yet these numbers say little without a look at the distribution of wealth. Fourfifths of all Christian heads of household listed in the declaration—married men, widowers, widows, unmarried women, unmarried men—had some form of home ownership: the share of individuals ranged from one-eighth of a house (Sebastian Gaspar, Johannes Groß, Jacob June, the single woman Madgalene Decker) to two and a half houses (widow Margarete Decker). Among Jewish families, barely a third could call a house or a share of a house their own. They included Abraham Jacob, who owned two houses in Steinbiedersdorf along with landholdings "in imperial, French, and Lorrainese territories."[58]

Many of the Jewish residents presumably lived in very cramped conditions. Among them must have been the four or five families who lived in Louis Keller's house and quarreled with their neighbors because of the cramped living situation.[59]

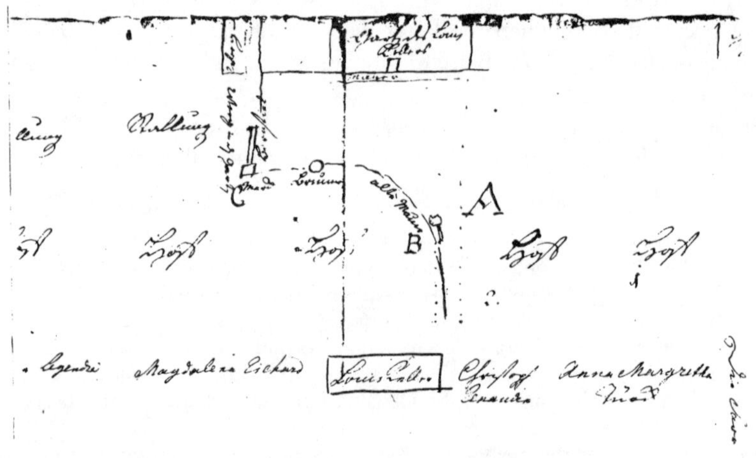

Illustration 2: Plan of the house of Louis Keller in which four or five Jewish families lived in cramped proximity to Christian families[60]

---

[57] AD Mos. 10 F 429: Steinbiedersdorfer Deklaration, 1775.

[58] AD Mos. Actes judiciaires Pontpierre B 10062: Testament von Abraham Jacob, 1775.

[59] See p. 251f.

[60] AD Mos. Actes judiciaires B 10054: Fiscalis Amtsankläger gg. Peter Finickel wegen eines von ihm dem Juden Louis May geschlagenen Pferds, 1755. On the Christian neighbors see p. 77, table 1.

Those who took up residence with widows who were renting out living space to pay debts or secure their livelihood are also unlikely to have encountered large quarters. Rather, judging from the above-mentioned complaint by the priest of Kriechingen, we should assume that at least some widows rented single rooms in their dwellings to Jewish neighbors. Other Jewish villagers found space with their parents or children. These included Malquem, one of Abraham Jacob's daughters, who in 1750 had married Heym Levi Meringen, the son of Berman Levy Meringen of Trier. In the *ketubah* (marriage contract), Abraham Jacob guaranteed the couple that they could live in his house for two years free of charge, and another two years at the cost of their living expenses.[61] Numerous such wedding contracts are still extant.[62]

Jacob Katz has emphasized that having newlyweds live in the house of parents or in-laws provided an opportunity to prepare the couples, who had married young because of religious law, for life outside.[63] However, we should not exaggerate the influence that religious rules propagating early marriages had on the marriage age.[64] If they had any influence at all, it would appear that richer families were guided by them, external conditions permitting.[65] Meyer's study of Metz, which is based on a broad range of demographic material, has shown

---

[61] AD Mos. E 3 6016, fol. 237: Ehe zwischen Heym Levy Meringen, Sohn des Berman Levy Meringen, aus Trier und Malquem, Tochter des Jacob Abraham, Kaufmann, von Steinbiedersdorf, 15.9.1750. The couple received a dowry of 1,000 Reichstaler.

[62] Relevant stipulations are frequently mentioned in the wedding contracts collected by Fleury, *Contrats de Mariage*, and Fraenckel, *Memoire*, although they require systematic analysis. The available sources for Steinbiedersdorf are too scanty to allow for generalizing statements. Gershon David Hundert mentions that in Optow in Poland, about 12 percent of families in 1755 had married sons or sons-in-law living in their households: Hundert, "Jewish Children and Childhood in Early Modern East Central Europe," in David Kraemer, ed., *The Jewish Family: Metaphor and Memory* (Oxford, 1989), 81–94, here 85.

[63] Jacob Katz, "Mariage et vie conjugale à la fin du Moyen Age," in Shmuel Trigano, ed., *La société juive à travers l'histoire*, vol. 2: Les liens de l'alliance (Paris, 1992), 385–411, here 388.

[64] A number of studies make statements about the marriage age that are guided by normative prescriptions or goals formulated at some time or another, which are usually accepted as universally binding with no consideration as to their geographic or temporal validity. See, for example, Katz, *Mariage*, 387f., and Herweg, *Die jüdische Mutter*, 45f. In this passage, Herweg bases herself especially on tannaitic teachings and a modern interpretation of them. For a similar discrepancy between the (lower) norm for the age of Jewish girls or women at marriage and a considerably higher real marriage age, see the analysis of age indications in late-antique Jewish inscriptions by Greg H. R. Horsley, *New Documents Illustrating Early Christianity*, vol. 4: A Review of Greek Inscriptions and Papyri Published in 1979 (Marrickville, 1987), 221–229.

[65] Fraenckel, *Memoire*, XVII; Meyer, *La communauté juive de Metz*, 226. Hundert, "Jewish Children," 89, came to a similar conclusion about Eastern Europe: "Members of that class [Jewish artisan guilds], though, tended to marry later than wealthier members of society."

that it was the exception when girls married at the age of 13 or 14, and boys at 14 or 15. Even the supposed upper age limit of 20 or 24 for men was rarely adhered to. From 1740 to 1789, most men in Metz were between 23 and 29 years of age at their first marriage, while the marriage age for most women ranged from 17 to 24.[66] The findings for other communities in the region are similar and are probably also applicable to the villages of the county.[67]

The high marriage age meant that sons remained at home for a fairly long time, requiring living space and creating costs, unless they contributed to their living expenses, as did the stepson of Lion Pfalzburger. He was in a position to do so because, as the grandson of Abraham Jacob, he had received a modest inheritance after his grandfather's death. This inheritance he handed over to his mother and stepfather, securing in return the right to live at home until the time he got married. Although Lion Moses Pfalzburger was not rich, as long as he was alive he was able to feed and support his family.[68] Upon his death at the end of the 1770s, one son and one daughter were living away from home, and two grown sons were still at home, along with a daughter who was engaged and five minor children.[69]

Living with parents had financial advantages for sons. As long as "they eat their father's bread and do not maintain a separate household" they were not taxed by the Jewish community and were not required to pay protection money. Attempts by the seigneurial government to force unmarried young men to pay entry fees and fees to register their right of residence show that Lion Pfalzburger's stepson was no exception.[70]

The population statistics for Steinbiedersdorf in 1785 also reveal that sons remained at home longer than daughters. This "general table," drawn up as part of the exchange negotiations between France and the Holy Roman Empire,[71] confirms that more sons than daughters lived in Jewish households. In purely arithmetical terms, a Jewish household in 1785 had on average 4.7 members, and a Christian household 4.0. The 68 Jewish households in the Imperial County of Kriechingen had 185 children, 100 boys and 85 girls (ratio 54:46), while 699 sons and 686 daughters were counted in Christian households (ratio 50.5:49.5).[72] The difference was even more pronounced in Steinbiedersdorf: a

---

[66] Meyer, *La communauté juive de Metz*, 223.

[67] Ibid., 220. See also Françoise Job, "Les Juifs dans l'état civil de Lunéville (1792–1891)," in Gilbert Dahan, ed., *Les Juifs au regard de l'histoire. Mélanges en l'honneur de Bernhard Blumenkranz* (Paris, 1985), 343–357.

[68] AD Mos. 10 F 428: in 1776 his wealth amounted to 2,500 lb.

[69] AD Mos. Actes judiciaires Pontpierre B 10079: Verlassenschaft des Lion Moses Pfalzburger, 1779.

[70] AD Mos. Actes judiciaires B 9958.

[71] AD Mos. 10 F 70: Generaltabelle über sämtliche Population, den Viehstand und alle weitere Konsistenz, 1785.

[72] Ibid.

59:41 ratio of sons to daughters in Jewish families, compared to a nearly equal ratio (50.3:49.7) of boys and girls in Christian households.[73]

These numbers point to clear differences in the life paths of Christian and Jewish girls and boys. To a certain degree the reason for this difference surely lies with the significantly higher marriage age of men. Girls were married off young and usually left their parents' family and place of residence. In marriages in Niedervisse, 8 out of 12 women came from villages between 7 and 33 kilometers away.[74] As we have already seen in the context of mobility, in Steinbiedersdorf as well, daughters and sons were rarely married to someone from within the community. In only 3 of the 41 notarized marriages in the eighteenth century both the bride and groom came from Steinbiedersdorf.[75] A quick look at the bishopric of Speyer shows that the villages of Kriechingen were no exception when it came to marriage arrangements. In that bishopric, 32 children married outside the community between 1738 and 1743: 29 daughters but only 3 sons had to leave their familiar surroundings.[76]

Children who had the chance to get married would enjoy a higher social status as wives and husbands, even if they remained poor. By contrast, children whose parents could not afford to give them a marriage portion faced an uncertain future.

Many children from poor families could neither get married nor create a livelihood for themselves because their parents could not raise the necessary marriage portion. The sons of Christians could enter foreign military service to earn money. The sons of Jews could try to work outside the home, in the hope that, with a little luck, they might be able to create a living for themselves in trade, or earn their livelihood as beggars. Such activities were no obstacle to marriage; on the contrary, beggars and petty crooks usually had families that had a fixed abode and whom they supported with the proceeds from their migrant begging.[77]

For women and girls the situation was entirely different. If a family's livelihood fell short, they had to leave their families and seek out a job as a servant, where they could work at least until they had saved up the necessary dowry. But those who proved their worth did have a chance to receive help:

---

[73] AD Mos. 10 F 69: Statistiques générales concernantes le comté de Créhange en 1786: one hundred sixty-seven sons, one hundred sixty-five daughters.

[74] Jean Daltroff and Alphonse Cerf, "Traditions et coutumes de la communauté juive de Niedervisse de 1750 à 1930," *Almanach KKL Strasbourg* 36 (1988/5748): 143–155, here 143ff. It is not entirely clear whether the authors are referring to the eighteenth and/or nineteenth century.

[75] See p. 109.

[76] Joseph Eschelbacher, "Über jüdische Heiratsausstattungen im 18. Jahrhundert," *Mitteilungen der Gesellschaft für jüdische Volkskunde* 3 (1900): 97–103. In Metz, most marriages involved a spouse from a region within a fifty-kilometer radius around the city: Meyer, *La communauté juive de Metz*, 192ff.

[77] Glanz, *Geschichte des niederen jüdischen Volkes*, 186.

in his last will, Abraham Jacob stipulated that poor young men and girls eager to marry should be given funds to help them get started in life. Similar regulations also existed in the cities, where servant girls, after three years of loyal service, could be given a subsidy for their dowry.[78]

There are indications that poorer Jews, and to some extent also poorer Christians, sent their daughters off into someone else's service at a very young age.[79] Wherever possible, families surely tried to place their daughters and sons with relatives. Bernard Lipman, for example, had Gelle, his[80] wife's niece and the daughter of Nathan Levy of Saarburg, in his house as a maid. This service relationship also reveals how important the establishment of kinship networks was for Jewish society. Since Jews could never be safe from harassment and persecution even if they had good relations with their Christian neighbors, it was important to have far-flung connections.[81] The importance of supraregional and supraterritorial networks, for which the border region offered especially favorable conditions, probably explains the preference for exogamous marriages I have described. And it may also have been one reason for the higher rate of remarriage. In this respect, too, there were significant differences between Christians and Jews. In 1785, just under 25 percent of the 433 Christian households were headed by widows (94) or widowers (39), while only 15 percent of the Jewish households were headed by widows (8) or widowers (2).[82]

In 1775, Jewish families owned no landed property that was not tied to a house.[83] Still, it appears that they did have the opportunity to lease parcels of land.[84] How else can one explain how Jacob Salomon's wife was accused of mov-

---

[78] Hermann Pollack, *Jewish Folkways in Germanic Lands. Studies in the Aspects of Daily Life* (Cambridge, Mass., 1971), 32.

[79] Jeggle cites statistics from the early nineteenth century, according to which no Jewish men but four Jewish women emigrated from Jebenhausen between 1812 and 1822: Jeggle, *Judendörfer in Württemberg*, 84.

[80] AD Mos. Actes judiciaires Pontpierre B 10073: Acta in Denunciationssachen der Jüdin Gelle, dermalen zu Steinbiedersdorf sich aufhaltend ctra Jacob Meyer Cahens Sohn von da pcto impregnationis ac satisfactionis, 1784.

[81] A documentation of the anti-Jewish activities in the region, including the already mentioned ritual murder trial against Raphael Levy, can be found in Cahen, ed., *Catalogue: Les Juifs Lorrains*, 86ff.

[82] AD Mos. 10 F 70: Generaltabelle über sämtliche Population, den Viehstand und alle weitere Konsistenz, 1785.

[83] However, there is some scattered evidence for the region: one Jew had eight properties in Momersdorf; Abraham Jacob is said to have owned houses and parcels of land in Lorraine; in Forbach in 1781, one of the one hundred seventy-two landholders was a Jew: Henri Wilmin, *Forbach. La ville et le canton pendant la Révolution française. 1789–1799* (Forbach, 1980).

[84] Since the lease agreements were evidently not made by the seigneurial authorities, documentary evidence is rare. For example, the fact that women in Denting had leased their garden to a Jew in 1787 is mentioned only in the context of a quarrel over the tithe that arose in 1792.

ing fences in the garden?[85] We can thus assume that Jewish women, as well, were able to produce at least some of their food by growing it in herb gardens, hemp plots, and leased garden plots.[86] Apart from meat, however, they most likely procured most victuals by purchasing them or trading for them in the village or obtaining them from outside sources.[87]

A separate Jewish street did not exist in Steinbiedersdorf. Rather, the Jewish community could, or had to, develop in close neighborly proximity to the Christian community.[88]

Taxes and the protection fees

The differences in wealth that became visible in the description of the housing conditions are also found in the tax registers and lists of protection fees. They reveal an increasing polarization within Jewish society. It would appear that the 1724 tax burden on the ten families living in Steinbiedersdorf was still fairly evenly distributed: three households paid 24 livres each, four paid 20 livres each, and another three paid 10 livres each for the protection fee.[89]

The demographic trend, the immigration of poorer Jews, and the relentless rise in monetary demands by the lord and the community made the situation worse in the subsequent years, causing more and more Jews to descend into poverty.

In 1758, at most 12 to 15 of the families resident in the village were said to be reasonably comfortable; in 1776, only 8 or 10 of them supposedly had enough bread to live, while the "biggest bunch" was made up of beggars.[90] As early as the middle of the eighteenth century, a small upper stratum of rich Jews began to set itself apart more and more clearly from the others, chief among

---

[85] AD Mos. Actes judiciaires B 10081: Plaids annaux, Rapport zu 1761.

[86] LA Saarbrücken Mf 35: in 1688, a Jewish woman obtained the seigneurial garden at auction.

[87] AD Mos. Actes judiciaires B 10065: Uri Jacob owes Magdalena Bouché money for fruit he had bought from her, 1775. When it came to the purchase of bread, eggs, fruit, dairy products, beer, and wine from non-Jews, certain restrictions applied, of the sort that are recorded, for example, in the Shulchan Arukh. Normative restrictions applied also to the consumption of dishes prepared by non-Jews. The purchase of animals (for instance, chickens, geese, ducks) from non-Jews was in principle permitted, provided a few restrictions were observed. Information according to the Kizzur Shulchan Arukh, the short version of the Shulchan Arukh by R. Schelomo Ganzfried, chaps. 38, 46, 47.

[88] To maintain their cohesion, Jews, if they were not restricted to a ghetto, usually lived together in neighborhoods that were centered around communal institutions. In Steinbiedersdorf the house of Abraham Jacob had a certain centrality, although there is no indication that the Jewish houses were grouped around it. The living conditions seem to point rather to a more open settlement pattern. On the need of the Jewish community to set itself apart and the tendency toward physical proximity that this entailed see Katz, *Tradition and Crisis*, 11f.

[89] Flaus, *Comté*, 87.

[90] AD Mos. 10 F 373: Steinbiedersdorfer Deklaration, 1776.

them Abraham Jacob, whose wealth becomes apparent not only in his last will. At the beginning of the 1750s he already demonstrated his financial clout by advancing 4,465 livres to the count.[91]

A declaration of wealth from 1776 makes clear how great the gulf between rich and poor had become. In that year, all Jews throughout the entire county were forced, under oath, to provide information about their assets. Nineteen of the 29 heads of Jewish households were assessed the lowest level of protection money. Just under half of this group had paltry assets of a few hundred livres de France, and the other eleven declared that they were poor or desperately poor, that they owned nothing but the clothes on their backs or lived on charitable handouts. Since it was not only housefathers who were obligated to furnish information and were liable for taxation, but also sons if they were engaged in trade of their own, we can assume that some of those listed as indigent were the sons of better-off parents who were in the process of creating their own livelihood.[92] On the other hand, we see here the flip side of a "generous" settlement policy by the territorial lord. By evidently allowing the immigration of poorer Jews while assessing the taxes—which were based on the number of households—from the Jewish community as a whole, the territorial lord was able to increase the profit he extracted from the presence of the Jewish minority. The fact that the wealthier Jews had to pay the taxes for their poorer coreligionists exacerbated the conflicts that were emerging within the community over the assessment of the tax and heightened the process of polarization.[93]

A Jewish middle stratum was weak in Steinbiedersdorf: only 6 of the 29 Jewish heads of households had wealth between 700 and 9,000 livres de France. Four families had between 9,000 and 14,000 livres. The assets of this thin upper class comprised two-thirds of all the Jewish wealth recorded in the entire village.[94] A similar situation prevailed in Kriechingen: here there were 4 well-off and 18 impoverished Jews. By means of a skillful marriage policy, the upper class ensured that its wealth remained in the hands of a few. The tax statistics from the year 1786 offer a similar picture to the declaration of 1776: 11 percent of Jewish households paid taxes in the highest bracket, 21 percent in the middle bracket, and 68 percent in the lowest bracket.

The distribution of wealth was somewhat more equal among Christians. There were neither very rich nor very poor Christian villagers: 6 percent of all Christian households paid taxes in the top bracket in 1786, 32 percent in the middle bracket, and 62 percent in the lowest bracket.[95]

---

[91] AD Mos. 10 F 375: Communauté juive: Comptes 1741–1766.

[92] AD Mos. Actes judiciaires.

[93] See p. 274.

[94] AD Mos. 10 F 373: Steinbiedersdorfer Deklaration, 1776.

[95] AD Mos. 10 F 70: Statistiques, 1777–1785. It is questionable, though, whether the tax brackets are even comparable.

More important than the differences in the distribution of wealth reflected in the tax brackets was the fact that the Christian residents, unlike their Jewish neighbors, owned land, and that—as already mentioned—80 percent of Christian heads of households, but just under one-third of all Jewish heads of households, were able to call a house or a portion of a house their own.[96]

Among the Jewish house owners was Moses Deutsch, one of the village poor. Although he lacked money, like most of the Christians he did have a roof over his head and, presumably, the opportunity to procure some of his food by cultivating a garden. He managed to achieve a modest level of wealth through his marriage to Eva Hirsch. His example makes clear that the term "tax poverty" does not mean much, and that the ownership of a house and land, which was only indirectly recorded in the tax registers, by itself is not a useful indictor of economic circumstances.

If we combine tax brackets and house ownership, it becomes apparent that the common picture we encounter in scholarship on the region, namely that the Jews, with the exception of a few court factors who were usually from urban circles,[97] were poor, is not tenable.[98] Instead, a large group of fairly poor individuals was faced with a rural elite that shaped the economic, cultural, and religious life of the community. The Jewish community in Steinbiedersdorf is a particularly good example of this pattern.

Court and community

The rise in population since the beginning of the eighteenth century had created the conditions for the development of Jewish communities in some villages of the county. In the beginning the center of religious life was Kriechingen. Here Jewish men and women from the entire surrounding area gathered on the Sabbath for services at the synagogue.[99] It was owing to Abraham Jacob's piety, commitment, and wealth that a Jewish community (*kehila*) began to take shape in Steinbiedersdorf in the first half of the eighteenth century. A synagogue is mentioned for the first time in 1749; it was said to have offered space for twenty worshippers.[100] The question of whether the community had its own

---

[96] See p. 175f.

[97] See, for example, Battenberg, "Zwischen Integration und Segregation," 439.

[98] Kasper-Holtkotte, *Juden im Aufbruch*, 33; Albert Marx, *Die Geschichte der Juden im Saarland vom Ancien Régime bis zum zweiten Weltkrieg* (Saarbrücken, 1992), 40ff. To both of these scholars, the history of the Jews means the history of the territorial rulers' Jewish policy. We are told very little about the history of the Jewish communities and the Jewish families of the region. Extensive material on the latter was compiled by Fritz Jacoby, the city archivist of Saarbrücken, who unfortunately died an untimely death.

[99] The synagogue is mentioned in the protocol of the episcopal visitation in 1699: AD Mos. Fonds de l'évêché 29 J 69: Visitation 1699, Créhange.

[100] The comment that the synagogue was large enough for twenty people comes from an episcopal visitation protocol from 1749: AD Mos. 29 J 63/64: Archiprêtre de Morhange. Etats détaillés des paroisses, Pontpierre, Visite de 1749. It is quite possible that Abraham

mikvah (ritual bath), and if so starting when, must remain open for the time being.[101] The cemetery was located outside the village.[102]

Leadership of the community was vested in its head. In West Yiddish and German sources he is called *barnas, barnes, parnes,* head or leader of the Jewry; French translations refer to him as syndic or chef.[103] For fifty-seven years, Abraham Jacob was *parnas* of Steinbiedersdorf. His long tenure shows how closely the emergence of the Jewish community was related to his person. It is unclear whether he was appointed for life or was reelected by the community at regular intervals.

As *parnas,* Abraham Jacob was charged with collecting and assessing the taxes and exercising "policing functions." Similar to the bailiff (Meier) of the Christian community, he was at the same time the point of contact for the lord and bound to him through a special oath of office.[104] Beginning in 1763, at the latest, he had two deputies who provided assistance in assessing the tax and on all other internal Jewish matters.[105] The other communal officials we encounter are the cantor and the teacher.[106]

Jacob later set up a larger space for prayers. On the seating arrangements in the synagogue see p. 46f.

[101] A ritual bath was prescribed for women and men under certain circumstances. For men, if they had become impure in a spiritual sense, for women before their wedding, following menstruation, and after the birth of a child: Deventer, *Das Abseits als sicherer Ort?,* 48, with additional literature.

[102] AD Mos. 10 F 428, Nr. 4: Kriechingen.

[103] As, for example, in Ad Mos. Actes judiciaires B 10062: Testament von den wohlbestalt(ten) Oberbarnes Aberham Jacob in Steinbiedersdorff, 1775, and AD Mos. 17 J 29: Traduction d'une copie d'un testament hébraique faite par le defunt Sr. Abraham, fils d'Ezechiel, juif de Pontpierre, le 14 mars 1771 (henceforth referred to as Traduction, 1771); ibid., Actes judiciaires B 10057: Acta in Sachen Abraham Jacobs Erben von Steinbiedersdorf ctra den Feist Levy zu Kriechingen nachgehend der gesamten Judenschaft der Grafschaft, 1772–1780. On the function of the *parnas* see Siegfried Wolff, "Parnass," in *Jüdisches Lexikon* IV/I (Berlin, 1928), 821; Natan Efrat, "Parnas," in *EJ* 13, 123f.

[104] The oath of the *parnas* of Saarwellingen in 1756 has come down to us: Marx, *Juden im Saarland,* 27. Since Saarwellingen was part of the County of Kriechingen and in other spheres had the same regulations as the enclave in France, it is probably safe to infer that the oath of the *parnas* was the same throughout the county.

[105] The deputies were established through the official decree of February 12, 1763. The source does not reveal whether the appointment was the result of the territorial ruler's arbitrary action, or whether he responded to suggestions put forth by the communities. The decree is printed in Sittel, *Sammlung der Provinzial- und Particular-Gesetze,* 567. The appointment of the deputies can also be interpreted as the institutional consolidation of the Jewish communities, in which the *tovim* advised and supported the *parnassim*: Katz, *Tradition and Crisis,* 68. On the *tovim* see Daniel J. Cohen, "Landjudenschaft," *EJ* 10, 1405–1407, here 1406. *Tovim* (= viri boni) were among the "officials of the *Landjudenschaft* who constituted the Small Council."

[106] In 1764 there was nobody in Steinbiedersdorf who could perform a circumcision, which is why Moses Deutsch summoned someone from Niedervisse: AD Mos. Actes judiciaires B 10048: Moses Deutsch gegen Abraham Jacob wegen eines Arrests, 1764.

As I have already mentioned, the designation of Abraham Jacob as chief *parnas* points to the formation of a Landjudenschaft in the region of Kriechingen.[107] This presumption is also supported by a testamentary disposition of Abraham Jacob for marriageable daughters living "under the suzerainty of Your Grace, Count of Crichingen." At the same time he left money for all those girls whose parents "belong to the Jewry of the region (Landschaft) under the protection of Metz."[108] These two stipulations point to competing, supraregional organizational forms:[109] while the first refers to an entity established by the territorial lord, the second makes clear the connections with the Landjudenschaft of Metz, connections that transcended political boundaries.[110] Other stipulations in his last will—for example, regarding the administration of his estate and the origins

------

[107] An introduction to the institutions of Jewish self-administration can be found in Cohen, "Landjudenschaften," 151ff. On the Jewish communities in the county of Kriechingen see Flaus, *Comté*, 84–91. On Wied-Runkel see Bernhard Wachstein, "Das Statut der jüdischen Bevölkerung der Grafschaft Wied-Runkel (Pinkas Runkel)," *Zeitschrift für die Geschichte der Juden in Deutschland* 4 (1932): 129–149. Evidently there were no relationships between the Jewish communities in the counties of Kriechingen and Wied-Runkel, which were subject to the same territorial lord. Numerous references to Kriechingen can be found in Kasper-Holtkotte, *Juden im Aufbruch*. However, this work is not always reliable. That applies both to the history of the lordship and institutions of the county of Kriechingen and to the statistical material and its analysis. Steinbiedersdorf is wrongly identified as Kleinblittersdorf (a village belonging to Nassau-Saarbrücken), the lordship of Saarwellingen as a county (e.g., 107), the county of Kriechingen as a lordship (65). The list of villages belonging to the county of Kriechingen is incomplete (e.g., Momersdorf is missing), the relationship to Wied-Runkel (occasionally the author speaks of the lordship of Wied-Runkel [65] or simply of the lordship Wied-Runkel [68]) is left unclear, and the author seems unaware of the location of the county's villages as enclaves in France and the later inclusion in the Département Moselle and not in the Rhineland under French dominion. Table 6 (33 f.) on the state of the population diverges considerably from the statistical data for the same period that is contained in AD Mos., which suggests that the source was misread (see chap. 4, n. 19).

[108] Testament of Abraham Jacob: see Appendix 23 Q, (45).

[109] On this problem in general see Stefan Rohrbacher, "Organisationsformen der süddeutschen Juden in der Frühneuzeit," in Robert Jütte and Abraham P. Kustermann, eds., *Jüdische Gemeinden und Organisationsformen von der Antike bis zur Gegenwart* (Wiesbaden, 1998), 137–150; Jörg Deventer, "Organisationsformen der Juden in einem nordwestdeutschen Duodezfürstentum der Frühen Neuzeit," in Jütte and Kustermann, *Jüdische Gemeinden*, 151–172. On the Landjudenschaft in the bishopric of Trier see Kasper-Holtkotte, *Juden im Aufbruch*, 186–188.

[110] In contrast to the urban community, the history of the rural communities of the généralité de Metz has been hardly studied. And that is the case even though all of them were subject to the "taxe brancas," a special tax introduced at the beginning of the eighteenth century, and the resulting quarrels would provide a good starting point for taking a look at the Landjudenschaft. Any study would also have to ask whether and in what form the imperial lordships were integrated into this organizational form, and which role the borders between Lorraine, France, and the Holy Roman Empire played. A brief overview is provided by Roger Clément, "Aperçu de l'histoire des Juifs de Metz dans la période française," *Jahrbuch der Gesellschaft für jüdische Altertumskunde* 15 (1900): 33–45.

of the students—also show that the community headed by Abraham Jacob was oriented toward Metz. In institutional terms that was reflected in the area of legal jurisdiction.

As far as jurisdiction is concerned, the Jewish communities of the County of Kriechingen were dependent on outside rabbis until 1777. A complaint by the Jews of Kriechingen in the year 1736 reveals that at least for a time the rabbinical court in Metz was responsible for the villages of Kriechingen.[111] An official decree in 1743 installed Nehemier Reicher as the rabbi of the county.[112] Nehemier Reicher, a grandson of the Metz rabbi Jacob Reicher (1716–1733), was a *dayan* to the chief rabbi in Metz and had been elected first rabbi of the Duchy of Lorraine in 1737.[113] For his activity in Kriechingen he was paid by the Jews who resided there.

The decree does not reveal whether his appointment was something the Jewish communities or some of its members had asked for, or whether, as Cilli Kasper-Hotlkotte believes, it was an arbitrary decision on the part of the territorial lord.[114] However, his appointment could have been a response to a grievance by the Jews of Kriechingen in 1736, who complained that the journey to Metz was quite far, which is why some members of the community were not able to bring their complaints.[115] In any case, the appointment letter for Nehemier Reicher contained the government's directives to the Jews that they were obliged to answer his summons and pay the dues to him in two payments, which seems to indicate that he exercised jurisdiction at fixed times and possibly within the county.[116] That view would also find support from the fact that in Lorraine the great majority of Jewish families lived in the northeastern section of the duchy and thus in greater proximity to the villages and towns of the County of Kriechingen.[117] The jurisdiction of the rabbinical court was strictly limited to ritual and ceremonial matters.[118]

---

[111] AD Mos. 10 F 748, 1736.

[112] LHA Koblenz 701, 465: Herrschaft Crichingen und Saarwellingen (Geschichte der Herrschaft Saarwellingen von Dr. Matthias Sittel), fol. 95: Regierungs-Erlaß die Bestellung eines Rabbiners für die Judenschaft der Grafschaft Crichingen betreffend, 19.7.1743.

[113] Meyer, *La communauté juive de Metz*, 67; Cahen, "Les juifs dans le région lorraine," 70.

[114] Kasper-Holtkotte, *Juden im Aufbruch*, 67. The appointment of the rabbi by the territorial lord, or in Metz the approval from the governor, was the rule, though that does not rule out a preceding election by the community: Berg, *Histoire du rabbinat français*, 21.

[115] AD Mos. 10 F 748, 1736. It is also possible that the appointment of a new rabbi in Metz played a role. Jonathan Eibeschütz, suspected of being an adherent of the messianic movement of Sabbetai Zvi, had come to Metz as the new rabbi in 1742.

[116] LHA Koblenz 701, 465: Herrschaft Crichingen und Saarwellingen (Geschichte der Herrschaft Saarwellingen von Dr. Matthias Sittel), fol. 95: Regierungs-Erlaß die Bestellung eines Rabbiners, 19.7.1743.

[117] See p. 172.

[118] AD Mos. 10 F 748, 1752: complaint by the fiscal authorities against the rabbi of

While it was still explicitly stated in 1752 that the rabbinical court's authority extended only to "ceremonies and matters pertaining to the Jewish religion,"[119] in the following years its sphere of competence was increasingly restricted and in 1760 almost entirely abolished.[120] Step by step, the seigneurial authorities proceeded to inject themselves into Jewish marriage law and to punish premarital and extramarital pregnancies by Jewish women.[121] At times they were able to collect substantial sums of money in this way.[122] Although the rabbis and heads of the communities could continue to draw up inventories, the authorities had to be notified ahead of time. Moreover, the chancery fees had to be paid to them. The adjudication of inheritance disputes was shifted to the jurisdiction of seigneurial courts.[123] Nehemier Reicher was dismissed from his post in 1760 and the Jews of the county were prohibited from employing his services any further. Henceforth all complaints, with the exception of those relating to Jewish ceremonies, were to be brought before the county courts.[124]

Ceremonial jurisdiction remained unregulated for nearly a decade. Only after a petition by the Jewish communities in 1768 were they given permission to elect their own rabbis.[125] Any rabbi thus chosen had to be appointed by the count before he could assume office.[126] There are indications from the early 1770s that the Jews once again turned to the *bet din* (rabbinical court) of Metz for justice.[127] At the same time, however, acceptance of seigneurial courts was

---

Metz, who had drawn up an inventory in one of the villages of the county. This was regarded as interference in the seigneurial jurisdiction.

[119] Ibid.

[120] This was in line with the general trend, though it was also accelerated by the fact that Jews voluntarily sought out the seigneurial courts. Very instructive in this regard are the disputes between the rabbinical court and the parliament in Metz: Frances Malino, "Competition and Confrontation. The Jews and the Parlement of Metz," in Gilbert Dahn, ed., *Les juifs au regard de l'Histoire. Mélanges en l'honneur de Bernhard Blumenkranz* (Paris, 1985), 327–341.

[121] In the later negotiations concerning the County of Kriechingen, the right of imposing a fornication fine (along with the amount of money raised in this manner) was noted explicitly as a right of the territorial ruler and something that had to be accounted for in case an exchange took place.

[122] AD Mos. 10 F 429: Strafregister von 1754ff.: the authorities demanded 800 livres de France from the Jew Heym Bermann Mehring on account of fornication.

[123] AD Mos. Actes judiciaires Denting B 10007: Extract aus der neueren Judenordnung, Art. 8, 1777/78.

[124] However, another decree dealing with ceremonial matters was to follow: AD Mos. 10 F 373, 1760.

[125] Ad Mos. 10 F 373. The model was evidently the condition in Wied-Runkel. The Jews there belonged to the rabbinate of Friedberg. On the organization of their jurisdiction and administration and the restrictions imposed by state authorities in the eighteenth century see Cohen, "Landjudenschaften," 151ff.

[126] AD Mos. 10 F 373/4, fol. 6, and Cahen, ed., *Catalogue: Les Juifs Lorrains*, No. 136.

[127] Kerner, "Les régistres," 15 (in the manuscript version of his article: Metz AD Mos. J. 6999); see p. 209.

on the rise, with Jewish men and women turning to these courts also in cases which, under Jewish law, would have required a decision by a rabbi. This development could no longer be undone by a disposition in Abraham Jacob's last will of 1771, which made it possible for Steinbiedersdorf to become the local seat of a rabbi after his death. Abraham Jacob established in his house living quarters for a rabbi, who had to come from Metz or from a renowned German synagogue community. These living quarters were intended as compensation for the obligatory instruction of students.[128] This created the conditions for turning Steinbiedersdorf into at least a modest center of Jewish piety and learning.

The first rabbi of Steinbiedersdorf was Aaron Worms of Geislautern. He had been chosen by the leaders of the Jewish community in Metz and, in response to a petition from Abraham Jacob's heirs, was given permission to live in Abraham Jacob's house.[129] However, the cases involving questions of marriage and sexual morality that members of the Jewish community pursued in the seigneurial courts in the 1770s and 1780s reveal the limits of rabbinical jurisdiction during his tenure. All the more importance must therefore have attached to the function of the rabbi in the community, whose cohesion as a *kehila* in a non-Jewish environment was sustained and promoted by adherence to tradition.

Abraham Jacob, who comes across in his last will as a pious, tradition-conscious Jew, had made a number of other dispositions in addition to the establishment of a rabbinical seat and a small Talmud school. For example, he provided support for a brotherhood whose members in Steinbiedersdorf "are wont to study, every day in the evening after shul."[130] In addition to the cultivation of religion and social life, the support for the brotherhood was also intended to raise the modest educational level among the men of the community.[131] That women were excluded from the nightly visit to the synagogue and the communal learning that followed was so self-evident that it did not require special mention.[132] Still, a casual comment in a court protocol gives us an indication of the clear separation of the sexes—independent of social class—when

---

[128] See p. 158.

[129] AD Mos. Actes judiciaires B 9958: 1776.

[130] Appendix: Testament of Abraham Jacob, 4 D, fol. 36. In the larger Jewish communities, these kinds of brotherhoods (*havurot*) were organs of social control. On the significance of public prayer and the synagogue, which was also the regular meeting place for the male members of the community, see Katz, *Tadition and Crisis*, 152.

[131] In his stipulations concerning the kaddish, Abraham Jacob complained about the men of Kriechingen and Steinbiedersdorf, "if they are not learned men, each shall pray in the *Psalms of David* or some other prayers <according to his knowledge> on account of my *soul*, for which each shall receive 30 sous *de France*." Testament of Abraham Jacob: see Appendix (34b).

[132] Women were excluded from studying the Torah: Baskin, "Introduction," 20. There were a few exceptions, though; see Shoshona Pantel Zolty, *"And All Your Children Shall Be Learned." Women and the Study of Torah in Jewish Law and History* (Northvale, 1993).

it came to religious practice. After the evening meal, a witness in a trial testified, "all men" went from their homes to the shul, while the "women" stayed at home.[133] Much like clothing and language, the separation of the sexes that became visible to the Christian neighbors in this instance was one of the characteristics that highlighted the differences to non-Jews and could strengthen the religious and social cohesion of the community.

Illustration 3: Sabbath illustration from a *Sefer Mesholim*, 1679[134]

That the rigid gender separation in Jewish religious practice could be seen by Christian men and women as a distinguishing characteristic is revealed in a remark by the Benedictine monk Dom Calmet. In the middle of the eighteenth century, he penned a description of the synagogue in Metz and noted: "The women are separated from the men and are placed in the galleries, where they cannot be seen, but from where they can see what is being said and what is going on in the synagogue."[135]

---

[133] AD Mos. Actes judiciaires B 10073: Acta in Denunciationssachen der Jüdin Gelle, dermalen zu Steinbiedersdorf sich aufhaltend ctra Jacob Meyer Cahens Sohn von da pcto impregnationis ac satisfactionis, 1784.

[134] From Wiesemann, ed., *Genizah*, No. 92, p. 181.

[135] Dom Augustin Calmet, *Notice de la Lorraine* (Nancy, 1756), t. I, 828, quoted in Meyer, *La communauté juive de Metz*, 83. Meyer also mentions a similar observation by the Benedictine Dom Thierry Ruinart, who had taken part in a service at the Metz synagogue in 1696.

The subordinate role of women in the community and their exclusion from education and public religious life must not obscure the fact, however, that there were spheres both within and outside the house in which women took on religious and social tasks. As the example of Sara Isaak Goldschmied revealed, these included gifts of personal ornaments that were transformed into Torah decorations. Such gifts, which usually bore the name of the giver, were well suited to expressing a family's wealth to the community and keeping the memory of the family alive.[136] Oftentimes the cult objects presented to the community were elaborately embroidered.[137] This kind of needlework, along with the sewing of Torah scrolls and the embroidering of Torah binders, were among the tasks that fell to pious women in the community.

Illustration 4: Torah binder from Westheim, 1757[138]

Another social and religious area in which women were active is indicated by a donation that Abraham Jacob made to the "brotherhood in Crichingen that washes and buries the dead bodies." As a rule women could be part of such a burial society (*hevra kadisha*), which looked after the dead and prepared funerals. In the French translation, this brotherhood is called "la sainte confrairie des veritables bienfaits envers le prochain."[139] This much more expansive title chosen by the French translator alludes to the extensive activities in the area of welfare and the care of the poor and the sick that were part of the tasks of a Jewish community or various communal organizations.

The community's ability to look after the poor was enhanced by the funds provided in Abraham Jacob's last will. Abraham Jacob had seen to it that every year at Easter, 120 livres de France would be distributed to the poor of Kriechingen and Steinbiedersdorf. Additional funds were set aside to allow the poor to purchase the flour (*pesach* flour) needed to bake *matzah* (unleavened passover bread). He also stipulated that the poor of the village were to receive alms at the hour of his death.

---

[136] Katz, *Tradition and Crisis*, 153.
[137] Most of the Torah ornaments were made from expensive cloths.
[138] Copy, from Wiesemann, ed., *Genizah*, 7.
[139] AD Mos. 17 J 29: Traduction.

Provisions for the poor were also made at weddings: when Heym Jacob married the daughter of Jacob Meyer Cahen in 1776, he distributed 900 Reichstaler as alms, which was 10 percent of what his father and father-in-law had granted him in the marriage contract as his marriage portion.[140] Modest charity was extended also to the nonlocal poor: Jewish vagrants were given temporary shelter and food in the "sleeping quarters" before being sent on to the next community.[141]

The Steinbiedersdorf sources alone provide no indication of how the distribution of alms to the poor and the allocation of the "sleeping quarters" to "outsiders" was organized. There is no evidence of the existence of the kind of separate sisterhoods that we find in Metz, such as the "sociétés des Dames pieuses," the "couturières de linceuls," or Rebecca Hadamard's "société de Dames," which every year made twelve dresses for poor women.[142] It is hard to imagine, however,

Illustration 5: Torah curtain in the synagogue of Metz, 1760–1765. The names of the donors, Jacob Weis and his wife, appear in the center of the curtain, between the two lions.[143]

---

[140] AD Mos. 10 F 428: Droit de protection de Juifs.

[141] AD Mos. Actes judiciaires B 10055: In Sachen des Isaac von Boldian aus Curland, 1769.

[142] A few references to these groups can be found in Mayer, *La communauté juive de Metz*, 73.

[143] From Cahen, ed., *Catalogue: Les Juifs Lorraine*, Nos. 28, 19f., and 22, I.

that the women of Steinbiedersdorf did not take on any tasks in the broad sphere of charity and would have been content with contributing religious objects for the synagogue. As we have already seen, the synagogue community too benefited from the dowry that Sara Isaak Goldschmied brought into her marriage to Abraham Jacob. Moreover, the dowry from her first marriage allowed her to engage in her own economic activities as Jacob's wife. In 1759, she brought demands against Georg Schneider of Winden, in the district of Buchweiler. Sara Isaak Goldschmied affirmed on oath before the authorities in Kriechingen that he owed her money, barley, and wheat: she swore to this in the presence of the schoolmaster on the Five Books of Moses, in the form prescribed for a "Jew, male or female," by placing her right hand on her left breast and the left hand on her left hip.

The references to Sara Isaak Goldschmied, about whom we know far less than we do about her husband, lead us back initially into the house, to marriage and family, and thus to the spheres in which it is easier to find traces of women.

CHAPTER SIX

"WOMAN—SHE IS THE HOUSE": GLIMPSES OF JEWISH WOMEN'S LIVES

To begin the search for Jewish women not in the synagogue but in the house is a way of recognizing the importance of the house as the center of religious and family life. In tradition-bound Jewish society, religion and family formed a single entity.[1] A woman was assigned to her house, her husband, and her children, and she was responsible for educating the children, running the household, and sanctifying everyday life. Even if she had no voice in the synagogue and the language of the holy texts was foreign to her, she did have her own prayers that, if she was pious, accompanied her daily routine.[2] She was, as S. Ph. de Vries emphasized, "the mistress of the *house*, or, as the Talmud puts it aptly and concisely: Woman—she is the *house*."[3]

As long as work and house had not been completely separated, the house provides glimpses also of the world of work.[4] And here a broad spectrum of activities reveals itself. Moneylending transactions were often done in the house and the pawned goods kept at home. Wives had to carry on the business while their husbands were absent. That included pawnbroking as well as the keeping of the books and the sale of goods on site.[5] For women to be able to do

---

[1] Judging from numerous statements in his last will, Abraham Jacob appears as a pious, tradition-oriented person to whom rabbinical teachings were important. Presumably he also envisaged a gender order that corresponded to the "rabbinical design" (see Introduction, note 131).

[2] On the religiosity of Jewish women see Chava Weissler, "The Religion of Traditional Askenazic Women. Some Methodological Issues," *Association for Jewish Studies Review* 12 (1987): 73–94; Susan Starr Sered, *Women as Ritual Experts. The Religious Life of Elderly Jewish Women in Jerusalem* (New York, 1992); Sered, Priestess; also Debra Renee Kaufman, *Rachel's Daughters. Newly Orthodox Jewish Women* (New Brunswick, 1991).

[3] de Vries, *Jüdische Riten*, 19f.

[4] On the separation of work and house see van Dülmen, *Kultur und Alltag*, vol. 2, 231f.

[5] This has also been emphasized by Deventer, *Das Abseits als sicherer Ort?*, 47. An even broader spectrum of activities is mentioned by Howard Adelman for Jewish women in the Italian Renaissance: "The business included work as moneylenders, silk and button manufacturers and merchants, developers and sellers of cosmetics, . . . healers proficient in medicine, publishers of Hebrew books and occasional involvement with stolen goods." Howard Adelman, "Italian Jewish Women," in Judith R. Baskin, ed., *Jewish Women in Historical Perspective* (Detroit, 1991), 135–242, here, 142.

this work, the spouses had to keep each other continually informed about their business. That was all the more important as Jewish men traveled often, leaving the household and the household business, including all necessary decisions, to their wives for extended periods of time. Even those who did not travel had their wives represent them during the time they spent in the synagogue. During these periods the women did not even have the support of a servant.[6]

Quite apart from the work of their husbands, which they assumed in their absence, the tasks of women included looking after the house, the stable, and the garden, taking care of the children, supervising the servants, providing for boarders and guests, and, if there were animals, working in the stable, laying in stocks, and making dairy products.[7] Butchering was also done at home, and we can assume that women helped.[8] Moreover, we can be certain that Jewish wives, much like their Christian counterparts, engaged in needlework not only to meet their household needs and produce ritual objects, but also to earn money.[9] This is revealed by the example of two Jewish women from Bionville, who were reported to the authorities in 1766 because they had been knitting while a mass was being celebrated in the Catholic church.[10] The fact that they ran into trouble because of this reveals how problematic it is to distinguish between domestic work in the sense of nonpublic work and work outside of the house.[11] On the other hand, that sewing and spinning were not simply equated with work is something we learn from the above-mentioned description of the activities of Bremel, who testified in court that she tried to "earn a paltry living with sewing, spinning, and work."[12]

---

[6] Katz, *Tradition and Crisis*, 151.

[7] Specific evidence for Steinbiedersdorf could not be found. That the wives of Jewish cattle dealers in the nineteenth century occasionally made small, hand-formed cheese and earned a small side income by selling it is mentioned by Friedrich L. Kronenberger, *Die jüdischen Vieh- und Pferdehändler im Birkenfelder Land und in den Gemeinden des Hunsrücks* (Birkenfeld, 1983), 13.

[8] Many Steinbiedersdorf Jews seems to have earned a living exclusively from cattle trading or butchering. AD Mos. E Dépôt 553, Pontpierre, HH I, 1744: measures to contain a cattle plague. The participation of a wife is confirmed in AD Mos. Actes judiciaires B 10081: Rapport gg. Jacob Levy, 1754. Levy was butchering at home behind closed doors. He refused to comply with the request that he open the door. His wife insulted the village official.

[9] Davis, *Women on the Margins*, 13ff.

[10] Complaint against the wives of Moise of Trier and Salomon Worms, 1766, mentioned in Mendel, *Les juifs de Bionville*, 16. Conflicts over open spinning and knitting on Sunday are also mentioned by Martin Jung, *Die württembergische Kirche und die Juden in der Zeit des Pietismus (1675–1780)*. Studien zu Kirche und Israel 13 (Berlin, 1992), 130.

[11] The distinction between public and private is often emphasized in scholarship on Jewish women's history. See for example Adelman, "Italian Jewish Women," 139ff.

[12] See above note 399. In the Mishna Ketubot (5,5), which was normative for Jewish marriage arrangements, textile work is clearly defined as work (*melachah*): "These are the works the wife must do for her husband: she must grind, bake, wash, cook, nurse her child, make his bed, and work with wool."

The separation of male work and the house was most advanced in the families of beggars and crooks. Nearly all Jewish men in this group were married family men with a fixed residence who supported their families with the proceeds from their itinerant begging or criminal activity. They "honored the institutions of marriage and family in every way and lived according to the rules of society."[13] The main pillars of support for the familial and communal life of beggars and crooks were their wives.[14] Because of the requisite discretion of this profession we do not know whether any Steinbiedersdorf Jews were engaged in it.

The importance of the labor of women becomes most strikingly apparent in the petitions for a reduction in protection money because of a wife's illness or disability. In 1736, a Jew from Steinbiedersdorf submitted an urgent supplication to the count, pleading that he was poor because he was unable to earn anything on account of the war and because he was "inundated with children, and for a long time I have had with me my weak and disabled wife, who has never been able to lend me a helping hand in any way."[15] A Jewish man from the Palatinate who requested a remission of the protection money in 1774 also invoked his wife's "illness of many years" and "other unfortunate circumstances with no livelihood."[16] Widows were in any case expected to work and carry on their former husbands' business.[17] In Bionville, for example, we meet the "widow of David, who exercises the profession of butcher along with her children." She was punished because she had butchered a cow whose provenance she was unable to document.[18] That a woman would carry on her husband's butchering business, of all things, was not unusual in Jewish society, in which the slaughtering of animals is a ritual act. The rabbinical literature of the Middle Ages at least discussed the question of whether women were permitted to slaughter animals, and if so under what circumstances.[19]

More frequently we find women involved in moneylending. In 1741, "Eve Cahen, a Jewish woman, wife of Ury Cahen," loaned 62 talers Lorraine to Johannes Zechmeister, shoemaker in Freibous.[20] Perle Levy wanted to negotiate about a fine, which reveals her familiarity with business practices. Sara

---

[13] Uwe Danker, *Räuberbanden im Alten Reich um 1700. Ein Beitrag zur Geschichte von Herrschaft und Kriminalität in der Frühen Neuzeit* (Frankfurt, 1988), 267.

[14] Glanz, *Geschichte des niederen jüdischen Volkes*, 189.

[15] AD Mos. 10 F 428: Droit de protection des juifs.

[16] Arnold, *Juden in der Pfalz*, 41.

[17] Rainer Sabelleck, *Jüdisches Leben in einer nordwestdeutschen Stadt* (Göttingen, 1991), 82f.

[18] Mendel, *Les juifs de Bionville*, 16, referring to AD Mos. Actes judiciaires B 4854.

[19] As noted by Adelman, "Italian Jewish Women," 141. He emphasizes that this was acceptable only in special, private situations.

[20] AD Mos. Actes judiciaires, Pontpierre, B 11264. The register of Jewish protection money for 1737 lists "old Ohry Cahen" as a protected Jew. Perhaps his wife looked after the business because of his advanced age: AD Mos. 10 F 428: I. Droit de protection de Juifs, 1737. The marriage contract of her daughter Gidel and Jacob Markus was signed on October 20, 1741. At that time Eve was already a widow: AD Mos. 3 E 6015r/150.

Isaak Goldschmied, Abraham Jacob's second wife, was, as we have seen, involved in business activities. The oath she had to swear in a non-Jewish court shows that her commercial contacts with non-Jews compelled her, by necessity, to establish relationships with the outside world that went beyond the immediate business. We occasionally also meet Jewish women at the frequent auctioning of the goods of "rebellious" subjects of the Christian community.[21]

Gainful work outside of the home, on which poor women and girls depended, was hardly possible in Steinbiedersdorf.[22] A comment by Gmendele, the wife of Heym Neumark, points to some small-scale trading activity: she claimed to have discovered in Metz, in the house of the innkeeper Briden, a kerchief that her daughter had lost on her way there a few months earlier along with a whole package of clothes.[23] Employment in Jewish households was rarely available to girls from the village. Only two families in Steinbiedersdorf hired a maid, and three had a farmhand. Perle Levy also had a washerwoman. Bremele earned her livelihood with odd jobs, as did perhaps some of the other poor girls. The misery of those who had neither work nor family becomes visible only when we leave the narrow confines of the village and take a look behind the walls of the cities. Glanz suspects that a large proportion of poor Jewish women made their way into the class of domestics. Among the countless women and girls who were on the move during the time of the turnover of domestics were many impoverished Jewish women.

Cities provided the primary labor market. Here, of course, the demand for female labor was often linked with an interest in female bodies. Sometimes, girls could support themselves only with prostitution. To escape the supervision of community leaders and obtain "better" working conditions, servant girls and

---

[21] When the goods of several instigators were seized in 1763, three Jewish men and one Jewish woman came to take them in pawn: LHA Koblenz 56/491 lit. R: Kommissionsbericht in Sachen der Gemeinde Steinbiedersdorf gegen Herrn Grafen Christian von Wied-Runkel.

[22] According to the occupational statistics from 1840, Jewish women rarely pursued gainful work outside the home even in the middle of the nineteenth century. Sewing seems to have been the only such work available to them: AD Mos. J 5818, 17 J 44, Nr. 15: Etat nominatif de tous les individus israélites domiciliés dans la commune de Pontpierre, 1840; 17 J 45: Etat nominatif de la population israélite de la commune de Pontpierre, 1846.

[23] AD Mos. Actes judiciaires, Pontpierre, B 10049, 1765: Acta in Denunciationssachen Heym Neumarks Ehefrau gegen Isaak Israel und dessen Sohn pcto. inj. realia. It would appear that Gmendle used her work to earn some rainy-day money that her husband was not supposed to know about. The latter lived in wretched circumstances and could contribute nothing to his upkeep. To engage in at least some minor trading, he regularly asked his wife for money. Since Heym Neumark's wife did not want her husband to know that she still had reserves, she asked the *parnas* Bernard Lipman to care for her husband and to give him an advance: AD Mos. Actes judiciaires B 10073: Acta in Denunciationssachen der Jüdin Gelle, dermalen zu Steinbiedersdorf sich aufhaltend ctra Jacob Meyer Cahens Sohn von da pcto impregnationis ac satisfactionis, 1784.

prostitutes seem to have coveted baptism. By changing religions they also tried to improve their chances and to force men to honor promises of marriage.[24]

The mention of servant girls is another reminder that the house was not only a place of peace or piety. It was also a place where conflicts were carried out, where power was exercised—also by women over women. To get a grasp of this, and to gain access to the spheres of agency of Jewish women and their varying experiences in a rural society that was strongly differentiated according to background, education, and wealth, we must turn our eyes to the interior of the houses.

Interior views: the houses of Abraham Jacob and Jacob Cahen

Among the Jewish houses and dwellings in Steinbiedersdorf, two stood out above all others: the house of the *parnas* Abraham Jacob, and that of the merchant Jacob Cahen. Thanks to a last will in one case and an inventory in the other, we are well informed about both of them.

Abraham Jacob owned a handsome estate in Steinbiedersdorf, complete with a horse stable, courtyard, and garden. His last will provides us an approximate idea of his property:[25] apart from a school and a study, Abraham Jacob, as we have already seen, had also set up living quarters for the rabbi in his house, consisting of a heated room, a kitchen, a bedroom, and sections of the garden, courtyard, and cellar. Another dwelling in Abraham Jacob's house was set aside for Baruch Nauviller from Alsace, who was studying in Steinbiedersdorf in 1771.[26] He had been promised the hand of Abraham Jacob's granddaughter in marriage. Other rooms or portions of the stable, courtyard, and garden were to be rented out, with the income used to pay for future repairs.[27] Abraham Jacob's house represented a social or religious center of the Jewish community, where business was also transacted with non-Jewish partners. At the same time, it makes clear how inappropriate it is to distinguish between the inner world and the outside world, between public and private. Abraham Jacob's house provided living space to several families; simultaneously, it was a place for activities— such as studying—that were reserved for men. House, community, and business

---

[24] Glanz, *Geschichte des niederen jüdischen Volkes*, 157. For Metz: Meyer, *La communauté juive*, 87; Kerner, *La vie quotidienne*, 212.

[25] See Appendix; AD Mos. 17 J 29: Traduction, 1771.

[26] Nauviller = Neuwiller-Lès-Saverne. The French text speaks of Sr. Baruch Nauviller de la Province d'Alsace. The German text, which contains many corrections and amendments, probably inserted at the request of Abraham Jacob, always speaks of Baruch Levy of Nauwiller (= name of the groom of Abraham's granddaughter Teille but Levy was subsequently crossed out in every instance). The Steinbiedersdorf declaration of 1775 mentions Baruch Levy as the owner of half a house: AD Mos. 10 F 429.

[27] AD Mos. Actes judiciaires B 10048: Fiscalis gg. Abraham Jacob, dessen Ehefrau und Hausgesinde pcto geschändeten Sabbats und vorgenommenen Hochzeitsschießens, 1766.

life were not strictly separated, and it is hard to imagine that the women and daughters living in Abraham Jacob's house played no role in the community.[28]

Jacob Cahen, Abraham Jacob's son-in-law, also owned a substantial house with a cellar, attic, hayloft, stable, and garden. Since an inventory was drawn up for his house in 1757, we are fairly well informed about its furnishings. They may offer us a first glimpse of how well-to-do Jewish people lived in Steinbiedersdorf.

> In keeping with the ducal decree of March 23, 1757, we the undersigned repaired to the house of Jacob Cahen in Steinbiedersdorf for the purpose of drawing up an inventory of all effects therein and to seize them. We found the following:

No. 1

First, in the hindmost room off the kitchen

1. Three feather beds, among them one of fustian, then three small and 3 large pillows, of which 3 had striped and three plain covers, in addition two quilts with striped covers, and 2 linen sheets, along with one flour and two hay sacks, also an oak bed together with a blue and yellow striped curtain and a small pine chest.
2. An oak extension table along with a bench and 2 chairs, one straw armchair.
3. Two brass Sabbath lamps.

No. 2

In the front room [Vorderstube]

4. a house clock and a blue-covered sofa, along with an oak extension table and 4 oak chairs.

No. 3

In the kitchen

5. two copper kettles in the kitchen, ein Bethpfand [?] a tart pan, a barrel for washing, two soup tureens and 11 pewter plates, a mortar [Krauthstein], one pewter pitcher, one teapot, one small pewter bowl, 2 small copper kettles, a coffeepot warmer and einem stred eißen [?], a copper bowl.

---

[28] In context we should recall that business transactions included eating and drinking (see p. 246). Even if women are not explicitly mentioned in the sources, we can assume that—like Christian village women—they were not excluded from these activities, especially since the houses where wine was served were not likely to have been licensed establishments. English ale houses, which were usually run by women as part of their household economy, reveal that there existed a sphere of women's activities especially in this hard-to-define area of "hospitality": Keith Wrightson, *English Society, 1580–1680*. Hutchinson Social History of England (London, 1982), 63, 76, 89, 166, 167–170, 182, 213, 215; Judith M. Bennett, *Ale, Beer, and Brewsters in England. Women's Work in a Changing World, 1300–1600* (New York, 1996).

No. 4

in the wash room

6. two pewter bowls and one coffepot, three iron kettles, one pewter
   chamber pot (Portchambre)

No. 5

in the back room

7. 3 tables that go together and covered with a blue wax cloth, a pine
wardrobe, an oak hottele [?] along with 5 chairs and one cotton cover.

No. 6

in the upper room toward the garden

8. 7 copper kettles, 3 tart pans, one casserole, one bed, one tea machine,
   6 large wall lamps in addition to a menorah, 30 plates, 3 soup tureens
   with handle, 7 bowls, 10 glasses, 1 large pewter pitcher, one copper
   bowl, one copper jam casserole, one copper pot with its lid, 12 paper
   signs [?] [Schilder] with . . ., 11 with glass, a small oak bed, and 2 chairs.

No. 7

in the adjoining windowless room

a bed with a blue-yellow trimmed curtain, one feather quilt and bed and
   2 pillows,
a chest with 18 packages of pledges [Pfänder], sealed.

No. 8

in the adjoining back room toward the courtyard

six feather quilts and beds, three with cover, along with 10 pillows and
an oak bed, one wardrobe made of pear-tree wood with bed and table
linen, one copper coffee and milk can along with a sugar box and six
chairs covered in yellow, a table with yellow wax cloth

No. 9

in the upper room in the very front

one feather fustian bed along with a bed and a curtain decorated in red
and white, six embroidered chairs along with three armchairs, 2 pairs of
copper brandreitel [?], three copper kettles
4 red window curtains
8 blue dyed curtains, one cotton cover, one yellow-coated wardrobe, in
which are the woman's clothes
one mirror with a golden frame

No. 10

in the dark storage room [?] (dunkelkammer)

2 copper kettles, dishes, 2 pine wardrobes, in one white table linen and
kitchen linen for passover, 2 iron pots, one mortar and one copper coffeepot warmer and 2 roasting grills

in the front attic
4 pewter trays, 11 plates, one large and one small kumpf [?], 2 measur-
ing cans, about 10 quarters of wheat, one grübele [?], one flour box

in the back attic
2 kitchen pans, 2 iron pots, one iron kettle, 1 copper mug

in the cellar
one cask of wine and various vats and empty barrels

in the hayloft
one level with hay

in the stable
one she-goat and one billy-goat

wood
about 12 cords

One house together with an adjoining garden in the rear.[29]

It is quite obvious that the officials who came to Jacob Cahen's house to inventory his possessions did not record everything they found in this household,
but only those things that had a certain value also to Christians and were at
the same time dispensable. It is striking, in any case, that this large, well-
appointed house is not supposed to have had a stove, a spinning wheel, books,
or individual items of clothing. As far as the stove is concerned, the house was
presumably heated by a chimney, which was part of the house, not the furnishings. Perhaps clothes, books, and ritual objects—only a few candlesticks,
especially two Sabbath lamps, are recorded—were simply of no interest to
Christian officials.[30] Other things, such as water tubs, well buckets, or chickens were presumably so much taken for granted in a rural household that they
were not noted in the inventory.

---

[29] AD Mos. Actes judiciaires B 10048: Fiscalis gg. Jacob Cahen, 1757.

[30] The absence of any mention of items that were important in Jewish life is especially striking if one reads, by way of comparison, a description of a dwelling written
from a Jewish perspective. This one comes from the 1620 autobiography of the Jewish
mohel, kosher butcher, and teacher Ascher Levy: "In the house that I built for myself
and acquired with the help of God, praised be He, to the glory of God and the glory
of my faith, I built three things: 1) a small room where I could study and pray regularly and put the books God has granted me as my possession, as I will relate in its
proper place, 2) a small baking oven wherein to bake the unleavened bread ... Moreover,
in this baking oven there was a smaller (oven) to warm every Friday and to bake therein
the sabbath bread in honor of sabbath for the blessing of ha-motzi, and also to keep
the dishes for the sabbath warm. 3) A small bathroom behind the winter stove for profound reasons, especially because the brutish custom prevails here that the non-Jews go
into the same room with their wives, as do the Jews and their wives who go to the
non-Jews and their wives. In contrast, I strove, to the glory of God, and built myself a
room in my house where I could relax on Friday or go if I needed to be bled, or woman
needed to put on white robes and the like, so that it would be ready at all times." *Die
Memoiren des Ascher Levy aus Reichshofen im Elsaß (1589–1635)*. Edited, transl., and
annotated by M[oses] Ginsburger (Berlin, 1913), 48f.

The numerous beds, which were distributed among five rooms, indicate that a fairly sizeable number of people lived, or could live, in Jacob Cahen's house. No room was used exclusively for sleeping; rather, the beds stood where one ate or spent time, or they were kept in the storage room, which is also where pawned goods were kept. The largest and best-furnished room, where the residents also spent the Sabbath and which served as a dining and sleeping room for at least three persons, lay in the back, "adjoining the kitchen," which means that it was most likely continuously heated by the chimney in the kitchen. The colorful curtains on some of the beds indicate a desire for luxury, privacy, and intimacy. In general, the many curtains no less so than the table cloths, the armchair, the blue-covered sofa, the house clock, and the pewter dishes attest to the owner's wealth and proximity to bourgeois ways of life.[31] The kitchen utensils that are mentioned, including a tea machine, convey a sense of how well-appointed the household was and the importance that was accorded to domestic life and thus to house and kitchen work. The observance of Jewish ritual laws required a large number of objects and utensils.

As for dietary habits, it is apparent that the people living in this house drank coffee with milk and sugar, tea, and wine, and that they made jam and pickled cabbage. The she-goat and the billy-goat in the barn allowed for a minimum of self-sufficiency in milk and meat. Along with the consumption of meat, which was taken for granted, other sources show that herring also played a certain role as a food. From the large array of dishes and table linen we can infer that special importance was placed on setting a refined table. On the whole, the inventory conveys a sense of the level of domestic living in the better-off social strata of the village, a lifestyle that was largely shaped by women. Among these women was Perle Levy, Jacob Cahen's daughter-in-law, a quarrelsome woman who, much like Katharina Legendre, kept the seigneurial courts busy.

Spheres of agency: Perle and Särle—a widow and her maid
Perle Levy was one of the few well-to-do Jewish women in Steinbiedersdorf. She was the daughter of Ausser Levy, the *parnas* of Kriechingen, and the sister of Feist—who succeeded to his father's office—and Frommet Oster Levy, the wife of Bernard Lipman. In 1759 Perle Levy married Ahron Cahen, the widowed husband of Abraham Jacob's daughter Shiva.[32] Her dowry consisted of 1,000 talers of French currency, one belt, as well as clothes, linen, and furniture

---

[31] On living conditions in the early-modern period see van Dülmen, *Kultur und Alltag,* vol. 2 55ff.; Allain Collomp, "Families: Habitations and Cohabitions," in Philippe Ariès and Georges Duby, eds., *A History of Private Life,* vol. 3: Passions of the Renaissance, transl. Arthur Goldhammer (Cambridge, Mass., 1989), 493–530. Similar objects are not mentioned in the inventories of Catholic villagers that I have looked at.

[32] The marriage contract between Ahron Cahen and Shiva, the daughter of Abraham Jacob, had been signed on January 31, 1754: Fleury, *Contrats de Mariage,* 29. In Abraham Jacob's last will it says Scheba or Lady Heba instead of Shiva: AD Mos. 17 J 29: Traduction, 1771; Testament of Abraham Jacob: see Appendix.

worth a total of 1,200 livres de France. After her husband's death she would have complete control of the possessions and money.[33]

Perle Levy may have already known her future husband before they got married, since Ahron was evidently a brother-in-law or nephew of her father and had business contacts with him.[34] Ahron came from a wealthy family that had suffered some financial setbacks. In 1755 Ahron's father Jacob had been accused of engaging in improper business activities. To avoid punishment, he had to present the government with a gift worth 200 pounds. Two years later, Jacob Cahen was again accused of usury and sentenced to a fine of 400 pounds for charging commission and excessive interest.[35] Then Ahron suffered some misfortune of his own: in 1759 his house burned down.[36] He had a coal-fired baking oven in his house, which was not very common at the time. His "people," who were still inexperienced in the use of the oven, had taken out the coals after the "pie and cheese baking" and had extinguished them with water. However, the embers had rekindled themselves later, setting fire to the small bake room, in which there were also wood and cupboards. Ahron was able to save his papers and most of his possessions and to transport them to Kriechingen, where Perle Levy's parents lived. For his carelessness he was assessed a fine of 200 pounds.[37] His petition that the fine be forgiven "seeing that he was just

---

[33] LA Saarbrücken Mi 35/36 Collection Steinthal des Bestandes des Leo Baeck-Instituts: AD Mos. B 9928: marriage contract between the Jew and widow Ahron Cahen and his second wife, Perle Levy, the daughter of Ausser Levy, the *parnas* of the Jews of Kriechingen, 1759. The contract is not mentioned in Fleury, *Contrats de Mariage*. According to the Takanoth Choum, the custom in the Rhenish Jewish communities, the sum of the dowry should be the same in all publicly read *ketubbot*: 1,200 florins for a girl, 600 florins for a widow. In addition, special conditions were negotiated in the *tenaïm*, and in many cases these were formulated to the advantage of the women (for example, with respect to inheritance law): Fraenckel, *Memoire*, XV.

[34] The kinship connections are mentioned in files about a usury trial in which Ahron's father, the merchant Jacob Cahen, was involved: AD Mos. Actes judiciaires B 11262, Bailliages Sarreguemines: Procès contre Joseph Salomon et Jacob Cahen, juifs accusés d'usure.

[35] AD Mos. Actes judiciaires B 10045: Fiscalis gg. Jacob Cahen; 1756; ibid., 10 F 429: Strafregister de annis 1754–1761. Jacob Cahen had been accused of loaning 24 Reichstaler but making the debt certificate out for 28 Reichstaler and charging 24 percent interest on that sum, although only 12 percent was allowed: Sittel, *Sammlung der Provinzial- und Paricular-Gesetze*, 556, no. 10: Verordnung in Betreff des Handels mit Juden und der Form der Errichtung desfalsiger Schuldbekenntnisse, 1756.

[36] The marriage contract was formalized by a notary in Kriechingen on October 25, 1759: LA Saarbrücken Mi 35/36 Collection Steinthal des Bestandes des Leo Baeck-Instituts: AD Mos. B 9928: Heiratskontrakt zwischen dem Schutzjuden und Witwer Ahron Cahen und dessen zweiter Ehefrau Perle Levy, der Tochter des Kriechinger Judenvorstehers Ausser Levy, 1759. The house burned down ten days later, Nov. 4–5: AD Mos. Actes judiciaires B 10047: Fiscalis contra Ahron Cahen, Schutzjude pcto in deß Behausung aufgekommenen Brands, 1759.

[37] AD Mos. 10 F 429: Strafregister de annis 1754–1761: the fine amounted to 133 pounds and 6 plus the treasury's third.

starting out and was quite innocent of the whole matter" was turned down.[38] We are not told anything about Perle Levy, who was just as much affected as her husband by the fire in the house. If the marriage had already been sealed, which is likely given the date of the notarized marriage contract, Perle, as the mistress of the household, was responsible for the maids, although her husband was legally liable. Ahron tried in vain to defend himself by pointing out that he was innocent. His comment that he was just starting out could indicate that he had lived and worked in the house of his in-laws or parents during his first marriage. As we have seen, such an arrangement was one way of preparing young couples for life on their own.[39] In 1759, at the time of his second marriage, Ahron was already a successful businessman. When he realized that he could no longer control the blaze, "he tossed entire packages of papers out of the window, which the Jews all gathered up, and he himself climbed out of the window and down the ladder with several boxes under his arms."[40] The "packages of papers" were debt certificates and thus his surety. They point once again to the importance of the house as a place of work.

It seems that Perle Levy and Ahron Cahen soon settled back into Steinbiedersdorf, for already in July 1760, Ahron Cahen, in his father's name, was punished in Steinbiedersdorf for disobedience. A short time later he incurred further penalties for clandestine and prohibited tapping of wine.[41] We hear virtually nothing about the marriage of Perle and Ahron, which lasted less than ten years. When Ahron was killed in Metz in the early 1770s, the children of Perle Levy and Ahron were "not grown."[42] In 1779, his daughter Fraidgen married Zacharie Levy, the son of Nathan Levy of Fenétrange.[43]

After the death of Ahron Cahen, Perle Levy was a wealthy widow who now begins to appear in the documentary sources. She was the only Jewish woman listed as a house owner in the Steinbiedersdorf Tax Declaration of 1775.[44] Her house was certainly not small. Although its tax assessment was only half that of the house of Abraham Jacob, it was double the assessment of the houses of

---

[38] AD Mos. Actes judiciaires B 10047: Fiscalis contra Ahron Cahen, Schutzjude, pcto in deß Behausung aufgekommenen Brands, 1759.

[39] See p. 177.

[40] Ibid., statement by Nicolas Arnoud.

[41] AD Mos. 10 F 429: Strafregister de annis 1754–1761: 1760, one fine of 24 pounds, one of 16 pounds, plus the treasury's third.

[42] In 1772 Perle Levy is a widow with two small children, Fraidgen and Jacob: AD Mos. Actes judiciaires B 10055: Acta in Sachen Samuel Samuel, Knecht by dem Abraham Jacob zu Steinbiedersdorf ca. Feist Cahen and andere pcto injuria realia, 1772.

[43] Fleury, *Contrats de Mariage*, 118, mentions the marriage contract of June 22, 1779, between Zacharie Levy and Fraidgen Cahen, the daughter of the late Ahron Cahen and Perle Levy. Fraidgen Cahen was accompanied by her uncle, Oury Levy of Kriechingen, and by her stepfather, Samson Mayer of Steinbiedersdorf: AD Mos. Fenétrange, 3 E 1752 R/147.

[44] It is likely that she was living in her father-in-law's house described above.

the other Jews.[45] Perle Levy was one of the few women in the village who had the help of a maid and a washerwoman. In 1773 she decided to remarry "so as to be able to raise her young children more properly." Samson Mayer from Rappoltsweiler/Ribbeauvillé in the Alsace, the son of the local *parnas*, had asked for her hand.[46] For Perle this offered another chance to contract a marriage in keeping with her social status. Perle Levy and her maid journeyed to Bouquenom/Bockenheim to negotiate the details of the marriage contract.[47]

According to a claim by the government's advocate, Braun, the courtship process was not without controversy: at the beginning of 1774 Perle Levy was pregnant, and in early February she ignominiously threw her maid Särle out of the house at the beginning of Sabbath,[48] after three years of loyal service. Särle could not even take her belongings with her. We have every reason to believe that there was a connection between Perle Levy's extramarital pregnancy and the sudden dismissal of the maid who would have been privy to what had happened.

After she had been thrown out of the house, Särle went straight to Abraham Jacob, the first person one would approach to mediate problems within the Jewish community.[49] Much like Nannette Schilling,[50] Särle got the help she asked for, especially since Perle Levy's lifestyle, her independent-minded behavior, and her relationships with non-Jews suggest that the pious, tradition-bound *parnas* had an interest in putting her in her place, if need be with the help of non-Jewish courts.[51] Abraham Jacob or another member of the community drew up a petition for Särle to the count's authorities, which she signed in person. In it, Särle begged the Oberamtmann, in his capacity as father to the orphans, to show mercy, to help her, and to give her justice so that she might regain her good name and all that she earned by the sweat of her brow. What follows is a lengthy excerpt from this petition, which was in all likelihood drafted by a Jewish clerk.[52]

---

[45] AD Mos. Actes judiciaires B 10070: Roll pertaining to the district taxes announced on February 9, 1775, to which Steinbiedersdorf had to contribute 1747 pounds, 6 sol. 2 den. de Lorraine.

[46] AD Mos. Actes judiciaires B 10061: Acta in Sachen Perle Levy, Ahron Cahens Wittib zu Steinbiedersdorf, Klägerin, ca. Samson Meyer zu Rappoltsweiler, Beklagten, pcto Stupri et promissi matrimonium, 1774.

[47] AD Mos. Actes judiciaires B 10061: Acta in Sachen Perle Levy von Steinbiedersdorf ca ihre gewesene Dienstmagd Särle Levy von da pcto rückständigen Lohns; 4.2.1774.

[48] "As the sabbath was about to begin," that is, on Friday evening.

[49] The task of "maintaining order and discipline" within the Jewish community had been conferred upon him by the territorial ruler (see 183), but it also resulted from the function of the *parnas* as a lay judge; on this see Menachem Elon, "Misphar Irvi," *EJ* 12, 109–151: 127f.

[50] See 164.

[51] The constellation seems to me quite comparable to that in the Christian community, where women in conflicts with men appealed to the authorities, who granted help for the simple reason that their interference weakened the position of the housefather.

[52] Unlike some interrogations, this petition speaks of the "leader" and not of the "Jewish leader." This seems to me a clear indication that this document was written from a Jewish perspective.

> To the Right Honorable Lord Oberamtmann and Councillor of the County
> of Kriechingen etc.
>
> A submission to the Right Honorable Lord by Zerrel Levy, washer-
> woman and maid in service to the widow Berrel Levy for three years and
> a half, having been in other services eighteen years, loyal and honest in
> conduct, with never a complaint from anyone. Until today she also served
> three and a half years honorably and loyally with Berrel Levy, as is known
> to all, both Jews and Christians, she showed Levy much loyalty in her
> illness, as is known, and to her entire family. And when she had resolved
> to enter into another marriage, I went along with her to Bocknon and
> sat up front on the coach box, enduring rain and cold the entire way,
> taking everything upon me out of love. But today, as the Sabbath was
> about to begin, Levy treated me with remarkable words of abuse and
> curses and threw me out of her house, saying that I would have to leave
> that same Sabbath. Willingly, I asked her for my clothes and my other
> belongings and the pay I earned, which comes to 15 French talers, and
> about 3 French talers in my drawer, and 7 in earned wages, as well as
> three pairs of new shoes. But she drove me from her house by force, all
> but proclaiming me and charging me with being a thief. I immediately
> went to the leader Abraham Jacob, I drafted my response to our honor-
> able lord and (and) hope to win your mercy and your help in obtaining
> justice, because I am a servant in foreign lands and have no one who
> will speak for me, and You are the father of the poor orphans, to help
> me obtain my expenses and wages, which I earned by the sweat of my
> brow, and my honorable name, which I have had all my life, and I plead
> with our right honorable sovereign to understand me and help me, a
> poor maid servant, Zerrel Levy from [?][53]

Although Särle's term of service ended with an irreconcilable row and she
found herself on the street suddenly, the unusually long service relationship indicates that she had better working conditions than the maids in other households. From her perspective she had served honorably and loyally, doing not
only what was required but taking on other tasks: when Perle Levy had been
ill, she had looked after the entire family, and she had accompanied Perle to
Bouquenom/Bockenheim. Evidently there were things she did in addition to her
required work, presumably out of a sense of loyalty and responsibility. That she
went along to Bouquenom/Bockenheim would indicate a relationship of trust
between Perle and Särle, even if the maid was made to feel her lowly status
by having to suffer rain and cold while sitting up front on the box for the entire
trip. She was paid 5 talers for coming along, one-tenth of which, 3 livres de
France, she had to give to a woman who did her work back in Steinbiedersdorf
while she was in Bouquenom/Bockenheim.[54] Särle was emphatic in noting that
she had always behaved honestly and loyally, and that it was important to her
to have her good name restored.[55]

---

[53] AD Mos. Actes judiciaires B 10061: Acta in Sachen Perle Levy von Steinbiedersdorf
ca ihre gewesene Dienstmagd Särle Levy.

[54] AD Mos. Actes judiciaires B 10061: Acta in Sachen Perle Levy, Ahron Cahens
Wittib zu Steinbiedersdorf, Klägerin: Schreiben von Regierungsadvokat Braun im Namen
seiner Mandantin v. 12.3.1774.

[55] The catalogue of virtues for Christian servants demanded that they be loyal,

The quarrel over the clothes also points to what must have once been a good work climate: Perle Levy had given her maid a blue cloth and had new shoes made for her ahead of time. The women quarreled over possession of the white cap as though the question of ownership was not entirely clear, as though the mistress occasionally loaned her maid some clothing.

The extended and evidently good working relationship reinforces the suspicion that the maid Särle had to leave because her mistress Perle Levy was having problems. As the maid, Särle must have known about Perle Levy's sexual liaison with Samson Meyer or another man, and possibly also about the impending difficulties. After a fierce quarrel had erupted for reasons that are not mentioned, and Perle Levy had showered her maid with invectives and curses, Särle left the house, forced to leave behind her belongings. They consisted of "15 French talers, one Perßenen Rock und Caraque [?], one wattenen Vortuch [some kind of cotton cloth], two muslin kerchiefs, one blue kerchief, two white caps, cloth for seven shirts, four old shirts, one pair of new shoes, and, lastly, two books."[56]

Särle, who was an outsider in Steinbiedersdorf and suddenly found herself on the street, filed a complaint with the officials for payment of her wages and the return of her clothes. What she got in return for now was a countersuit: her employer claimed that Särle had stolen from her. By bringing this charge she simultaneously undermined the maid's credibility in case she revealed any secrets. Perle Levy stated that after her maid had left, she noticed that she was missing ten new kitchen towels, one pair of silk gloves, and three measures (Stab) of yellow ribbon. Moreover, she claimed that the two white caps belonged to her and not the maid. As a witness she named her washerwoman. She also challenged the new shoes: supposedly these had been made for the coming year, since Särle was given new shoes only when her old ones were worn out. After the quarrel the two women no longer spoke. Perle Levy charged the seigneurial bailiff five times to bring Särle her belongings. On each occasion, Perle Levy later claimed, Särle had refused to take them. Eventually the two women were summoned to the seigneurial court to settle their quarrel. The court costs were charged to Perle Levy, who wanted to negotiate before paying. Rigobert Crepeaux, an official, noted in the files: "Berle Levy protested against these costs and wants to bargain with Your Highness about them, and offers to pay them herself if

---

obedient, hard-working, and pious: Otto Ulbricht, "Zwischen Vergeltung und Zukunftsplanung. Hausdiebstahl von Mägden in Schleswig-Holstein vom 16. bis zum 19. Jahrhundert," in Ulbricht, ed., *Von Huren und Rabenmüttern*, 139–170, here 141. The description of Särle's conduct while in service agrees largely with this catalogue of virtues, but the concept of honor has central importance ("served honorably and loyally," "honorable name"). On the catalogue of virtues for maids and manservants and the importance of honor see also Renate Dürr, *Mägde in der Stadt. Das Beispiel Schwäbisch Hall in der Frühen Neuzeit*. Geschichte und Geschlechter 13 (Frankfurt, 1995), esp. 114–126, 139–141, 220–265.

[56] On book ownership see 158.

she is guilty."[57] The quarrel with Särle had still not been resolved when Perle Levy had a run-in with Ahron Levy's farmhand. The details have come down to us in the charge she filed and which was written for her by the village clerk, the apothecary Schaupp. We read there:

> To the most honorable government of the count,
> On the 21st of the month passed, many young people were invited to the Jewish wedding held here in Steinbiedersdorf, and my daughters were also present. To watch over my daughter's conduct I went there and saw how some young people were embracing. Whereupon I said to the same that it was unseemly for them to do this in the presence of so many still innocent children, whereupon Jacob Ahron Levy's farmhand immediately responded that this was better than embracing the pelawer [?].
> Should this kind of talk go unpunished, I fear I could suffer further insults from others, and I would be ashamed to show myself on the street. To prevent this from happening, I direct my most humble and urgent plea to Your Most Honorable Government to summon Jacob Ahron Levy's farm-hand quietly to Kriechingen and not to sue him, but to make an example of him, to impose a penalty of eight days in the tower, as Your Most Honorable Government sees fit and deems agreeable, Your most humble servant.[58]

Apothecary Schaupp, who wrote the letter and may have also influenced its formulation and argumentation, had himself been assessed a fornication fine two years earlier, because he had had intercourse with his future wife and she had given birth only five months after they got married.[59] There is much to suggest that his own life experience furthered his willingness to take the side of the pregnant widow. In any case, together with Perle Levy he drafted a letter with which she tried to silence the gossip in the village. She asked that the farmhand who had mocked her because of her relationship be quietly imprisoned in the tower for eight days without a trial. Given the trivial nature of the offense and the inhuman conditions in the tower in Kriechingen, this was exceptionally harsh punishment. That a Jewish woman not only humbly asked the authorities for help, as she was entitled to do, but went on to make suggestions about procedure and the severity of the punishment, can be seen as inappropriate, although the authorities did not take exception to it, at least not in writing.[60] One explanation might be that the quarrel between Perle Levy and Särle offered a government eager to carry out reforms an opportunity to

---

[57] AD Mos. Actes judiciaires B 10061: Acta in Sachen Perle Levy, Ahron Cahens Wittib, zu Steinbiedersdorf, Klägerin: Dekret v. 17. März 1774.

[58] AD Mos. Actes judiciaires B 10061: Acta in Sachen Perle Levy von Steinbiedersdorf ca. Jacob Ahron Levy Knecht von da pcto injuriarum, 1774.

[59] AD Mos. Actes judiciaires B 10057: Acta in Denunciationssachen gegen den Apotheker Schaupp pcto anticipati concubitus, 1772.

[60] That Perle Levy did not turn to the *parnas* or try to obtain a rabbinical ruling on this quarrel within the Jewish community indicates that there was conflict between her and the Jewish community or its leader.

intervene in Jewish affairs and to weaken the *kehila* that was just then in the process of consolidating itself.[61]

In response to Perle Levys submission, the seigneurial officials set the required steps in motion and summoned the two parties. Since the farmhand denied the charge and demanded proof, Perle Levy suggested two witnesses who should be questioned.

Then, on March 12, Perle Levy got the Regierungsadvokat Braun involved, who drafted two letters for her. In one he accused the maid Särle of theft and thereby silenced her, and in the other he requested, on formal legal grounds, a temporary suspension of the proceedings against Lion Meyer Levy, Ahron Levy's farmhand: as he had no possessions of his own, should he be found guilty, he could take flight, in which case his client "would come away empty-handed." In the quarrel involving Nannette Schilling and her employer, which I have mentioned elsewhere, the lawyer had argued the exact opposite and had called for equal justice for the maid. Whether to hear a complaint and require the posting of bondsmen was an area in which the judge had procedural leeway, which he could use especially against the poor and outsiders.

In the present case, Perle Levy and her lawyer were evidently not interested in a public trial involving witness testimony, since she had explicitly asked that the farmhand be summoned "quietly." His punishment was to be a warning to others, so that she would not be insulted further and would not have to be ashamed to walk in the street.[62]

While premarital pregnancies did occasionally occur in Steinbiedersdorf, they were punished more harshly under the Jewish religion than in the Christian community.[63] There are two possible explanations why Perle Levy reacted so strongly: either she wanted to keep her pregnancy a secret until the marriage to conceal it from her fiancé or his father, or her marriage plans had already fallen apart and the village knew that the no longer young widow was carrying an illegitimate child. Perhaps by filing the complaint she was trying to

---

[61] As we have seen above, there certainly were analogous conflicts with the Christian community.

[62] AD Mos. Actes judiciaires Pontpierre B 10061: Acta in Sachen Perle Levy von Steinbiedersdorf ca. Jacob Ahron Levy Knecht von da pcto injuriarum, 1774.

[63] On the strictness of Jewish marital and sexual morality, which regarded any kind of extramarital sex as a violation of the religious laws and saw marriage as the only place of purity, see Katz, "Mariage," 385ff.; Herweg, *Die jüdische Mutter*, 38ff. Kerner's analysis of the Jewish court of the Jewish community in Metz shows that the legal practice in that city was indeed quite severe in the eighteenth century: "Le conseil se montrait particulièrement sévère à l'égard des servantes 'débauchées.' On les expulsait dans les 48 heures du moment où l'on avait découvert leur faute, même s'il agissait d'une faute commise dans le passé" [The council behaved with particular severity toward 'debauched' servants. They were expelled within forty-eight hours after the discovery of their wrongdoing, even if it was a wrongdoing committed in the past]. Kerner, *La vie quotidienne*, 212.

secure the support of Christian villagers and to find out what her chances were in the seigneurial courts.

Sometime in the spring or summer of 1774, the preparations for the wedding had been made in Steinbiedersdorf, supposedly at considerable expense. Samson Mayer arrived with his father. Since the bride "was, by her own admission, pregnant," Samson refused to get married, allegedly at the instigation of his father. Braun wrote:

> When the day that had been set for the actual wedding had arrived, the groom and his father arrived in Steinbiedersdorf. However, instead of the wedding taking place, for which my client had incurred considerable expenses, his father incited him against my client, filed a claim of indemnification against her, and along with other ill-disposed people advised him against contracting the marriage, from all kinds of pernicious intentions, and surely, as there is reason to suspect, to increase the promised dowry.[64]

Samson Meyer and his father invoked Jewish law, which demanded that cases like this be settled through a rabbinical decision.[65] An effort was made to involve the rabbi of Metz, though he "had soon grown so tired of the case from the intrigues and the demonstrated recalcitrance of the opposing parties that he wanted nothing more to do with it."[66]

Perle Levy gave birth to her child at the beginning of October, after having once again declared, under pain of birth and in the presence of the bailiff (Johann Georg Becker) and the clerk (apothecary Schaupp), "that she had been impregnated by Samson Meyer as her betrothed, and that none other than he was this child's father." She further affirmed her statement with an oath.[67] Already prior to the birth, Perle Levy had instructed the advocate Braun to bring a marriage and paternity suit against Samson Meyer, and he made every effort to bring the suit to a successful conclusion. Braun, who took cases of subjects only if he had been formally retained by them, defended Perle Levy with powerful eloquence, understanding, and energetic commitment.[68] To win the case, he employed the conventional gender prejudices, to which a woman like Perle Levy gave the lie by her behavior. Braun's report stated the following, among other things: "In the guise of the wooing that was taking place,

---

[64] AD Mos. Actes judiciaires B 10061: Acta in Sachen Perle Levy, Ahron Cahen's Wittib, zu Steinbiedersdorf, Klägerin.

[65] Marriage to a pregnant widow was and is prohibited in the religious laws: Lewittes, *Jewish Marriage*, 26.

[66] AD Mos. Actes judiciaires B 10061: Acta Jud Samson Meyer von Rappoltsweiler ca Ahron Cahens Witwe perle Levy von Steinbiedersdorf in specie Anschreiben von der zweibrückischen Kanzlei zu Rappoltsweiler, 1774.

[67] Ibid.; on the "Genießverhör" see chap. 3, n. 61.

[68] A brawl in Denting reveals that Braun was not especially liked by the subjects, among other reasons because he was ruthless in seizing distrained property: Ulbrich, "Traditionale Bindung," 117ff.

this young man did not lose the opportunity, with all kinds of flattery, to persuade her to follow his will, and since the love between the two contracting parties had finally grown so strong, she, a weak woman, allowed herself to be blinded by this into anticipatory coition with him."[69] The man appears as the active party who has "his will," the woman as the weaker party who allows herself to be blinded and who follows "his will."[70] This was councilor Braun's usual argument to defend women and girls suing for marriage.[71] Perle Levy, however, was not only a "weak woman," but also a "lonely widow," a widow, moreover, who came from a respected and influential Kriechingen family. One could not but conclude, Braun argued, that Samuel wished "to cheat her out of her wealth as a lonely widow and to leave her in disgrace." His client could swear before God "that this Samson Meyer induced her, a weak woman, with the most precious promises and carried out the impregnation, consequently he was the lawful father of the child she was now carrying under her heart."

To prevent Perle Levy and her entire respected family from being disgraced by the failed marriage, the lawyer was suing Samson Meyer for immediate enforcement of the promise of matrimony. In case Samson refused, he should be compelled to support the child, restore Perle's honor, and pay damages. Samson Meyer renounced the marriage obligation—either voluntarily or under paternal pressure—by invoking Jewish law, though at least he never denied in the seigneurial courts that the child was or could be his. He and his father merely insisted on clarification from a rabbi, something that Perle Levy and her family sought to prevent, for reasons that are not entirely clear.

Perle Levy must have gotten pregnant right around the time she negotiated the marriage contract with Samson Meyer. This makes it rather unlikely that she was trying from the outset to "foist" someone else's child on him through the planned marriage. Either the marriage was blocked not by Samson Meyer but by his father, who rejected his son's bond of matrimony with a pregnant widow for religious reasons or who did not agree with the marriage contract and saw in the bride's premarital pregnancy legal grounds to undo or correct his son's decision; or Perle Levy had a relationship that was known to Särle, possibly also the neighbors, but not to the future husband living at a considerable distance. Her family and her economic conditions could have forced her to enter into a marriage in keeping with her social status. The strongest support for this version of the story comes from her quarrel with Lion Meyer Levy. His comment that the embraces among young people were better "than embracing the pelawer [?]" was undoubtedly an allusion to some relationship of Perle Levy's. Unfortunately, or perhaps revealingly, the term of abuse or the name that Lion Meyer had used was written down by the clerk Schaupp in an illeg-

---

[69] AD Mos. Actes judiciaires B 10061: Acta in Sachen Perle Levy, Ahron Cahen's Wittib, zu Steinbiedersdorf, Klägerin.

[70] On this argumentative pattern see Lyndal Roper, "'Wille' und 'Ehre'," in Wunder and Vanja, *Wandel der Geschlechterbeziehungen*, 180–197.

[71] On the connection between femaleness and weakness in the argumentations in court see p. 74.

ible manner, because he either did not, or did not *want* to, understand it. After all, what had been said between the two was not to be publicly disseminated further through the legal proceedings. The widow's overreaction, her fear that she could no longer show herself in the streets, and her suggestion that an example be made of Samuel by punishing him with a week in the tower, quietly and without a trial, indicate that Samuel knew something that neither Samson Meyer nor the village was to find out. As an adult Jewish woman from a well-respected family and a mother of two children, Perle Levy was not free to live any way she wanted. She had to mind her honor and show regard for her family. Braun also pointed to the family's power, and he was happy to use the familial circumstances to support his case: Perle Levy's entire, well-respected family would be disgraced if the marriage did not take place, "which is something the family does not intend to tolerate."[72]

In the end the family had its way: in 1776 Samson Meyer was listed as a resident of Steinbiedersdorf. In terms of his wealth he was still among the top one-third of the Jews of Steinbiedersdorf. In 1779 he signed the marriage contract for Perle Levy's daughter as her stepfather. Whether the marriage was also a success for Perle Levy and Samson Meyer, or whether one or both were merely obeying economic and familial pressure, must remain an open question.

Perle Levy was the only woman of Steinbiedersdorf who fought a successful marriage suit in the eighteenth century. That was surely no coincidence. Although Perle Levy was Jewish, she came from a respected and wealthy family, and that helped bridge the gap between the religions in Steinbiedersdorf in the second half of the eighteenth century. Through her family, and undoubtedly also through the social contacts she cultivated as the wife of Ahron Cahen, Perle Levy had connections she could use in case of conflict. Above all, however, she was able to get the non-Jewish authorities to represent her interests: the sergeant acted as the intermediary between her and her maid; the clerk drafted her report and, along with the bailiff, came into her house at the time she gave birth to allow her to make the proper legal declaration of paternity; the advocate defended her; the government heard her libel and marriage complaint and decided to forego a fornication fine; even the count pondered how the case should be decided. Perle Levy may have been a persuasive woman, but that alone would not have been enough to assert oneself successfully in society, least of all if someone like Perle Levy had violated the prevailing norms. As we can see from the cases of the other Jewish girls in Steinbiedersdorf who became pregnant out of wedlock, her story would have been a different one without her family background and social standing.[73] Of course only a small minority of Jewish women enjoyed the privilege of belonging to such a favored social class.

---

[72] AD Mos. Actes judiciaires B 10061: Acta in Sachen Perle Levy, Ahron Cahen's Wittib, zu Steinbiedersdorf, Klägerin.

[73] To that extent it would be shortsighted if one tried to explain the active involvement by the authorities in this case simply by saying that they were taking advantage of an opportunity to further squeeze out Jewish jurisdiction.

How very differently the opportunities and risks of life were distributed among Jewish women becomes clear if we compare the life of Perle Levy with the little we are told about her maid Särle. Perle Levy had to yield to her family's interests to a much greater degree than Särle, of whose family we hear nothing, and who, on the contrary, points out that as a maid in a foreign land she had nobody who would take up her case. As a wife Perle Levy stood under the wardship of her husband and lived in a sphere of male authority barely regulated by laws and controlled more by the power of her family than by outsiders.[74] As an employer she had power over her maid, whose chances of marriage she could destroy simply by accusing her of theft.[75] As a widow she had noticeably broader leeway, yet as an adult woman, mother, and widow she had to be careful not to embarrass her family. Given the uncertainties with which the Jewish community lived, it was important to have a family and to be bound into kinship networks.[76]

Networks: marriage connections of the Jewish upper stratum

Wealth was not something one could rely on in Jewish life.[77] Not even Perle Levy, who owned an entire house, could be sure that she might not lose all her wealth from one day to the next. That was something she had to experience, at the latest, upon the death of her first husband, who had passed away in Metz. Although she came from a wealthy family that had given her a dowry and secured a good marriage contract for her, as a widow Perle Levy found herself in a difficult situation.

Ahron Cahen's children from his previous marriage, Jacob and Teille, were still unmarried when he died. It is not clear whether they lived in the house of Perle Levy after their father's death or with their grandfather, Abraham Jacob. The latter had provided for the children's future by setting aside a dowry and a marriage portion for them in his last will. In addition, he had negotiated a marriage contract for Teille. She was to marry Baruch Nauviller from the Alsace, who was studying in Abraham Jacob's house. A marriage to a scholar had also been arranged for his second granddaughter, Ester: she had been promised to Wolf Seligmann, who came from the Jewish academy in Fürth (in Franconia) and was working as a schoolmaster in Steinbiedersdorf.[78] These

---

[74] Herweg, *Die jüdische Mutter*, writes in her study, which over long stretches takes an a historical approach, that marriage in Jewish tradition should be understood as an equal partnership organized around a division of labor and tasks, and that the spheres of men's and women's tasks were organized in a complementary fashion. The story of Perle Levy, who did not live her life in strict accordance with religious norms, makes clear that this romantic view of the past cannot be readily applied to the practice of everyday life.

[75] Girls could receive a contribution to their dowry only if they had served at least three years honorably and faithfully.

[76] See 169.

[77] Davis, *Women on the Margins*, 44.

[78] AD Mos. 17 J 29: Traduction d'une copie d'un testament hébraique faite par le

planned marriages document once again the high esteem that male learning enjoyed in Jewish society, and the avenue it provided for men from lower social strata to rise in society.

Abraham Jacob had provided for all his grandchildren, including Teille and Jacob. When he arranged the disposition of his wealth, he made no distinction between granddaughters and grandsons or between the children of his son and those of his daughter in regard to a dowry or marriage portion. The four boys and two girls were all to receive 4,000 livres de France on the day of their wedding. This put the granddaughters in a good position, though not on an equal footing with the grandsons: at least in inheritance law, granddaughters were disadvantaged vis-à-vis grandsons.[79]

Although Abraham Jacob had not excluded his granddaughters from the inheritance of land and movable possessions, "in accordance with Jewish ritual and law" they received only half of what was bestowed upon grandsons.[80] If Abraham Jacob promised his granddaughters in marriage to scholars, that decision may also have had something to do with the economic inequality of women and men as grounded in inheritance law. Abraham Jacob made sure that his granddaughters would live in respected families.

When it came to Jacob and Fraidgen, the children of Ahron Cahen's marriage to Perle Levy, Abraham Jacob had made provisions only within the framework of general dispositions in favor of relatives. They were the responsibility of Perle Levy, who had been guaranteed in her 1759 marriage contract that she would have control of her husband's money and property after his death. Even if we cannot find any traces of her activities in the sources, we can assume that Perle, as a widow, carried on her deceased husband's business. However, Perle Levy did not remain single for long. As we have seen, she arranged a marriage to Samson Meyer, the son of the *parnas* of Ribbeauvillé in

---

def. Abraham, fils d'Ezechiel juif à Pontpierre le 14.3.1771. The "academy" was probably the yeshiva in Fürth, which, as Fritz Leopold Steinthal has said, "for a long time exerted a great attractiveness on many Jews": "Fürth," in *Jüdisches Lexikon*, II (Berlin, 1928), 852–854, here 853.

[79] Fraenckel, *Memoire*, XIII. In practice this principle was not consistently observed. However, a serial analysis of the marriage contracts must be left to a subsequent study.

[80] According to Jewish law, in theory—not in practice—only the paternal family was entitled to inherit. The husband was heir to his wife, the father heir to his children, the sons heirs to their parents. Instead of an inheritance, the woman was entitled under property law to payment of the sums provided for in the *ketubah*, and, as the case may be, support and a dwelling. In place of an inheritance, daughters received a dowry and marriage portion, which the father, grandfather, or brother in many cases negotiated with the father of the future bridegroom many years before the possible conclusion of a marriage. The unequal treatment of men and women in legal theory, which was based on old Biblical law, does not allow us to draw any conclusions as to practice. Since the late Middle Ages, at the latest, women were also to a certain extent legally entitled to inherit. On changes in the right of inheritance of the Jewish daughter and wife see Marcus Cohn, "Erbrecht," in *Jüdisches Lexikon*, II (Berlin, 1928), 442–456 (esp. 449ff.).

the Alsace. With this choice she continued the marriage alliances that were customary in her family.

Perle Levy came from a family of *parnasim*. Her brother had succeeded their father in the office of *parnas*, and her sister was married to Bernard Lipman, the successor to the *parnas* Abraham Jacob.[81] The background of her first husband, Ahron Cahen, is uncertain, although his first wife had been the daughter of the *parnas* Abraham Jacob. The social endogamy that becomes apparent here corresponds with the marriage pattern that Meyer was able to document on a broader basis for Metz: of 135 marriages that took place in Metz between 1720 and 1789, 53 (39.2 percent) were concluded between children or grandchildren of *parnasim*.[82] Since the families of the *parnasim* as a whole constituted only a relatively small group, marriage partners—as the example of Perle Levy also attests—were recruited from distant regions.[83] This practice was facilitated by the shared language and culture that linked the Ashkenazic Jews.[84] Circumstances permitting, it allowed a small stratum of wealthy Jews to insulate itself from the rest of the community.

A second marriage pattern noted by Meyer in Metz is discernible in Steinbiedersdorf only in an attenuated form: a preference given to scholars as marriage partners for daughters and granddaughters. The families of Metz *parnasim* tried to establish marriage alliances with families of rabbis. Given the high status that male learning enjoyed within Jewish society, this was an expression of piety and prestige.[85] Moreover, as marriage partners rabbis were of considerable practical importance as judges and business contacts. As we have seen, this marriage pattern, which helped to a certain extent to ameliorate the inequality between women and men in inheritance law, is also apparent with Abraham Jacob's granddaughters and in an interesting variation even in his own life. Abraham Jacob took as his fourth wife Hentla, the daughter of the "highly learned Samuel Willstätt." It is entirely conceivable that the high regard for learning played a role also in this choice of a spouse. But Hentla Samuel Willstätt, Abraham Jacob's companion in the last years of his long life, was poorly rewarded.[86] Before he married her, Abraham Jacob had drawn up his last will

---

[81] The transfer of the office from father to son was no exception. Meyer has good evidence for this practice also in Metz: Meyer, *La communauté juive de Metz*, 208. It is better known with respect to rabbis: Avraham Grossmann, "From Father to Son: The Inheritance of Spiritual Leadership in Jewish Communities of the Middle Ages," in Kraemer, *The Jewish Family*, 115–131.

[82] Meyer, *La communauté juive de Metz*, 204f.

[83] Ibid, 211.

[84] Katz, *Tradition and Crisis*, 127.

[85] Meyer, *La communauté juive de Metz*, 213ff. In Metz, physicians were, next to rabbis, a group with whom the families of the *parnasim* strove to establish marriage ties.

[86] Willstadt was the name of a well-known Jewish family in Metz that had assumed the name Lambert in the eighteenth century: Pierre Mendel, "Les Noms de juifs français modernes," *Revue des études juives* 10 (1949/50), 15–63, here 49; Meyer, *La communauté juive de Metz*, 147. Glikl mentions in her memoirs Reb Isai Willstatt, who had leased the mint of the Duke of Lorraine: Glückel of Hameln, *Memoirs*, 259.

Illustration 6. Bernard Lipmann (*Bouxwiller, Bas-Rhin, 1740/41, †September 27, 1817, Metz) and his wife Fromette Levy (*Kriechingen, Dep. Moselle, 1745, †April 24, 1806, Metz). Portraits in oil, exact date unknown. The pictures belonged first to their son, Isidor (1788–1864) then his daughter, Laure Nathan, then her son, the Paris publisher Fernand Nathan, and finally their nephews, Raoul Nathan and Jean-Pierre Blum. The photograph is in the possession of Bernard Lyon-Caen, who kindly granted permission to have it reproduced here. A copy is in the Archives Départementales de Meurthe et Moselle in Metz.

and disposed of his entire estate.[87] Since there was no one who would say *kaddish* for him now that his son was dead, Abraham sought to ensure through his testamentary arrangements that every year, on the day of his death, a *minyan* in Metz and Kriechingen would pray for his soul. In distributing his wealth he also thought of his more distant relatives, which he preferred over other poor.[88] But it would appear that he did not provide well for his wife who took care of him when he was very old. He allegedly promised her during his lifetime that he would "provide for her well and honorably" and had given her presents. Yet Abraham, or his legal heirs, and Hentla Samuel Willstätt had very different ideas of what it meant to be provided for "well and honorably." The heirs offered her money, which she turned down. Presumably this was the share to which she was legally entitled. Hentla Samuel Willstätt was unwilling to accept that after the death of her "dearly beloved husband, the late Jewish *parnas* Abraham Jacob . . . the loyal marital duty she had shown to her late husband was so poorly compensated."[89] With the help of the secular authorities, with tenacity, persistence, and imagination, she fought to obtain a larger share of the estate. Preserving her status was important not only for her own life, but also for her daughter's marriage prospects.

When the will was read, Hentla Samuel Willstätt initially rejected the money allocated to her "because of the idea in her head that she was with child," and contented herself with an interim sum. By claiming, or perhaps hoping, that she was carrying the child of her aged, deceased husband, she managed to postpone the execution of the will. The government believed her, "not for her own sake," as it insisted, "but because of the largeness of her body."[90] For two months the matter was in limbo, then it was regarded as certain that Hentla Samuel Willstätt was not pregnant. She was ordered to content herself with the money she had been offered.

But Hentla Samuel Willstätt did not accept this decision. She was able to retain advocate Braun to represent her case and to shut out the rabbi of Metz. Braun, who did not know enough about Jewish marital law to make a competent judgment of the situation, adopted Hentla Samuel Willstätt's version. He emphasized that the marriage between Abraham and Hentla Samuel Willstätt had been contracted in legally valid form and presented a witness who saw the handing over of the wedding ring. As usual he built his argument on the image of the poor widow. In his brief he painted a picture of how the widow did not know where she would obtain bread and other food, how when she wanted to

---

[87] Testament of Abraham Jacob: see Appendix.

[88] Katz explains the reason for the obligation to support one's relatives by noting, among other things, that in the face of the uncertain legal status, no Jewish family was able to ensure a uniform socioeconomic status for all its members: *Tradition and Crisis*, 126.

[89] AD Mos. Actes judiciaires Pontpierre B 10061, B 10063.

[90] AD Mos. Actes judiciaires Pontpierre B 10061: Acta in Sachen der Witwe des verstorbenen Vorstehers Abraham Jacob zu Steinbiedersdorf ctr. dessen hinterlassenen Erben allda pcto dotis et illatorum, 1774.

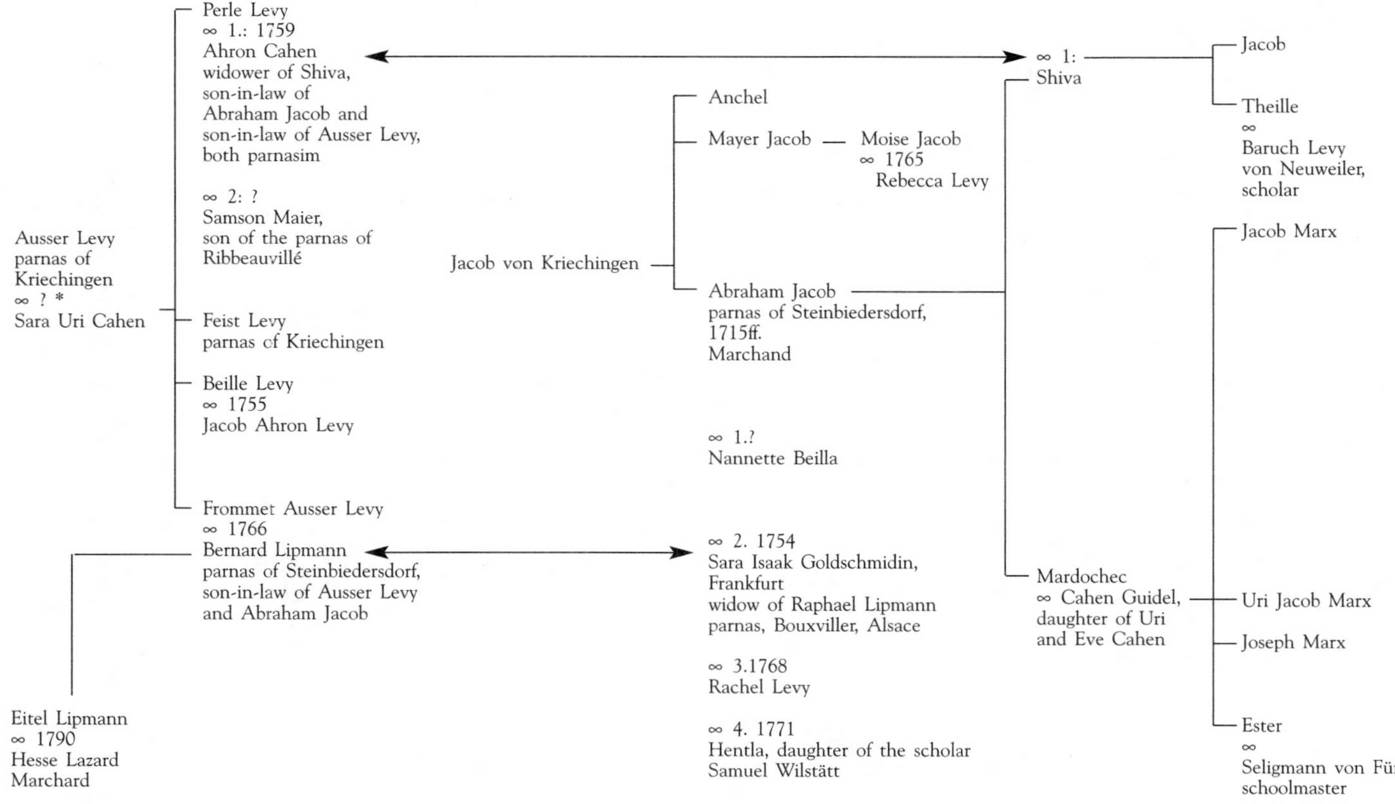

Table 6. Kinship ties between the parnasim of Kriechingen and Steinbiedersdorf

buy something she was compelled "to sell the clothes off her body," and how it was "a sin crying out to heaven" that she had been cut off from the necessary victuals.[91] He asked that she be awarded the set of silver cutlery Abraham had given her during their marriage. In addition, the 50 talers that had been promised to her daughter for her marriage would have to be separated from the estate and some capital secured to provide for her support.

As it would have been much better for the heirs if the rabbinical court in Metz settled the inheritance quarrel in accordance with Jewish law, they tried to pave the way for just such a settlement. Hentla Samuel Willstätt, on the other hand, benefited from the political developments, appealed to the court of the count, and as "a most humble supplicant" approached the count in his capacity as the patron of widows and orphans.[92] Did the advocate Braun and the Christian court fail to understand the marriage that Hentla Samuel Willstätt had entered into? Was Hentla Samuel Willstätt quite consciously able to use the ignorance or misunderstanding on the part of the Christian authorities to her advantage? Were there other reasons why the advocate took up the case of Hentla Samuel Willstätt and presented arguments that could carry weight under a Christian but not a Jewish understanding of marriage? These are questions we are hardly in a position to answer. At any rate, there was an overlap between the interests of Hentla Samuel Willstätt, who wanted to preserve her status as the widow of the rich Abraham in economic and sociocultural terms, and the interests of the secular seigneurial court, which was eager to suppress rabbinical jurisdiction and be accepted as a court with jurisdiction in this case. Hentla Samuel Willstätt was able to benefit to some degree from this partial concordance of interests. For years the government paid considerable attention to her, since the trial dragged on for a long time without a decision.

The example of Hentla Samuel Willstätt reveals the fragility of the life plans of Jewish women and their dependence on familial constellations. Although I was not able to reconstruct Hentla's familial connections on the basis of the existing material, there are numerous indications that she came from a respected, though not necessarily wealthy, family. As the legal proceedings showed, the living standard she could expect as the widow of Abraham Jacob did not correspond to her own ideas. The marriage to the aged Abraham had given her the possibility of moving up (again) socially, yet the chance of marrying off her daughter a little bit "higher up" depended on the life expectancy of Abraham, whose care was in her hands. Even if Hentla Samuel Willstätt was, much like Perle Levy, a woman who did not accept circumstances as they were and knew how to fight, her prospects for success were not the same.

------

[91] AD Metz, Actes judiciaires Pontpierre B 10061: Unterthänige Remonstration . . . in Sachen Abraham Jacob's hinterlassener Wittib von Steinbiedersdorf gegen die Vormünder and Erben, 1775.

[92] AD Metz, Actes judiciaires Pontpierre B 10061: Acta in Sachen der Witwe des verstorbenen Vorstehers Abraham Jacob.

How poorly Abraham Jacob had provided for his fourth wife becomes clear if we compare her situation to that of Eva Hirsch. On the occasion of her second marriage, the widowed Eva Hirsch had concluded a contract with the widower Moses Deutsch. They agreed that if Eva Hirsch were to die childless, her husband would inherit everything, although he would leave a certain sum of money to her sister and her brother.[93] The dispute over the inheritance of Teille, Abraham Jacob's granddaughter, shows that such stipulations for the benefit of the wife's family were by no means self-evident. When Teille died childless soon after the wedding, her husband laid claim to his wife's inheritance. Since Teille's brothers would not accept that wealth should flow out of their family after so short a time, the case ended up in court.[94] Eva Hirsch had preempted these kinds of problems.

Eva Hirsch, who had brought into the marriage 1,800 livres de France (partly in money, partly in furniture), a fully outfitted bed, as well as "womanly items of clothing belonging to her," concluded her marriage contract with Moses Deutsch "in the presence" of the Jew Herz Levy, a member of the count's government. As was customary, the contract made sure that Eva Hirsch would also be provided for as a widow. Upon the death of Moses Deutsch, the considerable capital that she had brought into the marriage would be kept in a chest to which only she and her husband's sons had a key. Her stepsons were to invest the money for her benefit. If they failed to do so conscientiously, Eva Hirsch was entitled to appoint guardians to administer her funds. If the assets she had brought with her were reduced during the marriage, she was allowed to access her husband's possessions, given to her as a mortgage to guarantee her own property, to make up the difference. Her right of residence was also settled in the contract. The agreement stipulated that she could live in her husband's house until such time as she remarried. Eva Hirsch agreed in the contract that after her death, her estate would pass to her husband's grandchildren. In return the surviving sons, along with their children and guardians should give her a proper burial, keep a light burning for her in the synagogue for a whole year, and during that time have prayers said for her soul in the morning and in the evening.[95] According to Jewish ritual customs, only a father and a mother were and are entitled to a one-year period of mourning and a commemorative candle.[96] Eva Hirsch, who was childless after her first marriage and evidently did not expect to have children in her second marriage, was able to use her wealth to compensate to a certain extent for the disadvantages she would incur as a

---

[93] AD Mos. Actes judiciaires Pontpierre B 10077: Acta Eheabredung und Schenkung auf den Todesfall zwischen dem Schutzjuden Moses Deutsch von Steinbiedersdorf und dessen Ehefrau Eva Hirsch von da, 1788.

[94] AD Mos. Actes judiciaires Pontpierre B 10059: Acta in Sachen Baruch Levy von Steinbiedersdorf ca. die Erben des Abraham Jacob und deren Vormünder pcto Debiti, 1774.

[95] AD Mos. Actes judiciaires Pontpierre B 10077: Acta Eheabredung und Schenkung auf den Todesfall.

[96] de Vries, *Jüdische Riten*, 320f.

childless woman and to secure intercessory prayers from her second husband's sons and grandchildren. Like Abraham Jacob, the childless widow made sure that *kaddish* would be said for her after her death.

Eva Hirsch and Moses Deutsch had their marriage contract notarized, thus investing it with the highest possible degree of mutual legal security that was valid also in non-Jewish courts. Their example demonstrates once more the significance of the house as a place of business affairs. In the house were kept not only promissory notes but also the dowry and the inheritance—highly important assets for securing and transferring wealth in a society whose member, as Jews, were unable to acquire land (or could do so only with great difficulty).[97] As we saw earlier, it was not unusual for these circumstances to give rise to the possibility of extensive economic activities, whereby women who pursued them also benefited from kinship networks.[98]

Disappointed hopes: the lives and fates of maids

Few Jewish families could afford to employ servants. The census of 1785 counted only four Jewish manservants and three Jewish maids in all the villages of the county.[99] Six, four manservants and two maids—worked in Steinbiedersdorf. Given the small number of servants, the frequency of conflicts is striking: the court records of Kriechingen over a period of fifteen years contain eight cases in which a manservant or maid was fired from the job. Among them Särle was an exception in that she had quarreled with her mistress and had been accused of theft. In most other cases, maids had gotten into trouble because they had, willingly or unwillingly, become involved in sexual relationships. Although the problem was essentially always the same, each case was different, for each young woman had placed different expectations and hopes on the relationship, had sought others ways of resolving the conflict and found different sources of help. Where the stories resemble each other again is in their outcome, when the young women, pregnant or with an illegitimate child, left the village and set out toward an uncertain future.

---

[97] A woman's dowry represented a special kind of security because it could not be touched by a husband's creditors. As long as marriage contracts were not notarized, it happened, according to Fraenckel, that indebted men altered the marriage contract in favor of their wives in order to protect as much of their wealth as possible. Women were not mere "objects" in these business arrangements, for the reason alone that these contracts affected the assets they would have as widows: Fraenckel, *Memoire*, XIV.

[98] Luciano Allegra has demonstrated this convincingly in the case of Turin: Allegra, "A Model of Jewish Devolution: Turin in the Eighteenth Century," *Jewish History* 7/2 (1993): 29–58.

[99] AD Mos. 10 F 69: Tableau général de la population et de la constitution du Comté de Créhange, 1786. By comparison, the Christian households had seventy-nine maids and thirty-nine manservants. The numbers do not include Saarwellingen.

Zarle, or the classic road to misery

Zarle, the daughter of "cross-eyed Isaac" (schelen Isäckel) of Steinbiedersdorf, had found employ and lodging with Feist Levy, the head of the Jewish community in Kriechingen. Apart from her, one manservant and, it would seem, the Jewish schoolmaster Simon Nathan from Wetzlar lived in the house of Feist Levy, who was a brother of Perle Levy. The neighbor Magdalene Stoffel, the wife of Martin Becker, came frequently to Feist Levy's house to help out. They all knew Zarle, watched her, and were aware that the girl had been sick for a while, had required medication, and had been bled twice. Moreover, they must have known that talk of Zarle's pregnancy had been "going around the village" for some time. If Zarle was asked about the pregnancy, she steadfastly denied it. As far as the men and women of the village were concerned, that was the end of the matter.

But when it became known in the fall of 1777 that Zarle, who must have been in her fifth or sixth month of pregnancy, "had suddenly disappeared and was staying with her father, known as the cross-eyed Isaac of Steinbiedersdorf," the interest of the authorities was aroused and the neighbors suddenly remembered: since the girl had not reported the pregnancy within the required time period, she had incurred criminal liability and exposed herself to the "suspicion of abortion." As the authorities were concerned with disciplining their subjects, it was only natural that they did not let the matter rest.

The government sought a report from doctor Fickelscherer, who made the following, unusually detailed statement:

> Fourteen months ago, at a time when I was still living in Pottier's house, the maid of Feist, the head of the Jews, had come to me and told me that she was no longer properly having her menses. Whereupon I had the suspicion that she might be pregnant, for it seemed to be true, judging from her external appearance. Thereupon I gave her medicines to strengthen the child. Whether she subsequently used alia remedia ad procurandum abortum is not something I can know. Four months later she came to me again and complained about the same conditions. She explained to me again what they were, namely that she felt heavy in all her limbs and asked me to bleed her, which is not allowed: when she realized that I would not do the bleeding, she said to me: Doctor, you are a rare kind of doctor! One would think you should help people, and I see that I am getting bigger by the day. To which I responded that such treatments cost money. She answered: and if it costs 6 Louis d'or, I would pay it. I responded: You are only a maid, how would you be able to give 6 Louis d'or? Whereupon she said: My master will pay it. I told her in reply: talk to your master, he should speak to me. Whereupon he spoke to me and promised me 6 Louis d'or pro aborte of his maid. I promised him to do it, but I was thinking something else. That man considered me a bad man by having the temerity to suggest such a black deed, Heaven protect me from it!"[100]

---

[100] AD Mos. Actes judiciaires B 10069: Acta in Deunciationssachen gegen des sogenannten scheelen Isäckels Tochter Zarle von Steinbiedersdorf pcto facto declarationis nec non adulterii, 1778.

For ten months Doctor Fickelscherer kept his outrage that one considered him capable of a "black deed" to himself. He filed a report and formal charge only in response to a formal request from the authorities. This circumstance casts a dubious light on his emphatic rejection of the allegation that he had negotiated an abortion. If Fickelscherer had been concerned solely about morality, he would not have entered into this devious agreement with Feist Levy in the first place, or he would have reported the case after Zarle had come to see him. Yet Fickelscherer wanted the authorities to believe that all he did was determine the intention of the Jewish householder and convict him by means of a fictitious agreement, after which, however, he kept this knowledge to himself. This story is not very convincing, especially since Fickelscherer claims that his honor had been insulted.

If we give credence to Zarle's version, which is only indirectly reported in the text, however, it must have been common knowledge in the village that women looking to abort a child could get help from Fickelscherer. It is therefore quite plausible that suspicion had fallen on him and that he was now under pressure to explain himself. Perhaps that is why he used his report to make himself appear like the guardian of good order and to emphasize his integrity. But if that was so, he had laid his plans without Zarle, for she had made sure that there were witnesses in good time. She had asked the doctor for a bleeding in the presence of the Jewish schoolmaster, after which she had spoken secretly with the doctor outside his door. The clandestine conversation between the maid and the doctor had not escaped the Jewish schoolmaster's attention, nor does it appear that it was supposed to, since Zarle complained to Simon Nathan: "The doctor is a scoundrel. I have already paid him in advance, I must have been to see him six times, but I cannot find him." Magdalene Stoffel, Martin Becker's wife, was also aware of the treatment.

Given the existence of witnesses, Fickelscherer had no choice but to admit the deed and to recast his involvement as responsible behavior on his part, as though his only concerns had been to strengthen the child and to convict Feist Levy, the head of the Jewish community, of the planned abortion. Whether the dialogue with the maid ever took place in the way he reported it, whether Zarle wanted the abortion or Feist had forced her into it—these are questions to which our sources provide no answers, especially since Zarle does not speak for herself. Instead, we have the witness testimony of Magdalena Stoffel, who had worked with Zarle. Magdalena knew that Fickelscherer had bled the maid twice at the foot, and that she had pretended to be sick without lying in bed. She did not notice her cooking a potion, however, and she also claimed to have been unaware of the forty-year-old woman's pregnancy, "because she was not paying attention." By claiming ignorance, she was asserting that there were areas in which neither the authorities nor the (male) neighbors should meddle; pregnancy was more than a biological condition that one could see.[101]

---

[101] Schulte, "Gerede," 69.

At the same time, she was protecting herself against punishment. For had she become aware of the attempted abortion, she would have been obligated to report it. By keeping quiet, Magdalene proclaimed her solidarity with the Jewish maid and protected her for now against the authorities eager to impose a punishment. In so doing she was also protecting a sphere of freedom which the community was still claiming for itself in the eighteenth century.

Extramarital sexual relationships generally did not escape the notice of the women of the village. But recourse to the authorities was only sought if they were needed to settle a conflict: if a girl wanted to marry the man by whom she was pregnant or sued for support, if the honor of another person had been harmed through false testimony, or if a crime had been committed and a newborn had been killed, a charge was brought or the villagers saw to it that the gossip became legally relevant.[102] In the case of the maid Zarle, however, the talk became impossible to ignore only after she had left the village and was thus out of danger.

The charge now implicated chiefly two men who had no difficulty talking their way out of it thanks to their social standing and gender: the doctor and the *parnas*. Doctor Fickelscherer placed the blame on the maid, and Feist Levy escaped further inquiries in spite of his dubious conduct. Levy was exonerated by the schoolmaster working in his home: Simon Nathan claimed to have noticed that the maid often went to the chamber of Feist Levy's manservant. At the same time he informed the government about a visit that Zarle's brother had paid to Feist Levy. Zarle had sought refuge with her brother during her pregnancy. After she had refused to tell even him who the father of her child was, he asked her point blank: "Was it your former master, the Jewish leader Feist Levy himself, who got you pregnant?" The brother claimed that Zarle tearfully admitted that the *parnas* was the one. Feist Levy claimed to know nothing about the matter, and the brother and sister probably thought it better, in view of the impending punishment, not to set foot again in Kriechingen. Much like urban servant maids, Zarle had been able to hire out her labor only together with her body, and her "reward" had been disgrace instead of honor. As an unmarried pregnant woman she was released from service, losing her livelihood and lodgings. To the extent that the relationship had involved an emotional aspect, she had to suppress her feelings since the pregnancy or failed abortion. It would seem that Feist Levy, as *parnas*, could take certain liberties with the girl. After all, he knew from his sister Perle Levy that the ability of the rabbinical court in Metz, which imposed harsh penalties for transgressions against Jewish marital and sexual morality, to intervene in the county of Kriechingen was slight, and that it was difficult for women to successfully bring a charge of paternity.[103] His calculation proved correct: the dispute ended without a decision.

---

[102] Silke Gösch, "'Vielmahls aber hätte sie gewünscht, einen andern Mann zu haben.' Gattenmord im 18. Jahrhundert," in Ulbricht, ed., *Von Huren und Rabenmüttern*, 313–334.

[103] This is not meant to imply that morals in the Jewish community became looser

It would appear that Zarle from the very outset did not aspire to marriage. At least she did not bother to inform the local courts and enlist them as allies in the pursuit of a claim for support or an action for marriage. She seems to have taken her fate upon her own shoulders and to have returned to her paternal family following the failed abortion.[104] Her continued presence in the house of the leader of the Jewish community was not tolerated. Zarle had, voluntarily or not, become involved in a relationship that had no prospects of lasting.[105] In so doing she had violated the prevailing social norms, which imposed on her as a woman the responsibility for the moral conduct of men, even when, as was the case here, the social, cultural, and economic distance between the two parties was enormous. At least in this regard, power and responsibility were distributed unequally at the expense of women.

It would seem that girls who insisted on a promise of marriage in due time, as in the following stories, were in a better starting position. But here, too, there was a wide gulf between theory and practice.

Failed efforts: Madl and Gelle

At around the same time in 1784, two maids in Steinbiedersdorf came to believe they were pregnant. Both attempted to secure the possibility of marriage by filing a complaint. While Gelle was supported by her aunt Frommet Oster Levy, Madl, who was cast out by her brothers, had to fend for herself. Madl, who worked as a maid in the house of Jacob Meyer Cahen, left nothing undone in her effort to deal with her difficult situation.

In December 1784 Madl duly declared her pregnancy and sued Meuschel Levy, the son of the Jew Mortgen, to compel him to keep his promise of marriage. Since Meuschel denied engaging in any sexual relations with Madl, the maid gave a detailed account of her relationship and presented witnesses who provided additional information. Madl claimed that Meuschel had pursued her for a long time, trying to seduce her into unlawful intercourse. Finally, he had his way, "and within a period of eight days he slept with her and impregnated her on four successive occasions, sometimes in her bed, having come into her chamber through the window, and sometimes in the hay, where they slept, having found the door locked at night."

Margarete Bildhauerin, the Sabbath maid, confirmed the meetings. We sense very little of the broad tabooing of sexuality that some scholars have ascribed

---

as a result of the suppression of the jurisdiction of Jewish courts. The sources are not sufficient to detect a development.

[104] I was unable to find any information about the birth and subsequent fate of the child.

[105] Jacob Katz prefers to see the causes rather in the economic difficulties that poor girls faced in raising the necessary dowry for a marriage. For that reason they were more willing to break sexual taboos: Katz, "Marriage," 408.

to people in the eighteenth century.[106] She readily and candidly explained to the men of the court that she had watched as the defendant had "lifted the skirt" of the plaintiff, who was still resisting a little, "and had touched her body with his bare hand under the skirt. Another time, eight days previously, she had seen the two standing very close to each other at the crib in the stable, and though she does not know what they were doing, it seemed suspicious to her."

Margarete further alleged that Meuschel had come in through the window of Madl's chamber. However, two Christian girls who had been summoned as witnesses did not confirm that statement. The nearly seventeen-year-old Margarete claimed she had to work during the day and was not allowed out of the house at night. Her fifteen-year-old sister testified that all she saw was that Madl and Meuschel had spoken with each other on several occasions. Since the testimony was not clear-cut, Meuschel was permitted to take an oath. He insisted that he had not had any sexual relations with Madl and was acquitted.[107]

At first Madl had no choice but to plead that the court costs be forgiven, but then the story took a surprising turn. Madl left Steinbiedersdorf and found shelter first in Rimmingen near Saargemünd.[108] There she related that she had accused Meuschel unjustly and that she was pregnant by Gembel, her employer's son. Gembel's father had promised her money if she put the blame on Moses Leib (Meuschel Levy), but he had subsequently sent her away with a very small sum of money. Furthermore, she alleged that her employer had also paid the Sabbath maid to make a false statement. Evidently Jacob Meyer Cahen had sufficient influence on his domestics. His power and Madl's need for money seem to have been such that Madl initially went along with the plan.

As an unmarried pregnant woman, Madl had to depend on the help of others. New men entered her life and tried to profit from her difficult situation. One of them, whom she followed all the way, tried to convince her to blackmail Gembel's father so that they both would get "their passover matzah." As a reward he held out the prospect of marriage and thus of a more or less stable existence. In Rimmingen, Herz May had secured a promise of marriage for the pregnant Madl on the condition that she raise 100 talers within a fortnight. In response she tried to obtain a dowry. She wrote a letter to her brothers in the Alsace, who did not take up her cause and explained that they no longer recognized her as their sister. The attempt to extort a dowry from Jacob Meyer Cahen also failed. Not even the hope of receiving 50 Louis d'or, "from

---

[106] This is the contention of Richard van Dülmen, for example, who largely follows Norbert Elias's theory of the civilizing process in his explanation of early modern sexuality: van Dülmen, *Kultur und Alltag*, vol. 2, 184ff.

[107] AD Mos. Actes judiciaires B 10073: Acta in Denunciationssachen der Madl Meyer von Steinbiedersdorf ca. Meuschel Levy von da, Beklagter, pcto impregnationis, 1784.

[108] Rimmingen near Saargemünd is presumably Rémering-lès-Puttelange, about twenty kilometers from Steinbiedersdorf.

which she could live even if she did not get married," materialized.[109] None of the Jews in Rimmingen received Madl in their home for very long, especially since Jewish families were forbidden from taking in strangers for long periods. Madl had to change her lodgings repeatedly. At the request of the wife of Herz May she was allowed to stay at least fourteen days in his house, at which time he refused further support. It is not clear whether he took any further interest in the girl's case once the prospects of a dowry had evaporated. Although it was beyond doubt that one of the young men of Steinbiedersdorf had gotten her pregnant, Madl declined to bring a new charge and bore her fate alone. Oury Cahen, who was frequently on the road because of his cattle trading and who had passed on her letters, had to pay a steep fine because he had stirred up a case that had already been settled and had thus injured Gemble's honor and good name once again.[110]

Madl's case is an impressive demonstration of the extent to which women were dependent on men. That Madl still made various attempts to enter into a marriage suggests how much greater her troubles would be if she remained single. Whereas it is possible that the first relationship involved feelings and hopes of happiness, the sole goal that Madl pursued later was to get married. In a society in which marriages were arranged, women had learned to adapt to men. The idea of marrying someone who was more or less a stranger was thus surely less unusual and easier to bear than the burden of the expected disgrace of an illegitimate birth and the punishment from one's own religious community and the surrounding Christian world.

If unmarried Jewish mothers failed to contract a marriage, they could expect, at least as long as they remained within the sphere in which French laws held sway, that their children would be taken away, baptized, and raised as Catholics.[111] The legal basis for this was an edict by the French king from the year 1682, which concerned all illegitimate children whose father or mother belonged to a "heretical confession."[112] In 1762 this regulation was somewhat ameliorated

---

[109] AD Mos. Actes judiciaires B 10074: Acta in Sachen des Schutzjuden Meyer Jacob Cahen von Steinbiedersdorf, Imploranten, ca. den Schutzjuden Oury Abraham Cahen daselbst, Imploraten, pcto injuriam, 1785.

[110] Ibid.; also Acta in Denunciationssachen der Madl Mayer von Steinbiedersdorf ctra. Meuschel Levy von da, Beklagter, pcto impregnationis, 1784.

[111] This possibility was noted by Mendel, who studied the Jewish community of Bionville (not far from Kriechingen), where a Jewish maid sought refuge because of the imminent birth of her illegitimate child: Mendel, *Le juifs de Bionville*, 17.

[112] "Voulons et Nous plaisit que tous les enfants bâtards de la R. P. R. de l'un de l'autre sexe, de quelque âge et condition qu'ils soient, soient instruits et élévez à la Religion catholique Apostolique et Romaine." In *Receuil d'Edits, Declarations et Arrests tant du Conseil que du Parlement, et autre pièces, rendus au sujet de ceux de la Religion Pretenduë Reformée* (no date or place of publication, unpaginated). The edict is connected with several decrees against the Huguenots shortly before the repeal of the Edict of Nantes. According to these decrees, marriages between Catholics and members of the reformed religion were declared to be invalid, and their children were excluded from the right of

for members of the Jewish religion: if the parents legalized their marriage within five years after the birth of their child, they were allowed to keep it.[113] But even within their own religious community, single mothers could hardly hope for sympathy until the end of the eighteenth century.[114]

In Jewish religion, a positive view of sexuality within marriage was confronted by a strict rejection of extramarital sexual relations.[115] Matchmaking was embedded within a ritual in which parents and partners were involved.[116] Apart from religious obstacles, there were also political, economic, and social obstacles to the sort of traditional forms of matchmaking that were found in Christian communities, some of which were practiced against the will of the church or against the will of the parents: in Jewish society, residence permits and the right of protection or domicile were existential questions in a way that was very different from the surrounding Christian world. Although the religious prohibitions and the legal regulations concerned men and women equally, Madl, much like Zarle, was forced to discover that women were punished more harshly for transgressions against marital and sexual morality. On this point the court of the count differed but little from the rabbinical court in Metz.[117]

---

inheritance and raised as Catholics. I would like to thank Ursula Fuhrich-Grubert for calling my attention to these sources in the Huguenot Archive.

[113] The laws are mentioned (though without any specification as to the areas where they were valid) in Rod. Reuss, "L'histoire d'Élias Salomon de Dauendorf et de Iedelé d'Obernai. Une page d'histoire de l'antisémitisme en Alsace (1790–1792)," *Revue des études juives* 68 (1914): 235–245.

[114] Claudia T. Prestel has stated, not least through recourse to data from the Jewish community in Berlin, that illegitimate children and single mothers were "a not unusual form of family formation" in the eighteenth century even within the Jewish minority: "Uneheliche Kinder und ledige Mütter in der jüdischen Gemeinschaft im 20. Jahrhundert: Eingliederung oder Ausschluß? Ein Beitrag zur deutsch-jüdischen Frauengeschichte," *L'Homme Z. F. G.* 5, No. 2 (1994), 81–101, here 81. The situation in Metz was different. Here only six illegitimate births were registered throught the entire eighteenth century, three of which occurred in the 1780s. The rate of illegitimacy in the Christian community stood at 15 percent at the time. In part the low illegitimacy rate in the Jewish community is explained by the harsh punishment meted out to pregnant girls by the rabbinical court. The girls were excluded from the community (*cherem*) and expelled: Meyer, *La communauté juive de Metz*, 130f. Paula E. Hyman also assumes a low illegitimacy rate among Alsatian Jewish families in the nineteenth century: *Emancipation*, 52f. Prestel has shown that a social breakdown of single mothers can lead to very different conclusions: illegitimacy was a rare phenomenon (about 4 percent) also in the community of Fürth she studied. The situation was different within the lower class (about 12 percent), which led her to conclude: "As far as the birth of illegitimate children as a form of deviation from the bourgeois moral code is concerned, it became largely the norm in Fürth": Prestel, "Jüdische Unterschichten im Zeitalter der Emanzipation, dargestellt anhand der Gemeinde Fürth, 1826–1870," *Aschkenas* 1 (1991): 95–134, here 118.

[115] See note 63.

[116] Herweg, *Die jüdische Mutter*, 38ff.

[117] Meyer, *La communauté juive de Metz*, 87.

The real winner, if we can say such a thing, was Jacob Meyer Cahen, Madl's employer and Gembl's father. He had prevented the marriage between his son and the maid, had deflected disgrace and dishonor from his house, and had preserved for this son the possibility of a better match.[118] Jacob Meyer Cahen evidently did a poor job of raising his son: while the father was still busy foisting Madl's child onto Meuschel, Gembel was already facing the next paternity suit.

There was another girl in the village who pinned her hopes on Gembel. In the days when Madl was declaring her pregnancy, sixteen- or seventeen-year-old Gelle claimed that she had gotten pregnant by Gembel. She allegedly met the young man at a wedding in Finstingen, where she worked in a tavern in which Gembel now and then drank tea. Gembel, as she later maintained, had occasionally made "improper propositions" and had also given her money on one occasion. With this claim, Gelle, who was much better represented in her suit than the other girls, advanced an important argument, one that substantially improved her chances of success. Not only did she point out that Gembel had played an active role while she had been passive, by referring to the money that changed hands she was alleging that there had been a serious attempt to establish a relationship. Later she also mentioned a formal promise of marriage.

It was certainly no coincidence that Gelle was able, a short time later, to procure employment in Steinbiedersdorf in the household of her aunt, Frommet Oster Levy. Gelle recounted that already on the second Sabbath following her arrival, Gembel had slept with her in the bed in the lodgings of the schoolmaster. Prior to that he had promised that he would marry her if she worked for just another year. The following Tuesday was "the time of her monthly purgation, but she did not get it, and from this she concluded that she was pregnant."

At the beginning of December, Bernard Lipman's wife came to suspect that her maid might be pregnant. She immediately told the cantor and Ahron Cahen: her maid had been in the basement together with her daughter and the cantor's son. There they had made fun of another girl who had recently gotten pregnant, probably Madl. The boy—in pure jest, as he later insisted—supposedly said to Gelle: "I think you too have a thick belly." The daughter related this to the mother, who questioned the maid and extracted a confession. The plan now was to have this confession made before witnesses. To that end, Frommet Oster Levy, whose husband was in St. Avold at the time in question, hid the two men, the forty-eight-year-old cantor and the thirty-three-year-old Ahron Cahen, in a wardrobe, called the maid, and told her to make the bed. As Gelle was working, Frommet questioned her: "You come from honorable people, and you have inflicted such disgrace on us. Tell me now, I want

---

[118] It is rather doubtful whether he succeeded in arranging a better marriage. In Fleury, *Contrats de Mariage*, in any case, we do not find any indication of a notarized marriage contract. This does not rule out the possibility, however, that other indications might be found in the Kriechingen material, which I was not able to analyze in its entirety for the present study.

to know, and speak the whole truth. You must not think that you can finger a rich man, because God knows everything."

After the maid had confessed to being pregnant by Gembel, the two witnesses came out of the wardrobe. The maid did not react further, finished her work, and left. Frommet Oster Levy, however, remained seated and was shouting. Marx Jacob Levy, the cantor, who related the situation in his testimony, from the outset did not quite believe the whole story. When Frommet Oster Levy told him the maid had been in her service for two months and since that time had not had her "regular purgation," that she never thought this was good yet believed it was caused by an injured foot, Marx Jacob Levy laughed and asserted that this was no sure sign. He knew from his wife that the purgation could be absent for two or three months and it might not mean anything.[119] Ahron Cahen confirmed the testimony of his fellow witness in part, but he claimed that when they were in the wardrobe, Frommet Oster Levy had asked the maid, "Tell me, why do you want to write a letter to your father, I want to know." In response she received the confession about the pregnancy.

The subsequent interrogations were as unusual as this first one. Many very detailed accounts were given, fragments of verbatim conversations were reported, topics were discussed that we today would assume would not have been spoken about in an eighteenth-century male society. The fact that Marx Jacob Levy talked to Frommet Oster Levy, who had an almost fully grown daughter, about whether one could infer a pregnancy at so early a date could indicate that in Jewish society menstruation and pregnancy were openly discussed even among men.[120] That both men, in spite of their differences of opinion about the signs of pregnancy, made themselves available as witnesses shows that "the wife of said Jewish leader" had a certain influence within her social environment, that she shared in her husband's status and power.

Immediately upon his return from St. Avold, Bernard Lipman was informed of the events by his wife, Frommet Oster Levy. Bernard Lipman questioned the girl harshly, obtained a confession, and the next morning sent for her father to discuss the matter and make a declaration. The testimony of the manservant and of one of the two schoolmasters also pointed the finger of blame at Gembel.

---

[119] This corresponded to the contemporary view that the absence of the menses could also be a sign of impending illnesses. See Barbara Duden, *The Woman Beneath the Skin: A Doctor's Patients in Eighteenth-Century Germany* (Cambridge, Mass., 1991), 159; Maren Lorenz, "'... als ob ihr ein Stein aus dem Leib kollerte ...' Schwangerschaftswahrnehmungen und Geburtserfahrungen von Frauen im 18. Jahrhundert," in Richard van Dülmen, ed., *Körper-Geschichten. Studien zur historischen Kulturforschung* (Frankfurt am Main, 1996), 99–121, and idem, "Devianz und Gesellschaft. Selbst- und Fremdwahrnehumg von Körper und Seele im Spiegel gerichtsmedizinischer Fallsammlungen des 18. Jahrhunderts," Ph.D. dissertation (Saarbrücken, 1997).

[120] In this context one should recall the importance of purification in Jewish life. As I have already mentioned, I have not been able to find any sign of a mikvah in Steinbiedersdorf, a clear indication that central issues of Jewish life were not addressed or written down in Christian courts.

The eighteen-year-old manservant remembered that Gembel asked him on the Sabbath in question: "Did you already try your maid?" When he denied this indignantly, Gembel supposedly boasted: "I've already tried her." Schoolmaster Philip Heym even claimed to have heard Gembel bragging: "No other young Jewish chap in the village, and no Jewish schoolmaster, shall have the honor of having the new maid Gelle, she was to be his alone." He stated that he saw Gembel and Gelle in his bedroom. The other schoolmaster vehemently contradicted that account: at the time in question, he had been drinking schnapps with Gembel. Three children were brought in as additional witnesses: they had spent the Sabbath, as they usually did, with Gelle, Gembel, and other young people. All they knew was that Gelle and Gembel had laid down on the bed in jest, and that the bed broke. But other than that, Bremele asserted, nothing happened.

Frommet Oster Levy, the wife of the head of the Jewish community, who had extracted a confession from Gelle in the presence of concealed witnesses and had given crucial impulses to the talk in the village, stayed away from the court. Her husband excused her on account of the bad weather and because he did not have a "chaise" for her. Gelle, who was afraid of ending up in the tower, tried to stay out of the proceedings. She refused to go to Kriechingen on the grounds that she did not have any shoes, which finally led the official (dechant) to declare that she should be provided with the necessary shoes or, if necessary, be put on a horse.

The fact that there was a trial at all was entirely the result of Jacob Mayer Cahen's paternal concern. He had been informed that the girl intended to name his son, "whom he surely knew to be innocent, as the cause of her pregnancy." That was the reason why the girl's father had announced that he would come to see him that day. To resolve the case and to prevent the witnesses from colluding, Jacob Mayer Cahen demanded that the girl be immediately removed from her employer's house and taken to another house, where she was to be guarded until the following day by two people, one of whom would be the dechant. He was to make sure, above all, that Gelle did not secretly speak "Hebrew or Jewish-German" (Yiddish) to anybody.

The quick complaint brought by Jacob Mayer Cahen, who at the same time had to defend his son also against Madl's paternity suit, and who may have believed that Gembel was "innocent" at least in this case, was successful. Gembel, who insisted in court that he did not even know "this immature woman" and that he had never socialized with such bad people, was cleared of the charges. His request to have his honor restored was granted. Since Gelle had grossly violated the honor and good name of the defendant, without even knowing whether or not she was pregnant, she was given a warning and sentenced to court costs. She had solely her indigence and youth to thank for this comparatively light sentence.[121]

---

[121] AD Mos. Actes judiciaires B 10073: Acta in Denunciationssachen der Jüdin Gelle,

By successfully fending off the paternity suit, Jacob Meyer Cahen had once again prevented his dissolute son from being forced into a marriage that was unfavorable to the family. To Gembel it was a matter of honor to seduce the maids, as they were objects he claimed for himself. The expectations of the girls were very different: like Madl, Gelle had been hoping for marriage. Unlike Madl she had the support of her aunt in the case. Frommet Oster Levy, the wife of Bernard Lipman, was the real driving force: it was she who, in her husband's absence, tried to initiate the negotiations between the fathers of Gelle and Gembel. Although there was no urgent need to take any action, as soon as she found out about the relationship between Gelle and Gembel, she summoned the two witnesses, hid them in the wardrobe, and extracted a confession from the girl. It is not clear whether she wanted to contract a good marriage for her niece whom she had taken into her home, or whether she was trying to protect herself and her house from disgrace. Be that as it may, she was concerned that the "affair" between Gembel and Gelle be resolved as quickly as possible through a marriage. In this she had her husband's unconditional support. Having returned from St. Avold, he immediately initiated the necessary steps (questioning the girl, informing the father). By taking such resolute action, the Lipmans, who had a marriageable daughter of their own, were defending the strict Jewish marital and sexual morality with its existing system of arranged marriages. This system stabilized the power of parents over their children, guaranteed the continuity of property, but also improved the matrimonial prospects of marriageable girls of the social stratum whose financial circumstances allowed their children to get married. Especially within Jewish society, whose conditions of settlement were subject to strict control and were highly restricted, this kind of thinking was not merely an outgrowth of religious attitudes and inner need for social control and isolation, but also a reaction to outside coercion.

When it came to the defense of arranged marriages, the Lipmans were of a mind with Jacob Meyer Cahen. The system of arranged marriages presupposed a world in which boys and girls were strictly separated from a certain age and in which the rules of chastity were respected and observed.[122] The young people of Steinbiedersdorf did not pay much heed to such concerns. The young men, who married much later than the girls and who formed a clear majority, were, at least in the estimation of the twenty-year-old schoolmaster Philip Heym from Arnsberg, "unruly and badly bred." Boys and girls, sons and daughters, maids and manservants, poor and rich played on the Sabbath while the parents were resting. They also took walks together[123] or had musicians from out-

---

dermalen zu Steinbiedersdorf sich aufhaltend ctra Jacob Meyer Cahens Sohn von da pcto impregnationis ac satisfactionis. Aussage des Ahron Cahen, 1784.

[122] Extensive rules of chastity were formulated also for married couples: Katz, "Mariage," 403ff.; Herweg, *Die jüdische Mutter*, 42f.

[123] AD Mos. Actes judiciaires B 10057: Acta in Sachen Samuel Samuel, Knecht bei

side the village play for a dance during their parents' absence, which was prohibited.[124] On other days, as well, they visited in each other's houses. Samuel,
for example, who had been involved in a brawl with another young Jew, was
supposedly in the house of a female witness until ten o'clock at night, coach-
ing her on her testimony.[125]

Weddings, which were always celebrated elaborately by the Jewish population,[126] provided another welcome opportunity for young people to enjoy each
other's company. Gelle stated that she met Gembel at a wedding in Finstingen.
In Steinbiedersdorf, the wedding of Bernard Lipman was a major event in 1766.
Accompanied by a raucous band of young men, the bride was led from Kriechingen to Steinbiedersdorf. In the process, eight or ten fireworks were set off,
one of which injured a Jewish boy. The "entire village" attended the spectacle.[127]

Jewish weddings came under growing criticism in the eighteenth century,
because excessive alcohol consumption created disorder, young and old men
danced with strange women, and young women and men spent the night in
the same room.[128] In Steinbiedersdorf it was Perle Levy, of all people, who took

---

Abraham Jacob zu Steinbiedersdorf contra Feist Cahen und Gembel Cahen anstatt seines
Sohnes Samuel Cahen pto. injuria realia, 1772. The manservant Samuel had been out
on a walk with the two maids of Jacob Ahron Levy and Ahron Cahen's widow when
a brawl occurred. The reports about mixed-gender walks in the village are also interesting in that they cast a different light on the thesis of Gudrun M. König with regard
to the urban bourgeoisie. König has argued that the modern habit of going on walks is
a practice that was propagated during the Enlightenment and arose from the burgher
class: König *Eine Kulturgeschichte des Spaziergangs. Spuren einer bürgerlichen Praktik
1780–1850.* Kulturstudien, Sonderband 20 (Vienna, 1996).

[124] AD. Mos. Actes judiciaires B 10043: Jacob Levy zu Steinbiedersdrof wegen Tanzen
und Spielen, 1751. On the importance of music in Jewish culture see Walter Salmen,
"... *denn die Fiedel macht das Fest." Jüdische Musikanten und Tänzer vom 13. bis 20.
Jahrhundert* (Innsbruck, 1991).

[125] AD Mos. Actes judiciaires B 10057: Acta in Sachen Samuel Samuel, Knecht bei
Abraham Jacob: the brawl broke out when one of the young men said, "I don't have
as many lice in my beard as you."

[126] Joseph Gutmann has emphasized that wedding customs were very different in the
various countries: "Jewish Medieval Marriage Customs in Art: Creativity and Adaptation,"
in Kraemer, *The Jewish Family,* 47–61.

[127] AD Mos. Actes judiciaires B 10048: Acta in Sachen Fiscalis gg. Abraham Jacob,
dessen Ehefrau und Hausgesind pcto beschädigten Sabbats und vorgenommen Schießens,
1766.

[128] Wachstein, "Das Statut," 139; Pollack, *Jewish Folkways,* 39. In Illingen, as well,
there was trouble on account of a Jewish wedding that was held during Lent. The pastor was offended that the Jews "in their Jewish manner" had entertained themselves
"with jumping and dancing, not without vexation to the Christian folk," while the
Amtmann noted: "It is known that at Jewish weddings the Jews generally go crazy and
perform their copulation, if one may say so, out in the open, which brings many young
people running and makes them laugh about their buffonery." Quoted in Robert Kirsch,
Die Juden in der Herrschaft Illingen. Die Kerpische Judengemeinde im 18. Jahrhundert
(Illingen, no date), 104.

offense at this riotous festiveness. In the spring of 1774 she attended a wedding "to which many young people had been invited" in order to keep an eye on her daughters. She was upset that some were embracing in the presence of "minor children." As we have seen, when Lion Meyer Levy answered her reproach by alluding to her own relationship, she brought a charge against him. Like Jacob Meyer Cahen and later the Lipmans, she enlisted the seigneurial court in an effort to defend not only her honor and standing, but also the system of arranged marriages, and to reinforce parental control over the young.

Suspicious company: love among domestics

The resolve with which the Jewish upper stratum defended itself against uncontrolled, freely chosen relationships among their children and domestics becomes clearer still in a conflict that took place three years later in the house of Bär Lipman. This time it was not only the maid who was involved, but also the farmhand. Relationships among domestics were strictly prohibited in both the Jewish and the Christian village community.[129] By foisting paternity for a pregnant maid's child onto a farmhand, one could rid oneself of both domestics and thus keep any suspicion away from one's own social class. Heaping blame on the farmhand provided Christian and Jewish society with a successful model for regulating conflict, although it naturally presupposed a relevant confession by the maid. Such a confession seemed to exist in Bär Lipman's house.

In 1787 yet another maid in the household of Frommet Oster Levy and Bernard Lipman was pregnant. Evidently a rumor had arisen in the village that the farmhand Abraham Benedikt had engaged in "suspicious conduct" with the maid Frommet Ahron. When Frommet Oster Levy and Bernard Lipman heard about it, they confronted their maid. As soon as they had extracted a confession, Bernard Lipman summoned the bailiff and the clerk into his house and asked them to question the maid about the child's father. Initially the girl was reluctant to admit anything, but eventually she made the following statement: "Yes, last night my master talked me into naming the farmhand as the child's father. However, on my conscience I cannot say that." Upon hearing this, Frommet Oster Levy flew at the girl and slapped her while remarking: "What, scoundrel, did we incite you to do?" As the maid refused to confess, Bernard Lipman threatened the farmhand: "You, farmhand, get out of my house or I will get three farmers and have you removed." He chased the farmhand away without paying him his outstanding wages.[130]

---

[129] On the connection between marriage possibilities, the organization of labor, and illegitimacy rates see Michael Mitterauer, *Ledige Mütter. Zur Geschichte unehelicher Geburten in Europa* (Munich, 1938), 67ff.; on illegitimacy within the Jewish lower stratum see note 114.

[130] AD Mos. Actes judiciaires B 10075: Acta in Sachen Benedict Isaak und Abraham Benedikt von Dentingen ca. den Barnes Bär Lipman von Steinbiedersdorf pcto schuldigen Lidlohns, 1788.

The maid was allowed to stay, at the intercession of the bailiff and the court, but she had been forced, under threats, to make a declaration in the office of the court clerk about her pregnancy, and to name the farmhand Abraham Benedikt as the father: she stated that about six months previously, the farmhand "had lain with her twice and she had conceived by him."[131] Although Frommet Ahron had to pay a fine for committing the sexual offense until such time as she could prove that Abraham Benedikt was the father, she wisely did not take any steps to do so.

The farmhand, outraged that the "whore" had initially been allowed to remain in the house while he had been driven out, sued unsuccessfully for his wages and his savings with help from this father, a "desperately poor" man. The court also denied him the satisfaction he demanded for the insults he had suffered. Instead, he was accused of being litigious. Frommet Ahron, who came from Ribeauvillé/Rappoltsweiler in the Alsace, many hours from Steinbiedersdorf, was probably permitted to carry her child to term in the house of the Lipmans, but after that she appears to have left the area.

With help from advocate Braun, who was very favorably disposed toward the Jewish upper stratum, the honor of the Lipman house was thus reestablished, at least on the outside. Even though Bernard Lipman, as a Jew, stood outside the system of social estates, he was, like advocate Braun, a member of a wealthy elite that strove to defend its privileged social position against intruders, and to use its power to keep those of lower social standing at a distance.

This becomes clear also from the form of address used by the domestics: "Herr and Herrschaft." Frommet Oster Levy, Bär Lipman's wife, identified with the interests of her husband, together with whom she exercised domination in the house over farmhands and maids. In her we come closest to finding the respected, independent Jewish woman "who is the house" and whom I described at the beginning of this chapter. Frommet Oster Levy was concerned no less than her husband about the honor of the house, which she defended by force if necessary. While he was away on business, she looked after the household, the children, the farmhand, and the maid, and she condemned their moral transgression no less forcefully than he did. As a member of a privileged class, she had special reason to fear the dissolution of the social order. A loosening of morals and the relinquishing of arranged marriages put her power as mistress of the house in question, and with it the privileges precisely of those members of the "weaker" gender who had a structural advantage over others because of status, background, family, or wealth, and who had learned through a specifically female upbringing and education to gear their expectations towards their husband, to accommodate themselves to him and identify with his interests. Within

---

[131] Ibid., 10.9.1787: Deklaration vor dem Tabellion und herrschaftlichen Meier von Steinbiedersdorf.

the house she exercised power in mutual agreement with her husband.[132] She used her position not only to defend order in the house and thus simultaneously her honor, but also tried, as has become clear in the case of Frommet's niece Gelle, to establish and take advantage of social networks and to use her influence to promote the interests of her own family.[133]

Although in the present case the farmhand was initially punished more harshly than the maid, it seems remarkable how many maids—compared to the total number of domestics working in the households—were confronted with existential problems from an illegitimate pregnancy. The chances of the girls to obtain legal redress were slim. It made no difference to them whether they were condemned by the seigneurial court or by the rabbinical court in Metz. Those who sat in judgment over them were in every instance men whose attitudes toward female honor and sexuality were similar, and who received the support of their wives.[134] The girls could try to end the pregnancy through abortion, to force the father of the child into a marriage by making a declaration, or to convict him through public talk—in the end they were all losers. Except for Perle Levy. The wealthy widow was the only one who successfully prosecuted a complaint of marriage in spite of all the difficulties she faced.[135] She fought not only for economic but also symbolic capital, which related not only to herself but her entirely paternal family. For the role of honor and status was no less important in Jewish society than it was in Christian society. As Natalie

---

[132] On the shared household as an element of social order and part of the "political" public arena see Wunder, *He is the Sun, She is the Moon*, esp. chapter 12.

[133] On the importance of power relationships see Knapp, *Macht und Geschlecht*, esp. 301f.

[134] In this respect, as well, the limits to the usefulness of theories of difference between the two genders become clear. See on this the critical remarks by Gildemeister and Wetterer, "Wie Geschlechter gemacht werden," 201ff.

[135] Immediately prior to the period of the revolution, one maid in Denting won at least a modest victory in the court. Madeleine from the Alsace sued her employer, Ausser Worms, who had "dismissed her from service under the pretext of an alleged pregnancy, who had beat her in the process and refused to pay her wages." Ausser Worms attempted to defeat the charge with the help of the court. He invoked the existing law by which a person from the outside could initiate proceedings in Kriechingen only if he or she was able to provide a security deposit. Wealthy Christians and Jews had always used this rule to their advantage, as it allowed them to turn away complaints by the poor and domestics. Bernard Lipman had also tried to defend against a complaint brought by a farmhand by demanding a security deposit. The court, however, had considerable leeway on this question, hence whether or not a complaint was accepted depended also on what kind of relationship the plaintiff and defendant had to the Amtmann. Madeleine was fortunate: she was allowed to swear an oath, and the court accepted her clothes, which she kept in Boulay, as a security deposit. She was at least able to initiate proceedings, but it would seem that the case was swept away by the upheavals of the revolution: AD Mos. Actes judiciaires, Denting, B 10075: Acta in Sachen die Jüdin Madeleine aus dem Elsässischen gegen Ausser Worms betr., 1789.

Zemon Davis has emphasized: "Honor in its most general form was often coupled with riches."[136]

The lawsuits of Perle and Särle, of Madl, Gelle, Frommet, and Benedikt lead us back to the Christian community and to Christian domination, which Natalie Zemon Davis has described as "encircling the Jews with their institutions and worldly control."[137]

---

[136] Davis, *Women on the Margins*, 34.
[137] Ibid., 38.

CHAPTER SEVEN

FROM THE MARGIN TO THE CENTER: CHRISTIAN-JEWISH RELATIONS

The influx of Jewish immigrants into German Lorraine should not obscure the continuing existence of a latent—and occasionally open—hostility between Christians and Jews. Religious bias was still alive when an increasing number of Jews came to settle in German Lorraine in the second half of the seventeenth century. Jews were still demonized as members of a religious minority and confronted with accusations of ritual murder.[1] Throughout the eighteenth century, rumors about ritual murders, charges of host desecration, and accusations of witchcraft helped to nourish anti-Jewish feelings that were more than economic in nature. As late as 1761, when the wave of witchcraft persecutions across Europe had long since died down, three Jews were burned as wizards in Nancy.[2]

The debate over the political emancipation of the Jews was also accompanied by anti-Jewish feelings, which escalated at the beginning of the French Revolution.[3] After 1789 the Jews of eastern France "had to defend themselves not only against verbal but also physical attacks, which were fed by the horror clichés of the ugly, stinking, cheating, and usurious Jews."[4] It would seem that many of the expressions of anti-Jewish sentiment originated in the cities rather than the countryside. There are numerous indications that the guilds were especially hostile toward the Jews.[5]

The enormous financial need of the territorial ruler was one reason why the Jewish villagers of Steinbiedersdorf could hope for his protection in times of conflict as long as they had sufficient monetary resources. Still, there are many

---

[1] Evidence for the hostility of the population of Lorraine toward Jews in the seventeenth and eighteenth centuries is in Cahen, ed., *Catalogue: Les Juifs Lorrains*, 28ff., and in Behre, "Raphael Levy," 19ff.

[2] Cahen, "La region lorraine," 106ff.

[3] Badinter, *Libres et égaux*, esp. 55; Girard, *La Révolution Française*, 148ff.

[4] Wolfgang Schmale, "Frankreich und die Erklärung der Menschen- und Bürgerrechte 1789 im Lichte der französischen Forschung 200 Jahre danach," *ZHF* 20 (1993): 345–376 (quote 363).

[5] This has been noted, among others, by Behre, "Raphael Levy," 19–44; Badinter, *Libres et égaux*, 32, 40; Girard, *La Révolution Française*, 32.

indications that the Jews—notwithstanding their importance to the economy of the territory and in spite of the continuous expansion and consolidation of the Jewish community—were always aware of how fragile Christian-Jewish coexistence was. That fragility became especially apparent during the Kriechingen Rebellion described earlier, which meant for many Christian neighbors a descent into poverty. Since the rebellion was a conflict between the Christian community and the authorities, the Jewish villagers were not directly involved. It would seem, however, that they followed the events closely, and that at least one of them acted as an informant. Like Katharina Richard, Jacques Levy had picked up and passed on the rumor that the villagers were planning to free their fellow villagers from the seigneurial prison.[6] When soldiers entered Steinbiedersdorf a short while later, the Jews were also out in the streets. Before the soldiers began to seize property, the official messenger (Amtsbote) was dispatched to Abraham Jacob, who was to see to it "that all Jews get off the street, whereupon they ran off so quickly as though chased by someone out to beat them."[7]

After a man from Lorraine who happened to be present during the enforcement action was shot and killed, Abraham Jacob donated the lumber for a coffin. Perhaps this was a gesture of apology, since the fact that Jacques Levy had passed on information would invariably be seen as the Jews taking the side of the submitted and the territorial lord against the "rebellious" subjects.[8] The Jewish villagers knew only too well how easily conflicts could turn into anti-Jewish unrest, as we learn a few years later in very different circumstances.

One evening in 1771 Magdalene Wagner, a "woman in an advanced state of pregnancy," was accosted by a stranger. She fled in a panic, exerting herself so much that she put her life and the life of her child in danger. This incidence caused quite a stir in the village. Magdalena Wagner's husband, Peter Richard, testified "that it is not right at all that nobody is safe in the streets, and it is very bad to harass a woman, and a woman who is very pregnant no less, seeing as his wife is an honorable[9] woman. Moreover, having been so badly frightened she is in great danger, not only of losing the child, but also of losing her own life. He thus humbly asks the count's government to provide complete satisfaction for his wife against such highwaymen."[10]

----

[6] LHA Koblenz 56/491, fol. 154: Kommissionsbericht in Sachen der Gemeinde Steinbiedersdorf gegen Herrn Grafen Christian van Wied-Runkel, Lit. C: Extr. Protokoll v. 23.3.1763.

[7] LHA Koblenz, 56/1301: In Sachen sämtlicher Untertanen und Dorfschaften der Grafschaft Kriechingen gg den Grafen von Wied-Runkel. Mandatis, 1764, fol. 208.

[8] That could also explain the considerable fear they were evidently feeling.

[9] The reading of this word is not entirely clear. Since the clerk did not distinguish between e and r, the word could be "eheliche" ("married") instead of "ehrliche" ("honorable").

[10] AD Mos. Actes judiciaires Pontpierre B 10059: Acta in Sachen Magdalena Wagner, Peter Richards Ehefrau von Longeville ca. Feist Jacob von Steinbiedersdorf pcto an ihr verübten Exzesses auf der Straße, 1774.

Magdalena Wagner claimed that a strange, unknown voice had addressed her in the field with "rough and many godless words of abuse": "Where are you from you—pardon the expression—whore, Lutheran person, just wait, I'll cure you of running about at night."[11] When she made her statement, Magdalena Wagner already knew that the strange voice had been that of Feist Jacob. Still, in her testimony she made no connection between her fear and the Jew. Apparently she become so frightened because the person addressing her was a stranger and had a voice she did not recognize, and because she was especially afraid of such encounters and insults on account of her pregnancy. The superstitious belief that such frightening experiences could harm the unborn child had not been eradicated.[12] But even if Magdalena Wagner had recognized the other person as a Jew, had regarded him—because of her prejudices—as the messenger of evil and a danger to her child and had therefore fled in fear of her life, the authorities avoided using this as an official argument.

Although not a single word in the court protocol gave any indication that the accused was a Jewish villager,[13] the Jews seemed to have sensed the danger. Feist Jacob, who claimed he had merely addressed the person walking ahead of him to find out who she was, was clearly afraid that there could be a great uproar among the people. He and his father-in-law offered the woman a present as a token of reconciliation, a gesture that was interpreted in court as quite the opposite, namely an admission of guilt.

Even if the attempt to settle a conflict in its early stages through a gift failed in this instance and Feist Jacob was punished, the case points to forms of

---

[11] Ibid.

[12] Vartier, *La vie quotidienne*, 75ff. However, the evidence of superstitious beliefs concerning pregnancy, birth, and lying in in the nineteenth century is no sure indication that such ideas also shaped the thinking of people in the eighteenth century. On this see also Eva Labouvie, *Andere Umstände. Eine Kulturgeschichte der Geburt* (Cologne, 1998), 65ff.

[13] In the protocol he is identified in familial terms as the stepson of Lion Pfalzburger and not with respect to his religion. The same is true for a whole series of other Kriechingen court documents, which means that only an analysis of the names can determine whether the accused were Christians or Jews. This raises the question whether the government in Kriechingen is an exception in this regard, or whether it is not more likely that many Jews are today no longer identified as such because of a lack of clues. For example, in the introduction to his widely cited essay on brawling (*Raufhändel*), Bernhard Müller-Wirthmann mentions a brawl from the year 1684 between one Samuel Mayr and one Georg Kienle. The name Samuel Mayr suggests that one of the two brawlers was a Jewish fellow: Müller-Wirthmann, "Raufhändel. Gewalt und Ehre im Dorf," in Richard van Dülmen, *Kultur der einfachen Leute. Bayerisches Volksleben vom 16. bis. 19. Jahrhundert* (Munich, 1983), 79–111. If that is the case, the problem about the exclusion of Jews from conflicts of honor would have to be rethought. Dülmen has argued that Jews had been excluded from such conflicts: *Kultur und Alltag in der Frühen Neuzeit*, vol. 2: *Dorf und Stadt. 16–18. Jahrhundert* (Munich, 1992), 175ff. In Steinbiedersdorf, however, there were brawls and quarrels of honor between Jews and between Christians and Jews (see p. 252f.).

conflict resolution within the village that were of existential importance to the Jewish villagers. To avoid endangering the delicate balance between Christian and Jewish neighbors, the Jewish villagers had to acquire an extensive knowledge of the prevailing power relationships and social networks. This forced them to seek contact with their Christian neighbors. Members of different religions coming into closer contact was a situation that disturbed the ideas of the proper order of things held by the Christian authorities, who were concerned to draw lines of separation.[14]

Fear of contact: the representatives of the church

Representatives of the church, in particular, paid attention that relationships between Christians and Jews did not become too intimate. For example, the priest in Woippy in Lorraine, not far from Metz, complained during the visitation of 1698 that his parishioners were helping the Jews in their preparations for the Feast of Booths. In his view, by doing so they were not only ignoring the commandments of the church, but also supporting the superstition of the unbelievers.[15] While church representatives in Denting and Steinbiedersdorf confined themselves to complaining about the nonobservance of Sunday rest (apart from the Jews, who were mostly engaged in cattle and meat trading, numerous Christian traders also came into the villages on Sundays),[16] Gaspard de la Croix, the priest of Kriechingen, lamented in 1716 that his parishioners did not even shy away from sharing a table with the Jews:

> The intercourse with the Jews is so extensive that the Christians drink and eat with the Jews, and rent to them not only houses, but also rooms within their houses, which have nine or ten families. One Jew bought a house of his own which he renovated. They hold regular assemblies every Friday evening, Saturday morning and evening, and on other days, in a synagogue they have made with scandal not only to the entire parish, but also to the entire neighborhood, from where the Jews come in groups to this synagogue of Crehange, which is even more scandalous. A good way of preventing this would be to prohibit the Christians from going to assist the Jews in the course of their assemblies and exercises in accordance with the statutes, and from renting them houses. The Jews are profaning the feast days and Sundays with their trading.[17]

Clearly the priest of Kriechingen had a host of complaints, all of which can be reduced essentially to the same denominator: cohabitation with a minority of a different faith bothered him because it injected disorder into his world. The mere fact that the Jewish community in Kriechingen had built a synagogue

---

[14] Battenberg has pointed to the importance of demarcation in the thinking of Christian authorities: "Zwischen Integration und Segregation," 423.

[15] Cahen, ed., *Catalogue: Les Juifs Lorrains*, no. 17.

[16] AD Mos. 29 J 63: Archiprêtre de Morhange: États détaillés des paroisses, 1699–1700.

[17] AD Mos. 29 J 69: Fonds de l'évêché: Visitation 1699, Créhange. Scattered evidence for Christians and Jews living together is also in Jeggle, *Judendörfer in Württemberg*, 12, and Battenberg, "Zwischen Integration und Segregation," 425.

constituted in his eyes a nuisance to the community and the neighborhood.[18] It was no less scandalous in his mind that the Jewish faithful from the entire surrounding area—which no doubt included also the French and Lorrainese vicinity—gathered in Kriechingen to hold services.[19] But he delivered the same verdict on a series of Christian customs: the public dances on Sundays and feast days, which were still practiced, chiefly at the initiative of the young men, and organized sometimes as an alternative to attendance in church; the May ride (Maiumritt); and weddings during Lent—all these things he described as a vexation. Since in his eyes the women and girls with their nightly gatherings were also causing "desordre," the number of "regular" parishioners who gave no cause for scandal seems to have been small. In principle only the housefathers were exempted from the priest's criticism, at least as long as they did not sell or rent their houses or living space to Jews. Given his many complaints about the deplorable state of affairs all around, we should not, at any rate, attach too much importance to his criticism of the Jewish population.

There are no statements about the Jews by priests from Steinbiedersdorf. It would appear that this is not merely a problem with the sources. A village priest in the eighteenth century had only limited influence on the religious attitudes of his parishioners; if he wanted to be effective at all, he had to accommodate their needs and ideas.[20] Father Richard from Steinbiedersdorf had to discover in 1719 what it could mean to oppose the convictions of the parishioners when he tried to enforce the episcopal prohibition against the weather procession: if his complaints are to be believed, a few members of the parish nearly smashed down the church door to get the banner. In addition, he was called a seducer of the people and a thief. Even if the primary defendant later denied having used such abusive language and asked for forgiveness in writing, these words had been introduced in court. The person accused of uttering them was not exactly a pious, church-going parishioner. How little attention Nikolas Krämer paid to prohibitions issued by the church is also revealed by the fact that he was renting his house and his hemp garden to a Jew.[21]

When it came to the Jewish villagers, Father Richard appears to have confined his complaint to the observance of Sunday rest. Beyond that, he tried, like other representatives of the authorities and the community, to derive personal financial advantage from the presence of a religious minority. However, his demand for a yearly payment from the Jews was turned down by the territorial ruler.[22]

---

[18] See chapter 5, note 99.

[19] Coming immediately after the war, this comment could have also had this political meaning. An examination of the connection between religious organization and political borders must be left to another study.

[20] Beck, "Pfarrer," 107ff. For parts of the bishopric of Trier see Hahn, "Rezeption," 42ff.; Ulbrich, "Frauen und Kleriker," 155ff.

[21] AD Mos. Actes judiciaires Pontpierre B 10041: Fisc. entgegen Nicolas Bernard und Cons., 1719.

[22] See p. 268.

The tenure of his successor witnessed one of the severest tests of the relationship between Christian and Jewish men and women in Steinbiedersdorf. During the night of July 6–7, 1757, the parish church was robbed. The burglars made off with a liturgical vestment, a new canopy, the monstrance, and the ciborium. Suspicion immediately fell upon a few "godless and unscrupulous Jews." A search was conducted in all the houses in which Jews lived; eventually, the monstrance, the ciborium, and the consecrated hosts were found in the forest of Steinbiedersdorf. The Christian community gathered immediately and returned the stolen items to the church in a procession. Further investigation solidified the suspicion that outside Jews, "an insolent, dissolute pack of thieves," were responsible for the robbery. However, all searches of Jewish homes in the county of Kriechingen came up empty. And yet: if the Christians in Steinbiedersdorf or in the other villages of the county had been harboring serious ill-feeling toward their Jewish neighbors, the burglary at the church would surely have been an opportune moment to allow potential latent tension to turn into open hostility, since a charge of host desecration had often triggered pogroms in the past.[23] In Steinbiedersdorf in 1757, however, the situation apparently remained calm. Still, the fact that fellow villagers had to put up with searches of their homes merely on the basis of their religious affiliation and were seen as a "pack of thieves" points to the hostile images underlying this action.

Interestingly enough, this event was given a different spin in the traditional recounting. The following version appears in a modern Lorraine guidebook, which provides no source that would allow further investigation:

> In the parish church of Pontpierre, the ciborium with the consecrated wafers was stolen in 1733. There was great agitation. A few workers soon found them at the edge of a forest, radiating brilliant white. The priest went to the spot in a festive procession, and the hosts were returned to the church accompanied by singing, the ringing of bells, and prayers. A wooden cross marks the location. It disappeared during the Revolution. In 1803, a new cross of stone was set up "in atonement," and next to it was built a chapel "To the lost Lord."[24]

At the center of this recounting is not the desecration of the host but its resplendent return to the church, the erection of a cross, and later of a chapel. Unlike other tales of similar incidents, the Steinbiedersdorf hosts did not bleed but radiated a brilliant white, which is more reminiscent of a miracle than a desecration. Only the name "in atonement" indicates that this was a very serious incident, that the locals wished to beg God's forgiveness by erecting the cross and wanted to build in the forest a place of prayer, a small pilgrimage site of local significance.

---

[23] Jonathan I. Israel has shown that we cannot speak of a continuous development with respect to Christian-Jewish relations: *European Jewry in the Age of Mercantilism* (Oxford, 1985).

[24] Günter Metken, *Liebe zu Lothringen. Horizonte und Hügel* (Karlsruhe, 1985), 104.

Even if this version of the story did not arise until the nineteenth century, it casts a revealing light on the religious attitude of the Steinbiedersdorf Catholics, who were pious but whose piety was not church-focused. This is further confirmed by the previously mentioned remarks by Monseigneur de Mondéville, who admitted outright in 1777 that his parishioners held the hermit who dwelled in the chapel at the outskirts of the village in far greater esteem than they did him: "Our hermit is worshipped and highly venerated among all the country folk, such that it is he who is their counselor, and they listen to him more so than to me."[25]

In view of these recorded differences of opinion between priests and parishioners, and the low level of church piety, it should now be clear that anti-Jewish statements from clergymen, which are generally used to prove the anti-Jewish sentiments of the "people," do not allow us to jump to any conclusions about the relationship between Christian and Jewish neighbors. Such conclusions emerge only from a thorough contextualization, one that also analyzes the forms of day-to-day interactions and the power structures concealed therein.[26]

Neighborliness and the village public

Simple spatial proximity and the reciprocal work and commercial relationships made it impossible for Christian and Jewish men and women to remain strangers to each other: those who wanted to live in peace with their neighbors, rent out their houses, engage in trade, or borrow money had to know the individuals they were dealing with, had to know whether they had a good name, honor, and credit-worthiness. Villagers met in the street, in the market, at the fountain, in the tavern, and in their houses. They knew each other, quarreled, reconciled, and helped each other out in times of need. It is small occurrences, recorded almost by accident, that make this clear: on Sunday mornings, Christians and Jews met in the house of Abraham Jacob, where they not only did business but also drank wine.[27] The house of the *parnas* was also open to Jews and Christians during the week. Here the men could while away their time "with cards and drinking."[28] Michel Mangin's combativeness is the only reason we know that the chief juror and the court juror (Meisterschöffe and Gerichtsschöffe),

---

25 AD Mos. 10 F 751.

26 There are many parallels here to women's history and gender history, especially with regard to methodology and the problems of the sources. See my reflections in the introduction.

27 As we have seen, Abraham Jacob had two houses, one of which was the center of the Jewish community. The brawls may have occurred in this house. It is possible that Abraham Jacob's second house, which he left to his brother in his will, was a tavern. In this connection it is interesting that Ahron Cahen, Abraham's stepson, was fined in 1760 for illegally serving wine (see p. 203).

28 We can assume that card-playing was also popular among Jewish men. References to forms of Jewish sociability that were very similar to Christian ones come from Pinkas Runkel—for example, Wachstein, "Das Statut," 139.

the Heimmeier, and the bailiff of the Christian community participated in this sociability: on one such occasion he "grabbed the dechant Charles Wilbourg by the hair without cause," while the clerk "got a good slap in the face for his troubles, the traces of which are still visible in his face."[29]

A "Christian girl" was sitting in the kitchen of Louis May when a stranger appeared and wanted to sell spirits.[30] Feist Jacob sent a young lad by the name of Nicolas Pirra to Falkenburg with four quarters of meat. Since Feist Jacob referred to him as "his lad," we can assume that Nicolas Pirra was working for him.[31] A Jewish boy called Schitteler Feist was with Nicolas Metzinger's wife to buy oil when a detachment of soldiers appeared to seize property on account of an unpaid fine.[32] A very different, though by no means unusual, form of cooperation was practiced by a Jewish lad from Steinbiedersdorf: he and a Christian fellow attacked an itinerant Jewish beggar who had spent the night in the village, robbed him of the bread he had scrounged, and threatened him with a knife until he handed over all the ducats sewn into his frock.[33] Another Jewish man engaged in activities with a "Christian girl" that were no less dubious: he gave her two hindquarters of a cow, intended for the butcher, so that she could sell them.[34]

These incidentally recorded clues reveal the varied spheres in which Christian and Jews, men and women, established work and business relationships. Special significance attaches in this context to the "shabesfroy," "Sabbath-woman," or "shabbes maid."

Gossip: neighbor women and shabbes maids

Since Jewish women and men were prohibited by religious law from working on the Sabbath, they employed Christian domestics to perform the tasks that had to be accomplished on the Jewish days of rest.[35] The duties of the shabbes

---

[29] AD Mos. Actes judiciaires Pontpierre B 10048: Fiscalis gegen Michel Mangin und Johannes Decker und Konsorten wegen Kartenspiel, 1766.

[30] AD Mos. 10 F 172 Steinbiedersdorf: In Sachen Fiscalis ca. Niclas Becker zu Steinbiedersdorf pcto Branntweinverkaufens von Ausländischen, 1755.

[31] AD Mos. Actes judiciaires B 10059: 1774.

[32] LHA Koblenz, 56/1398: In Sachen der sämtlichen Untertanen und Dorfschaften der Grafschaft Kriechingen gegen den Grafen von Wied-Runkel, Mandati, fol. 801f.

[33] AD Mos. Actes judiciaires Pontpierre B 10055. On the cooperation of Christians and Jews in gangs of crooks see Rudolf Glanz, *Geschichte*, and Uwe Danker, *Räuberbanden im Alten Reich um 1700. Ein Beitrag zur Geschichte von Herrschaft und Kriminalität in der Frühen Neuzeit* (Frankfurt a. M., 1988).

[34] AD Mos. Actes judiciaires B 10047: 1761.

[35] Sabbath services were a controversial issue among Jewish scholars. Jacob Katz has traced the intense discussion over the question of whether Jews were permitted to let non-Jews work for them on holidays when it was a matter of necessary activities or the Jews in question would have suffered economic harm by interrupting their work: *The Shabbes Goy. A Study in Halakhic Flexibility* (Philadelphia, 1969). On the shabbes maid see also Glückel of Hameln, *Memoirs*, 138f.

maid or "shabbes goy" included lighting a fire in the house and the candles in the synagogue.[36] Poor women, especially, could earn a little extra money as shabbes maids. Their work gave them an inside look at Jewish homes, let them participate in domestic life to a certain extent, and at the same time gave them an important intermediary function within the intravillage network of communication. The representatives of the church, concerned with drawing lines of demarcation, were always suspicious of Sabbath services provided by Christians.[37] Since they could not prevent them, they at least wanted to exercise some control over them. In 1747, for example, the bishop of Metz issued a decree for three communities in Lorraine, stipulating that irreproachable poor widows over the age of forty were permitted to earn their living in Jewish services: "Consequently, you may permit one or two poor women of your parish to render to the Jews who are resident there the services listed below, on the condition that the women are poor, widowed, and above the age of forty, and after the Jews have chosen from among them, they shall be presented to you so that you may examine whether there is anyone inappropriate among those selected."[38]

In 1765 the General Vicariate decided to extend this regulation to Niedervisse. With this permission of shabbes services, limited as it was, the principle of strict separation had been broken.[39]

We have already seen this in the two cases in the Steinbiedersdorf court files in which shabbes maids appeared on record: one was Magdalena Stoffel, the wife of Martin Becker, who was questioned as a witness in 1774 in the proceedings against the pregnant Jewish maid Zarle; the other was Margarethe Bildhauerin, the fifty-six-year-old widow of the seigneurial forest hand Peter Arnoud of Steinbiedersdorf, who testified in the 1784 paternity suit brought by the Jewish maid Madl.[40] Both Christian maids took the side of the Jewish maids, who were many years their junior. Magdalene Stoffel defended Zarle, who had been accused of attempted abortion. In court she testified emphatically that she had never heard any ill spoken of the maid, knew nothing about potions, and had not noticed the pregnancy. She made these statements despite the claim of the Jewish schoolmaster that there had been a rumor in the village about Zarle's pregnancy. By noting that she did "not pay attention" to the pregnancy,

---

[36] Daltroff and Cerf, *Traditions et coutumes*, 143–155.

[37] Criticism of the service in Jewish households was also voiced in Protestant areas: Davis, *Women on the Margins*, p. 244, n. 135; Jung, *Die württembergische Kirche*, 166ff.

[38] Quoted in Touba, *Dörfer*, 21.

[39] It would appear that the local clergy was at times even stricter than the bishop in its rejection of shabbes services. In Illingen, which was also part of the bishopric of Metz, the curate threatened in 1776 that he would no longer admit to confession the women who were performing shabbes services. Four years later, another prohibition of shabbes services was issued, once again with the threat that Easter communion would be denied. In both instances, the local clergy was not able to prevail over the General Vicariate or the territorial ruler: Kirsch, *Juden in der Herrschaft Illingen*, 104f.

[40] See p. 224ff.

the married Magdalene Stoffel was defending a female sphere of knowledge beyond the boundaries of religious status, a sphere in which neither the authorities nor the male villagers should interfere.[41]

Margarete Bildhauerin, Jacob Meyer Cahen's shabbes maid, was much more talkative. She alleged that Jacob Meyer Cahen had given her money to spread the rumor that a certain Jewish lad was the father of Madl's child. The behavior of Margarete Bildhauerin, who went along with the deal, makes clear that relationships of trust and solidarity could exist between the shabbes maid and the Jewish family she worked for. Margarete undoubtedly disseminated her knowledge to more than only the Jewish homes. We can assume that the morals and customs of the Jewish villagers were also a topic of discussion in her spinning room. And as we learned in connection with the fire in the house of Ahron Cahen, neighborly relationships existed beyond the working relationships I have mentioned. Information about the events leading up to the fire had passed from Heym Neumark's wife to Katharina Richard, and from her to her husband, who initiated the investigation.

While at least some Christian women got a glimpse of Jewish homes, the contacts and thus the knowledge of men was focused more on business relationships and leisure activities. Anyone who wanted to engage in commerce and take out a loan had to know with whom he or she was dealing.[42] Unless men wanted to rely solely on the information provided by their wives,[43] they had to gain insight into the Jewish world. And since they frequented the same taverns and walked the same streets, one can assume that they could not remain strangers anyhow.

Commensality

There are a number of indications that Jacob Cahen ran a tavern that was also frequented by Christians. In 1775, for example, he quarreled with a Christian debtor. Cahen had to appear in court because, among other things, he had taken six Louis d'or from his guest's pocket for "the consumed wine."[44] In 1760 we find further clues to a tavern in the seigneurial penal register: on two occasions, Jacob Cahen or his son Ahron were punished for the clandestine and prohibited serving of wine.[45] Since Ahron Cahen's first wife was Shiva, the daughter of Abraham Jacob, it is possible that they were living in one of his father-in-law's houses.[46] In any case, a very revealing quarrel allegedly took place there in 1766.

---

[41] See p. 222.

[42] On the importance of honor see 263ff.

[43] In 1751, for example, Jacob Gouvé turned down a horse trade with a Jewish business partner on the grounds that he was unsure "whether his wife would be satisfied with this trade": AD Mos. Actes judiciaires Pontpierre B 10043, 1751.

[44] See p. 264.

[45] See p. 203.

[46] It is also possible that he purchased the house from Abraham Jacob.

On June 22, 1755, the bailiff Dominique Richard, the juror Johann Philipp Gaspard, the sergeant Charles Wilbourg, and Peter Richard as witness and clerk (tabellion) submitted the following report:

> On this day and date, after mass, the seigneurial bailiff Dominique Richard, the court juror Jean Philip Caspar, and the dechan Charell Wilbourg were in the house of the head of the Jews, Abraham Jacob, and together drank wine. There were several other Christians and Jews in the house, including Michel Mangin, who openly insulted the bailiff, calling him an animal, the court juror a wastrel, and the dechan a publican, and saying that all three of them were dog cunt. The head of the Jews, Abraham Jacob, was surprised that such a man could utter such things against the court, and said he would have him removed unless he apologized. He said he stood by what he had said, and herewith we submit our report as we are duty-bound to do.[47]

It would appear that Christian and Jewish men spent the hours after Sunday mass together, though not necessarily in each other's company. Those present undoubtedly used the opportunity to do business. All this surely included the consumption of alcohol and thus a certain level of sociability. Work and leisure were not—or at least not always—clearly separated. For that reason it is not possible to unambiguously categorize the gatherings in the house of Abraham Jacob. They were surely part of the sphere of business contacts that had always existed between Jews and Christians; however, the environment of these contacts also points to social contacts transcending this sphere.

Perhaps we should recall, at this point of our interpretation, the complaint lodged by Gaspard de la Croix, the priest of Kriechingen, in 1716: "The intercourse with the Jews is so extensive that the Christians drink and eat with the Jews."[48] Although Christians, unlike Jews, had no restrictive dietary rules, except during Lent and on certain fast days, the priest objected to Christians and Jews sharing the same table.[49] That he was not alone in his criticism is revealed by a police decree of 1740, which, in an effort to prevent an injurious scandal ("le scandale prejudiciable à la religion catholique"), explicitly forbade all Christian subjects to eat and drink in Jewish homes. Violations were punishable by a fine, payable by both the Jewish hosts and the Christian guests.[50] Since neither of the two sources elaborates on what this scandal might have been, we must fall back on conjectures involving certain aspects of hospitality that I have already mentioned in a different context.[51]

---

[47] AD Mos. Actes judiciaires Pontpierre B 10048: Fiscalis contra Michel Mangin, 1766.

[48] See p. 175.

[49] On food laws see chap. 5, n. 87.

[50] LHA Koblenz 701 465: Herrschaft Crichingen und Saarwellingen (= Geschichte der Herrschaft Saarwellingen von Dr. Matthias Sittel), fol. 80: Verordnung in Betreff der Religion, der Wirtshaus- und Feldpolizei, 1740. However, the text appears to have survived only in a copy in Sittel's papers that can not be unambiguously classified.

[51] On hospitality see K. D. Sievers, "Gastfreundschaft," *HRG*, vol. 2 (Berlin, 1990), cols. 1389–1391.

When Christians went into the homes of Jews to share a meal or a drink, they submitted themselves to the hospitality of the house.[52] They brought honor to their host[53] and were to a certain extent entitled to the latter's protection, which seems to have been the case in the quarrel mentioned above. This turned the unequal order between Christians and Jews on its head—and that did not agree with the ideas held by the Catholic priest or the Protestant ruler, who made himself into the defender of the interests of the Catholic religion. It may therefore have been not only proximity that troubled the priest and the authorities, but also the social asymmetry that was challenged to some extent by this hospitality.

However, sharing food and drink was also a problem within Jewish society. The issue was not shared eating and drinking, but adherence to the ritual dietary laws. Observance of the laws was only guaranteed if Jewish guests who went to Christian homes to eat and drink brought along some of the tableware, dishes, and drinks.[54] But as the Jewish Enlightenment thinker Zalking Hourwitz, who had spent some time in Metz as a student of the Talmud, emphasized, one ought not infer from this a culture of separateness.[55] He rejected the charge by the Göttingen scholar Johann David Michaelis that the Jews were keeping themselves apart by pointing out that while the law prohibited the Jews from consuming certain foods, it in no way forbade them to eat the permitted foods with non-Jews: "Moses forbade only certain animals, along with fat and blood; however, he in no way forbade eating non-prohibited foods with strangers. Thus the Jews make it a daily custom to take drink (with the exception of wine, for the reason indicated above), bread, vegetables, dairy products, and fish with Christians . . . and they also invite the latter to their tables. Thus, abstention from certain foods in no way renders the Jews more unsociable than the Brahmins, the Muslims, or the Christians during Lent."[56]

---

[52] Until now, hospitality has rarely been a topic of historical research. On hospitality in ancient Christianity and ancient Judaism, in pagan antiquity, as well as in the Middle Ages and the early modern period, see also the references in Martin Leutzsch, *Die Bewährung der Wahrheit. Der dritte Johannesbrief als Dokument urchristlichen Alltags.* Bochumer Altertumswissenschaftliches Colloquium 16 (Trier, 1994), 159f. The works of Felicity Heal deserve to be singled out especially: "The Idea of Hospitality in Early Modern England," *Past & Present* 102 (1984): 66–93; idem, *Hospitality in Early Modern England* (Oxford, 1990).

[53] Davis, *Women on the Margins,* 34.

[54] In the Steinbiedersdorf sources there are only few indications of Jewish guests in Christian taverns (see for example note 76).

[55] Anna-Ruth Löwenbruck, "Zalkind Hourwitz—Ein jüdischer Aufklärer zur Zeit der Französischen Revolution," *Tel Aviver Jahrbuch* 20 (1991): 77–101, on shared meals, 86.

[56] Zalkind Hourwitz, *Apologie des Juifs en réponse à la question: Est-il des moyens de rendre les Juifs plus heureux & plus utiles en France? Ouvrage couronné par la Société Royale des Arts & des Sciences de Metz* (Paris, 1789; reprint, Paris, 1968), 51f. With regard to wine, he notes elsewhere: "here is the reason for their abstaining from the wine of the Christians and Muslims, even though the Talmud prohibits only that of [unclear] . . . they use only wine manufactured, put into barrels, sealed, and sent with great care by a Jew, which costs them much more than ordinary wine" (ibid., 28f.).

As we know from ethnological studies, this commensality did not abolish the differences between the various cultures,[57] but it does cast the house in a different light. The house was not only the place where—as I have emphasized above—the seemingly separate spheres of inside and outside, of subject and lord, of men and women, were interwoven; it was also the place were working relationships, business relationships, and neighborly relationships were established between Christian and Jewish residents. From this perspective, the Christian prohibition against sharing a table fits into that series of normative sources that postulated the complementarity of the spheres of men's and women's tasks,[58] regulated the domestic order, and sought to strengthen the authority of the housefather.

Neighborly aid

These reflections on commensality have made it clear once more that the conflicts between Christian and Jewish villagers were more than incidental encounters. The reciprocal relationships of work and business, and the integration of the two unequal groups into the same contexts of seigneurial authority, called for more extensive contacts in order to ensure a stable coexistence. And these contacts excluded neither conflicts nor mutual neighborly aid. There are numerous documented instances of such aid in the sources. One of the reasons I will discuss them here is because this aspect of Christian-Jewish coexistence has received far less attention in scholarship than has been devoted to anti-Jewish outrages.

Neighborly aid was extended in various ways, even if seigneurial laws and prohibitions were violated in the process. For example, Johannes Kremeter helped his Jewish neighbor transport the bier bearing the deceased Jewish schoolmaster to Kricchingen at five o'clock on a Sunday morning. Because he did this without permission from the ecclesiastical and secular authorities, and on a Sunday to boot, he got into trouble. His wife asked the dutiful village warden (Dorfschütz) who wanted to bring a complaint: "What business it was of his, he had such a big mouth."[59] However, she ended up with a complaint against herself for making this remark, with which she was defending the villagers' autonomy in their dealings with each another against the seigneurial

---

[57] The importance of hospitality as been noted especially in ethnological studies. See, for example, Werner Schiffauer, *Die Gewalt der Ehre. Erklärungen zu einem türkisch-deutschen Sexualkonflikt* (Frankfurt, 1983), 72f.; he discusses the signficance of the ritual of hospitality for the boundaries between inside and outside and notes that the boundaries are erected in the house itself as long as the guest is there. It would be worth investigating whether such explanatory approaches are also useful for historical scholarship.

[58] Interesting in this context are the sociological reflections by Albert O. Hirschman, *Tischgemeinschaft. Zwischen öffentlicher und privater Sphäre* (Vienna, 1997), 11–33, who, drawing on the ideas of Georg Simmel, situates shared eating at the intersection between the public and the private sphere.

[59] AD Mos. Actes judiciaires B 10081: Plaids annaux, 1755.

attempts at exerting control. Even the influence of Abraham Jacob was not enough to dissuade the warden from lodging his complaint.

Commonalities existed also in the sphere of medical treatment. Christian and Jewish women, smiths, shepherds, and old Jews were skilled in the art of healing. Using "old practices" (Brauchen in German and scho'rmen in Yiddish), they tried to cure disease in humans and animals.[60] The attempt by the old widow of the miller Claude Jeanbille from Denting to help Josef Israel by preparing a potion for a sick cow points to beliefs and practices shared by Jewish and Christian men and women.[61] Evidently there existed ways of dealing with everyday life that stubbornly resisted the normative prescriptions of faith laid down by the church and the authorities and knew no barriers imposed by religion.[62]

Beyond the neighborly and work relationships, the fact that both groups participated in constituting the village public, which claimed a "right to know," established another bond between the Christian and Jewish villagers.[63]

Since everyday contacts existed between Jews and Christians, Jewish women and men could also invoke the protection and help of the Christian village public. Once again, the sources provide a number of examples. When an inebriated Peter Köhler was told that the Jew Isaak Kain was unable to pay his rent (Hauszins), he beat him so severely that the bailiff and the court felt compelled to file a report with the government.[64] During the brawl between Christian

---

[60] Fox, *Volkskunde*, 296.

[61] AD Mos. Actes judiciaires Denting B 10006: 1766. Legal proceedings came about only because Josef Israel slaughtered the cow, sold the meat, and refused to take it back after the fraud became known.

[62] On the importance of magic among Jews see W. J. Cahnmann, "Der Dorf- und Kleinstadtjude als Typus," *Zeitschrift für Volkskunde* 70 (1974): 169–193, here, 191. The novella "Die Judenbuche" by Annette Droste-Hülshoff, which is based on an incident from the early nineteenth century, is regarded as an especially striking example of the belief of Christian peasants in Jewish magic. The influences that the non-Jewish environment exerted on the practices of Jewish magic are noted by Pollack, *Folkways*, 113ff., with extensive bibliographical references. As early as 1971, Pollack was calling for a differentiated analysis of both superstitious and magical practices, of the internal conditions that gave rise to them, and of their mutual interdependence with the non-Jewish environment (197f.). A study of Christian and Jewish customs of popular magic, which would provide important insights into relations "independent of religion," remains a desideratum of historical scholarship. For our region, though with no reference to the Jewish population, see Eva Labouvie, "Wider Wahrsagerei, Segnerei und Zauberei. Kirchliche Versuche zur Ausgrenzung von Aberglaube und Volksmagie seit dem 16. Jahrhundert," in Richard van Dülmen, ed., *Verbrechen, Strafen und soziale Kontrolle. Studien zur historischen Kulturforschung* (Frankfurt a. M., 1990), 15–55, here 15ff. On the forms of healing magic see Dies, *Verbotene Künste. Volksmagie und ländlicher Aberglaube in den Dorfgemeinden des Saarraums (16.–19. Jahrhundert)* (St. Ingbert, 1992), 95–110.

[63] Schulte, *Village in Court*, 116. The phrase "village public" does not refer to a fixed entity. The (village) public was formed depending on the situation, among other things, through gossip; on this see Patricia-Anne Anderson, *Gossips. Ale-wives, Midwives and Witches* (Ann Arbor, Mich., 1992).

[64] AD Mos. Actes judiciaires B 10045: Fiscalis entgegen Peter Köhler von Steinbiedersdorf pcto injuria realia, 1755.

men in Abraham Jacob's house, "nearly the entire village had been in an uproar."[65] After Heym Neumark's wife had been beaten by another Jew, she ran to the village clerk "covered in blood, such that one didn't know whether this was a person or not," having first raised a hue and cry in the village. She immediately had her wounds bound by the Christian barber-surgeon Johannes Ladner, who also drew up a statement about the severity of her injuries.[66] The aid of Johannes Ladner was also solicited by another Jewish woman, who had been so frightened at night by a drunken lad that she feared giving birth prematurely.[67] Finally, the Jewish maid Särle Levy, in a petition to the territorial ruler, expressed the hope that "all people, among both Jews and Christians" knew how loyally she had served her mistress.[68]

Särle implied in her letter that Jews and Christians would be able to provide information about the quality of her work as a maid. Even if she was employing merely a turn of phrase, it had to be within the bounds of possibility. This means that the village public not only mitigated brawls through its controlling presence and active intervention and was informed about transgressions of the law, extramarital pregnancies, abortions, or infanticides, but also knew about less important goings-on within the Jewish community. The brawl in the house of Abraham Jacob revealed there may also have been some kind of Jewish village public that became involved in a mediating role in quarrels among Christians. Jacob's intervention and attempt to restore order were described in detail in court. This could be an indication that—at least in the eyes of the Jewish minority—there existed a public that was not limited to the Jewish or the Christian community. As we shall see, this public takes on clearer outlines in the context of honor and shame.

Fields of conflict

Noting the close relationships between Jews and Christians and the willingness to accept others in their otherness does not imply that the coexistence of Jews and Christians was free of conflict or devoid of the issue of power. On the contrary, the nature and frequency of conflicts is further evidence for the capacity of early modern society to engage in them.

One revealing example is a quarrel in the house of Louis Keller, home to four or five Jewish families. This house included a stable that was not separated from the neighboring courtyard. As a result, the tenants with their animals could pass through the courtyard of the neighbors Christoph Renaudin and Anna Maria Türk.[69] In 1755 Louis May led a horse—which, as he insisted to the court, he had "purchased for his own most urgently needed use"—to

---

[65] AD Mos. Actes judiciaires B 10048: Fiscalis gegen Michel Mangin und Johannes Decker und Konsorten wegen Kartenspiel, 1766.
[66] AD Mos. Actes judiciaires B 10049: 1765.
[67] AD Mos. Actes judiciaires B 10047: 1760.
[68] AD Mos. Actes judiciaires B 10061: 1774.
[69] See p. 176.

drink at the shared well located behind the house of his landlord and that of the oil miller Peter Finickel. When old Finickel, who was sitting in his son's barn and picking out flax seeds, noticed what his neighbor was doing, he assaulted him verbally: "Get the hell out of here with your old nag, what business do you have being at this well?" To which Louis May responded: "My horse won't eat the well, and there is plenty of water in the trough." Whereupon Finickel came running out of the barn with a hay fork and gave the horse such a blow that it suffered an injury. Since the horse had to be taken to the knacker, Louis May lodged a complaint against Peter Finickel. Although he later settled with him, it was too late to avoid legal proceedings and punishment.[70] In a futile attempt to avoid punishment, Finickel's daughter went to Kriechingen to excuse her father on the grounds of age and incapacity, and to convey the message that he had realized his "crime" and had settled with his neighbor. Although the excuse and the settlement were accepted, Finickel still had to pay a fine to the authorities.[71]

At the initiative of Peter Finickel's widow, the case was laid before the Imperial Chamber Court a few years later as part of legal proceedings brought by the subjects. Years after the fact, Katharina Finickel countered Louis May's argument that he had purchased the horse for his own urgent need by claiming that it had been a "mangy horse" that Louis May had led to the trough from which she had to draw her drinking and cooking water. Her husband had avoided a trial simply "from stupidity and age" and had settled with the neighbor, but then had to pay a seigneurial fine of 73 Louis d'or.[72] Such an inordinate fine was apt to create rifts between neighbors who previously had been perfectly capable of tolerating and settling conflicts with each other.[73]

Many examples have indicated that living side by side led to quarrels and disagreements, and that the contending parties did not always treat each other with kid gloves. Apart from neighborly conflicts, one can identify three other types of confrontations: the first type arose within the village public and concerned primarily young lads who caused disturbances, sometimes also "quarrelsome women." Other conflicts were grouped around the problematic issue of Sunday and feast day rest. These tended to touch more on the relationship between the moralizing authorities and the community, but also on relations between Christian and Jewish villagers. The third type concerns conflicts that arose in the area of business relationships, most of which were caused by failure to repay loans on time, sometimes also by excessively high demands.

---

[70] LHA Koblenz, 56/1398: In Sachen der sämtlichen Untertanen und Dorfschaften der Grafschaft Kriechingen gegen den Grafen von Wied-Runkel, Mandati, fol. 512.

[71] AD Mos. Actes judiciaires Pontpierre B 10045: Fiscalis Amtsankläger gg. Peter Finickel wegen eines von ihm dem Juden Louis May geschlagenen Pferds, 1755.

[72] LHA Koblenz, 56/1398: In Sachen der sämtlichen Untertanen und Dorfschaften der Grafschaft Kriechingen gegen den Grafen von Wied-Runkel, Mandati, fol. 512.

[73] On the context of penal measures by the authorities, which should in no way be understood as an expression of an anti-Jewish attitude, see p. 114f.

Drunken lads and quarrelsome women

Disturbances within the village were caused chiefly by young men, and alcohol was involved in most of their violent confrontations.[74] In 1755 a quarrel arose in the house of Jacob Cahen after several Christians, who had to settle some loan affairs, gathered there during Vespers and drank wine.[75] A fight broke out between Johannes Bernard and Salomon Cahen after the latter had entered the tavern.[76]

Peter Mangin, who had been enrolled in a Swiss regiment by a recruiter, engaged in a lot of mischief in the village by "getting drunk every day, waving around the naked sword of said recruiter, and acting like a madman." One November evening he went to the house of Moses Deutsch and ordered schnapps. When Moses Deutsch asked him to sheath his sword on account of his children, Mangin gave him such a blow that Moses Deutsch ended up with bruises and a bump on his head. Peter Mangin was forced to give the Jewish villager satisfaction and was additionally fined for his violent act.[77]

One night, some unmarried Christian men, a social group that was prone to violence and whose members brawled frequently over issues of honor, invaded a house inhabited by Jews, demanded herring and drink, and terrorized or injured several people. The authorities in Kriechingen forbade such "almost daily acts of godlessness committed by such dissolute rakes" and countered them in part with harsh fines and shaming punishments.[78] These punishments, too, make clear that the Jews were included, at least to some extent, in the honor code within the village.

Now and then women too were involved in quarrels, most of which appear in the sources more or less by accident. The only reason we are told that Margarete Bildhauerin had quarreled openly in the street with the Jew Meuschel is because Meuschel recounted the incident in arguing that she should not be admitted as a witness against him.[79] The wives of Hans Georg Becker and

---

[74] AD Mos. Actes judiciaires Pontpierre B 10047: The Swiss soldier Johannes Becker was drunk when he invaded a house inhabited by Jews and caused a mortal fright to a women who was in the late stages of her pregnancy, 1760.

[75] AD Mos. Actes judiciaires Pontpierre B 10045: Fiscalis gegen Jacob Cahen, Schutzjuden zu Steinbiedersdorf, pcto dem Christoph Kiefer von Laningen aus Sack genommenen 6 Louis d'or, 1755.

[76] For example: AD Mos. Actes judiciaires Pontpierre B 10049: 1766. Brawl between Johannes Bernard and Salomon Cahen when the latter came into the tavern.

[77] AD Mos. Actes judiciaires Pontpierre B 10051: Acta in Sachen Michel Mangin und Anna Maria Richard von da, 1767.

[78] As note 67. A brief overview of the discussion about the treatment of Jews in Christian courts can be found in Otto Ulbricht, "Criminality and Punishment of the Jews in the Early Modern Period," in R. Po-chia Hsia and Hartmut Lehmann, eds., *In and out of the Ghetto. Jewish-Gentile relations in late medieval and early modern Germany* (Cambridge, 1995), 49–70.

[79] AD Mos. Actes judiciaires Pontpierre B 10073: Acta in Denunciationssachen der Madl Meyer von Steinbiedersdorf c. Meuschel Levy von da pcto impregnationis, 1784.

Jacob Meyer Cahen traded vicious insults in a garden in 1754.[80] Because they
were caught in the act by the warden, Jacob Meyer Cahen's wife ended up
having a report filed against her. Hans Georg Becker gave the following account
at the Jahrgeding: "Yesterday on the Feast of the Assumption during High
Mass, Jacob Meyer Cahen's wife pulled onions in her garden and took herbs
from other gardens, when his wife came upon her and asked what she was doing
in her garden. She responded with a hundred insults what it was to her, such
that she had to retreat from her."[81]

At this same Jahrgeding a charge was brought against Jacob Levy's wife, who
had mocked and insulted the police warden: when she and her husband had
been caught in the act of butchering behind closed doors, she called out of
the window for the warden to go right ahead and open the door, as they had
butchered a wolf.[82] If Jacob Levy himself had spoken such words, the couple
surely would not have gotten off so easily. His wife, however, could exploit a sphere
of freedom made possible by an honor code that was differentiated according
to gender.[83] Since the recipient of her insults was not a common member of the
community, but a sworn deputy of the lord, her vituperative words no longer
belonged unambiguously into the context of personal conflicts among villagers,
but were instead situated at the level of relationships of power and domination.

Sabbath, Sunday, idleness

In addition to the neighborly conflicts, the minor quarrels among women, and
the acts of young lads that can be seen within the context of their latent aggres-
sion (further heightened by the consumption of alcohol) and their claim to exert
control over the life of the community, there were numerous other conflicts
whose causes lay not so much in the different religions per se as in the way
they affected daily life, economic activities, and politics. The nonobservance of
Sunday rest on the part of the Jews and occasionally also their idleness on the
Sabbath, a Christian work day, which was manifested not in passive idleness
but in public or publicly noticeable entertainment, dancing, or promenading,
posed a problem also in the prerevolutionary period.[84] However, the issue here
was not, as it would be in the cultural revolution of Year II, an attempt to cre-

----

[80] AD Mos. Actes judiciaires Pontpierre B 10081: Plaids annaux, Pontpierre, 1754.

[81] Ibid.

[82] Ibid.

[83] See the pathbreaking reflections by Nicole Castan, "La criminalité dans le ressort
du Parlement de Toulouse. 1690–1730," in *Crimes et criminalité en France sous l'ancien
régime, 17./18. siècles*. Cahiers des Annales 33 (Paris, 1971): 91–107.

[84] AD Mos. Actes judiciaires Pontpierre B 10081: Plaids annaux: complaints about
nonobservance of Sunday rest, 1755, 1759, 1761; complaint because a Jew had shared
a drink with a traveler during mass, 1789; B 10049, 1766: complaint because a Jew had
washed meat at the fountain in public on Sunday; B 10053, 1769: complaint against
Ahron Cahen and Bernard Lipman regarding the profaning of the Sabbath—they had
talked business with a tailor.

ate equality by abolishing cultural peculiarities; instead, these were first of all pragmatic problems caused by differences in work and feast days.

Most of the complaints about the violation of Sunday rest reflect the fear that the Jews could secretly do business, or commit theft or engage in other unlawful acts, while the Christian community was at mass. Occasionally this did happen.[85] Carl Pied, for example, complained that something had been taken from a locked container during mass. His young daughter, who had remained at home, had told him that a tall Jew with a big beard had been in the house. He left behind his *tefillin* (phylacteries) and his Jewish prayer book during the theft; however, because he moved away from the village for several years, he could not be brought to justice.[86] Not only men, but women, as well, took advantage of the favorable moment. As we have already seen, Jacob Meyer Cahen's wife had harvested onions and herbs in the neighbor's garden during high mass. During Vespers on Sunday, a Jewish woman from Denting had beaten the children of Margarethe Crusem so severely "that the poor women heard the screaming of the children all the way in church." Margarethe Crusem became alarmed, ran from church believing that some great calamity had happened, and ended up pummeling the Jewish women so severely that the latter lodged a complaint with the authorities.[87] Incidentally, problems resulting from the nonobservance of the Christian feast day commandment were created not only by the Jews and children, who were not obligated to attend mass, but also by herders. The latter took the opportunity to lead their animals onto forbidden pastures during mass.[88]

Fear of clandestine activities or the claim of supervisory authority can only go so far in explaining why Sunday rest was watched over and enforced by the seigneurial officials and their village representatives, the police wardens. Committing theft in their own village was exceedingly risky for Jews, since they had to fear that transgressions against the law on their part could result, rather quickly, in banishment from the territory.[89] For their own safety, they had to be vigilant that no outside Jews came into the village to steal something. Theft, brawls, and damage to crops are thus, by themselves, not a sufficient concern to explain why so much emphasis was placed on the observance of Sunday rest.

---

[85] One can assume that such occurrences were reported to the autorities; however, there are few traces in the sources. See, for example, the quarrel over the children of Margarethe Crusem (see note 87).

[86] AD Mos. Actes judiciaires Pontpierre B 10057: Acta in sachen Carl Pied von Einsweiler ca. Salomon Hirsch von Steinbiedersdorf pcto Furti, 1772.

[87] AD Mos. Actes judiciaires Pontpierre B 10012: Niederwiesener, Dentinger, Momersdorfer Jahrgedingsprotokolle, 1754ff.

[88] For example, ibid., the complaint that the horseboys sent their animals out during mass, and, because nobody could watch them, were causing damage.

[89] For example, Isaak Israel and his son, who were reported to the authorities by the wife of Heym Neumark because they had beaten her, were banished from the territory for two years: AD Mos. Actes judiciaires Pontpierre B 10049, 1765.

Rather, this demand provided an opportunity to force the Jews to submit to the decrees of a Christian authority and to respect the Christian calendar of feast days.[90]

Yet the cultural hegemony of the Catholic Church and an order sustained by a Christian authority had to be enforced not only among the Jews, but also among the Catholic Christians. In the eighteenth century, the latter not infrequently preferred their own forms of piety to a church-controlled, disciplined, and disciplinary religiosity, or, as was apparently the case with many herders, they were indifferent toward the church and did not attend mass. Exuberant celebrations, which unquestionably had a group-stabilizing function, troubled the authorities, regardless of whether they occurred among Jews or Christians. Members of both confessions were forbidden, on pain of a fine of 10 Reichstaler, to set off fireworks at kermis, weddings, baptisms, and on New Year or other feast days. As a result, Georg Court and Georg Decker, no different from Abraham Jacob, his wife, and his domestics, ended up with a complaint against them because they had set off fireworks. The former had celebrated their name day with the noisy explosions, the latter a wedding. Christian and Jewish lads were both punished for prohibited dancing. The former had arranged a kermis dance and had auctioned off dances to the highest bidder, the latter had hired outside musicians on the Sabbath and had them play at successive dances in two different houses.[91]

When it came to festive celebrations, the Catholic priests, who were closely tied to the villagers by background and way of life, and the Protestant officials, who came from a remote elite of functionaries, by no means saw eye to eye. For much to the chagrin of the secular authorities, the priests, too, had a liking for extravagant feasts, as long as they were able to maintain control. For example, on the feast of the patron saint, the priest of Saarwellingen, "on his own presumptuous authority," had four French soldiers parade "with unsheathed swords and wearing their soldier's hats." The government saw this as an encroachment on its ius armorum, accused the priest of having "infringed upon the powers of the territorial authority in a punishable manner," and issued a reprimand.[92]

---

[90] In this context belong the complaints, for example, that a Jew was washing meat in public on a Sunday, even though "the Jews are expressly forbidden, and it is inserted into their letters of protection, that on our Sundays and feast days they may not engage in any commerce, nor run about the alleys or the street, but should conduct themselves quietly and noiselessly in their houses": AD Mos. Actes judiciaires Pontpierre B 10049, 1766, and B 10048, 1768: Acta in Sachen Abraham Jacob, dessen Ehefrau und Hausgesind pcto verschändeten Sabbats und vorgenommen Schießens. "Sabbat" means "Sunday" (see note 97).

[91] AD Mos. Actes judiciaires Pontpierre B 10043: Fiscalis gegen Jacob Levy zu Steinbiedersdorf wegen Tanzen und Spielen, 1751 and B 10048: Fiscalis gegen Wagner Peter Schmidt und der Witwe Magdalena Bommersbach ihre Söhne zu Steinbiedersdorf pcto ohne herrschaftliche Erlaubnis aufgeführten öffentlichen Kirmestanzes, 1762.

[92] LHA Koblenz K 26 Nr. 64 1779. I would like to thank Dr. Weißgerber for calling my attention to this source.

The situation was different when it came to Sunday rest, something the priest too was interested in.[93] It was not only Jews who made Christian feast days into market days and bestowed an important economic function on them.[94] Jean Richard, the priest of Steinbiedersdorf, felt compelled in 1699 to complain about the fact that the parishioners throughout the diocese worked more on Sundays and feast days than they did on work days, on account of which they were often staying away from Mother Church.[95] In Saargemünd, as well, the complaints about the profaning of Sunday referred to both Jews and Christians: while some opened their stores, loaded their carts, or butchered calves, others opened their taverns, baked bread, played cards, or quarreled.[96] As usual, the authorities subsumed all transgressions against the laws pertaining to Sundays and feast days, including those that occurred explicitly and demonstrably on a Sunday, under the heading "Sabbath desecrations."[97] The claims of the secular authorities to govern and supervise their subjects surely extended also to the Sabbath, since the enforcement of good order demanded that all subjects, Jews and Christians, fulfill their different obligations and not live as Jewish or Christian heretics.[98]

In general, the "daily crimes" denounced as "Sabbath desecrations" do not seem to have bothered the Christian villagers very much. The police warden Nicolas Finickel was very understanding that Abraham Jacob had meat carried from one of his houses to another on Whitsunday, two days before his son's wedding. He refrained from filing a report and got into trouble with the authorities, who alleged that he had seen the "Sabbath desecration" with his own eyes. Abraham Jacob's argument that while the sale of meat was prohibited on Sundays and feast days, "the use of meat for his own need" was not, surely made sense to the villagers, even if the authorities refused to accept it.[99]

Considering the conflicts over Sunday rest I have mentioned, it becomes clear that the battle over adherence to the Sunday and feast day ordinance must be

---

[93] AD Mos. Actes judiciaires Pontpierre B 10049: Fisc. gg Georg Becker, Schlosser und Georg Court zu Steinbiedersdorf pcto gegen Verbot vorgenommen Schießens im Dorf, 1766, and B 10048: Acta in Sachen Abraham Jacob, dessen Ehefrau und Hausgesind pcto verschändeten Sabbats und vorgenommen Schießens, 1768.

[94] On the discussion over feast days see P. Hersche, "Wider 'Müssiggang,'" 97–122.

[95] AD Mos. 29 J 63, Archiprêtre de Morhange, Visitationsprotokolle, 1699–1700.

[96] Henri Hiegel, *La paroisse Saint-Nicolas de Sarreguemines* (Sarreguemines, 1969), 82.

[97] The phrase "Sabbath desecration" (Sabbatschänderei) did not refer to the Jewish Sabbath but to the Christian Sundays and feast days: "Sabbath-Entheiligung bzw. Sabbaths-Schändung," in Zedler, *Universallexikon*, vol. 33 (1742), cols. 88ff., 92.

[98] As mentioned above, the head of the Jewish community had to swear an oath to the territorial ruler, which contained among other things the obligation "to maintain good law and order among the Jews" (see chap. 6, n. 49). This requirement, which was aimed at disciplining the subjects, most likely also included the duty to supervise the adherence to the religious laws and thus of Sabbath rest. We know that the Christian authorities paid attention to this since the late Middle Ages; see also the reflections of Burghartz, *Leib, Ehre und Gut*, 183ff.

[99] AD Mos. Actes judiciaires B 10048: Fisc. gg. Abraham Jacob, dessen Ehefrau und Hausgesinde pcto geschändeten Sabbats und vorgenommenen Hochzeitsschießens, 1766.

seen within the larger context of secular and ecclesiastical attempts to discipline the population. This battle was not only, perhaps not even primarily, against the Jews. Rather, its goal was to establish a uniform, Christianized, church-controlled way of life that was supervised by the Christian authorities. The existence of a religious minority was no obstacle to this goal, as long as it was "preserved in a suppressed state in order to testify to the truth of Christianity."[100]

In view of the many poor Jewish beggars, it was presumably not difficult to assert the superiority of Christian culture. But the fact that the unquestionably richest man in Steinbiedersdorf was a Jew, that his wife came from an urban milieu, and that he boarded a graduated scholar in his house who did not earn a living but devoted himself solely to study[101] could challenge claims of cultural hegemony, regardless of whether they were articulated by the community, the church, or the authorities.[102] The same can be said for the fact that even a poor Jewish maid could sign her own name,[103] and that all Jews, men and women, rested from work for an entire day each week. There is much to suggest that the interest of the Christian authorities, the Catholic priest, and the Protestant territorial lord in preventing too great an intermingling of Christian and Jewish worlds had its origins here.

Controversial business dealings

The Christian population was highly dependent on the work of Jewish men and women, who supported themselves and their families chiefly by trade and moneylending. The large number of loans that women and men took out from Jews speaks for itself. Without the possibility of going into debt, the spheres of action of individual villagers (both men and women) and of the Christian community as a whole would have been significantly more restricted. The loans advanced by Jewish women and men helped not only to bridge short-term emergencies, they also allowed the community to get involved in costly legal proceedings against its lord. In 1789 a critic, speaking about German Lorraine, noted that the Jews were the chief cause of the emigration that was occurring only where Jews were present. One would have to supplement this observation by adding that wherever Jews were present, the economic spheres of action for

---

[100] Jacob Katz, *Out of the Ghetto: The Social Background of Jewish Emancipation, 1770–1870* (New York, 1978), 14.

[101] AD Mos. 17 J 29 PR 119: Traduction d'une copie d'un testament hébraïque faite par le def. Abraham fils d'Ezechiel juif à Pontpierre le 14.3.1771.

[102] The difference is to be found in the various spheres of activity more so than in religion. Peasants could not heed Sundays and feast days in their work cycles.

[103] The maid Särle Levy signed a petition to the lordship in her own hand in Hebrew letters. Her meager possessions included two books: AD Mos. Actes judiciaires Pontpierre B 10061: 1774. Before the Jewish woman Gelle, who had accused Gembel of getting her pregnant, was questioned, careful attention was paid lest she secretly spoke Hebrew (what was probably meant was Yiddish) to anyone: AD Mos. Actes judiciaires Pontpierre B 10074, 1784.

Christians, along with the attendant risks of taking on too much debt, were far greater than in regions in which rural inhabitants were not able to borrow money.[104] While this may have been an annoyance to the authorities and the well-off among urban and rural dwellers, the money borrowed from the Jews offered Christians a chance to survive emergencies, to break out of poverty, and to create a livelihood for themselves.[105] Christian women were no less dependent on this option than men, for the simple reason that they were legally liable for debts incurred by their husbands, which meant that they were all too often confronted by the choice between dipping into their own inheritance or going into debt with a Christian or Jewish moneylender. But even the everyday money needs of Christian women could be readily managed through short-term pawn transactions or trade with the Jews.[106]

That credit transactions were not one-sided affairs, that Jews also borrowed money from Christians, is something we learn purely by chance in the quarrel between Louis May and Peter Finickel over the joint use of a well. Finickel, who had struck Louis May's horse, settled with his Jewish neighbor out of court. As his widow later recounted, Finickel returned to May a document stating that the Jew Louis May owed the Christian Peter Finickel 5 new talers.[107] The question of whether such a credit transaction was the exception or indicates a more common practice would require further study.

Irrespective of whether the loan business went one way or both ways, one must note that the interests of Christian and Jewish rural dwellers complemented each other in the economic sphere, and that in most cases people dealt with each other pragmatically and without prejudice.[108] In their sales strategies, Christian peasants and Jewish merchants were equals.[109] Of course, the balance established by trade and money interests was a very fragile one, and there were also many quarrels within the orbit of credit transactions, repayment demands, or auction sales. These quarrels were related to the nature of the business, to

---

[104] René Paquet, *Bibliographie analytique de l'histoire de Metz pendant la Révolution (1789–1800)* (Paris, 1926), 1086.

[105] Jean Daltroff has studied the money transactions of the Alsace Jew Samuel Levy and found that the vast majority of his debtors (85 percent) came from the rural population. Most needed the money to refinance their debt because other repayments were coming due: Daltroff, "Samuel Levy de Balbronn. Un riche prêteur d'argent juif de Basse Alsace au dernier siècle de l'Ancien régime," *Revue des études juives* 148 (1989): 53–68.

[106] See, for example, the trade between Magdalena Bouché with a Jewish fellow lodger: AD Mos. Actes judiciaires Pontpierre B 10065, 1776.

[107] LHA Koblenz, 56/1398: In Sachen der sämtlichen Untertanen und Dorfschaften der Grafschaft Kriechingen gegen den Grafen von Wied-Runkel, Mandati, fol. 512.

[108] Cahnman, "Dorf- und Kleinstadtjude," 188, emphasizes that "the Jews and the peasants were dependent on each other, in buying and selling, loaning and borrowing, as creditor and debtors, whereby each participating party soberly weighed advantages and disadvantages."

[109] Ibid. Numerous pieces of evidence for the character of these relatively stable relationships of exchange can also be found in the literature: see, for example, J. P. Hebel.

poverty and the inability to pay, to attempts to obtain extensions of credit or wrangle more out of a transaction than was permissible.[110] In general, these quarrels were settled in court. This aspect of Christian-Jewish relations is undoubtedly most densely documented. Measured by the number of transactions that were carried out, accusations of usury are rare. There were a few large trials that were initiated by fraudulent Christian businessmen. Using targeted propaganda, activists were able to mobilize many small debtors who testified against the Jews and entertained hopes that their debts would be forgiven and they would escape having to repay them.[111] For example, Jacob Cahen of Steinbiedersdorf, who was accused of usury, claimed that there was a personal connection between the great usury trials in Saargemünd and in Vic: in both cases, he alleged, the indebted rural dwellers had been bribed by the same man into making false statements.[112] In 1756 an official messenger (Amtsbote) from Boulay ran through the villages, rang the bells to call assemblies in the king's name, rounded up the communities, and forbade the peasants to pay the Jews anything. In response, forty-seven peasants brought charges of usury against Jews of Kriechingen.[113] In 1775 an Amtsbote from Thionville tried to harm the Jews by lodging an accusation of usury, but they found an open-minded defender in Metz in Pierre-Louis Roederer.[114]

Precisely because of this link between going into debt and clearing oneself of debt that is becoming apparent in most of the individuals involved in these cases, the conflicts over usury reflect the descent of large segments of the rural population into poverty much more so than shady business practices on the part of the Jews. Still, the 'cahiers de doléances' that were drawn up in 1789 had a decidedly aggressive thrust.[115] Here the two sources of anti-Jewish feel-

---

[110] In this context one must recall that cases of fraud as a whole increased in the eighteenth century, and, in addition, that unlawfulness as such was a "condition of the political and economic functioning of society": Foucault, *Discipline and Punish*, 82. If, in reading the sources about usury and moneylending, one frees oneself from the notion or prejudice that these were typically Jewish business practices, and if one locates the conflicts within the contemporary context and problem of fraud, delinquency, and unlawfulness, it becomes clear how normal these conflicts were.

[111] AD Mos. Bailliage Sarreguemines B 11262–11265: Procès contre Joseph Salomon et Jacob Cahen de Pontpierre, juifs accusés d'usure, 1756ff.

[112] Ibid. Pierre Kranz of Freibous and a former merchant from Püttlingen were supposedly behind the affair.

[113] D. Clessienne, "La justice dans le bailliage de Boulay (1751–1789)," *Les cahiers lorrains* (1984): 2–3, 162.

[114] Cahen, ed., *Catalogue: Les Juifs Lorrains*, no. 118.

[115] On the anti-Jewish tendencies in the cahiers of Lorraine see O. Möckelt, *Lothringen nach den Cahiers de doléances von 1789 unter besonderer Berücksichtigung der wirtschaftlichen und sozialen Fragen* (Bamberg, 1927), 141ff.; Fr. W. Hussong, "Cahiers de doléances des communautés en 1789. Bailliages de Boulay et de Bouzonville," *Jahrbuch der Gesellschaft für lothringische Geschichte und Altertumskunde* 24 (1912): 1–166, here, 143ff.; Johannes Schmitt, "Französische Saarregion vor der Revolution," in idem, ed., *Revolutionäre Spuren . . . Beiträge der Saarlouiser Geschichtswerkstatt zur Französischen Revolution im Raum*

ings, the charge of usury and religious intolerance, entered into a symbiotic relationship that would have been scarcely conceivable in the decades preceding the Revolution. The following accusation was leveled against the French Jews of Niedervisse, to whom many residents of Kriechingen were indebted:[116] "As for the Jews, we do not know or cannot begin to make clear the misfortunes that cursed people is causing us . . . They have ruined our fathers through their usury; and because we have inherited nothing but misery, it is very easy for them to trap us with their ruses in our distress."[117]

In their cahiers, the French peasants even went so far as to ask the estates to exclude the Jews from tolerance, to tear down their synagogues, to forbid them once again from confiscating real estate and engaging in usury. Moreover, they were to extend the current loans for ten years at no interest.[118] What is striking is that these cahiers no longer pondered the causes of this rural pauperization but targeted their criticism at the weakest link in the chain, the Jews. This indicates that the arguments employed here were very strategic: even after 1789, a complaint against Jewish moneylenders had far greater prospects of being successful than a complaint against their Christian counterparts.

The communities in the County of Kriechingen had been repeatedly compelled to take out loans from Jews to settle the extensive demands of Christian creditors.[119] In 1788 the peasants of Niedervisse who lived on the side of the Holy Roman Empire and were subjects of the county were no longer able to repay the interest on the debts they had incurred in their lawsuits against the territorial rulers. The better part of them lived "in the most dire poverty and wretchedness" and were struggling to "put bread on the table."[120] To pay their debts and thus prevent imminent legal action, they had procured some of the needed money from a Jew at interest. They intended to pay the rest by selling a piece of communal land, provided the ruler gave his permission. The distress of the poor grew worse as a result of the extremely harsh winter in early 1789. Jewish merchants had purchased what little grain was still available in the region and supplied it to the cities. The prospects of clearing one's debt and thus providing temporary relief were much better if one brought a charge

---

Saarlouis (Saarbrücken, 1991), 37f. Anti-Jewish tendencies were even more pronounced in Alsace, home to two-thirds of all French Jews prior to 1789. Especially in the Upper Alsace, hatred against the Jews vented itself in numerous uprisings: Roland Oberle, "L'emancipation de juifs," *Saisons d'Alsace* 33/104 (1989): 113–123.

[116] LHA Koblenz 56/493 e, fol. 117ff. Auffstellung der Schulden, Waldnersches Kapital.

[117] Etienne Charles, *Cahiers de doléances du bailliage de Vic*, T. 1 (1907): 551–556.

[118] Despite the anti-Jewish tenor of the cahiers of Niedervisse, the synagogue there remained a center of Jewish life until its destruction by the Germans in 1944: Daltroff and Cerf, *Traditions*, 143ff.

[119] The prohibition for Christians against taking interest that is often mentioned in the literature, along with the claim that they did not participate in money transactions, does not match the reality of the eighteenth century.

[120] LHA Koblenz 56/493 b: Beschwerde von Niedervisse, 8. Mai 1788.

of usury against the Jews rather than against Christian creditors, although the same accusation was also leveled against the latter.

The Christian women and men who had loaned money, some belonging to the nobility, some to the village,[121] had much better prospects than the Jews of being able to enforce their interests through the court and to get their hands on their creditors' land and real estate if the latter were unable to pay. Jews who sued for payment of their loans could not be sure that they would win: for one, corruption in the courts played no small part in the decision-making process, and for another, proof of usury was enough to escape repayment of the debts.[122] Jewish creditors also tried to get their hands on real estate in a roundabout way through money transactions and thus make up for their legal disabilities in this regard.[123] For example, Abraham Jacob kept the seigneurial bailiff Dominik Richard and his wife Anna Wahl from losing their house and farm by taking over their considerable debts, while at the same time insisting that he be given the house and the garden as surety.[124] Through this action, which was in keeping with the usual business practices, Abraham Jacob could simultaneously solidify his power in the village, since the bailiff was, after all, the extended arm of the territorial lord. The fact that Jews, unlike Christians, could not invest their money in land, may have led to the situation in which they were chiefly interested in real estate, houses, and residential units if their debtors fell behind on their payments. This kind of behavior must have been a crucial element in the intensifying anti-Jewish feelings. The request in the cahier of Niedervisse that the authorities renew the prohibition against the seizure of real estate points in this direction.

Finally, it is possible that the border location of the village exacerbated the conflicts. Complaints and accusations similar to those in Niedervisse were also voiced in other villages of the border region of Thionville-Boulay-Sarrebourg.[125] Given the intertextual dependence of the individual cahiers of the region, it is more than questionable whether these complaints reflect the attitudes of the relevant local populations at all.[126] The concentration of anti-Jewish complaints along the language boundary could also have something to do with the fact

---

[121] It would appear that widows, who had relatively few opportunities to invest their money, played no small role in credit transactions. The subjects of Kriechingen financed a large portion of their legal proceedings through loans from the Rittmeisterin Waldner from St. Johan (LHA Koblenz 56/493 e, fol. 117ff.: Aufstellung der Schulden, Waldnersches Kapital), and from Madame Lacapelle from Saarbrücken (AD Mos. Actes judiciaires B 10051, 1767).

[122] AD Mos. Bailliage Sarreguemines B 11262–11265: Procès contre Joseph Salomon et Jacob Cahen de Pontpierre, juifs accusés d'usure, 1756ff.

[123] Sabelleck noted that the Jews in Nienberg were intensely interested in acquiring real estate: *Jüdisches Leben*, 90f.

[124] AD Mos. Actes judiciaires Pontpierre B 10057, 1772.

[125] Jean-Bernard Lang, "L'images des Juifs à travers des cahiers de doléances," *Les cahiers lorraines* (1989): 315–322, here 319f.

[126] Maurice Liber, *Les juifs de la convocation des États généraux (1789)* (Paris, 1989), first published in *Revue des études juives* (1912, 1913).

that the border region was a favorable environment for swindlers and crooks, but it would require an extensive study of the sources to substantiate this hypothesis. At this time not even the question about the diffusion of smuggling, gangs, and criminal activity in the border region has been sufficiently investigated.[127]

Honor and shame

The central importance of honor is reflected in page after page of the court documents relating to the Jewish population.[128] It is not rare for the term itself to appear in the statements—recorded verbatim—of witnesses and defendants. Frommet Levy is reported to have begun the questioning of her pregnant maid Gelle with the words: "You come from honest folk, and you have brought such shame on us."[129] In the tension between honor and shame established by these words, Frommet Levy not only indicated the importance that the family of origin had for the sense of Jewish honor, but at the same time also connected it with the resultant expectations about her maid's conduct. Elsewhere we hear of reputation, honor, and honorableness, of an honorable name, of honor and credit, or of how someone was honorably taken care of or was serving honorably and loyally.[130] As the flipside of honor we hear, apart from shame, about

---

[127] The presence of criminal gangs in this region has not been adequately researched. However, one must assume that the border region was an especially advantageous area for such activity. A gang of eighteen crooks, among them fourteen Jews, was executed in Nancy in 1760: Cahen, *Catalogue: Les Juifs Lorrains*, 132, 133. References to individual thieves and Jewish vagrants are also found in the Steinbiedersdorf sources.

[128] This is not unique to the County of Kriechingen or to the eighteenth century. In her 1990 doctoral issertation, Burghartz demonstrated that honor and shame were central categories in the judgment of behavior in quarrels that were brought before the Ratsgericht in Zurich: Burghartz, *Leib, Ehre und Gut*, 200. The memoirs of Glikl bas Judah Leib are striking and well known testimony to the high esteem in which honor was held among Jews in the late seventeenth century (see note 130). Statements that Jews were "devoid of honor" (ehrlos)—Friedrich Zunkel, "Ehre, Reputation," in *Geschichtliche Grundbegriffe* II (1975): 16; van Dülmen, *Dorf und Stadt*, 202—can be understood only from a Christian perspective, according to which Jews—who were not members of estate-based society—were excluded from the honor that attached to the various estates. However, this should not be confused with "dishonorable" or "dishonest." A general overview of Jewish honor is also provided by Robert Jütte, "Ehre und Ehrverlust im spätmittelalterlichen und frühneuzeitlichen Judentum," in Klaus Schreiner and Gerd Schwerhoff, eds., *Verletzte Ehre. Ehrkonflikte in Gesellschaften des Mittelalters und der Frühen Neuzeit* (Vienna, 1995), 144–165.

[129] AD Mos. Actes judiciaires B 10075: Acta in Sachen Benedict Isaac und Abraham Benedikt von Dentingen ca. den Barnes Bär Lipman von Steinbiedersdorf pcto schuldigen Lidlohns, 1788.

[130] These findings point to differentiated notions of honor, of the sort that we also find in Glikl bas Judah Leib. Honor as a sign of respect, esteem, uprightness, and honesty in matters of business are central aspects throughout Glikl's memoirs. Glikl, too, applied honor to Jews and non-Jews. As Davis has written of Glikl, "so sure is she of the quality of Jewish honor that she almost always uses the Hebrew-derived noun *koved* rather than the German-derived er (from Ehre), even doing so in those few cases where her cast of characters is made up entirely of non-Jews": Davis, *Women on the Margins*, 49f.

dishonor (Unehre) and dishonoring (Verunehrung). The manner and frequency with which honor becomes a topic in court shows that honor was conceived of within a context that also included the surrounding Christian world. The same is true for domestic conflicts in which maids were involved.

The uncompromising severity with which Jewish and Christian employers or courts treated Jewish maids who were pregnant out of wedlock reveals the close connection between sexuality, the honor of women, the honor of the house, and the honor of the family. That connection points beyond the narrower domestic context to the realm of social coexistence and economic life. As a minority in a non-Jewish world that confronted them with reservations and prejudices, Jewish housefathers and housemothers had to be careful not to cause any offense or scandal. Simply considering the importance of the house as a place of work and business, and of the dowry as a medium for the transfer of property, "disorder" in the house threatened the financial foundation of families. For Jews who lived from trade, and for Christians who had to appraise their business partners and trust them, honor was and remained the central foundation of business. Maids who were pregnant out of wedlock or broken promises of marriage by sons represented threats to honor and thus to success in business.

Since the honor of Christian and Jewish business partners was reciprocally related, it was imperative to develop a shared code of honor for the realm of conduct and to enforce it publicly with the help of the secular courts. For example, in a quarrel between the Jews Louis May and a debtor living in France, the seigneurial court demanded "that each declare the other a honorable man, wherefore they shall shake hands here before the court."[131]

This quarrel over honor between a foreigner and a Jewish subject offered the court an opportunity—much like its interference in domestic Jewish conflicts— to benefit from the conflictual nature of rural society and to demonstrate its competency as a mediating body. Conversely, however, Christian and Jewish subjects used the courts as an instrument in pursuit of their own interests. For example, when Jacob Cahen, Perle Levy's father-in-law, was accused of theft by Christoph Kiefer, he tried to restore his honor by asking the court to demand that the plaintiff "by public recantation of his false accusation restore the honor and good name he sought to take thus . . . and to pay for the wine he drank."[132]

A year later, Jacob Cahen was accused of usury. He had a petition drawn up, affirming that he was honorable, upright, and honest: "His reputation is established, it is the most happy fate of a man of business (homme d'affaires),

---

[131] AD Mos. Actes judiciaires B 10054: Inquisitionssachen des Barthel Sidot im Französischen und des fiskalischen Amtsklägers gegen den Schutzjuden Louis May in pcto errichteter falscher Handschrift, 1756.

[132] AD Mos. Actes judiciaires Pontpierre B 10045: Fiscalis entgegen Jacob Cahen, Schutzjuden zu Steinbiedersdorf in puncto dem Christoph Kiefer van Laningen aus dem Sack genommen 6 Louis d'or, 1775.

one to which one attains only by the probity and honorableness of one's conduct."[133] In this formulation, his honor relates no longer to his Jewish religion but to the professional honor of an "homme d'affaires." This reveals how similar the sense of honor was among Christians and Jews. Särle's petition to the Christian authorities likewise indicates a similarity in values. When she invokes everyone "among both Jews and Christians" as witnesses to her claim that she served her employer faithfully and honestly, the supposed boundaries between inside, where she worked as a maid, and outside, the realm of the judging public, between Christian and Jews, between men and women became blurred.

A final example, taken from the will of the pious and tradition-bound Abraham Jacob, will show that this openness to a public that transcended religion should not be equated with integration. Abraham Jacob stipulated that his will be "written publicly in the open market," and that it be signed "in the open street," "lest it be said that this was done in secret, or clandestinely; rather, it shall be open and known to all and sundry."[134] The public nature of the will and thus its legal validity was to be guaranteed, not by the synagogue, but by the open market and the open street as spheres of special law used jointly by Christian and Jewish subjects. The choice of this location shows the contours of a shared system of reference that—though related to the Christian authorities—was placed above both the Christian and Jewish communities. The indication of various kinds of public realms shows once again that in a social order built on inequality and grounded in plurality (as was the one I have been describing), it was conceivable to pursue simultaneously integration in the sense of incorporation into the state, and segregation as an "effort to ensure the cohesion of one's own group."[135] In some respects, as I will show, segregation as community-formation was one precondition for integration into the state.

---

[133] AD Mos. B 11262 Bailliage de Sarreguemines: Procès contre Joseph Salomon et Jacob Cahen, juifs accusés d'usure. By linking honor, reputation, and a good name, which he describes as the highest good fortune of every man of business, not to external honor but to internalized, individualized virtues, to uprightness and honesty, Jacob Cahen was adopting an enlightened notion of honor, of the sort that was promulgated as early as 1724 by the Hamburg weekly *Der Patriot*: "A businessman of credit and repute, who is honest and punctual in all his affairs, has much more honor and possesses much more genuine nobility than a wild, wasteful Junker who shows off with a lot of titles and costly accoutrements" (quoted in Zunkel, "Ehre," 2).

[134] Testament of Abraham Jacob: see Appendix (51).

[135] Battenberg, *Zwischen Integration und Segregation*, 431, 452. Battenberg's argument that Christian-Jewish cultural contacts comparable to the ones I have been describing were "accidental phenomena, created invariably by the collision of two different groups," does not make sense for the simple reason that the relationships were structurally conditioned. Moreover, it seems to me that the above-mentioned testamentary disposition by Abraham Jacob, especially, provides evidence that one cannot link state and religion so closely that one could speak, as Battenberg does, of two cultural systems. Rather, I believe that in spite of the inequality and difference of religion, one can speak here of a triadic relationship: Christian community, Jewish community, territorial lord.

Lordship and communities

The Jewish population in Steinbiedersdorf was under the direct authority of the territorial lord through the person or office of the *parnas*. Despite its cohabitation within the boundaries of the village, the Jewish population was not tied into the community that was formed by the Christian housefathers and integrated into the structure of domination through the person or office of the bailiff.[136] This constellation, the product of seigneurial rights and not of communal needs of inclusion and exclusion, led to numerous conflicts that we can trace back to structural and economic causes.[137] While the ecclesiastical and secular authorities—the priest, the territorial lord, and the officials—tried to derive the greatest possible economic benefit from the presence of a Jewish minority, for the Christian community the settlement of Jews meant a curtailment of its resources. Every house that was purchased by a Jewish neighbor reduced the capacity of the Christian community to generate taxes, since the Jewish owner had to pay his levies directly to the territorial ruler or his officials.

The problem already began with the admission of Jewish community members, which was at the discretion of the territorial authority. Although it was always a central concern for communities to acquire the ability to have some say in the admission of strangers, evidently neither the Christian nor the Jewish community was able to assert itself successfully on this issue.[138] The fact that

---

[136] The only reason why I speak of a Christian community in the following discussion is to express that there also existed in the village a Jewish community whose position within the structure of lordship is, in my view, not correctly described with terms such as "corporation." If we follow Peter Blickle and assume that village and community are synonymous, the equation ceases to apply if a second body arises within the village to which the territorial lord assigns tasks such as protecting the law and maintaining peace: Peter Blickle, *Deutsche Untertanen. Ein Widerspruch* (Munich, 1980), 30f. This becomes clear in the oath of the *parnas* (see chap. 5, n. 103).

[137] This is not meant to question that the relationship between Christians and Jews was unequal and hierarchical. However, it does not make sense to me to derive this, as Battenberg does, from the status of "protected Jew" (*Zwischen Integration und Segregation*, 424), especially since Battenberg himself notes elsewhere that "the status of a protected Jew could assume privileged forms" ("Schutzjude," *HRG* 4 [Berlin, 1990], 1535–1541). While Battenberg, with reference to Katz, mentions the Jewish community (*kehila*), he discusses it only within the context of a coherence model applied to Jewish society. He does not discuss the integration of the *kehila* into the lordship, which, on a structural level, placed the two communities into an analogous relationship to the territorial lord and ruled out the authority (not power) of the Christian community over the Jewish community. On the division of authority under the old order see Renate Blickle, "Die Tradition des Widerstands im Ammergau. Anmerkungen zum Verhältnis von Konflikt- und Revolutionsbereitschaft," *ZAA* 35 (1987): 138–59, here, 144f.

[138] The right to control the admission of Christian outsiders was the subject of the Kriechingen unrest (see chap. 4, n. 110). Whether the Jewish community demanded the right to limit the inflow of Jewish outsiders is not documented. However, it becomes clear from the work of Meyer, *La communauté juive de Metz*, 27ff., what sort of interests the Jewish community had in setting limits. Since the reception of outsiders placed a financial burden on the local residents and could constrain their options, the recep-

the territorial ruler arrogated to himself the right to settle in the village and place under his direct authority individuals over whom the Christian community had no direct control, and on whom it could place no demands, led to continuous complaints from the Christian community.

A principled dispute had occurred as early as 1708. Since the Jewish villagers were allegedly wealthier than their Christian counterparts at the time, the bailiff sought to force the Jews to bear a part of the war costs imposed on the community as a whole. With the argument that it was the duty of the stronger to support the weaker, he was able to override the agreement made in peacetime that the Jewish population was not required to contribute to communal taxes and levies. The Jewish residents were forced to assume one quarter of the contributions to the war expenses.[139]

Nearly a decade later, in 1717, the government again demanded that the Jewish villagers contribute to an extraordinary tax over and above the payments they had already made. Regierungsrat Schiff defended them against the demands of the Christian community, which hardly wanted to see the postulate of the obligation of the stronger applied to itself. Most of the Jews, he wrote, "are poor and struggle mightily to raise their usual dues (Schatz-Geld), over and above which they must contribute like the Christians to the imperial and district levies." Moreover, they had been "treated rather harshly" in the earlier wars.[140]

The Christian community, however, was unwilling to exempt the Jews, who were exploited by the territorial lord, from the communal tax burden, and throughout the eighteenth century it repeatedly tried to enforce the claim through the courts. The fact that the lieutenant of the généralité de Metz during the réunion had briefly imposed on the Jews the obligation to pay dues in the communities in which they lived, must have strengthened the hand of the communities: they were now in a position to invoke a "customary" law.[141]

The Christian communities objected especially to the fact that the Jews in the villages of Kriechingen had acquired from the lord the right to pasture their animals. They argued that the pasturing of animals was reserved for long-established peasants and residents, who in return performed certain services for the communal good, such as guard duty and road building. A territorial ruler had no right to dispose of such "bona communia universitas." The Jews had no right to the common; they had to meet their need for fodder by bidding for the excess

---

tion of a large number of Jews into a lordship should not be equated necessarily with a pro-Jewish policy, as is frequently done in regional historical scholarship. In general, the territorial rulers also tied the inflow of outside Jews to a certain level of wealth, which means that a generous immigration policy should always be interpreted also within a context of the economic interests it entailed.

[139] AD Mos. E Dépot 553 Pontpierre CC 1: 1708.

[140] AD Mos. 10 F 120: Bericht von Rat Schleiff und die Fürstin, 1717.

[141] LA Saarbrücken Mi 35/36 Collection Steinthal des Bestandes des Leo Baeck-Instituts: Klage des Fiscals, daß die Kriechinger Juden 5 Taler für Wohnrecht und 10 Franken für die Beherbergung Auswärtiger zu zahlen hätten, 1683.

rowens. The revenue generated in this way would be distributed among the community.[142] This particular quarrel in 1750 reveals, more clearly than later clashes, a close relationship between complaints about the settlement of Jews in the village and their participation in communal levies, on the one hand, and conflicts of interests and spheres of authority between the community and the authorities, on the other hand. It shows that in the final analysis this was not only about the rights of the Jews, but also about the distribution of power between the Christian community and the territorial lord.

While the financial interests were one important aspect in this conflict, they must be seen within the context of the power interests and hegemonic claims they entailed, and they were fundamentally different from the clashes in the nineteenth-century state, which held a monopoly of power.

The territorial lord demanded from all Jews to whom he granted a letter of protection not only arrival and departure fees, but also levies such as protection, synagogue, and burial money, sometimes also pepper, ginger, and sugar, and he placed them under obligation to buy their salt from him.[143] The residency permit for the Jews depended not only on the correct payment of fees and dues and conduct in accordance with the laws, but also on the favor of the lord and the good will of the officials. Like the priest, the lord prohibited Christians and Jews from sharing meals and demanded that the Jews respect the Christian feast days and provide no cause for complaint in the communities in which they lived. In return, he promised protection against insults and harassment from Christian neighbors.[144]

Relations between the Jews and the territorial lord, no different from those of the Christians, were characterized by an emotionalized patriarchal relationship that cast the ruler as a merciful lord. In numerous humble petitions, Jewish women and men addressed him as the merciful father of those who were poor and forsaken, like widows and orphans.[145] However, in a register of seigneurial rights, "the Jews" were listed in conjunction with the beverage tax, the salt monopoly, hunting, and fishing as a profitable source of revenue.[146] Still, a decree issued in 1723 concerning the admission of strangers and valid for both

---

[142] AD Mos. Actes judiciaires B 11058: Gravamina die Juden betr.

[143] LA Saarbrücken Mi 35/36 Collection Steinthal des Bestandes des Leo Baeck-Instituts.

[144] LHA Koblenz 701, Nr. 465: Herrschaft Crichingen und Saarwellingen (= Geschichte der Herrschaft Saarwellingen von Dr. Matthias Sittel), fol. 80: Verordnung in Betreff der Religion, der Wirtshaus- und Feldpolizei, 1740.

[145] In a petition to the territorial lord, the Jew Leib Cahen addressed him "as a father of the poor and forsaken subjects": AD Mos. 10 F 428. In 1774 the maid Särle applied the father image even to the Oberamtmann when she complained "because I am a servant in foreign lands and have no one who will speak for me, and you are the father of the poor orphans" (see p. 205).

[146] AD Mos. 10 F 429: Supplikation der Einwohner von Steinbiedersdorf und Büdingen beim Reichskammergericht, 1716.

Christian and Jews makes clear that they were not placed on a par with "wandering gypsies and thieves."[147]

Lest the financial dependence of the lord on his financiers challenge the power relationship between them, the latter had to practice gestures of subservience and submission: one Kriechingen Jew who was in jail and was to be expelled because he had refused to honor an action for eviction, was advised in 1682 to win a pardon by begging the countess (Madame La Comtesse) for forgiveness bareheaded and on his knees.[148] The rights to the Jews, no different from other seigneurial rights, were objects of business transactions in which each side wanted to maximize its profits. In 1724, for example, the Admodiator [Administrator] Hugo, who had purchased at an auction the right to collect the Jewish protection money for the current year, demanded from the Jews of Steinbiedersdorf not only the fees to which he was entitled and which had been contractually agreed upon, but also a sugarloaf. Since the Jews, who intended to deliver their money in Kriechingen on schedule, were not willing to pay the legally unjustified sugar levy, Hugo refused to accept the money offered to him. Instead, he invaded the village under arms and forced the bailiff to allow an enforcement action to take place. It would appear that the bailiff tried to avert the calamity by claiming that he was unable to find anyone to carry out the action. Eventually, five men who were cutting wood were discovered and enjoined to enter the houses of their Jewish neighbors, bring out seized property and sell it, throw everything else of the Jews out of the house, and tell them that they would have to leave the village within three days.

They obeyed the order, but argued in their defense that they had acted under duress and had asked the Jews to give up something voluntarily to make the enforcement action less severe. The bailiff also complained that he had not been able to defend himself against the Admodiator, who was lashing out with his rifle, and he called upon one of the affected Jews to seek legal recourse. Since this case also involved the interests, the reputation, and the honor of the government—Hugo had high-handedly (propria auctoritate) arrogated to himself the right to carry out the seizure and had claimed that he was lord and did not ask about the government—the officials were willing to protect the Jews. They arranged for the seized property to be returned to the injured parties.[149]

As we have already seen, the priest also tried to enrich himself at the expense of the religious minority. In 1728 he claimed that the Jews were required to pay him a yearly levy. His demand was rejected when the government pointed out that this regulation had been abolished when the count entered the

---

[147] LHA Koblenz 701 465: Herrschaft Crichingen und Saarwellingen (= Geschichte der Herrschaft Saarwellingen von Dr. Matthias Sittel), fol. 68.

[148] LA Saarbrücken Mi 35/36 Collection Steinthal des Bestandes des Leo Baeck-Instituts.

[149] AD Mos. 10 F 428 Nr. 4: Admissions de Juifs, droit de protection dans le comté en général, Supplik v. 19. Mai 1724.

territory—which means simply that with the consolidation of the count's power after the Peace of Rijkswijk, the count himself laid claim to all payments from the Jews.[150] In return, he was willing to protect the Jewish population against claims and demands from third parties.[151]

The situation was very different if the interests of the officials themselves were affected. In 1748 Kammerrat Köppel sued the Jews because they had given the Oberamtmann of Kriechingen, but not him, two silver cups as a New Year's present. This violated one of the count's directives, according to which officials had to be treated equally when it came to the obligatory New Year's presents. Köppel demanded compensation from the two *parnasim*.[152] It is not surprising that he, of all people, was putting on airs vis-à-vis the Jews, seeing as he could show no qualifications of any kind for his office; it was also said "that he is considered a good cameralist because he has delivered a few 100 Reichstaler as prepayment for future rent to my lord and Your Excellency the Princess (Fürstin), and has now promised further to loan 100,000 fl. on the lordship of Criechingen."[153]

While it is true that the arbitrary behavior of officials was curtailed when Count Christian Ludwig assumed the reins of government in 1754, the intensification of seigneurial rule that now began and the resultant lawsuits before the Imperial Chamber Court confronted the Christian subjects with a new set of problems.

The need for money caused by legal costs and increased taxes and levies had to be covered through loans, with the end result that many Christians found themselves in a situation of financial dependence on Jewish creditors.[154] A small Jewish upper stratum was able to benefit from these developments and acquire houses. Ownership of real estate or land entailed the obligation to pay a share of imperial and county taxes, since these levies were never assessed on individuals but only on houses. In addition to the Jews, nonresidents (forenses) and officials were also exempt from payment. The calculation was simple: the more houses came into the possession of Jews, nonresidents, and officials, the higher the share of taxes that would fall on the remaining houses.[155]

Pressure from seigneurial taxes and levies, the destruction of the basis of exist-

---

[150] AD Mos. 10 F 755.

[151] See, for example, AD Mos. E Dépôt 553 Pontpierre HH I: complaint by the Jews of Steinbiedersdorf, who for the most part made their sole living as cattle traders, against foreign butchers, especially those from Falkenburg, 1740.

[152] Ibid., Supplik v. 1748.

[153] AD Mos. 10 F 140: Criechingische Bedientenansetzung und übler Zustand der Grafschaft, 1742–43.

[154] Part of the debts to pay for trial costs had been taken out from the Jews of Niedervisse: LHA Koblenz 56/493, fol. 117ff.: Aufstellung der Schulden, Waldnersches Kapital.

[155] The connection between house ownership and participation in paying imperial and county levies becomes clear, for example, in the demand by the official of Saarwellingen in 1741 (AD Mos. 10 F 373).

ence through military enforcement actions, restrictions on rights of forest usage and thus fewer opportunities to make money—all this led to a deterioration of the social climate. It was not a different culture that made the Jews into outsiders in the village but their "special status." The lawyers for the subjects who articulated the complaints of the peasant communities devoted a good deal of space to the problems arising from the Christian-Jewish coexistence. This kind of emphasis, which was surely not imprudent in terms of legal strategy and potential success in the court, does not necessarily reflect the views of the Christian population.[156]

The declared goal of the complaints by the subjects was to get the Jews to share in the "common burdens"[157] and to assess them as well for the costs incurred by the subjects' legal case.[158] Complaints were voiced "that various villages in the lordship of Kriechingen were overpopulated with Jews, for example, in Kriechingen, Steinbiedersdorf, and Saarwellingen there are thirty or more Jewish households in each place, which causes a great annoyance to the subjects."[159]

The chief complaint was still that "the Jews, with whom the land is very overpopulated, and who enjoy the water and the pasture like every other member of the community, have so far contributed nothing to the costs of war."[160] Jews were accused of putting more animals than was allowed onto the pasture and depriving the subjects of their sustenance.[161] Moreover, the Jews were reproached for charging high interest rates and for having driven once well-off subjects into financial ruin with their demands.

Many had to experience to their misfortune that the government, with its excessive fees, bore a considerable part of the blame for this process of impoverishment. There was the case of one Jacques Wilhelm, for example, once a comfortable subject of Kriechingen. The chancery auctioned off his entire belongings, even though their value far exceeded the debts he owed to a Jew. This seigneurial enforcement action, which was never accounted for, ruined him, forcing him to earn a living as a day-laborer to scrape together enough to feed himself, his wife, and their six children.[162]

---

[156] See on this the fundamental reflections by Göttsch, "*Alle für einen Mann . . .*," 284ff., and idem, "Konstruktion," 443–452.

[157] LHA Koblenz 56/489, fol. 138ff.: Urteil von 1778.

[158] AD Mos. Actes judiciaires B 10047: Gemeinde Steinbiedersdorf gegen die Judengemeinde: Forderung, daß die Judengemeinde 12% der Kosten für das Kreiskontingent übernehme; LHA Koblenz 56/493, fol. 191ff.: Forderung, daß Juden und Auswärtige die sog. Pacifikationsgelder mittragen, 1758.

[159] LHA Koblenz 56/1301, fol. 490.

[160] LHA Koblenz, 56/491, fol. 1014: Beschwerde von 1764.

[161] Ibid., fol. 1034. As already mentioned in chap. 5, n. 53, in Steinbiedersdorf in 1767 the complaint was also voiced that only Christian members of the community had been ordered to muzzle their dogs, while the dogs of Jews were exempt, "by which not only the entire hunt has been spoiled, but it is also possible that there could be damage to people and cattle in the village": AD Mos. Actes judiciaires B 10081: Plaids annaux, 1767.

[162] LHA Koblenz, 56/491, fol. 1020f.

Magdalena Bouché had also discovered that legal proceedings, once set in motion, could not be stopped. In her case a Jew was the injured party: in 1776 Magdalena Bouché complained to the bailiff that Uri Jacob had purchased fruit from her but had failed to pay for it. After a few inquiries, the bailiff submitted a report to the government. A few hours later, Magdalena Bouché got her money. Uri Jacob had paid her as soon as he had been able to get his hands on some cash. Magdalena Bouché immediately went to the bailiff and informed him that the matter had been resolved. She was told that it was no longer her business, that punishment would invariably follow upon a report once it had been submitted.[163] The example demonstrates to what extent the reforms of Christian Ludwig, aimed at modernizing and intensifying government, affected the coexistence of people in the village and caused legal quarrels and legal uncertainty.

Like its Christian counterpart, the Jewish community also suffered from the increasing reach of government since the middle of the eighteenth century. In the space of a few years, the Jewish protection fees were raised from 12 to 20 talers, which amounted to a de facto restriction on Jewish immigration.[164] The contribution of the poor was more than doubled, rising from 12 to 26 pounds. The officials collected the levies with ruthless severity. In order to obtain a share of the money transactions of the Jews and control them, the government, in 1754, compelled them to write all contracts on stamped paper.[165] Christians, too, were required to use stamped paper not only for court documents, but for all affairs within the community.[166]

While the Christians brought a case before the Imperial Chamber Court over this innovation, the Jewish community was able to purchase a partial release from this imposition, obtaining exemptions at least for money transactions with foreigners and for smaller loans to locals. However, the relevant charter, dated April 18, 1755, was revoked ten months later, and failure to observe the new law was made subject to a heavy punishment.[167] Following another petition from the Jewish community, Jewish money lenders were eventually permitted, "by a special act of grace," to draft debt certificates from outside debtors themselves or have it done by an outside clerk, though they were still required to use the stamped paper that required a fee. This easing of the law was intended to prevent commercial disadvantages that would have weakened the financial health of the Jewish minority. Money transactions within the county had to be carried out in front of the seigneurial clerk, as they had always been.

---

[163] AD Mos. Actes judiciaires B 10065: 1776.

[164] This observation goes against Marx, *Juden im Saarland*, 36, who argues that the counts of Kriechingen practiced a comparatively generous admissions policy and never seriously impeded the settlement of Jewish families.

[165] Sittel, *Sammlung der Provinzial- und Particular-Gesetze*, 554ff., nos. 7–10: decrees concerning trade with the Jews.

[166] Cramer, "Wetzlarische Nebenstunden 100," 71.

[167] Sittel, *Sammlung der Provinzial- und Particular-Gesetze*, V, nos. 7–10, 554–556: Decrees of April 18, 1755, February 14, 1756, February 18, 1756, and April 9, 1756.

The interest rate was limited to 12 percent. In this way the territorial lord secured for himself a piece of the credit transactions between Jews and Christians.

New sources of revenue were soon tapped. The government eventually compelled Jews to furnish horses for the travel needs of the lord and his officials, pay postal fees, and purchase seigneurial horses against their will. The *parnasim* complained about these impositions when Christian Ludwig assumed the reins of government, and the Jews of Kriechingen were exempted in 1758 in return for a special tax of 100 Louis d'or.[168] At the same time they were able to deflect a demand from the Christian community to pay a share of the imperial and county levies and taxes, which had risen sharply at the time. Once again, the territorial ruler had granted the Jewish community a privilege at the expense of its Christian neighbors.

The Christian community, deeply in debt from legal proceedings, enforcement actions, and higher tax impositions, refused to accept the situation. It, too, wanted a share of the Jews. In 1769 the community decided to seize the property of Jews who refused to pay the communal fees voluntarily, or to confiscate the assets of their landlords, which happened in at least one case. The widow Maria Morell had property confiscated because of her tenant Jacob Alexander, while Katharina Richard and Margaretha Decker were evidently able to prevent worse from happening by speaking "well" of their tenants. The cantor Max Levy resisted the confiscation and demanded to see an order from the territorial authorities. In response, the peasants attacked him and punched his fifteen-year-old son in the face.[169]

When district taxes were assessed in 1775, the community imposed obligatory contributions on 258 men and women from the village. Among them were seven Jewish house owners (five men, one widow, and one group of joint heirs), who had to pay a comparatively modest sum.[170] In 1776, one year after Abraham Jacob's death, the Jews were asked to pay quite a bit more. They were accused of having sent their horses illegally to graze on the rowens. For this transgression they had to pay the rowens wine: according to an old tradition, the community gathered after the first yield had been cut to drink a pint of wine for each member of the community. The small Jewish community, which had grown financially poorer after Abraham Jacob's death, was to foot the wine bill for the Christian community, which had 120 members at the time.[171] We cannot rule out the possibility that this was a reaction to the fact that Abraham Jacob had most of his assets invested and administered in Metz, and that a number of his Jewish neighbors had received a sum of money, if a modest one, from the estate after his death.

---

[168] LA Saarbrücken, Mi 35, with reference to AD Mos. Actes judiciaires B 9566.

[169] AD Mos. Actes judiciaires B 10079: 1769.

[170] AD Mos. Actes judiciaires B 10070: Rolle zu den vom 9. Febr. 1775 ausgeschriebenen Creisgelders, wozu Steinbiedersdorf 1747 lb. 6 sol. 2 den. de Lorraine beizutragen hat.

[171] AD Mos. Actes judiciaires B 10065.

Although the Jews were approached with additional demands for payments, in the end the Christian community's demand that the Jews contribute to the taxes and levies was not successful. In this conflict, as well, the territorial lord held the better hand. While the community had to resort to fines, as in the case of the rowens wine, the lord continued to consolidate his authority over the Jews and tried to bring all aspects of Jewish life under his control. His most important points of contact with the Jewish community were the *parnasim*, who had taken an oath to him, and who held a position that was comparable to that of the Christian bailiffs.[172]

In both cases, proximity to the lordship enhanced the status of the officeholders. In 1762, when the Jew Louis May called Abraham Jacob "the biggest thief and rogue in the world," he was severely punished by the secular authorities as a "dishonorable liar." For anyone who attacked Abraham Jacob, according to the argument in court, simultaneously insulted the territorial lord who had installed him as the head of the community.[173] A similar line of reasoning was employed in 1764 in a defamation case involving the seigneurial bailiff: when a Christian member of the community called him a liar, the bailiff maintained that he could not put up with such a serious insult, all the less so because it indirectly violated the respect that was owed the territorial lord. Since a member of the community did not have the right to utter insults against his superiors, the bailiff was demanding punishment: the man was sentenced to two twenty-four-hour periods in the tower and had to restore the official's injured honor through an apology.[174] The identical argumentation shows how similar the status of both men was within their respective reference systems, in spite of the legal disability from which the Steinbiedersdorf Jews suffered.

Finally, the *parnasim* were authorized to collect money from their subjects through the seizure of property without the need to ask for prior permission. The seigneurial bailiffs and officials were to assist them in their official capacity.[175]

The Jewish community did not accept the growth in the power of the *parnasim* without objection. Conflicts arose over the assessment of taxes. After a number of Jews had complained to the government in 1763, Regierungsrat Reusch ordered that Abraham Jacob had to use a government-provided for-

---

[172] AD Mos. Actes judiciaires B 10062: Einsetzung von Bernard Lipman als Nachfolger von Abraham Jacob zum Parnes der Juden von Steinbiedersdorf. It is not documented whether the installation of Lipman as the new *parnas* was preceded by an election.

[173] AD Mos. Actes judiciaires Pontpierre B 10048: Fiscal gegen den Juden Louis May wegen der Injuria atroci et verbalia gegen Abraham Jacob; AD Mos. 10 F 429: Rechnung des Sekretär Stammel über eingenommene Strafgelder und Einzug samt Juden Copulationsgebührnissen, 1762.

[174] AD Mos. Actes judiciaires Pontpierre B 10048: In Sachen Dominik Richard, Meier, Kläger, gegen Nicolas Bommersbach, Beklagten, pcto injuria verbalia, 1764.

[175] LA Saarbrücken, M 35, 1761 Sept.: the leader of the community of Dentingen is empowered, like the other leaders of the county, to collect money from his subjects through the seizure of property without the need to ask for permission.

mula to assess taxes: one-third of the money should be assessed as a capitation tax, the rest as a wealth tax. Since Abraham Jacob did not adhere to this prescription, he was ordered to call in two Christian deputies when making his tax calculations. Abraham Jacob would not accept this either, and it would appear that in the end he was successful in fending off this kind of interference in inner-Jewish affairs.[176]

In 1790 a quarrel erupted in Denting over the question of how to assess taxes on sons who were still part of a household but were already engaged in commerce of their own. Some members of the community believed that the *parnas* had violated the principle of equality and had unjustly exempted his sons from the obligation to pay taxes.[177]

A few years earlier a quarrel had erupted in the same village because the *parnas*, who had his eldest daughter instructed by a private tutor, refused to pay her share of the costs for the schoolmaster. The manner in which this conflict was resolved reveals that the higher authorities cooperated, if necessary: Regierungsamtmann Reusch, to whom the case had been assigned, solicited advice from the chief rabbi of Metz before making a decision.[178]

In other cases, as well, officials were quite willing to provide each other "official assistance" or at least declare their solidarity. In this context we should recall a quarrel in the house of Abraham Jacob in 1766 during which the bailiff and the court were insulted. We read in the report: "The head of the Jews, Abraham Jacob, was surprised that such a man could utter such things against the courts, and said he would have him removed unless he apologized."[179] Abraham Jacob intervened in the quarrel in a mediating role not only as the owner of the house, but also on behalf of the political elite of which he felt himself a member.

His bond to the territorial lord also becomes evident in the last will he drafted a few years later. In addition to leaving extensive bequests to Jewish institutions and providing for his family and community, he included non-Jews in his will: to the count he left 600 pounds, to the chief bailiff 300 pounds, with the request that the latter ensure that the provisions of the testament be carried out correctly. While this testamentary disposition still reflects utilitarian thinking relating to the legal enforcement of the will, another bequest is more difficult to interpret: Abraham Jacob set aside a small sum "for poor Christians living here in Steinbiedersdorf as well as in Crichingen," an act that would have been entirely unthinkable in the late Middle Ages.[180]

---

[176] AD Mos. Actes judiciaires Pontpierre B 10048: Markus Vancour von dahier Kläger gegen Abraham Jacob pcto. das Ratione betr., 1764.

[177] AD Mos. Actes judiciaires Denting B 10010: Schutzjude Itzig gegen den Judenvorsteher Josef Cahen, 1790.

[178] AD Mos. Actes judiciaires Denting B 10008: 1786.

[179] AD Mos. Actes judiciaires Pontpierre B 10048: Fiscalis contra Michel Mangin, 1766.

[180] Testament of Abraham Jacob: see Appendix; and AD Mos. 17 J 29: Traduction

Abraham Jacob provides no explanation for his charity toward the poor of a different faith, which means one has to resort to speculation: behind this gesture there could also be an economic or legal utilitarian thinking, in so far as the bequest to the poor was something the count and the Christian community very much desired. Especially if we think about the rise in status that the *parnas* experienced during his tenure of more than fifty-seven years, one suspects that Abraham Jacob, who had been given a share of his lord's power, was also seeking to participate in his generosity, a gesture that expresses not only benevolence but also superiority.

A final example may show that cooperation between Christians and Jews was not linked exclusively to the person of Abraham Jacob. When Leib Cahen of Kriechingen was unable to pay his protection money in 1791, the Jewish community decided to expel him. They asked the official in Kriechingen to throw his furniture out into the street and to return the key to the owner of the house.[181] This minor incident shows that the Jewish community certainly used the long arm of the lordship to rid itself of fellow Jews who were a burden on the community.

What emerges in all the examples I have recounted is that the cohesion between the higher social strata in the late eighteenth century began to overlay the rift between the religions. From a Jewish perspective the increasing interference by the state constituted—at least over the long term—the beginning of political integration into the state. On the Jewish side this integration was borne by a rural elite that felt committed to Jewish culture and education and was tied to Jewish society beyond their villages through kinship bonds. Its ideas of a "civilized" life were evidently much closer to those of Regierungsadvokat Braun than the ideas of both were to the attitudes of most of the peasants, artisans, merchants, and poor living in the countryside.

In 1787, when Braun was defending Bernard Lipman against an accusation from his farmhand in connection with the extramarital pregnancy of the maid Frommet Ahron, he offered the following justification for the conduct of the *parnas*:

> Surely no one will question that a housefather may castigate his domestics appropriately, nor will anyone deny the defendant the right to expel his domestics for such serious transgressions as he was afflicted with. Every housefather who loves discipline and respectability seeks to cleanse his house from such dissolute people, and one would be highly suspect of my client if he had permitted and provided opportunity for his farmhand and maid to continue their immorality.[182]

---

d'une copie d'un testament hébraïque faite par le def. Abraham fils d'Ezechiel, 1775. Jacov Guggenheim emphatically called my attention to this provision, which seems completely unimportant at first glance.

[181] AD Mos. Actes judiciaires Créhange, B 9924, 1791.

[182] AD Mos. Actes judiciaires B 10075: Acta in Sachen Benedict Isaak und Abraham Benedikt von Dentingen, 1787.

If one ignores the context in which these statements were made, they could easily be understood as an expression of a hegemonic Christian culture. After all, Braun, the Christian lawyer who had brought the quarrel between the Jewish householder and his Jewish farmhand before a Christian court, could or had to move argumentatively on the level of prevailing Christian norms. Possible differences—if he even perceived them or wanted to perceive them—he could regard with indifference.

More striking than the argumentative approximation is therefore the circumstance that Christian officials, the bailiff and the court clerk, were asked into the house of the Jew to question the maid, that the bailiff had considerable influence on the decision to keep the maid in the house, and that the *parnas* threatened to get some peasants who would throw the farmhand out. Bernard Lipman, the son of the wealthy Frankfurt woman Sara and stepson of the pious *parnas* Abraham Jacob, did not quite fit into rural society with his ideas of honor and good manners, and in his lifestyle he evidently identified far more with the Christian upper stratum than with his fellow Jews in the village. In his condemnation of the sexual immorality that had occurred and in the importance he attached to the honor of the house, he had the support of his wife, the daughter of the *parnas* of Kriechingen. By slapping the maid she expressed very clearly on whose side she stood. Bernard Lipman was one of the first to take advantage of the opportunities offered in 1791 in the emerging laical-republican France by the new law granting the Jews legal equality: he left Steinbiedersdorf with his family and settled in Metz. His grandsons and great-grandsons were able to pursue careers in Metz, Lille, and Paris that had been closed to his own generation as long as it remained bound to the Jewish religion.[183] Those who did not follow him to Metz voted in the winter of 1792–93 for the incorporation of the county's villages into France and thus for their legal equality.

The incorporation petition from Kriechingen has survived. The ninety-one individuals who supported this step included twelve Jews. They signed as a group right after the procureur, and only then came the signatures of the other villagers and the local nobility.[184] The revolutionary nature of the act is indicated even by the sequence of signatures. As an expression of the integration of the Jews into the newly created municipality, the *parnas* of Kriechingen was henceforth given a seat on the conseil municipal.[185] The fact that he had previously already held an important office as *parnas* was probably a crucial prerequisite for the smooth integration of the Jewish community.

---

[183] Benjman Lipman's grandson was the chief rabbi of Metz and later of Lille; one great-grandson, Fernand Nathan (1859–1949), was a publisher in Paris, who published, among other things, books for children and young adults: Cahen, *Catalogue: Les Juifs Lorrains*, 108, 349–350.

[184] AN Paris, sect. mod., F 7, 4401: 22.2.93.

[185] Ulbrich, "L'impact," 434.

It would appear that the communal council in Steinbiedersdorf did not admit a Jew. This is likely connected to the fact that the political representative of the Steinbiedersdorf Jewry had left the village, and along with him probably also the wealthier Jews. There now began for Steinbiedersdorf a period of increasing cultural impoverishment. The village became "rustic" and the Jews turned into a socially marginal group. By 1846 only 84 Jews were still living in Steinbiedersdorf; 39 of them were below the age of 20, and 9 above the age of 60. They made a living as middlemen and brokers, while only a scattered few were still cattle traders. Six women supplemented their income as seamstresses,[186] and the others were, as one woman had once put it during questioning, "ad cetera bene."[187]

---

[186] AD Mos. 17 J 45: Etat nominatif de la population israélite de la commune de Pontpierre.

[187] AD Mos. 10 F 166: Verhör der Nannett Berger, 1729.

CHAPTER EIGHT

Concluding Reflections

The present study was premised on the notion that early modern society was a complex structure grounded in pluralism. This microanalysis of a single village demonstrates an empirically not only the diversity of experiences and the complexity of relationships that existed in it, but also the extent to which an estate-based society that was built upon inequality and privileges allowed room for cultural plurality. This insight changes our understanding of what difference meant. The principles by which the society I have examined was constructed included the willingness—especially in the legal system—to adopt new things without giving up the old.

One result was the kind of contradictions that became apparent in the quarrel over the estate of Pierre Schmidt. While one party invoked territorial law, the other party looked to local custom. In the end, though, the question was not which law was valid and applicable, but which party had the requisite institutional knowledge, who was tied into which networks, and who could mobilize whom. This conflict, which dragged on over many years and eventually occupied the highest courts of the Holy Roman Empire, is one of many which show that the idyllic picture of rural society as a cohesive community devoid of conflict is not grounded in reality. The same is true for the homogenizing idea of a coherent rural culture.

The microhistorical approach reveals that the community, even if it acted as a single entity toward the outside world, was not free of conflicts but capable of engaging in them. The complex and partly contradictory rules that were produced and reproduced in daily life gave rise to continuous disagreements. That was true even for seemingly mediating rules such as division, drawing of lots, or auction at candlelight that were used in quarrels over inheritance. This finding shifts our perspective: what is important is no longer the social order as such, which can be read from norms and institutions, but who had what sort of options for living with these norms and institutions, infusing them with meaning, and either affirming or changing them in his or her daily (conflictual) behavior. In this constellation stability appears not simply as the continuation of existing conditions and thus the opposite pole to development, but as the result of an active process of appropriation.

The capacity to resolve conflicts created one important precondition for living with differences and thus also for the coexistence of Christians and Jews. Steinbiedersdorf's Jews, men and women, did not live separate lives. As the discussion of hospitality, work relationships, tenant relationship, brawls, and quarrels over honor has shown, the Jews had multifaceted relationships with their Christian neighbors, both male and female. These relationships bound the villagers into an economy of everyday life that presupposed shared spheres of action and values. We see this in the petition of the Jewish maid Särle, in which she invoked Christians and Jews as witnesses to her loyalty, and in the complaint that Jacob Cahen filed to force his opponent, a Christian, to publicly recant his accusation. Numerous brawls and quarrels over honor between Christians and Jews point to a concept of honor that was related to the community and transcended the boundaries of social status and religion, and which existed alongside ideas that were specific to religion, gender, and estate.

Even if Christian-Jewish coexistence was based on a hierarchical relationship, it was possible, depending on the situation, to dissolve or invert this relationship. For example, in his testament Abraham Jacob referred to the open market and the open street as spheres of special law that were jointly used by Christians and Jews, while the priest of Kriechingen criticized the practice of Christians and Jews sharing food and drink. The priest's disapproval raises the question of whether the hospitality extended to Christian neighbors in Jewish houses may have temporarily challenged or abolished the asymmetry between Christians and Jews postulated by the majority culture. And I am not necessarily talking about spectacular events like the brawl that occurred in the house of Abraham Jacob: when a Christian member of the community insulted the Christian village authorities in the presence of the head of the Jewish community, this gave the Jewish elder an opportunity to intervene in the quarrel and to take the side of the Christian authorities. It is not very likely that Abraham Jacob's intervention and testimony would have been relevant if the quarrel had occurred in a Christian house. The choice of the places where Christian and Jewish villagers interacted, and their significance to the economy, argue against those interpretations that seek to reduce Christian-Jewish relations to accidental encounters or to a coexistence shaped by pragmatism.

Hospitality and shared food and drink in Jewish houses are symptoms of an interweaving of Christian and Jewish realms of work and life, an interweaving that made it possible to stabilize the fragile balance between the Christian and Jewish populations. At the same time, this created an important precondition for the institutionalization of the Jewish community. In the eighteenth century, the Jewish men and women of Steinbiedersdorf succeeded in establishing and consolidating a separate Jewish community. This community had its social and religious center in the house of Abraham Jacob, and it was integrated into the territorial lordship through the office of the *parnas*.

While the cohesiveness of this community proved itself in many situations, my study has also shown that a small Jewish upper stratum set itself apart from the majority of its coreligionists. Its cooperation with the Christian officials points to a cultural closeness, which was probably grounded in the functions they exercised in their respective communities and in their shared orientation toward bourgeois values. The Jewish upper stratum had links to Jewish families from the urban milieu through marriage alliances and brought a certain bourgeois element into the village. As the founding of a Talmud school made possible by Abraham Jacob reveals, that element also included wealth and learning. At the same time, the existence of the Talmud school makes clear that the Jewish upper stratum of Steinbiedersdorf, which was connected to the wealthier Jewish families of the region, did not accommodate itself to the Christians in the sense of assimilation; it did not smooth out differences or give up its close ties to its own religion. On the contrary, the findings in Steinbiedersdorf suggest that especially the members of the Jewish elite who cultivated close contacts to the Christian world in their business dealings lived their lives according to the religious laws. Abraham Jacob lived a pious life and adhered to the Jewish ideals of learning and honor.

In contrast, the extramarital pregnancies in the village point to a "loosening of morals." The question of whether the explanation for the out-of-wedlock pregnancies of Jewish girls lies in a change in mentality that began to emerge with the Enlightenment must remain open for now.

What has become clear, however, is that the Jewish upper stratum of the eighteenth century lived a life that was strongly influenced by religious laws and sought its cohesiveness in the Jewish community, which had at least rudimentary forms of institutionalization. But this did not rule out an interweaving with the Christian population in the realms of work, business, and neighborly relationships. And what is important here with respect to the gender order is that hospitality, as an important foundation of these interwoven networks, leads into the house and thus into a sphere in which the seemingly separate spheres of inside and outside, higher and lower, women and men were intertwined.

In this context the house appears as the starting point of the analysis and not as the model or counterpole to the order of the state. The reconstructed biographies in this book, which place the worlds of women's experiences in the center, should have made clear that the house forms the basis from which politics, economic life, and society can be studied. The traces of women have led from the house into the street, the court, the church, or the synagogue. What has become visible along the way are contexts of agency and areas of conflict that point far beyond the house. Let us recall the midwife Anne-Marie Decker, whose testimony as to whether or not Anne-Marie Pierrard's child had lived after birth could profoundly influence the devolution of the mother's inheritance; or Katharina Legendre, whose attempt to pay her debts with assignats takes us into basic problems of the economic history of the French Revolution; or Hentla Willstätt, whose battle for a share of Abraham Jacob's wealth points to the world of court Jewry. We should also recall those maids who, pregnant out of wedlock, were expelled by their employers and families and who shed a revealing light on the idea—still widespread in scholarship—that the house was a harmonious living arrangement or existential community.

The stories of these unfortunate young women revealed the fragility of the domestic order and helped to uncover the multitude of constellations in which men and women exercised power within the house. If the example of the Jewish widow Perle and her maid Särle shows the means that Perle employed to assert her interests, if necessary at the expense of her subordinates, the look inside the house of Johannet Wahl makes clear how women were able to accumulate power as wives and mothers-in-law. Her example, like that of Marie Charlotte, the mother-in-law of the territorial lord Johann Ludwig Adolf, shows that women did not restrict their power to the house, but exercised it also vis-à-vis neighbors and subjects: Johannet Wahl by placing three women in a difficult situation when she named them as witnesses, and Marie Charlotte by increasing the taxes and levies of the subjects no less than her son-in-law had done.

The analysis of patriarchal institutions like church and community has demonstrated how closely the possibilities of self-expression for women were tied to the significance of the house or referred back to it. Writing the history of the community from various perspectives has made clear at the same time how one's point of view alters the results of the inquiry. In this sense the history of Steinbiedersdorf remains an "open history."

Last Will of Abraham Jacob

Last will of the esteemed chief parnas Aberham Jacob in Steinbiedersdorff, a translation word for word from the Hebrew.[1]

(27) *As an eternal attestation and* remembrance, there came before us, the undersigned witnesses, on this day, the fifth day of the week, the twenty-eighth day in the *month of Ader* in the year 5531 since the creation of the world, as we reckon here in Steinbiedersdorff, there came the esteemed *parnas* and leader of the Jews, *Abraham* by name, the son of *Jacob* of Crichingen, of blessed memory, and said to us: since a person's life on earth is brief and his days go by like the shuttle of the weaver's loom [Job, 7.6] and since the learned *rabbis* who came before us spoke and explained in their writings,

(27b) that the man who has the fear of *God* in him during his lifetime shall take heed of his last days and hour, and shall prepare provisions for the path that all humans must tread, to stand before the *king* of all the world, and thereby protect his body from exile on earth, and simultaneously to bring the immortal *soul* up to heaven, to the source of its dwelling, to be connected there in the eternal and immortal realm, to soothe oneself and take joy in the light of His *Divine Majesty* <the king of the living{eternal}>, as I too am old and hoary, and have arrived at the days of suffering, on account of my sin, that [approx. one-half line illegible]

---

[1] The last will was drafted in 1771 and notarized in 1775. The German translation is found in AD Mos. Actes judicaires Pontpierre, B 10062. A French version of the text has survived in AD Mos. 17 J 29: Traduction d'une copie d'un testmant hébraïque faite par le def. Abraham fils d'Ezechiel, 1775. The Hebrew original appears to be no longer extant. This text was taken from the German edition of 1775, which contains a number of underlined passages, additions, crossed-out words, and words that were highlighted in some way. These textual peculiarities are reproduced in the following ways: <written above the line>; {crossed out}; *in italics in the original*; [editors additions]. Some of the passages are no longer legible. As far as possible, I have tried to decipher the meaning with the help of the French translation. Even so, the translation of some sections proved extraordinarily difficult. Many passages remain unclear and require further discussion and examination. The text is characterized by a high degree of intertextuality. I was able to identify a few biblical passages, which are noted in brackets. On how to situate the text historically see esp. p. 216.

(28) and the joy has been taken from my eyes. My wife and sons and daughters have died, I alone am left behind. I have not a single heir to dispose of my wealth, only my children's children. And on account of this my heart trembles . . . [several lines of unclear meaning]

(28b) who will have the strength to be a *defender* or intercessor on your behalf, to speak of your righteous works, through which your sin will be expunged, and your misdeeds be forgiven? [Daniel 9.24; Lamentations 4.22] Wither shall I turn or look for a son who will intercede for his father through prayer, they are at rest and have exchanged the world for eternity, and your sin pursues you and pulls you to punishment? But my son, hear my voice, I will counsel you, thus *God* will be with you, share your wealth with the needy and poor of your people, and leave behind you a gift that bestows blessing upon the pious and the learned [about one and a half lines illegible]

(29) the same will be with you in secret, to protect your body from destruction, and thus even to lift you to the highest flowering in name, beauty, and renown, for when righteousness precedes you, the [enemy] soldiers, who were once created on account of your sin, will be destroyed and dispersed, they will thus be lost, but you attain eternal rest until the time when our redeemer for whom we yearn will come.

On account of this you are my true and honest witnesses, and take from me the *mandel griff*[2] from here on, and write this in every possible way

(29b) that it may last for ever. And you shall affirm this with your own signature to give permanence to the alms and the gifts to the learned, as well as the other *gifts* <articles> that are provided in this *contract* and *testament*, that not one *dot* or syllable should go missing or be lost. And you shall be a true witness that I have done this willingly and with the utmost forethought and good will, without any coercion or other motivations, but with my entire heart <good will, and sound mind>, and you profess yourselves true witnesses on this day and date, and this shall have as much force as though it had been done before the highest court . . . (30) . . . and I will not depart from such *provisions*, or change my mind, from this day and forever. That in all truth I oblige myself through the above mentioned *mandelgriff* and take upon myself the obligation, as do those who shall act for me on my authority, and likewise my heirs, to place my entire estate under mortgage <with due obligation and truthfully>, that all following provisions mentioned in this contract and testament shall be carried out as they have been ordered.

---

[2] Mantelgriff or *kinjan* is a way of acquiring real estate. The transfer of property and the establishment of rights takes place through a symbolic act of acquisition (fictive real contract). Apparently, the contracting parties, instead of shaking hands, took hold of a corner of each other's coats, a symbolic act that carried greater legal force.

(30b) No. I A

And this shall be the first *provision*, concerning my aforementioned obligation, immediately upon my *death*, there shall be taken from the estate, and so on with all possibility <possible speed>, *both from my moveable and immovable goods* the *sum of 13,000 Livres de France*, and this *sum* shall be delivered and handed over to the esteemed [?] heads of the Jewry of Metz, and this sum shall remain in their hands forever from generation to generation, until our *messiam* for whom we yearn comes, *and loan it at interest* <as far as we are allowed to do so>

(31) namely to take 5 *procento* yearly of the sum which the entire *sum* yields every year = 650 *Livres [de France]*, and this interest shall be divided according to the following *provisions* <yearly>: namely 500 *Livres {de France}* of the indicated interest shall be set aside and given to a *rabbi* for his yearly support, and the same rabbi *with his wife and children and any other fellow lodgers* [*hausgenossen*] shall have his lodgings in the house in which I now live. However, this *rabbi* must have received the title of rabbi from the chief *rabbi* of Metz or from some other chief *rabbi* from a respectable Jewish community in German lands. And this [about one-third line illegible] *function* shall consist of

(31b) that the same shall study three days and nights, in the room in my house which has been {for a long time} set up for this purpose, which is below the school, and, not counting this study room, the lodging for him and his wife and children in my mentioned house shall be as follows, namely *one room, one kitchen* = and another room for his bedroom, as well as a part of the garden, and courtyard, and cellar, and attic in my aforementioned house, and all this <entirely free> *without the least bit of payment*, over and above the mentioned bequest of 500 l: {*de France*} yearly, as long as the *rabbi* lives in my house as stated, and I transfer [approx. half a line illegible]

(33b) to other {*particular*} Jews of Metz <wealthy and known as such to all people> at 5 *procento*, which the chief *rabbi* in consultation with the other rabbis of Metz shall choose, shall take the indicated *sum* in hand {but not any other Jews}. And the *rabbi* chosen with the aforementioned conditions is obligated to study in *compagnie* with the *very learned* <student> and groom *Baruch {Levi}* of Nauweiler in the *Alsace*, who is currently studying in my house, and the two are obligated to study the 5 books of *Moses*, and the *prophets*, and the *psalms of David* = and the *Talmud*, {and the same} for an hour a day <at a set time and also on> the *sabbath* {and other feast days}

(34) not counting what the *rabbi* is otherwise obligated to study with the aforementioned school children.

And account of the teaching of the aforementioned learned Jewish student and groom {*Baruch Levi*}, I have already committed myself with the utmost obligation to give to the latter as a dowry, on the wedding day of my granddaughter *Teille*, the *sum* of 2,400 *Livres* in cash. I now affirm the above obligation and the stipulations intended for the marriage *contract* with all force and power, from this day on I obligate myself to <bring in> to the mentioned {*Baruch Levi*} on his wedding [about one-third line illegible] dowry {to give} the *sum* of 2,400 *Livres*

(34b)

Also, from the yearly <aforementioned> {Metz} *interest* 30 *Livres* {*de France*} shall be taken and the same distributed to the learned and the poor, that they may study every year on the anniversary of my death, and say a prayer for my *soul*, namely ten Jewish students from Metz, and ten people from Crichingen, and {ten} from here in Steinbiedersdorff <together>, of the latter two places, if they are not learned men, each shall pray in the *Psalms of David* or some other prayers <according to his knowledge> on account of my *soul*, for which each shall receive 30 sous *de France*.

The remaining 120 *Livres* {*de France*} of the aforementioned *interest* shall every year before Easter [approx. one-third of a line illegible]

(35) be distributed to the poor in Crichingen and Steinbiedersdorff, namely those who are related to me in the second degree, a man shall be given =6= lb and a woman 3 lb {*de France*}, and the other poor in {Crichingen u Steinbiedersdorff} <the two villages mentioned > a man 3 lb and a woman 30 S: {*de France*} and this money shall be part of the alms for the purpose of buying flour for matzah, but with this condition that in every case in Crichingen and Steinbiedersdorff my relatives shall be given preference over the others.

No. II B

At the time when my days and hours have been accomplished, and I shall go the way of all human beings, there shall be taken from the estate and distributed

(35b) 248 two-Sou pieces, as much as my name *abraham* written in *Hebrew* <40/5/200/2/1> [numerical values written above the Hebrew letters of his name: mem he resch bet alef] has in number, namely half of it to the poor here in Steinbiedersdorff in the last hour of my life, and the other half to be distributed to the poor at the time of my funeral in Crichingen.

{No. III} C

To the *brotherhood* in Crichingen that washes and buries the dead bodies shall be given the *sum* of 12 lb *de France* from my estate.

{No. IIII} D

To the assembled *brotherhood* here in Steinbiedersdorff

(36) which is used to studying here every day after the evening prayer in the synagogue, 24 lb *de France* shall be given from my estate.

{No. V} E

In the first 30 days following my death, 10 people <of Steinbiedersdorf> shall engage in study twice a day for the sake of my *soul*, namely in the morning and at night after the prayer in the synagogue, and each shall receive from the estate 6 *Livres* {*de France*}, and these ten people shall include the aforementioned *rabbi*, who is to come into and live in my house as *rabbi*, along with the learned *Baruch* {*Levi*}, aforementioned as the groom, and likewise on the yearly anniversary of my death, as mentioned, the *rabbi* and {Baruch Levi} <the aforementioned student> shall be included.

(36) {No. VI} F

The entire house in which I presently live, the stables and barns along with the house, and all rooms and chambers in the house, and the courtyard and the garden behind the courtyard, with all entrances and exits, the cellar and the attics and the roof, from the ground to the top, everything without the least exception, I give through the aforementioned highest obligation, and through all power and strength, according to the [juridical power] used by learned rabbis of old, from this day on and one hour before my death, as a *sacred* gift, as follows,

Namely the aforementioned *rabbi* already has his lodgings as stipulated and provided for, and to the learned groom *Baruch* {*Levi*} I have in like manner already obligated myself in the marriage *contract*

(37) To the latter I have transferred his half lodging in my aforementioned house according to the marriage *contract* that was written on the 5th day of the week on the 9th day in the *month of Ellel* in the year 5530 from the creation of the world.

{No. VII} G

And the remaining living space in my house in which I currently live, without the two stipulated dwellings of the *rabbi* and {*Baruch Levi*} <the aforementioned student and groom>, shall be leased year by year forever, and the income from the house shall be used to pay for the *maintenance* of the house, and if there should be anything left over after the *maintenance*, every year on the day of my death it shall be distributed to the poor in Crichingen (37b) *and Steinbiedersdorff*, and in every case relatives of mine shall have priority in this distribution.

{No. VIII} H

And none of my surviving heirs or my descendants shall have the least claim or demand, no matter what their name, either against the assigned housing and everything connected with it, starting with the house and ending with the garden, and <horse> stables and barns and attic, or against the rent of the house from the remaining dwelling, they shall have no *claim* or demand, in *sum*, no matter what their name may be.

(38) {No IX} J

And seeing that after my *son Marx* exchanged mortal with eternal life and left behind three sons by name of *Uri Marx Jacob* = and *Joseph Marx* = and *Jacob Marx* = and one daughter called *Ester*, and I have already spent on my grandson *Uri Marx Jacob* on the day of his wedding the *sum* of 4,000 *Livres de France*, and have already obligated myself to my granddaughter *Ester*, to give her on the day of her wedding a dowry of 4,000 *Livres de France* in accordance with the wedding *contract* that was drawn up between her and the groom *Selligman*, the son of *Feiber* of Jeitz, it is therefore no less right that my other grandchildren shall receive the same and suffer no disadvantage.

(38b) On account of which I give from my estate from this day on and one hour before my death to the other two grandsons mentioned above, *Joseph Marx* and *Jacob Marx*, the *sum* of 8,000 *Livres de France*, namely to each 4,000 *Livres {de France}*, and this *sum* shall be to the same a bride gift, but no sooner than on the day of their wedding.

{No. X} K

And as my daughter *Scheba* of blessed memory has left behind a son and a daughter called *Jacob {aron cain}* and *Teille*, both children of the late *Aron Cain* of blessed memory, and I have already obligated myself in the marriage *contract* of my granddaughter *Teille* to issue a promissory note on her wedding day

(39) in the amount of 3,000 *Livres de France* to pay such a *sum* one hour before my death, thus, as a further security and affirmation, I give from my estate from this day on and one hour before my death to my grandson by *Teille* the *sum* of 4,000 *Livres de France*, which *sum* is to include the aforementioned promissory note which I have obligated myself to give on her wedding day {of 3,000 L}, and the expenses *Teille* is yet to incur on behalf of my grandson, clothing and other ornaments, and the wedding costs shall be subtracted from these same 1,000 lb *de France* that are over and above the aforementioned promissory note.

(39b) {No. XI} L

In the same manner I give from this day forth and one hour before my death from my estate to my grandson *Jacob {Aron Cain}*, the son of my daughter *Scheba* of blessed memory, the *sum* of 4,000 *Livres de France* for a bridal gift and no earlier than his wedding day, just as I now affirm to pay the obligation to my granddaughter *Ester*, daughter of my son *Marx* of blessed memory, the aforementioned *sum* from my estate, but in the same manner not before the day of her wedding.

{No. XII} M

And may *heaven* forbid that one or the other [approx. two-thirds of a line illegible; "of my"? (40) grandchildren of my *son Marx* of blessed memory shall die before reaching their wedding day, I henceforth give the portion of the

deceased, or even more, to those who are still alive among the four grandchildren of my son *Marx* of blessed memory, to distribute amongst themselves
in equal shares the portion of the deceased over and above the portion I have
bequeathed them as described. And, heaven forbid, should all three <afore-
mentioned> grandchildren {of my son *Marx*} die before reaching their wedding day, I give their entire portion to my two grandchildren from my daughter
{*Scheba*} of blessed memory to distribute amongst themselves the portion of
the deceased [about one-third of a line illegible] or to the one of the

(40b) two who is still alive, and may *God* forbid that one = or the other =
of my two grandchildren of my daughter *Scheba* of blessed memory should die
before reaching their wedding day, I give the portion of the deceased to the
brother or sister who is still alive over and above their inheritance, but if, *God*
forbid, both grandchildren of my daughter of blessed memory should die before
reaching their wedding, I give their entire portions to all the grandchildren of
my son *Marx* of blessed memory, to those who are still alive, to divide amongst
themselves, the brothers and the sister, in equal parts, over and above their
inheritance.

(41) {No. XIII}

The esteemed and highly learned *chief rabbi* of Metz, whoever it may be at the
time, in consultation with the lower *rabbis*, shall choose guardians who shall
take control of all the aforementioned *sums* for my grandchildren of both my
son and my daughter of blessed memory, and invest them at interest rates to
be determined at their discretion, and the entire *sums* shall remain in their hands
until the wedding day of each of my grandchildren.

{No. XIIII}

To my two brothers *Anschel* and *Mayer* I give from my estate from this day and
one hour before my death

(41b) the *sum* of 2,000 *Livres de France*, namely to each 1,000 lb. as a sincere
gift, with all my power.

{No. XV}

To the leaders and the entire Jewry of Metz, whoever it may be at the time,
I give from my assets and estate from this day on and one hour before my
death the *sum* of 300 *Livres de France*, which shall be used for the expenses of
the Jews of Metz, in return for which I ask that my name be inscribed in the
memorial book, that my *soul* be remembered well on *the sabbath* and other feast
days as is the custom <there>,

(42) however, with this bequest, as well, I reserve the right on the condition
that the lords parnasim in Metz agree to take the aforementioned *capital* of
13,000 lb at 5 *procento*, and should the lords parnasim, on the contrary, be unwilling to take the *capital* at 5 *percento*, this bequest of 300 lb shall be null and
void from this day on.

{No. XVI}

To the highly learned lord chief *rabbi*, whoever it may be at the time, I give from my estate from this day on and one hour before my death the *sum* of two *Louis d'or*, on condition however, that the same shall make every effort that all the provisions listed in this *testament* are carried out, and not a word [two-thirds of line illegible: "shall perish"]

(42b) {No. XVII}

To His Lordship the Count and Ruler of the Land, under whose high authority we live here in Steinbiedersdorf and are protected, I give from this day on and one hour before my death from my assets and estate the sum of 600 Livres de France, and to the lord *Regierungsrat* of Crichingen <whoever it may be at the time> I give from this day on and one hour before my death the sum of 300 Livres de France from my wealth and estate, and I ask humbly and obediently <Your Grace and the Lord *Regierungsrat*> to grant me this favor

(43) by your justice and high power and authority to look out for the aforementioned provisions and articles dealt with in this testament, that not one word {large or small} shall perish.

{No. XVIII}

To the poor Christians living here in Steinbiedersdorf and in Crichingen I give from this day on and one hour before my death from my wealth and estate the sum of 12 sous de Lorraine to each.

(43b) {No. XVIIII} T

The shul in my house I make into an eternal sanctuary from this day on and one hour before my death, forever after. In return the protected Jews living here shall be obligated and bound to keep an eternal light burning for the sake of my soul from the hour of my death until our true and just redeemer shall come, and to pay the expenses they may rent out and lease the places in the men's and women's shul, and my surviving heirs have no more claim to the shul than all the other resident protected Jews. However, I reserve for myself that the place in the shul where I now stand shall be assigned to the rabbi for free, without him having to pay anything for it.

(44) Likewise the place where now stands the learned groom Baruch Nauweiller shall be his for his lifetime <for free>, likewise in the shul on the right side, counting from the front, the fourth place shall properly belong to my grandson Uri Marx, and three other places in the shul shall properly go to my three grandchildren, namely Joseph and Jacob of my son {Marx} and Jacob {Aron Cain} from my daughter {Scheba} of blessed memory, namely to each one place.

{No. XX} U

The house that also belongs to me, in which my brother's son Marx <Amschel> lives, the entire house shall from this day on and one hour before my death belong entirely as an inheritance to my {three} <all male> grandchildren, of [about two-thirds of a line illegible] and his sister [one line illegible]

(44b) of blessed memory shall have no claim, either to the house or to the revenues generated by it.

{No. XXI} V

To my farmhand and maid who are in my house, at the time of my death, I give from this day on and one hour before my death from the estate the sum of 15 lb de France jointly.

{No. XXII} W

To my brother's son Marx <Amschel> I forgive and renounce with all possible force all the debt claims I have against him, both the oral and the written claims, from this day on I give to the aforementioned brother's son [one and two-thirds lines illegible]

(45) {No. XXIII} Q

And after all the provisions and articles listed above and on all these pages have been carried out and taken from my wealth and estate, should there be anything left in my estate, be it houses or other real estate, whatever its name may be, whatever the mouth can speak or the heart can conceive <furniture, silver, gold, cash, debt certificates or other certificates, now or in the future, open or hidden>, in keeping with my aforementioned dispositions, the remaining wealth as indicated above shall be divided into five parts, namely two parts of this shall be taken by my grandchildren of my son Marx of blessed memory, and divided among themselves {according to Jewish ritual and law}, namely a man one whole part, and a woman half of that, and one part of the five parts shall likewise go to my grandchildren of my daughter Scheba of blessed memory, a man an entire part and a woman a half part [approx. one-third of a line illegible].

(45b) And two parts of the aforementioned five parts shall {be mine for my eternal memory} <belong to me>, through the following articles, and as far as my heirs are concerned, I order and command that they shall not, as I have said, let the remaining estate be sold at public auction, instead, they shall take discerning men <in appraising>, the same shall appraise all the furniture and house furnishings and the silver and gold, which will be in the remaining estate, according to their worth and estimation, and then everything shall be divided into five parts, and the grandchildren of my son of blessed memory shall take two parts, and my grandchildren of my daughter one part as mentioned, in kind and the two parts [one long word illegible].

(46) Shall be mine, to <me in [?] my name> *my eternal memory* as I have said, and it shall be given to a wealthy man in Metz and to no one else chosen by the chief rabbi, in consultation with the lower rabbis, or it shall be handed

over to the leaders of Metz if they so demand, thus they shall have priority over all others, and the leaders or the chosen man shall take control of these aforementioned two parts from the estate and sell it, and thereby the same shall have all the cash in their hands at 5 percent a year in accordance with <Jewish law>, and the interest from it shall be used as a help and dowry for the weddings of young girls, namely for the wedding of children whose parents are among the Jewry {and leaders} <of the *Landschaft*> standing under the protection of Metz, or also daughters, [approx. two-thirds of a line illegible] lordship (46b) under the authority and protection of Your Grace the Count of Crichingen, and so on.

Every year there shall be <given> from the aforementioned interest 3 lb, and to the daughters and those getting married from the aforementioned land and lordship, to each 30 sous, and to my kin to the second degree, not including the second degree, there shall be given to each {of those getting married} 24 lb, and to my kin in the second degree to each 12 lb, and in the third degree to each 6 lb, and at all times my kin shall be given priority, thus the aforementioned two parts shall remain in my name in the hands of these leaders of Metz or in the hands of a wealthy man, from generation to generation, at 5 percent a year, until the awaited redeemer comes, at a tax . . . [one or two words illegible].

(47) And I commit and bind myself to all the articles and provisions indicated above, and likewise on all the pages and places, both before myself as well as all my surviving heirs, and all my wealth from this day on, through the aforementioned *mandelgriff*, as a true obligation and committment, in every manner invented by our highly learned rabbis, to pay everything from my wealth and estate from today on and one hour before my death all the above mentioned articles, and reservations indicated above and on all pages, and what is intended above, to pay the interest of 500 lb {de France} to a rabbi who will be in my house, from the capital that will be in the hands of those leaders, or other wealthy men [?] of Metz as stated,

(47b) This provision shall be carried out right away after my death and from generation to generation, to be continued until the arrival of our just redeemer, the aforementioned rabbi shall study in my house, and for his support he shall have every year 500 Livres de France from the aforementioned interest, not counting the income which the rabbi can achieve over and above by teaching the students, as stated in the articles above, and thus the parnas Abraham tells us from now on I leave to each and every one mentioned in this contract, . . .

(48) with a pledge made in sound mind and through the above-mentioned *mandel griff*, I pledge all my holdings and possessions I have under heaven, what I have already purchased or will yet purchase from this day on, . . . everything shall be committed and pledged, from which is to be paid all the aforementioned provisions, even if I have to give the shirt off my back, from this day

on to all eternity, and all the provisions and reservations that are in this testament [aprrox. one-third of a line illegible] and on all pages [1 word illegible] (48b) I reserve, with a right and true reservation, and with a two-fold reservation, and with yes before no, . . . to affirm this document and contract, as with the reservation of the children of Gad and Ruve, and in accordance with all their laws, thus has also been done by me, from this time on each person man and woman shall most strongly affirm item by item as they are recorded above, . . . each one mentioned above shall be confirmed, in every manner as best can be, both against me and against those who are to come [part of the line illegible].

(49) All this shall be affirmed against my surviving heirs, even if they are young orphans—may God protect them from this, namely with respect to the payment of all sums that are mentioned here and the implementation of all provisions . . . The contract shall be confirmed by the tear of the chief rabbi and his colleagues, and on it they shall write that this testament is absolutely legal. And also he who has signed before us [approx. one-third of a line illegible] the parnas Aberham

(49b) renounces and voids all agreements, secrets, that he may have made with regard to these arrangements, or intends to do in the future, that go against them, even if it was done in front of witnesses, this the aforesaid parnas Aberham has affirmed, and these witnesses shall not be valid, whatever goes against this prescription, as is the customary tearing with a divorce letter between a husband and wife . . . just as our eminent and learned rabbis have decreed that it should be,

(50) and this contract shall not be destroyed, and its force shall not be diminished, . . . even if something should be out of order, even if something should be crossed out or erased, or there be a hole, or a tear that was not made by the rabbi, even if there should be one word too many or too little, either a syllable or a whole word, even if it were possible to interpret the entire document in two ways, none of that shall have any validity, instead the entire document shall be interpreted in accordance with the true intention [?], and affirmation [about half a line illegible: "to each and every"] item by item,

(50b) as they are intended in this contract, and forever after every one and all those articles mentioned above shall have the power and affirmation, both against me and those who should come after me, and also against my surviving heirs. The above mentioned parnas Abraham also told us witnesses, now I tell you witnesses the writing of this contract, write it and sign it, and even though one hundred should be written, and even though the chief rabbi with his colleagues have already affirmed it, continue until there issues forth from your hands one that is written rightly and properly the way it should, as confirmation of [approx. two words illegible] all points and articles,

(51) also {said the aforementioned parnas Aberham} write the contract publicly in the open market, and signed it in the open street, so that it may not be said that it was done in secret or clandestinely, rather it shall be open and known to all, as though it had been contracted by a rabbinic authority . . .

Thus we the undersigned witnesses have accepted a mantelgriff from the parnas Aberham on account of his obligations, first toward the esteemed parnasim in Metz, and to the chief rabbi, and to all the poor {Christians as well as Jews}, and to the students, and to the two brothers Anschel and Mayer,

(52b) <and my nephew Marx, the son of my brother Amschel> and to all my grandchildren, by they of my late son or daughter, and farmhand and maid, and the gift of a residential house as an eternal sanctuary, and all other articles, point by point, as they are given in the writing of this contract, all as mentioned above, described in detail on all the pages, especially as concerns the validation, as each and every shall be confirmed as listed and described, and this was done with a valid *mandelgriff*, and everything is correct and confirmed.

Aberham   Uri Feis: clerk of the Jewry of Metz, witness
son of Jacob   David Elinger: witness

We two, the undersigned Marx Vantous and Isac Worms, protected Jews in Criechingen, affirm herewith that the testament of the late Jew Abraham Jacob of Steinbiedersdorff, translated from the Hebrew, has been translated word by word from the Hebrew and is completely identical.

Criechingen, July 6, 1775   Marx Vantous
                                   [illegible]

BIBLIOGRAPHY

UNPRINTED SOURCES

Koblenz: Landeshauptarchiv (LHA Koblenz)
    56: Reichskammergericht 487–503, 505, 1801, 2987
    701 Pfalz-Zweibrücken: 465: Herrschaft Crichingen und Saarwellingen (Geschichte der Herrschaft Saarwellingen von Dr. Matthias Sittel)
Metz: Archives Départementales de la Moselle (AD Mos.)
    B: Juridiction d'Empire 9931, 10012–10013, 10041–10081, 10087–10088
    B Spire: Répertoire du Fond de la Chambre impériale de Spire et de Wetzlar, 10770/ 10771
    3 E: Notaires et Tabellions 6013–6035
    5 E: Régistres paroissiales, 1680–1865 (1 Mic EC 553)
    E Dépot 553: Archives communales: Pontpierre
    10 F: Fonds de Créhange, 1–820.
    Annexes: Archives anciennes des communes C:
    Pontpierre: AA1–CC1–DD 2, DD 3–FF3, FF4, FF 5
    17 J: 44/45: État nominatif de tous les israélites, 1840/1846
    29 J: Évêché: 63, 66, 69, 70, 657
    J 5818: Collection Richard
Paris: Archives diplomatiques (AD Paris)
    C.P. Allemagne, Petites Principautés,18: Créhange (1737–1774). Mémoires sur le comté de Créhange et correspondance relative aux transports de grains, aux réquisitions de la guerre de sept ans, aux recrutements, au libre passage de troupes d'Empire en vue d'executions militaires contre les sujets de Créhange; Affaires Duverdier; Projets d'échange etc.
    C.P. Allemagne, Petites Principautés,18: Créhange (1780–1825)
Paris: Archives nationales (AN Paris)
    Section moderne, sér. F (7): Comité de sureté générale (1787–an IV)
    Section ancienne, sér. Q (2): Domaines
Saarwellingen: Gemeindearchiv
    Pamphlets
Saarbrücken: Landesarchiv (LA Saarbrücken)
    MI 35/36 Collection Steinthal des Leo Baeck-Instituts
Wiesbaden: Staatsarchiv (STA Wiesbaden)
    172–3381: Akten den Abfall der Grafschaften Dillenburg und Crichingen von dem Hause Wied-Runkel und dem Deutschen Reich betr.
    Pamphlets
Wien: Haus-, Hof- und Staatsarchiv Wien (HHSTA Wien)
    Kleinere Reichsstände
    Reichshofrat, Obere Registratur

PRINTED SOURCES AND SECONDARY LITERATURE

Abel, Wilhelm. *Geschichte der deutschen Landwirtschaft vom frühen Mittelalter bis zum 19. Jahrhundert.* Deutsche Agrargeschichte 2, 3rd ed. Stuttgart, 1978.

Abu-Lughod, Lila. *Writing Women's Worlds. Bedouin Stories.* Berkeley, 1993.

———. "Gegen Kultur Schreiben." In *Wechselnde Blicke. Frauenforschung in internationaler Perspektive,* edited by Ilse Lenz and Andrea Germer, 14–46. Opladen, 1996.

Actenmäßige Geschichts-Erzählung und Deduction in Sachen des gewesenen Oberforstmeisters und Rechnungsführers Köppel contra den hochgebohrenen Grafen und Herrn, Herrn Christian Ludwig, regierenden Grafen zu Kriechingen. STA Wiesb. 3005–2244.

Adelman, Howard. "Italian Jewish Women." In *Jewish Women in Historical Perspective,* edited by Judith R. Baskin, 135–158. Detroit, 1991.

Algazi, Gadi. *Herrengewalt und Gewalt der Herren im späten Mittelalter. Herrschaft, Gegenseitigkeit und Sprachgebrauch.* Frankfurt am Main, 1996.

———. "Otto Brunner—'Konkrete Ordnung' und Sprache der Zeit." In *Geschichtsschreibung als Legitimationswissenschaft, 1918–1945,* edited by Peter Schöttler, 166–203. Frankfurt am Main, 1997.

Allegra, Luciano. "A Model of Jewish Devolution: Turin in the Eighteenth Century." *Jewish History* 7, no. 2 (1993): 29–58.

Anchel, Robert. *Les Juifs de France.* Paris, 1946.

Anderson, Patricia-Arnold-Anne. *Gossips. Ale-wives, Midwives and Witches.* Ann Arbor, Mich. 1992.

Arnold, Hermann. *Juden in der Pfalz. Vom Leben pfälzischer Juden,* 2nd ed. Landau, 1988.

Bader, Karl Siegfried. *Dorfgenossenschaft und Dorfgemeinde. Studien zur Rechtsgeschichte des mittelalterlichen Dorfes 2.* Weimar, 1962.

Badinter, Robert. *Libres et égaux. L'émancipation des Juifs sous la Révolution française (1789–1791).* Paris, 1989.

Bartsch, Robert. *Die Rechtsstellung der Frau als Gattin und Mutter.* Leipzig, 1903.

Baskin, Judith R. "Introduction." In *Jewish Women in Historical Perspective,* edited by Judith Baskin, 15–24. Detroit, 1991.

Battenberg, J. Friedrich. "Schutzjuden." *HRG* 4 (1990): 1535–1541.

———. *Das europäische Zeitalter der Juden. Zur Entwicklung einer Minderheit in der nicht-jüdischen Umwelt Europas.* Darmstadt, 1990.

———. "Zwischen Integration und Segregation. Zu den Bedingungen jüdischen Lebens in der vormodernen christlichen Gesellschaft." *Aschkenas* 6, no. 2 (1996): 421–454.

Baumann, Peter. *Macht und Motivation. Zu einer verdeckten Form sozialer Macht.* Opladen, 1993.

———. "Die Motive des Gehorsams bei Max Weber: eine Rekonstruktion." *ZfS* 22, no. 5 (1993): 355–370.

Beck, Rainer. "Der Pfarrer und das Dorf. Konformismus und Eigensinn im katholischen Bayern des 17./18. Jahrhunderts." In *Armut, Liebe, Ehre. Studien zur historischen Kulturforschung,* edited by Richard van Dülmen, 107–143. Frankfurt am Main, 1988.

———. "Frauen in der Krise. Eheleben und Ehescheidung in der ländlichen Gesellschaft Bayerns während des Ancien Régime." In *Dynamik der Tradition. Studien zur historischen Kulturforschung,* edited by Richard van Dülmen, 137–212. Frankfurt am Main, 1992.

Beck, Ulrich, and Elisabeth Beck-Gernsheim. *The Normal Chaos of Love,* translated by Mark Ritter and Jane Wiebel. Cambridge, Mass., 1995.

Becker, Peter. "'Ich bin halt immer liederlich gewest und habe zu wenig gebetet.' Illegitimität und Herrschaft im Ancien Régime: St. Lambrecht 1600–1850." In *Frühe Neuzeit–Frühe Moderne. Forschungen zur Vielschichtigkeit von Übergangsprozessen,* edited by Rudolf Vierhaus et al., 157–179. Veröffentlichungen des Max-Planck-Instituts für Geschichte 104. Göttingen, 1992.

Behre, Patricia, "Raphael Levy—'A Criminal in the Mouth of the People.'" *Religion* 23 (1993): 19–44.

Bennett, Judith M. *Ale, Beer, and Brewsters in England. Women's Work in a Changing World, 1300–1600.* New York, 1996.

Berg, Roger. *Histoire du rabbinat français (XVIe–XXe siècle).* Paris, 1992.

Bernard, Gildas at al. *Les familles juives en France. XVe siècle–1815.* Paris, 1990.

Blickle, Peter. *Deutsche Untertanen. Ein Widerspruch.* Munich, 1980.

———. *Unruhen in der ständischen Gesellschaft. 1300–1800.* Munich, 1988.

——— et al., eds. *Aufruhr und Empörung? Studien zum bäuerlichen Widerstand im Alten Reich.* Munich, 1980.

Blickle, Renate. "Die Tradition des Widerstandes im Ammergau. Anmerkungen zum Verhältnis von Konflikt- und Revolutionsbereitschaft." ZAA 35 (1987): 138–159.

———. "Hausnotdurft. Ein Fundamentalrecht in der altständischen Ordnung Bayerns." In *Grund- und Freiheitsrechte von der ständischen zur spätbürgerlichen Gesellschaft,* edited by Günter Birtsch, 42–64. Veröffentlichungen zur Geschichte der Grund- und Freiheitsrechte 2. Göttingen, 1987.

———. "Nahrung und Eigentum als Kategorien in der ständischen Gesellschaft." In *Ständische Gesellschaft und soziale Mobilität,* edited by Winfried Schulze and Helmut Gabel, 73–93. Schriften des Historischen Kollegs, Kolloquien 12. Munich, 1988.

———. "From Subsistence to Property: Traces of a Fundamental Change in Early Modern Bavaria." *Central European History* 25 (1992): 377–386.

Blumenkranz, Bernhard, ed. *Histoire des Juifs en France.* Toulouse, 1972.

Bock, Gisela. "Geschichte, Frauengeschichte, Geschlechtergeschichte." GG 14, no. 3 (1988): 364–391.

———, ed. *Lebenswege von Frauen im Ancien Régime.* Geschichte und Gesellschaft 18/4. Göttingen, 1992.

Bourdieu, Pierre. "Structures, *habitus*, practices." In P. Bourdieu, *The Logic of Practice,* translated by Richard Nice, 52–65. Stanford, 1990.

———. "Die männliche Herrschaft." In *Ein alltägliches Spiel. Geschlechterkonstruktion in der sozialen Praxis,* edited by Irene Dölling and Beate Krais, 153–217. Frankfurt am Main, 1997.

Bowman, William David. "Frauen und geweihte Männer: Priester und ihre Haushälterinnen in der Erzdiözese Wien, 1800–1850. In *Religion der Geschlechter. Historische Aspekte religiöser Mentalitäten,* edited by Edith Saurer, 245–259. L'Homme Schriften 1. Vienna, 1995.

Bradley, Harriet. *Men's Work, Women's Work. A Sociological History of the Sexual Division of Labour in Employment.* Cambridge, 1989.

Braudel, Fernand. *The Identity of France,* translated by Siân Reynolds, 2 vols. Vol. 1: History and Environment. New York, 1988.

Braun, Christina von. "'Der Jude' und 'Das Weib': Zwei Stereotypen des 'Anderen' in der Moderne." *Metis* 2 (1992): 6–28.

Breit, Stefan. *"Leichtfertigkeit" und ländliche Gesellschaft. Voreheliche Sexualität in der frühen Neuzeit.* Ancien Régime, Aufklärung und Revolution 23. Munich, 1991.

Briais, Bernard. *Contrebandiers du sel. La vie des faux sauniers au temps de la gabelle.* Paris, 1984.

Brunner, Otto. *Land and Lordship: Structures of Governance in medieval Austria,* translated from the fourth, revised edition by Howard Kaminsky and James van Horn Melton. Philadelphia, 1992.

———. "Das 'Ganze Haus' und die alteuropäische 'Ökonomik.'" In Otto Brunner, *Neue Wege der Verfassungs- und Sozialgeschichte,* 2nd edition, 103–127. Göttingen, 1968.

Burghartz, Susanna. *Leib, Ehre und Gut. Delinquenz in Zürich Ende des 14. Jahrhunderts.* Zurich, 1990.

———. "Jungfräulichkeit oder Reinheit? Zur Änderung von Argumentationsmustern vor dem Basler Ehegericht im 16. und 17. Jahrhundert." In *Dynamik der Tradition. Studien zur historischen Kulturforschung,* edited by Richard van Dülmen, 13–40. Frankfurt am Main, 1992.

Burguière, André, and François Lebrun. "The One Hundred and One Families of Europe." In *A History of the Family*, edited by André Burguière et al., translated by Sarah Hanbury Tenison, vol. 2, 11–94. Cambridge, Mass., 1996.

Burke, Peter. *Küchenlatein. Sprache und Umgangssprache in der frühen Neuzeit*. Berlin, 1990.

———— and Roy Porter, eds. *The Social History of Language*. Cambridge Studies in Oral and Literate Culture 12. Cambridge, 1987.

Cabourdin, Guy. *La vie quotidienne en Lorraine aux XVIIe et XVIIIe siècles*. Paris, 1984.

————. *Les temps modernes: de la paix de Westphalie à la fin de l'Ancien régime.* Encyclopédie illustrée de la Lorraine. Histoire de la Lorraine 3/2. Nancy, 1990.

Cahen, Gilbert, ed. *Catalogue: Les Juifs Lorrains: Du Ghetto à la Nation 1721–1871.* Metz, 1966.

Cahen, Gilbert. *Archives départementales de la Moselle. Répertoire numérique de la série F (Fond divers antérieurs à 1790, sous série 10 F [Fonds de Créhange]).* Metz, 1966.

————. "La région lorraine." In *Histoire des Juifs en France*, edited by Bernhard Blumenkranz, 77–136. Toulouse, 1971.

————. "Les juifs dans la région lorraine des origines à nos jours." *Les pays lorrain* 53 (1972): 55–82.

Cahnmann, W. J. "Der Dorf- und Kleinstadtjude als Typus." *Zeitschrift für Volkskunde* 70 (1974): 169–193.

Campe, Johann Heinrich. "Väterlicher Rat für meine Tochter (1789)." Reprinted in *Ordnung, Fleiß und Sparsamkeit. Texte und Dokumente zur Entstehung der 'bürgerlichen Tugenden,'* edited by Paul Münch, 260–271. Munich, 1984.

Carsten, Janet, and Stephen Hugh-Jones. "Introduction." In *About the House. Lévi-Strauss and Beyond*, edited by Janet Carsten and Stephen Hugh-Jones, 1–46. Cambridge, 1995.

Castan, Nicole. "La criminalité dans le ressort du Parlement de Toulouse. 1690–1730." In *Crimes et criminalité en France sous l'ancien régime, 17./18. siècles*, Cahiers des Annales 33, 91–107. Paris, 1971.

Charles, Etienne. *Cahiers de doléances du bailliage des Vic*, vol. 1, 551–556. 1907.

Châtelain, Victor. "Histoire du comté de Créhange." *Annuaire de la Société d'histoire et d'archéologie lorraine* (1891): 175–231; (1892): 66–115; (1893): 92–138.

Châtellier, Annick, and Louis Châtellier. "Les premières catéchistes des temps modernes. Confrères et consoeurs de la Doctrine chrétienne aux XVIe–XVIIIe siècles." In *La religion de ma mère. Le rôle des femmes dans la transmission de la foi*, edited by Jean Delumeau, 287–299. Paris, 1992.

Châtellier, Louis. "De 'la crise de la conscience européenne' aux missions rurales: Changement religieux dans les campagnes au début du XVIIIe siècle." *Histoire. Économie. Société* 8 (1989): 237–248.

————. "Les missions et le changement religieux des campagnes aux XVIIe–XVIIIe siècles aux pays de Sarrebourg." In *Die alte Diözese Metz—L'ancien diocèse de Metz. Referate eines Kolloquiums in Waldfischbach-Burgalben vom 21.–23. März 1990*, edited by Hans-Walter Herrmann. Veröffentlichungen der Kommission für Saarländische Landesgeschichte und Volksforschung 19. Saarbrücken, 1993.

Clément, Roger. "Aperçu de l'histoire des Juifs de Metz dans la période française." *Jahrbuch der Gesellschaft für jüdische Altertumskunde* 15 (1900): 33–45.

Clementi, Siglinde. "Die Aussegnung und die Unreinheit der Wöchnerin: zur Geschichte eines Kirchenbrauchs und seiner Idee." Dissertation, University of Vienna, 1994.

Clessienne, D. "La justice dans le bailliage de Boulay (1751–1789)." *Les cahiers lorrains* (1984): 2–3, 162.

Cohen, Daniel J. "Die Landjudenschaften in Hessen-Darmstadt bis zur Emanzipation als Organe der jüdischen Selbstverwaltung." In *Neunhundert Jahre Geschichte der Juden in Hessen. Beiträge zum politichen, wirtschaftlichen und kulturellen Leben*, 151–213. Wiesbaden, 1983.

Cohen, S. J. "Über die religiöse Bildung der Frauenzimmer jüdischen Glaubens." *Sulamith* 1 (1806): 473–490.

Cohen, Seymour J. *The Holy Letter. A Study in Jewish Sexual Morality.* Northvale, N.J., 1976.

Cohn, Marcus. "Erbrecht." *Jüdisches Lexikon* II: 442–456. Berlin, 1928.

Collomp, Allain. "Families: Habitations and Cohabitations." In A *History of Private Life*, IV: Passions of the Renaissance, edited by Philippe Ariès and Georges Duby, translated by Arthur Goldhammer, 493–529. Cambridge, Mass., 1989.

Contamine, Henry. "Les plaintes contre le clergé rural en Moselle sous le consulat et l'empire." *Annuaire de la fédération historique lorraine* 3 (1930): 101–112.

Cooperman, Bernard Dov. "Afterword: Tradition and Crisis and the Study of Early Modern Jewish History." In Jacob Katz, *Tradition and Crisis. Jewish Society at the End of the Middle Ages*, 237–253. New York, 1993.

Corfield, Penelope J. "Ehrerbietung und Dissens in der Kleidung. Zum Wandel der Bedeutung des Hutes und des Hutziehens." *Aufklärung* 6, no. 2 (1991): 5–19.

Coutumes de l'évêché de Metz. Nancy, 1761.

Cramer, Johann Ulrich Freiherr von. "Wetzlarische Nebenstunden 98: Bericht über die Entstehung und den Verlauf der Auseinandersetzung zwischen Graf Christian von Wied-Runkel als Besitzer der Grafschaft Kriechingen und den Untertanen dieser Grafschaft bis zum Einsatz des Exekutionskommandos im Juli 1758." New edition in *Bäuerlicher Widerstand und feudale Herrschaft in der frühen Neuzeit*, edited by Winfried Schulze, 290–294. Stuttgart, 1980.

———— "Wetzlarische Nebenstunden 100." Ulm, 1770. Reprinted in *Quellen und Beiträge zur Geschichte Saarwellingens* 27/29 (1972): 76–87.

Daltroff, Jean. *Les Juifs de Niedervisse. Naissance, épanouissement et déclin d'une communauté.* Sarreguemines, 1992.

————. "Samuel Levy de Balbronn. Un riche prêteur d'argent juif de Basse Alsace au dernier siècle de l'Ancien régime." *Revue des études juives* 148 (1989): 53–68.

———— and Alphonse Cerf. "Traditions et coutumes de la communauté juive de Niedervisse de 1750 à 1930." *Almanach KKL Strasbourg* 36 (1988/5748): 143–155.

Danker, Uwe. *Räuberbanden im Alten Reich um 1700. Ein Beitrag zur Geschichte von Herrschaft und Kriminalität in der Frühen Neuzeit.* Frankfurt am Main, 1988.

Davis, Natalie Zemon. "City Women and Religious Change." In Natalie Zemon Davis, *Society and Culture in Early Modern France. Eight Essays*, 65–96. Stanford, 1975.

————. *Women on the Margins. Three Seventeenth-Century Lives.* Cambridge, Mass., 1995.

Dekker, Rudolf. "Women in Revolt. Popular Protest and its Social Basis in Holland in the Seventeenth and Eighteenth Centries." *Theory and Society* 16 (1987): 337–362.

Delumeau, Jean. *Sin and Fear. The Emergence of a Western Guilt Culture, Thirteenth–Eighteenth Centuries*, translated by Eric Nicholson. New York, 1990.

————. *L'aveu et le pardon. Les difficultés de la confession XIIIᵉ–XVIIIᵉ siècle.* Paris, 1990.

Derks, Hans. "Über die Faszination des 'Ganzen Hauses.'" GG 22, no. 2 (1996): 221–242.

Desplat, Christian. *Charivaris en Gascogne. La 'morale des peuples' du XVIᵉ au XXᵉ siècle.* Paris, 1982.

Deventer, Jörg. *Das Abseits als sicherer Ort? Jüdische Minderheit und christliche Gesellschaft im Alten Reich am Beispiel der Fürstabtei Corvey (1550–1807).* Paderborn, 1996.

————. "Organisationsformen der Juden in einem nordwestdeutschen Duodezfürstentum der Frühen Neuzeit." In *Jüdische Gemeinden und Organisationsformen von der Antike bis zur Gegenwart*, edited by Robert Jütte and Abraham P. Kustermann, 151–172. Wiesbaden, 1998.

Dierse, U. "Religion, 18. Jh." In *Historisches Wörterbuch der Philosophie*, edited by Joachim Ritter and Karlfried Gründer, vol. 8, 623–713. Basel, 1992.

Dietz, Alexander. *Stammbuch der Frankfurter Juden. Geschichtliche Mitteilungen über die Frankfurter jüdischen Familien von 1349–1849.* Frankfurt am Main, 1907.

Driks, Maria. *Das Landrecht des Kurfürstentums Trier. Seine Geschichte und seine Stellung in der Rechtsgeschichte.* Cologne, 1965.

Dorvaux, N. *Les anciens pouillés du diocèse de Metz.* Nancy, 1902–1907.

Douglas, Mary. *Purity and Danger: An Analysis of Concepts of Pollution and Taboo.* London, 1966.

Duden, Barbara. *The Woman Beneath the Skin. A Doctor's Patients in Eighteenth Century Germany,* translated by Thomas Dunlap. Cambridge, Mass., 1991.

————. *Disembodying Women: Perspectives on Pregnancy and the Unborn,* translated by Lee Hoinacki. Cambridge, Mass., 1993.

Dülmen, Richard van. *Kultur und Alltag in der Frühen Neuzeit,* 3 volumes. Munich, 1990–1994.

Dürr, Renate. *Mägde in der Stadt. Das Beispiel Schwäbisch Hall in der Frühen Neuzeit,* Geschichte und Geschlechter 13. Frankfurt am Main, 1995.

Eder, Irmtraut. *Die saarländischen Weistümer—Dokumente der Territorialpolitik.* Veröffentlichungen der Kommission für saarländische Landesgeschichte und Volksforschung 8. Saarbrücken, 1978.

Efrat, Natan. "Parnas." *Encyclopaedia Judaica* 13: 123f. Jerusalem, 1971.

Elias, Norbert. "Wandlungen der Machtbalance zwischen den Geschlechtern. Eine prozeßsoziologische Untersuchung am Beispiel des antiken Römerstaats." *Kölner Zeitschrift für Soziologie und Sozialpsychologie* 38 (1986): 425–449.

Elon, Menachem. "Mishpat Ivri." *Encyclopaedia Judaica* 12: 109–151. Jerusalem, 1971.

Encyclopaedia Judaica, 17 vols. Jerusalem, 1979.

Eschelbacher, Joseph. "Über jüdische Heiratsausstattungen im 18. Jahrhundert." *Mitteilungen der Gesellschaft für jüdische Volkskunde* 3 (1900): 97–103.

Eschwege, Helmut. *Die Synagoge in der deutschen Geschichte. Eine Dokumentation.* Dresden, 1980.

Farge, Arlette, and Michel Foucault. *Le Désordre des Familles. Lettres de cachet des Archives de la Bastille.* Paris, 1982.

Fassbinder, Stefan. "Frömmigkeit. Entwicklung und Problemfelder eines Begriffs." *Saeculum* 47, no. 1 (1996): 6–34.

Fehr, Hans. *Die Rechtsstellung der Frau und der Kinder in den Weistümern.* Jena, 1912.

Filippini, Nadia Maria. *La nascita straordinaria. Tra madre e figlio la rivoluzione del taglio cesareo (sec. XVII–XIX).* Studi di ricerche storici 198. Milan, 1995.

Flaus, Pascal. *Comté et comtes de Créhange du XVIIe au XVIIIe siècle. Étude administrative, économique et sociale.* Mémoire de maîtrise. Metz, 1984.

Fleury, Jean. *Contrats de Mariage juifs en Moselle avant 1792. Recensement à usage généalogique de 2021 contrats de mariage notariés.* 1989.

Foucault, Michel. *Discipline and Punish. The Birth of the Prison,* translated by Alan Sheridan. New York, 1979.

Fox, Nikolaus. *Saarländische Volkskunde.* Bonn, 1927.

Fraenckel, André Aaron. *Memoire juive en Alsace. Contrats de Mariae au XVIIIème siècle.* Strasbourg, 1998.

François, Ch. "Les ermites en Lorraine." *La revue populaire* 18 (1977): 224ff.

Françoise, Etienne. "Alphabetisierung und Lesefähigkeit in Frankreich und Deutschland um 1800." In *Deutschland und Frankreich im Zeitalter der Französischen Revolution,* edited by Helmut Berding, Etienne Françoise, and Hans-Peter Ullmann, 407–425. Frankfurt am Main, 1989.

Franz, Adolph. *Die kirchliche Benediktionen im Mittelalter,* 2 vols. Freiburg/Br., 1909. Reprint, Graz, 1960.

Freitag, Winfried. "Haushalt und Familie in traditionalen Gesellschaften: Konzepte, Probleme und Perspektiven der Forschung." *GG* 14 (1988): 5–37.

Frevert, Ute. "Bürgerliche Meisterdenker und das Geschlechterverhältnis. Konzepte, Erfahrungen, Visionen an der Wende vom 18. zum 19. Jahrhundert." In *Bürgerinnen und Bürger. Geschlechterverhältnisse im 19. Jahrhundert*, edited by Ute Frevert, 17–48. Kritische Studien zur Geschichtswissenschaft 77. Göttingen, 1988.

———. *"Mann und Weib, und Weib und Mann." Geschlechter-Differenzen in der Moderne.* Munich, 1995.

Frishman, Judith. "Als Mann und Frau erschuf sie sie. Feminismus und Tradition." In *Jüdische Lebenswelten. Essays*, edited by Andreas Nachama, Julius H. Schoeps, and Edward van Voolen, 86–107. Berlin, 1991.

Frühsorge, Gotthardt. "Die Einheit aller Geschäfte. Tradition und Veränderung des 'Hausmutter'—Bildes in der deutschen Ökonomieliteratur des 18. Jahrhunderts." *Wolfenbütteler Studien zur Aufklärung* 3 (1976): 137–157.

———. "Die Begründung der 'väterlichen Gesellschaft' in der europäischen oeconomia. christiana. Zur Rolle des Vaters in der Hausväterliteratur des 16. bis 18 Jahrhunderts in Deutschland." In *Das Vaterbild im Abendland*, edited by Hubertus Tellenbach, vol. 1, 110–123. Stuttgart, 1978.

Gabbois, Geneviève. "'Vous êtes la seule consolation de l'église.' La foi des femmes face à le déchristianisation de 1789 à 1880." In *La religion de ma mère. Le rôle des femmes dans la transmission de la foi*, edited by Jean Delumeau, 301–325. Paris, 1992.

Gélis, Jacques, Mireille Laget, and Marie-France Morel. *Der Weg ins Leben. Geburt und Kindheit in früherer Zeit.* Munich, 1980.

Gerhard, Ute. "Die Rechtsstellung der Frau in der bürgerlichen Gesellschaft des 19. Jahrhunderts. Frankreich und Deutschland im Vergleich." In *Bürgertum im 19. Jahrhundert. Deutschland im europäischen Vergleich*, edited by Jürgen Kocka, vol. 1, 439–468. Munich, 1988.

———. *Gleichheit ohne Angleichung. Frauen im Recht.* Munich, 1990.

———, ed. *Frauen in der Geschichte des Rechts. Von der Frühen Neuzeit bis zur Gegenwart.* Munich, 1997.

Gibson, Ralph. "Le catholicisme et les femmes en France au XIXᵉ siècle." *Revue d'histoire de l'église de France* 79 (1993): 63–93.

Gierke, Otto. *Deutsches Privatrecht*, vol. 1. Munich, 1895.

Gildemeister, Regine, and Angelika Wetterer. "Wie Geschlechter gemacht werden. Die soziale Konstruktion der Zweigeschlechtlichkeit und ihre Reifizierung in der Frauenforschung." In *Traditionen Brüche. Entwicklung feministischer Theorie*, edited by Gudrun-Axeli Knapp and Angelika Wetterer, 201–254. Freiburg, 1992

Girard, Patrick. *La Révolution française et les juifs.* Paris, 1989.

Glanz, Rudolf. *Geschichte des niederen jüdischen Volkes in Deutschland. Eine Studie uber historisches Gaunertum, Bettelwesen und Vagantentum.* New York, 1968.

Gleixner, Ulrike. *"Das Mensch" und "der Kerl." Die Konstruktion von Geschlecht in Unzuchtsverfahren der frühen Neuzeit (1700–1760).* Geschichte und Geschlecht 8. Frankfurt am Main, 1994.

———. "Die 'Gute' und die 'Böse.' Hebammen als Amtsfrauen auf dem Land (Altmark Brandenburg, 18. Jahrhundert)." In *Weiber, Menscher, Frauenzimmer. Frauen in der ländlichen Gesellschaft. 1500–1800*, edited by Heide Wunder and Christina Vanja, 96–122. Göttingen, 1996.

Glückel of Hameln. *The Memoirs of Glückel of Hameln*, translated by Marvin Lowenthal, with a new introduction by Robert Rosen. New York, 1977.

Goody, Jack. *The Development of the Family and Marriage in Europe.* Cambridge, 1983.

Göttsch, Silke. "Zur Konstruktion schichtenspezifischer Wirklichkeit. Strategien und Taktiken ländlicher Unterschichten vor Gericht." In *Erinnern und Vergessen. Vorträge des 27. Deutschen Volkskundekongresses*, edited by Brigitte Bönisch-Brednich, Rolf W. Brednich, and Helge Gerndt, 443–452. Göttingen, 1989.

———. *"Alle für einen Mann . . ." Leibeigene und Widerständigkeit in Schleswig-Holstein im 18. Jahrhundert.* Studien zur Volkskunde und Kulturgeschichte Schleswig-Holsteins 24. Neumünster, 1991.

————. "'Vielmahls aber hätte sie gewünscht, einen andern Mann zu haben.' Gattenmord im 18. Jahrhundert." In *Von Huren und Rabenmüttern. Weibliche Kriminalität in der Frühen Neuzeit*, edited by Otto Ulbricht, 313–334. Cologne, 1995.

Griesebner, Andrea. "Interagierende Differenzen. 'Vergehen' und 'Verbrechen' in einem niederösterreichischen Landgericht im 18. Jahrhundert." Dissertation, University of Vienna, 1998.

Groebner, Valentin. "Außer Haus. Otto Brunner und die 'alteuropäische Ökonomik.'" *GWU* 46 (1995): 69–80.

Grossmann, Avraham. "From Father to Son: The Inheritance of Spiritual Leadership in Jewish Communities of the Middle Ages." In *The Jewish Family: Metaphor and Memory*, edited by David Kraemer, 115–131. Oxford, 1989.

Gruendlicher Beweiß, daß es dem Hochgeborenen Grafen und Herrn, Herrn Christian Grafen zu Wied, Isenburg und Criechingen nicht angemutet werden könne, aus alleiniger Versammlung der widerspenstigen Unterthanen der Grafschaft Kriechingen die Naturalmannschaftsaufstellung aufzuheben, und dieselbe mit einem verhaltungsmäßigen Geldbeitrag zu vertreten. STA Wiesbaden, 3005–2247.

Gutmann, Joseph. "Jewish Medieval Marriage Customs in Art: Creativity and Adaption." In *The Jewish Family: Metaphor and Memory*, edited by David Kraemer, 47–61. Oxford, 1989.

Habermas, Rebekka. *Wallfahrt und Aufruhr. Zur Geschichte des Wunderglaubens in der Frühen Neuzeit*. Historische Studien 5. Frankfurt am Main, 1991.

Hahn, Alois. *Die Rezeption des tridentinischen Pfarrideals im westtrierischen Pfarrklerus des 16. und 17. Jahrhunderts. Untersuchungen zur Geschichte der katholischen Reform im Erzbistum Trier*. Luxembourg, 1974.

Harris, William V. *Ancient Literacy*. Cambridge, Mass., 1989.

Hausen, Karin. "Die Polarisierung der 'Geschlechtercharaktere'—Eine Spiegelung der Dissoziation von Erwerbs- und Familienleben." In *Sozialgeschichte der Familie in der Neuzeit Europas*, edited by Werner Conze, 363–393. Stuttgart, 1976.

————. "Familie und Familiengeschichte." In *Sozialgeschichte in Deutschland*, edited by Wolfgang Schieder and Volker Sellin, vol. 2, 64–89. Göttingen, 1986.

————. "Frauenräume." In *Frauengeschichte-Geschlechtergeschichte*, edited by Karin Hausen and Heide Wunder, 21–24. Geschichte und Geschlechter 1. Frankfurt am Main, 1992.

Heal, Felicity. "The Idea of Hospitality in Early Modern England." *Past & Present* 102 (1984): 66–93.

————. *Hospitality in Early Modern England*. Oxford, 1990.

Herold, Hans. "Das Hebammenamt in rechtsgeschichtlicher Betrachtung." In Hans Herold, *Rechtsgeschichte aus Neigung. Ausgewählte Schriften aus den Jahren 1934–1986*, edited by Karl S. Bader and Claudio Soliva, 367–376. Sigmaringen, 1988 (first published 1968).

Hersche, Peter. "Intendierte Rückständigkeit: Zur Charakteristik des geistlichen Staates im Alten Reich." In *Stände und Gesellschaft im Alten Reich*, edited by Georg Schmidt, 133–149. Stuttgart, 1989.

————. "Wider 'Müssiggang' und 'Ausschweifung.' Feiertage und ihre Reduktion im katholischen Europa, namentlich im deutschsprachigen Raum zwischen 1750 und 1800." *Innsbrucker Historische Studien* 12/13 (1990): 97–122.

————. "Die protestantische Laus und der katholische Floh. Konfessionsspezifische Aspekte der Hygiene." In *Ansichten von der rechten Ordnung. Bilder über Normen und Normverletzung in der Geschichte*, edited by Benedikt Bietenhard, et al., 43–60. Bern, 1991.

————. "Devotion, Volksbrauch oder Massenprotest? Ein Literaturbericht aus sozialgeschichtlicher Sicht zum Thema Wallfahrt. Von der kirchlichen über die volkskundliche zur sozialgeschichtlichen Wallfahrtsforschung." In *Das achtzehntes Jahrhundert in Österreich*, 7–34. Jahrbuch der Österreichischen Gesellschaft zur Erforschung des achtzehnten Jahrhunderts 9. Vienna, 1994.

———. "'Klassizistischer' Katholizismus. Der konfessionsgeschichtliche Sonderfall Frankreich." *HZ* 262 (1996): 357–389.

Herweg, Rachel Monika. *Die jüdische Mutter. Das verborgene Matriarchat.* Darmstadt, 1995.

Hinsberger, Rudolf. *Die Weistümer des Klosters St. Matthias in Trier.* Quellen und Forschungen zur Agrargeschichte 34. Stuttgart, 1989.

Hippel, Wolfgang von. *Die Bauernbefreiung im Königreich Württemberg,* vol. 1. Boppard, 1977.

Hirschman, Albert O. *Tischgemeinschaft. Zwischen öffentlicher und privater Sphäre.* Vienna, 1997.

Hochgräflich Wied-Runkel- und Crichingischer Staats- und Haus-Kalender. Frankfurt am Main, 1767.

Hodler, Beat. *Das "Ärgernis" der Reformation. Begriffsgeschichtlicher Zugang zu einer biblisch legitimierten politischen Ethik.* Veröffentlichungen des Instituts für Europäische Geschichte 158. Mainz, 1995.

Hohkamp, Michaela. "Frauen vor Gericht." In *Frauen und Öffentlichkeit. Beiträge der 6. Schweizerischen Historikerinnentagung,* edited by Mireille Othenin-Girard et al., 115–124. Zurich, 1991.

———. "Häusliche Gewalt. Beispiele aus einer ländlichen Region des mittleren Schwarzwaldes im 18. Jahrhundert." In *Physische Gewalt. Historische Studien zu einer verschwiegenen Kontinuität,* edited by Thomas Lindenberer and Alf Lüdtke, 276–302. Frankfurt am Main, 1995.

———. "Wer will erben? Überlegungen zur Erbpraxis in geschlechtsspezifischer Perspektive." In *Gutsherrschaft als soziales Modell. Vergleichende Betrachtungen zur Funktionsweise frühneuzeitlicher Agrargesellschaften,* edited by Jan Peters, 327–342. HZ Beihefte NF 18. Munich, 1995.

———. "Macht, Herrschaft und Geschlecht. Ein Plädoyer zur Erforschung von Gewaltverhältnissen in der Frühen Neuzeit." *L'Homme.* ZFG 7/2 (1996): 9–17.

———. "Vom Wirtshaus zum Amtshaus." *Werkstatt Geschichte* 16 (1997): 8–18.

Holenstein, André. "'Local-Untersuchung' und 'Augenschein.' Reflexionen auf die Lokalität im Verwaltungsdenken und- handeln des Ancien Régime." *Werkstatt Geschichte* 16 (1997): 19–31.

Holenstein, Pia, and Norbert Schindler. "Geschwätzgeschichte(n). Ein kulturhistorisches Plädoyer für die Rehabilitierung der unkontrollierten Rede." In *Dynamik der Tradition. Studien zur historischen Kulturforschung,* edited by Richard van Dülmen, 41–148. Frankfurt am Main, 1992.

Honegger, Claudia. *Die Ordnung der Geschlechter. Die Wissenschaften vom Menschen und das Weib. 1750–1850.* Frankfurt am Main, 1991.

——— and Bettina Heintz, eds., *Listen der Ohnmacht. Zur Sozialgeschichte weiblicher Widerstandsformen.* Frankfurt am Main, 1984.

Honneth, Axel. *Kritik der Macht. Reflexionsstufen einer kritischen Gesellschaftstheorie.* Frankfurt am Main, 1985.

Horsley, Greg H. R. *New Documents Illustrating Early Christianity,* vol. 4: *A Review of Greek Inscriptions and Papyri published in 1979* (North Ryde, N.S.W.: Macquarie University, 1987).

Hsia, Ronnie Po-chia, and Hartmut Lehmann, eds. *In and Out of the Ghetto. Jewish-Gentile Relations in Late Medieval and Early Modern Germany.* Cambridge, 1995.

Hudemann-Simon, Calixte. *L'État et la santé. La politique de la santé publique ou "police médicale" dans les quatre départements rhénans. 1794–1814.* Sigmaringen, 1995.

Hufton, Olwen. *The Prospect Before Her. A History of Women in Western Europe, 1: 1500–1800.* Oxford, 1994.

Huhn, E. H. Th. *Deutsch-Lothringen. Landes-, Volks- und Ortskunde.* Stuttgart, 1875.

Hundert, Gershon David. "Jewish Children and Childhood in Early Modern East Central Europe." In *The Jewish Family: Metaphor and Memory*, edited by David Kraemer, 81–94. Oxford, 1989.

Hunt, Lynn. *Politics, Culture, and Class in the French Revolution.* Berkeley, 1984.

Hussong, Fr. W. "Cahiers de doléances des communautés en 1789. Bailliages de Boulay et de Bouzonville. Kritische Studien zur Vorgeschichte der Französischen Revolution im alten Lothringen." *Jahrbuch der Gesellschaft für lothringische Geschichte und Altertumskunde* 24 (1912): 1–166.

Hüwelmeier, Gertrud. "Gendered Houses. Kinship, Class and Identity in a German Village." In *Gender, Agency, and Change: Anthropological Perspectives*, edited by Victoria Goddard. London, 2000.

Hyman, Paula E. *The Emancipation of the Jews of Alsace. Acculturation and Tradition in the Nineteenth Century.* London, 1991.

Imhof, Arthur E. *Die gewonnenen Jahre. Von der Zunahme unserer Lebensspanne seit dreihundert Jahren oder von der Notwendigkeit einer neuen Einstellung zu Leben und Sterben.* Munich, 1981.

———. "Wiederverheiratung in Deutschland zwischen dem 16. und 20. Jahrhundert." In *Studien zur deutschsprachigen Leichenpredigt der frühen Neuzeit*, edited by Rudolf Lenz, 185–222. Marburg, 1981.

———. *Die Zunahme unserer Lebensspanne seit 300 Jahren und ihre Folgen.* Schriftenreihe des Bundesministeriums für Familie, Senioren, Frauen und Jugend 110. Stuttgart, 1996.

Isambert, François-André. "Empirische Vielfalt und ideologische Geschlossenheit: Populare Religion in Frankreich." In *Volksfrömmigkeit in Europa. Beiträge zur Soziologie popularer Religiosität aus 14 Ländern*, edited by Michael N. Ebertz and Franz Schultheis, eds., 192–211. Munich, 1985.

Israel, Jonathan I. *European Jewry in the Age of Mercantilism 1550–1750.* Oxford, 1985.

Jancke, Gabriele. "Publizistin-Pfarrfrau-Prophetin. Die Straßburger 'Kirchenmutter' Katharina Zell." In *Frauen mischen sich ein. Wittenberger Sonntagsvorlesungen*, edited by Peter Freybe, 55–80. Wittenberg, 1995.

———. "Die Sichronot (Memoiren) der jüdischen Kauffrau Glückel von Hameln zwischen Autobiographie, Geschichtsschreibung und religiösem Lehrtext. Geschlecht, Religion und Ich in der Frühen Neuzeit." In *Autobiographien von Frauen. Beiträge zur ihrer Geschichte*, edited by Magdalene Heuser, 92–134. Untersuchungen zur deutschen Literaturgeschichte 85. Tübingen, 1996.

———. "Die Kirche als Haushalt und die Leitungsrolle der Kirchenmutter, Katharina Zells reformatorisches Kirchenkonzept." In *Geschlechterperspektiven. Forschungen zur Frühen Neuzeit*, edited by Heide Wunder and Gisela Engel, 145–155. Königstein, 1998.

Jeggle, Utz. *Judendörfer in Württemberg.* Tübingen, 1969.

Jewish Encyclopedia, 12 vols. New York, 1901–1906.

Job, Françoise. "Les Juifs dans l'état civil de Lunéville (1792–1891)." In *Les Juifs au regard de l'histoire. Mélanges en l'honneur de Bernhard Blumenkranz*, edited by Gilbert Dahan, 343–357. Paris, 1985.

Jüdisches Lexikon. Ein enzyklopädisches Handbuch in vier Bänden, edited by Georg Herlitz and Bruno Kirschner. Berlin, 1927–1930.

Jung, Martin. *Die württembergische Kirche und die Juden in der Zeit des Pietismus (1675–1780).* Studien zu Kirche und Israel 13. Berlin, 1992.

Jütte, Robert. "Ehre und Ehrverlust im spätmittelalterlichen und frühneuzeitlichen Judentum." In *Verletze Ehre. Ehrkonflikte in Gesellschaften des Mittelalters und der Frühen Neuzeit*, edited by Klaus Schreiner and Gerd Schwerhoff, 144–165. Vienna, 1995.

Karant-Nunn, Susan C. *The Reformation of Ritual. An Interpretation of Early Modern Germany.* London, 1997.

Kaschuba, Wolfgang. *Volkskultur zwischen feudaler und bürgerlicher Gesellschaft. Zur Geschichte eines Begriff und seiner gesellschaftlichen Wirklichkeit.* Frankfurt am Main, 1988.

Kasper-Holtkotte, Cilli. *Juden im Aufbruch. Zur Sozialgeschichte einer Minderheit im Saar-Mosel-Raum um 1800.* Forschungen zur Geschichte der Juden A 3. Hannover, 1996.

Katz, Jakob. *The Shabbes Goy. A Study in Halakhic Flexibility.* Philadelphia, 1969.

———. *Out of the Ghetto. The Social Background of Jewish Emancipation, 1770–1870.* New York, 1978.

———. "Mariage et vie conjugale à la fin du Moyen Age." In *La société juive à travers l'histoire,* vol. 2: Les liens de l'allience, edited by Shmuel Trigano, 385–411. Paris, 1992.

———. *Tradition and Crisis. Jewish Society at the End of the Middle Ages,* translated and with an afterword and bibliography by Bernard Dov Cooperman. New York, 1993.

Kaufman, Debra Renee. *Rachel's Daughters. Newly Orthodox Jewish Women.* New Brunswick, 1991.

Kerner, Samuel. "La vie quotidienne de la communauté juive de Metz au dix-huitième siècle." Doctoral dissertation, University of Paris, 1979.

———. "Les registres inédits des tribunaux rabbiniques de Metz (1771–1779) et de Niedernai (1755–1777)." *Revue des études juives* 138 (1979): 495–497.

Kienitz, Sabine. *Sexualität, Macht und Moral. Prostitution und Geschlechterbeziehungen Anfang des 19. Jahrhunderts in Württemberg. Ein Beitrag zur Mentalitätsgeschichte.* Berlin, 1995.

King, Margaret L. *Women of the Renaissance.* Chicago, 1991.

Kirsch, Robert. *Die Juden in der Herrschaft Illingen. Die Kerpische Judengemeinde im 18. Jahrhundert.* Illingen, n.d.

Klayman-Cohen, Israela. *Die hebräische Komponente im Westjiddischen am Beispiel der Memoiren der Glückel von Hameln.* Jiddische schtudies 4. Hamburg, 1994.

Knapp, Gudrun-Axeli. "Macht und Geschlecht. Neuere Entwicklungen in der feministischen Macht- und Herrschaftsdiskussion." In *Traditionen Brüche. Entwicklung feministischer Theorie,* edited by Gudrun-Axeli Knapp and Angelika Wetterer, 287–321. Freiburg, 1992.

Koch, Elisabeth. "Pater semper incertus." *Rechtshistorisches Journal* 9 (1990): 107–124.

———. *Maior dignitas est in sexu virili. Das weibliche Geschlecht im Normensystem des 16. Jahrhunderts.* Ius Commune Sonderhefte: Studien zur europäischen Rechtsgeschichte 57. Frankfurt am Main, 1991.

König, Gudrun M. *Eine Kulturgeschichte des Spaziergangs. Spuren einer bürgerlichen Praktik 1780–1850.* Kulturstudien, Sonderband 20. Vienna, 1996.

Kraut, Antonie. *Die Stellung der Frau im württembergischen Privatrecht.* Stuttgart, 1934.

Kriedte, Peter, Hans Medick, and Jürgen Schlumbohm. *Industrialisierung vor der Industrialisierung. Gewerbliche Warenproduktion auf dem Land in der Formationsperiode des Kapitalismus.* Göttingen, 1977.

———. "Sozialgeschichte in der Erweiterung—Proto-Industrialisierung in der Verengung? Demographie, Sozialstruktur, moderne Hausindustrie: eine Zwischenbilanz der Proto-Industrialisierungsforschung," part 1: GG 18/1 (1992): 70–87; part 2: GG 18/2 (1992): 231–255.

Kronenberger, Friedrich L. *Die jüdischen Vieh- und Pferdehändler im Birkenfelder Land und in den Gemeinden des Hunsrücks.* Birkenfeld, 1983.

Krug-Richter, Barbara. "'Eß gehet die bauren ahn und nicht die herren.' Die Auseinandersetzungen um die Einführung neuer Dienste in der westfälischen Herrschaft Canstein 1710 bis 1719." In *Konflikt und Kontrolle in Gutsherrschaftsgesellschaften. Über Resistenz und Herrschaftsverhalten in ländlichen Sozialgebilden der Frühen Neuzeit,* edited by Jan Peters, 151–200. Veröffentlichungen des Max-Planck-Instituts für Geschichte 120. Göttingen, 1995.

Kühn, Hans-Joachim. "Notizen zur Reunion der Gemeinde Püttlingen mit der Französischen Republik am 14. Februar 1793." In *Revolutionäre Spuren . . . Beiträge der Saarlouiser Geschichtswerkstatt zur Französischen Revolution im Raum Saarlouis,* edited by Johannes Schmitt, 237–246. Saarbrücken, 1991.

La Torre, Michel de. *Guide de l'art et de la nature: Moselle.* 1985.

Labouvie, Eva. "Wider Wahrsagerei, Segnerei und Zauberei. Kirchliche Versuche zur Ausgrenzung von Aberglaube und Volksmagie seit dem 16. Jahrhundert." In *Verbrechen, Strafen und soziale Kontrolle. Studien zur historischen Kulturforschung,* edited by Richard van Dülmen, 15–55. Frankfurt am Main, 1990.

———. *Verbotene Künste. Volksmagie und ländlicher Aberglaube in den Dorfgemeinden des Saarraums (16.–19. Jahrhundert).* St. Ingbert, 1992.

———. *Andere Umstände. Eine Kulturgeschichte der Geburt.* Cologne, 1998.

Lang, Jean-Bernard. "L'image des Juifs à travers des cahiers de doléances." *Les cahiers lorrains* (1989): 315–322.

Laperche-Fournel, Marie-José. "Le mariage en pays mosellan au XVIIIe siècle: formation et rupture du couple." *Les cahiers lorrains* 3, no. 4 (1992): 389–401.

Le Moigne, François-Yves. "Versailles et Créhange au XXIIe siècle ou les aléas d'une politique frontalière." In *L'Europe, l'Alsace et la France. Étude réuni en l'honneur du Doyen Georges Livet,* 307–316. Strasbourg, 1986.

Le Play, M. Frédéric. *L'organisation de la famille selon le vrai modèle signalé par l'histoire de tous les races et de tous les temps.* Paris, 1871.

Leiber, Gert. *Das Landgericht der Baar. Verfasssung und Verfahren zwischen Reichs-und Landrecht. 1232–1632.* Veröffentlichungen aus dem Fürstlich Fürstenbergischen Archiv 18. Allensbach, 1964.

Leutzsch, Martin. *Die Bewährung der Wahrheit. Der dritte Johannesbrief als Dokument urchristlichen Alltags.* Bochumer Altertumswissenschaftliches Colloquium 16. Trier, 1994.

Levy, Ascher. *Die Memoiren des Ascher Levy aus Reichshofen im Elsaß (1598–1635),* edited, translated, and annotated by M[oses] Ginsburger. Berlin, 1913.

Lewittes, Mendell. *Jewish Marriage. Rabbinic Law, Legend, and Custom.* Northvale, N.J., 1994.

Liber, Maurice. *Les juifs et la convocation des États généraux (1789).* Paris, 1989. Originally in *Revue des études juives* (1912, 1913).

Lipp, Carola. "Überlegungen zur Methodendiskussion. Kulturanthopologische, sozialwissenschaftliche und historische Ansätze zur Erforschung der Geschlechterbeziehung." In *Frauenforschung–Frauenalltag. Beiträge zur 2. Tagung der Kommission Frauenforschung in der deutschen Gesellschaft für Volkskunde, Freiburg, 22.–25. Mai 1986, 29–46.* Frankfurt am Main, 1988.

———. "Alltagskulturforschung im Grenzbereich von Volkskunde, Soziologie und Geschichte. Aufstieg und Niedergang eines interdisziplinären Forschungskonzepts." *Zeitschrift für Volkskunde* 89, no. 1 (1993): 1–33.

Logette, Aline. "Naissances illégitimes en Lorraine dans la première moitié du XVIIIe siècle d'après les déclarations de grossesses et la jurisprudence." *Annales de l'Est* 35 (1984): 91–125.

Lorenz, Maren. "'... als ob ihr ein Stein aus dem Leibe kollerte ...' Schwangerschaftswahrnehmungen und Geburtserfahrungen von Frauen im 18. Jahrhundert." In *Körper-Geschichten. Studien zur historischen Kulturforschung,* edited by Richard van Dülmen, 99–121. Frankfurt am Main, 1996.

———. "Devianz und Gesellschaft. Selbst- und Fremdwahrnehmung von Körper und Seele im Spiegel gerichtsmedizinischer Fallsammlungen des 18. Jahrhunderts." Dissertation, University of Saarbrücken, 1997.

Lorenzi, Philipp de. *Beiträge zur Geschichte sämtlicher Pfarreien der Diöcese Trier.* Trier, 1887.

Löwenbrück, Anna-Ruth. "Zalkind Hourwitz—Ein jüdischer Aufklärer zur Zeit der Französischen Revolution." *Tel Aviver Jahrbuch* 20 (1991): 77–101.

Lüdtke, Alf. "Einleitung: Herrschaft als soziale Praxis." In *Herrschaft als soziale Praxis. Historische und sozial-anthropologische Studien,* edited by Alf Lüdtke, 9–63. Veröffentlichungen des Max-Planck-Instituts für Geschichte 91. Göttingen, 1991.

Luebke, David Martin. *His Majesty's Rebels: Communities, Factions, and Rural Revolt in the Black Forest, 1725–1745.* Ithaca, 1997.

Lütge, Friedrich. *Geschichte der deutschen Agrarverfassung vom frühen Mittelalter bis zum 19. Jahrhundert*. Deutsche Agrargeschichte 3. Stuttgart, 1967.

Maihofer, Andrea. *Geschlecht als Existenzweise. Macht, Moral, Recht und Geschlechterdifferenz*. Frankfurt am Main, 1995.

Malino, Frances. "Competition and Confrontation. The Jews and the Parlement of Metz." In *Les juifs au regard de l'Histoire. Mélanges en l'honneur de Bernhard Blumenkranz*, edited by Gilbert Dahan, 327–341. Paris, 1985.

Martin, Philippe. *Les chemins du sacré. Paroisses, processions, pélerinages en Lorraine du XVIe au XIXe siècle*. Metz, 1995.

Marx, Albert. *Die Geschichte der Juden im Saarland vom Ancien Regime bis zum Zweiten Weltkrieg*. Saarbrücken, 1992.

McLeod, Hugh. "Weibliche Frömmigkeit—männlicher Unglaube? Religion und Kirche im bürgerlichen 19. Jahrhundert." In *Bürgerinnen und Bürger. Geschlechterverhältnisse im 19. Jahrhundert*, edited by Ute Frevert, 134–156. Kritische Studien zur Geschichtswissenschaft 77. Göttingen, 1988.

Medick, Hans, "Biedermänner und Biederfrauen im alten Laichingen. Lebensweisen in einem schwäbischen Ort an der Schwelle zur Moderne." *Journal Geschichte* 1 (1991): 46–61.

———. "Buchkultur und lutherischer Pietismus. Buchbesitz, erbauliche Lektüre und religiöse Mentalität in einer ländlichen Gemeinde Württembergs am Ende der frühen Neuzeit. Laichingen 1748–1820." In *Frühe Neuzeit–Frühe Moderne. Forschungen zur Vielgeschichtigkeit von Übergangsprozessen*, edited by Rudolf Vierhaus, et al., 297–326. Veröffentlichungen des Max-Planck-Instituts für Geschichte 104. Göttingen, 1992.

———. "Entlegene Geschichte? Sozialgeschichte und Mikro-Historie im Blickfeld der Kulturanthropologie." In *Zwischen den Kulturen? Die Sozialwissenschaften vor dem Problem des Kulturvergleichs*, edited by Joachim Matthes, 167–178. Soziale Welt, Sonderband 8. Göttingen, 1992.

———. *Weben und Überleben in Laichingen 1650–1900. Lokalgeschichte als Allgemeine Geschichte*. Veröffentlichungen des Max-Planck-Instituts für Geschichte 126, 2nd ed. Göttingen, 1997.

——— and David W. Sabean. "Interest and Emotion in Family and Kinship Studies: A Critique of Social History and Anthropology." In *Interest and Emotion: Essays on the Study of Family and Kinship*, edited by Hans Medick and David Warren Sabean, 9–27. Cambridge, 1984.

Mendel, Pierre. "Les noms des juifs français modernes." *Revue des études juives* 10 (1949/50): 15–63.

———. *Les juifs de Bionville en pays messin du 17e siècle à nos jours*. Metz, n.d.

Metken, Günter. *Liebe zu Lothringen. Horizonte und Hügel*. Karlsruhe, 1985.

Meyer, Pierre-André. *La communauté juive de Metz au XVIIIe siècle: histoire et démographie*. Nancy, 1993.

Mitterauer, Michael. *Ledige Mütter. Zur Geschichte unehelicher Geburten in Europa*. Munich, 1983.

———. "Formen ländlicher Familienwirtschaft: Historische Ökotypen und familiale Arbeitsorganisation im österreichischen Raum." In *Familienstruktur und Arbeitsorganisation in ländlichen Gesellschaften*, edited by Josef Ehmer and Michael Mitterauer, 185–323. Vienna, 1986.

———. "The Myth of the Large Preindustrial Family." In Michael Mitterauer and Reinhard Sieder, *The European Family: Patriarchy to Partnership from the Middle Ages to the Present*, translated by Karla Oosterveen and Manfred Hörzinger, 24–27. Oxford, 1982.

———. "Geschlechterspezifische Arbeitsteilung." In Michael Mitterauer, *Familie und Arbeitsteilung. Historisch vergleichende Studien*, 58–148. Vienna, 1992.

Möckelt, O. *Lothringen nach den Cahiers de doléances von 1789 unter besonderer Berücksichtigung der wirtschaftlichen und sozialen Fragen*. Bamberg, 1927.

Molitor, Hansgeorg, and Herbert Smolinsky, eds. *Volksfrömmigkeit in der Frühen Neuzeit.* Munich, 1994.

Mommertz, Monika. "'Ich, Lisa Thielen.' Text als Handlung und als sprachliche Struktur— ein methodischer Vorschlag." *Historische Anthropologie* 4 (1996): 303–329.

———. "Handeln, Bedeuten, Geschlecht. Konfliktaustragungspraktiken in der ländlichen Gesellschaft der Mark Brandenburg (2. Hälfte des 16. Jahrhunderts bis zum Dreißigjährigen Krieg)." Dissertation, University of Florence, 1997.

Mori, Akiko. "Familiengrabpflege in ethnologischer Sicht: Eine Dorfforschung in Südostkärnten." *L'Homme. ZFG* 6, no. 2 (1995): 86–97.

Müller-Wirthmann, Bernhard. "Raufhändel. Gewalt und Ehre im Dorf." In *Kultur der einfachen Leute. Bayerisches Volksleben vom 16. bis 19. Jahrhundert,* edited by Richard van Dülmen, 79–111. Munich, 1983.

Münch, Paul. *Lebensformen in der Frühen Neuzeit. 1500 bis 1800.* Frankfurt am Main, 1996.

Nahmer, Wilhelm van der. *Die Land-Rechte des Ober- und Mittelrheins,* vol. 1. Frankfurt am Main, 1831.

———. *Entwicklung der rheinischen Territorial- und Verfasungsverhältnisse.* Frankfurt am Main, 1832.

Nipperdey, Thomas. *Religion im Umbruch. Deutschland 1870–1918.* Munich, 1988.

Oberle, Roland. "L'émancipation des juifs." *Saison d'Alsace* 33, no. 104 (1989): 113– 123.

Opitz, Claudia. "Neue Wege der Sozialgeschichte?—Ein kritischer Blick auf Brunners Konzept des 'ganzen Hauses.'" *GG* 20, no. 1 (1994): 88–98.

———. "Hausmutter und Landesfürstin." In *Der Mensch des Barock,* edited by Rosarion Villari, 344–394. Frankfurt am Main, 1997.

Ozment, Stephen. *When Fathers Ruled. Family Life in Reformation Europe.* Cambridge, Mass., 1983.

Paquet, René. *Bibliographie analytique de l'histoire de Metz pendant la Révolution (1789–1800).* Paris, 1926.

Pelaja, Margherita. *Matrimonio e sessualità a Roma nell 'Ottocento.* Rome, 1994.

———. "Praxis und Darstellungsformen sexueller Gewalt im Rom des 19. Jahrhunderts." *L'Homme. ZFG* 7/2 (1996): 28–42.

Penco, Gregorio. *Storia della chiesa in Italia,* 2 vols. Milan, 1988.

Perrot, Michelle. "Vorwort." In *Geschlecht und Geschichte. Ist eine weibliche Geschichtsschreibung möglich?,* edited by Alain Corbin, et al., 15–27. Frankfurt am Main, 1989.

Peters, Jan. "Der Platz in der Kirche. Über soziales Rangdenken im Spätfeudalismus." *Jahrbuch für Volkskunde und Kulturgeschichte* 28 (1985): 77–106.

Plongeron, Bernard. *La vie quotidienne du clergé français.* Paris, 1979.

Pollack, Hermann. *Jewish Folkways in Germanic Lands (1648–1806). Studies in the Aspects of Daily Life.* Cambridge, Mass., 1971.

Pomata, Gianna. "Partikulargeschichte und Universalgeschichte—Bemerkungen zu einigen Handbüchern der Frauengeschichte." *L'Homme. ZFG* 2, no. 1 (1991): 5–44.

Prestel, Claudia T. "Jüdische Unterschichten im Zeitalter der Emanzipation, dargestellt anhand der Gemeinde Fürth, 1826–1870." *Aschkenas* 1 (1991): 95–134.

———. "Uneheliche Kinder und ledige Mütter in der jüdischen Gemeinschaft im 20. Jahrhundert: Eingliederung oder Ausschluß? Ein Beitrag zur deutsch-jüdischen Frauengeschichte." *L'Homme. ZFG* 5, no. 2 (1994): 81–101.

———. "Geschichtsschreibung zur jüdischen Geschichte in Deutschland: Qualität oder Quantität?" *Archiv für Sozialgeschichte* 35 (1995): 457–494.

Pulz, Waltraud. *"Nicht alles nach der Gelahrten Sinn geschrieben"–Das Hebammenanleitungsbuch der Justina Siegemund. Zur Rekonstruktion geburtshilflichen Überlieferungswissens frühneuzeitlicher Hebammen und seiner Bedeutung bei der Herausbildung der modernen Geburtshilfe.* Munich, 1994.

Quéniart, Jean. "Alphabetisierung und Leseverhalten der Unterschichten in Frankreich im 18. Jahrhundert." In *Sozialgeschichte der Aufklärung in Frankreich,* edited by Hans

Ulrich Gumbrecht, Rolf Reichardt, and Thomas Schleich, part 2, 113–146. Ancien Régime, Aufklärung und Revolution 4. Munich, 1981.

Rang, Brita. "Zur Geschichte des dualistischen Denkens über Mann und Frau. Kritische Bemerkungen zu den Thesen von Karin Hausen zur Herausbildung der Geschlechtscharaktere im 18. und 19. Jahrhundert." In *Frauenmacht in der Geschichte. Beiträge des Historikerinnentreffens 1985 zur Frauenforschung*, edited by Jutta Dahlhoff, Uschi Frey, and Ingrid Schöll, 194–204. Geschichtsdidaktik-Studien, Materialien 41. Düsseldorf, 1986.

Raphäel, Freddy, and Robert Weyl. *Juifs en Alsace. Culture, société, histoire*. Toulouse, 1977.

Reck, J. St. *Geschichte der gräflichen und fürstlichen Häuser Isenburg, Runkel, Wied, verbunden mit der Geschichte des Rheintals zwischen Koblenz und Andernach von Julius Cäsar bis auf die neueste Zeit*. Weimar, 1925.

Recueil d'Edits, Declarations et Arrests tant du Conseil que du Parlement, et autres pièces, rendus au suject de ceux de la Religion Pretenduë Reformée (n.p., n.d.).

Das Reichsland Elsass-Lothringen. Landes- und Ortsbeschreibung, 3 vols. Published by the Statistisches Bureau des Ministeriums für Elsaß-Lothringen. Strasbourg, 1903.

Reuss, Rod. "L'histoire d'Élias Salomon de Dauendorf et de Iedelé d'Obernai. Une page de l'histoire de l'antisémitisme en Alsace (1790–1792)." *Revue des études juives* 68 (1914): 235–245.

Richarz, Irmintraud. *Herrschaftliche Haushalte in vorindustrieller Zeit im Weserraum* (Berlin, 1971).

———. *Oikos, Haus und Haushalt. Ursprung und Geschichte der Haushaltsökonomik*. Göttingen, 1991.

———. "Das ökonomisch autarke 'Ganze Haus'—eine Legende?" In *Haushalt und Familie in Mittelalter und früher Neuzeit*, edited by Trude Ehlert, 269–280. Sigmaringen, 1991.

Richarz, Monika. "Landjuden—Ein bürgerliches Element im Dorf?" In *Idylle oder Aufbruch? Das Dorf im bürgerlichen 19. Jahrhundert. Ein europäischer Vergleich*, edited by Wolfgang Jacobeit, et al., 181–190. Berlin, 1990.

———. "Die Entdeckung der Landjuden. Stand und Probleme ihrer Erforschung am Beispiel Südwestdeutschlands." In *Landjudentum im Bodenseeraum. Wissenschaftliche Tagung zur Eröffnung des jüdischen Museums Hohenems vom 9. bis 11. April 1991*, 11–21. Dornbirn, 1992.

———. "In Familie, Handel und Salon. Jüdische Frauen vor und nach der Emanzipation der deutschen Juden." In *Frauengeschichte—Geschlechtergeschichte*, edited by Karin Hausen and Heide Wunder, 57–66. Frankfurt am Main, 1992.

Riehl, Wilhelm Heinrich. *Die Naturgeschichte des Volkes als Grundlage einer deutschen Socialpolitik*, vol. 3: Die Familie. Stuttgart, 1855.

———. *Die bürgerliche Gesellschaft*, edited and with an introduction by Peter Steinbach. Frankfurt am Main, 1976.

Roberts, Michal. "Sickles and Scythes: Women's Work and Men's Work at Harvest Time." *History Workshop* 7 (1979): 3–28.

Rohan-Chabot, Alix de. *Les écoles de campagne au XVIIIe siècle*. Nancy, 1985.

Rohrbacher, Stefan. "Organisationsformen der süddeutschen Juden in der Frühneuzeit." In *Jüdische Gemeinden und Organisationsformen von der Antike bis zur Gegenwart*, edited by Robert Jütte and Abraham P. Kustermann, 137–150. Wiesbaden, 1998.

Roper, Lyndal. "'Wille' und 'Ehre': Sexualität, Sprache und Macht in Augsburger Kriminalprozessen." In *Wandel der Geschlechterbeziehungen zu Beginn der Neuzeit*, edited by Heide Wunde and Christina Vanja, 180–197. Frankfurt am Main, 1991.

Rublack, Ulinka. *Magd, Metz' oder Mörderin. Frauen vor frühneuzeitlichen Gerichten*. Frankfurt am Main, 1998.

Rudolph, Richard L. "The European Family and Economy: Central Themes and Issues." *Journal of Family History* 17, no. 2 (1992): 119–138.

Sabean, David W. "Young Bees in an Empty Hive: Relations between Brothers-in-law in a South German Village around 1800." In *Interest and Emotion. Essays on the Study of Family and Kinship*, edited by Hans Medick and David Sabean, 171–186. Cambridge, 1984.

———. *Property, Production, and Family in Neckarhausen. 1700–1870*. Cambridge Studies in Social and Cultural Anthropology 73. Cambridge, 1990.

———. "Soziale Distanzierungen. Ritualisierte Gestik in deutscher bürokratischer Prosa der Frühen Neuzeit." *Historische Anthropologie* 4, no. 2 (1996): 216–233.

———. *Kinship in Neckarhausen, 1700–1870*. Cambridge, 1998.

Sabelleck, Rainer. *Jüdisches Leben in einer nordwestdeutschen Stadt: Nienburg*. Göttingen, 1991.

Sahlins, Marshall. *Historical Metaphors and Mythical Realities: Structure in the Early History of the Sandwich Islands Kingdom*. Ann Arbor, Mich., 1981.

Salmen, Walter. *". . . denn die Fiedel macht das Fest." Jüdische Musikanten und Tänzer vom 13. bis 20. Jahrhundert*. Innsbruck, 1991.

Saurer, Edith. *Straße, Schmuggel, Lottospiel. Materielle Kultur und Staat in Niederösterreich, Böhmen und Lombardo-Venetien im frühen 19. Jahrhundert*. Veröffentlichungen des Max-Plack-Instituts für Geschichte 90. Göttingen, 1989.

———. "Frauen und Priester. Beichtgespräche im frühen 19. Jahrhundert." In *Arbeit, Frömmigkeit und Eigensinn. Studien zur historischen Kulturforschung*, edited by Richard van Dülmen, 141–170. Frankfurt am Main, 1990.

———. "Einleitung." In *Die Religion der Geschlechter. Historische Aspekte religiöser Mentalitäten*, edited by Edith Saurer, 7–14. L'Homme Schriften 1. Vienna, 1995.

Schäfer, Walter Ernst. *Johan Michael Moscherosch: Staatsmann, Satiriker und Pädagoge im Barockzeitalter*. Munich, 1980.

Schiffauer, Heinz. *Die Gewalt der Ehre. Erklärungen zu einem türkisch-deutschen Sexualkonflikt*. Frankfurt am Main, 1983.

Schilling, Heinz. "Die Konfesionalisierung von Kirche, Staat und Gessellschaft—Profil, Leistung, Defizite und Perspektiven eines geschichtswissenschaftlichen Paradigmas." In *Die katholische Konfessionalisierung: wissenschaftliches Symposium der Gesellschaft zur Herausgabe des Corpus Catholicorum und des Vereins für Reformationsgeschichte 1993*, edited by Heinz Schilling and Wolfgang Reinhard, 1–49. Gütersloh, 1995.

Schlieben-Lange, Brigitte. *Traditionen des Sprechens. Elemente einer pragmatischen Sprachgeschichtsschreibung*. Stuttgart, 1983.

———. "Schriftlichkeit und Mündlichkeit in der Französischen Revolution." In *Schrift und Gedächtnis. Archäologie der literarischen Kommunikation*, edited by Aleida Assmann, Jan Assmann, and Christof Hardmeier, vol. 1, 194–212. Munich, 1983.

Schlumbohm, Jürgen. "Familie, Verwandschaft und soziale Ungleichheit: Der Wandel einer ländlichen Gesellschaft vom 17. zum 19. Jahrhundert." In *Frühe Neuzeit—frühe Moderne? Forschungen zur Vielschichtigkeit von Übergangsprozessen*, edited by Rudolf Vierhaus, et al., 133–156. Veröffentlichungen des Max-Planck-Instituts für Geschichte 104. Göttingen, 1992.

———. *Lebensläufe, Familien, Höfe. Die Bauern und Heuerleute des Osnabrückischen Kirchspiels Belm in proto-industrieller Zeit, 1650–1860*. Veröffentlichungen des Max-Planck-Instituts für Geschichte 110. Göttingen, 1994.

Schmale, Wolfgang. "Frankreich und die Erklärung der Menschen- und Bürgerrechte 1789 im Lichte der französischen Forschung—200 Jahre danach." *ZHF* 20 (1993): 345–376.

———. "Vergleichende Analyse der Seigneurie in Burgund und der Grundherrschaft in Kursachsen." In *Gutsherrschaft als soziales Modell. Vergleichende Betrachtungen zur Funktionsweise frühneuzeitlicher Agrargesellschaften*, edited by Jan Peters, 101–125. HZ Beihefte NF 18. Munich, 1995.

Schmidt, Heinrich Richard. *Konfessionelle Institutionalisierung im 16. Jahrhundert*. Munich, 1992.

———. *Dorf und Religion. Reformierte Sittenzucht in Berner Landdgemeinden der Frühen Neuzeit*. Quellen und Forschungen zur Agrargeschichte 41. Stuttgart, 1995.

Schmitt, Johannes. "Französische Saarregion vor der Revolution." In *Revolutionäre Spuren . . . Beiträge der Saarlouiser Geschichtswerkstatt zur Französischen Revolution im Raum Saarlouis*, edited by Johannes Schmitt, 9–54. Saarbrücken, 1991.

Schnyder-Burghartz, Albert. *Alltag und Lebensformen auf der Basler Landschaft um 1700. Vorindustrielle ländliche Kultur und Gesellschaft aus mikrohistorischer Perspektive. Bretzwil und das obere Waldenburger Amt von 1690 bis 1750.* Quellen und Forschungen zur Geschichte und Landeskunde des Kantons Basel-Landschaft 43. Liestal, 1992.

Schorn-Schütte, Luise. "'Gefährtin' und 'Mitregentin.' Zur Sozialgeschichte der evangelischen Pfarrfrau in der Frühen Neuzeit." In *Wandel der Geschlechterbeziehungen zu Beginn der Neuzeit*, edited by Heide Wunder and Christina Vanja, 109–153. Frankfurt am Main, 1991.

"Schreiben aus Wetzlar vom 5. November 1790 betr. den Aufstand in der Grafschaft Kriechingen." *Göttingisches Historisches Magazin* 8 (1791): 399–402.

Schulte, Regina. *The Village in Court. Arson, Infanticide, and Poaching in the Court Records of Upper Bavaria, 1848–1910*, translated by Barrie Selman. Cambridge, 1994.

———. "Bevor das Gerede zum Tratsch wird." In *Frauengeschichte–Geschlechtergeschichte*, edited by Karin Hausen and Heide Wunder, 67–73. Frankfurt am Main, 1992.

Schulze, Winfried. *Bäuerlicher Widestand und feudale Herrschaft in der frühen Neuzeit.* Neuzeit im Aufbau 6. Stuttgart, 1980.

———. *Vom Gemeinnutz zum Eigennutz. Über den Normenwandel in der ständischen Gesellschaft der Frühen Neuzeit.* Schriften des Historischen Kollegs, Vorträge 13. Munich, 1987.

———. "Der Neubeginn der deutschen Geschichtswissenschaft nach 1945: Einsichten und Absichtserklärungen der Historiker nach der Katastrophe." In *Deutsche Geschichtswissenschaft nach dem Zweiten Weltkrieg (1945–1965)*, edited by Ernst Schulin, 1–38. Munich, 1989.

———. "Ego-Dokumente. Annäherungen an den Menschen in der Geschichte?" In *Von Aufbruch und Utopie. Perspektiven einer neuen Gesellschaftsgeschichte des Mittelalters. Für und mit Ferdinand Seibt aus Anlaß seines 65. Geburtstages*, edited by Bea Lundt and Helma Reimöller, 417–450. Cologne, 1992.

Schwab, Dieter. "Familie." In *Geschichtliche Grundbegriffe*, vol. 2, 253–301. Stuttgart, 1975.

Scott, James C. *Domination and the Arts of Resistance: Hidden Transcripts.* Yale, 1990.

Scott, Joan W. "Gender. A Useful Category of Historical Analysis." *American Historical Review* 91 (1986): 1053–1075.

Segalen, Martine. *Love and Power in the Peasant Family. Rural France in the Nineteenth Century*, translated by Sarah Matthews. Chicago, 1983.

———. "Aufgaben und Rollenverteilung bei Männern und Frauen im ländlichen Milieu des 19. und 20. Jahrhunderts: Frankreich und die Gesellschaften des Mittelmeerraums." In *Aufgaben, Rollen und Räume von Frau und Mann*, edited by Jochen Martin and Renate Zoepffel, 915–936. Freiburg/Br., 1989.

———. *Historical Anthropology of the Family*, translated by J. C. Whitehouse and Sarah Matthews. Cambridge, 1986.

Sered, Susan Starr. *Women as Ritual Experts. The Religious Life of Elderly Jewish Women in Jerusalem.* New York, 1992.

———. *Priestess, Mother, Sacred Sister. Religions Dominated by Women.* Oxford, 1994.

Sievers, K. D. "Gastfreundschaft." In *HRG*, vol. 2, cols. 1389–1391. Berlin, 1990.

Simon, Christian. *Untertanenverhalten und obrigkeitliche Moralpolitik. Studien zum Verhältnis zwischen Stadt und Land im ausgehenden 18. Jahrhundert am Beispiel Basels.* Basel, 1981.

Sittel, Johannes Matthias. *Sammlung der Provinzial- und Particular-Gesetze und Verordnungen, welche für einzelne ganz oder nur teilweise an die Krone Preußen gefallene Territorien des linken Rheinufers über Gegenstände der Landeshoheit, Verfassung, Verwaltung, Rechtspflege und des Rechtszustandes erlassen worden*, vol. 2. Trier, 1843.

Stein, Wolfgang Hans. *Untertan—Citoyen—Staatsbürger. Die Auswirkungen der französischen Revolution auf den rheinisch-pfälzischen Raum.* Koblenz, 1981.

————. "Die Einwirkung des französischen Notariats auf die freiwillige Gerichtsbarkeit im Westen des Reiches." In *Tradition und Gegenwart. Festschrift zum 175 jährigen Bestehen des badischen Notarstandes*, edited by Peter Johannes Schuler, 143–150. Karlsruhe, 1981.

————. "Die Archive des Departements Donnersberg. Eine Möglichkeit, die Methoden der französischen Sozialgeschichte für die deutsche Landesgeschichte nutzbar zu machen." In *Vom Alten Reich zu neuer Staatlichkeit. Alzeyer Kolloquium 1979. Kontinuität und Wandel im Gefolge der Französischen Revolution am Mittelrhein*, edited by Alois Gerlich, 152–177. Wiesbaden, 1982.

————. "Französisches Scheidungsrecht im katholischen Rheinland (1798–1803): eine unbemerkte Revolution." In *Palatia Historia. Festschrift für Ludwig Anton Doll zum 75. Geburtstag*, 466–488. Mainz, 1994.

Steinthal, Fritz Leopold. "Fürth." In *Jüdisches Lexikon* II, 852–854. Berlin, 1928.

Stockums, W. *Das Los der ohne die Taufe sterbenden Kinder.* Freiburg, 1923.

Suter, Andreas. *"Troublen" im Fürstbistum Basel (1726–1740). Eine Fallstudie zum bäuerlichen Widerstand im 18. Jahrhundert.* Göttingen, 1985.

————. *Der schweizerische Bauernkrieg von 1653. Politische Sozialgeschichte-Sozialgeschichte eines politischen Ereignisses.* Tübingen, 1997.

Tackett, Timothy. *Priest and Parish in Eighteenth-Century France. A Social and Political Study of the Curés in a Diocese of Dauphiné.* Princeton, 1977.

Die Teutsche Reichsgrafschaft Krichingen von Franzosen mishandelt. Ein historisches Bruchstück, 1793. A.D. Moselle 10 F 77.

Thompson, E. P. *Customs in Common.* New York, 1991.

Touba, Jacques. *Die vormals krieching'schen Dörfer Dentingen, Momersdorf und Niederwiesen.* Forbach, 1908.

————. *Die Kriechinger Unruhen. Aufruhr von 1768.* Forbach, 1911.

Troßbach, Werner. *Soziale Bewegung und politische Erfahrung. Bäuerlicher Protest in hessischen Territorien 1648–1806.* Weingarten, 1987.

————. *Bauern 1648–1806.* Munich, 1993.

————. "Das 'ganze Haus'—Basiskategorie für das Verständnis der ländlichen Gesellschaft deutscher Territorien in der Frühen Neuzeit?" *Blätter für deutsche Landesgeschichte* 129 (1993): 277–314.

————. "'Rebellische Weiber'? Frauen in bäuerlichen Protesten des 18. Jahrhunderts." In *Weiber, Menschen, Frauenzimmer. Frauen in der ländlichen Gesellschaft. 1500–1800*, edited by Heinde Wunder and Christina Vanja, 154–174. Göttingen, 1996.

Tyrell, Hartmann. "Soziologische Anmerkungen zur historischen Familienforschung (Literaturbericht)." GG 12 (1986): 254–273.

Ulbrich, Claudia. *Leibherrschaft am Oberrhein im Spätmittelalter.* Veröffentlichungen des Max-Planck-Instituts für Geschichte 58. Göttingen, 1979.

————. "La ribellione di Inzlingen (1600–1613). Un caso di resistenza contadina nella Germania sud-occidentale." In *Conflitti locali e idiomi politici a cura di Sandro Lombardini, Osvaldo Raggio et Angelo Torre*, 759–776. Quaderni storici 63. 1986.

———— "Traditionale Bindung, revolutionäre Erfahrung und soziokultureller Wandel. Denting 1790–1796." In *Revolution und konservatives Beharren. Das Alte Reich und die Französische Revolution*, edited by Karl Otmar Freiherr von Aretin and Karl Härter, 113–130. Mainz, 1990.

————. "Rheingrenze, Revolten und französische Revolution." In *Die französische Revolution und die Oberrheinlande, 1789–1798*, edited by Volker Rödel, 223 244. Oberrheinische Studien 9. Sigmaringen, 1991.

————. "Die Bedeutung der Grenzen für die Rezeption der französischen Revolution an der Saar." In *Aufklärung, Politisierung und Revolution*, edited by Winfried Schulze, 147–174. Pfaffenweiler, 1991.

————. "L'impact de la Révolution française dans le comté de Créhange, pays enclavé en Lorraine." In *Révolution Française 1988–1989. Actes des 113e et 114e congrès nationaux des soc. sav.*, 425–435. Paris, 1991.

————. "Frauen und Kleriker." In *Von Aufbruch und Utopie. Perspektiven einer neuen Gesellschaftsgeschichte des Mittelalters. Für und mit Ferdinand Seibt aus Anlaß seines 65. Geburtstages*, edited by Bea Lundt and Helma Reimöller, 155–177. Cologne, 1992.

————. "Grenze als Chance? Bemerkungen zur Bedeutung der Reichsgrenze im Saar-Lor-Lux-Raum am Vorabend der Französischen Revolution." In *Grenzöffnung, Migration, Kriminalität*, edited by Arno Pilgram, 139–146. Baden-Baden, 1993.

————. "Weibliche Delinquenz im 18. Jahrhundert. Eine dörfliche Fallstudie." In *Von Huren und Rabenmüttern. Weibliche Kriminalität in der Frühen Neuzeit*, edited by Otto Ulbricht, 281–311. Cologne, 1995.

————. "Die Jungfrau in der Flasche. Ländlicher Traditionalismus in Deutschlothringen während der Französischen Revolution." *Historische Anthropologie* 3, no. 1 (1995): 125–143.

————. "Überlegungen zur Erforschung von Geschlechterrollen in der ländlichen Gesellschaft." In *Gutsherrschaft als soziales Modell. Vergleichende Betrachtungen zur Funktionsweise frühneuzeitlicher Agrargesellschaften*, edited by Jan Peters, 359–364. H. Beihefte NF 18. Munich, 1995.

————. "Saufen und Raufen in Steinbiedersdorf. Ein Beitrag zur Erforschung häuslicher Gewalt in der ländlichen Gesellschaft des 18. Jahrhunderts." *HMRG* 8, no. 1 (1995): 28–42.

————. "Zeuginnen und Bittstellerinnen. Überlegungen zur Bedeutung von Ego-Dokumenten für die Erforschung weiblicher Selbstwahrnehmung in der ländlichen Gesellschaft des 18. Jahrhunderts." In *Ego-Dokumente. Annäherungen an den Menschen in der Geschichte*, edited by Winfried Schulze, 207–225. Selbstzeugnisse der Neuzeit 2. Berlin, 1996.

————. "Frauen im Aufstand. Möglichkeiten und Grenzen ihrer Partizipation in frühneuzeitlichen Bauernbewegungen." In *Schlaglichter Preußen—Westeuropa. Festschrift für Ilja Mieck zum 65. Geburtstag*, edited by Ursula Fuhrich-Grubert and Angelus H. Johansen, 335–348. Berlin, 1997.

————. "Zankapfel 'Weibergestühl.'" In *Historie und Eigen-Sinn. Festschrift für Jan Peters zum 65. Geburtstag*, edited by Axel Lubinski, Thomas Rudert, and Martina Schattkowsky, 107–114. Weimar, 1997.

Ulbricht, Otto. "Zwischen Vergeltung und Zukunftsplanung. Hausdiebstahl von Mägden in Schleswig-Holstein vom 16. bis zum 19. Jahrhundert." In *Von Huren und Rabenmüttern. Weibliche Kriminalität in der Frühen Neuzeit*, edited by Otto Ulbricht, 139–170. Cologne, 1995.

————. "Criminality and Punishment of the Jews in the Early Modern Period." In *In and Out of the Ghetto. Jewish-Gentile Relations in Late Medieval and Early Modern Germany*, edited by R. Po-chia Hsia and Haartmut Lehmann, 49–70. Cambridge, 1995.

————, ed. *Von Huren und Rabenmüttern. Weibliche Kriminalität in der Frühen Neuzeit.* Cologne, 1995.

Vartier, Jean. *La vie quotidienne en Lorraine au XIXe siècle.* Paris, 1973.

Veblen, Thorstein. *The Theory of the Leisure Class.* New York, 1899.

Vierhaus, Rudolf. "Die Rekonstruktion historischer Lebenswelten. Probleme moderner Kulturgeschichtsschreibung." In *Wege zu einer neuen Kulturgeschichte*, edited by Harmut Lehmann, 7–28. Göttinger Gespräche zur Geschichtswissenschaft 1. Göttingen, 1995.

Vogel, Barbara and Ulrike Weckel. "Vorwort." In *Frauen in der Ständegesellschaft. Leben und Arbeiten in der Stadt vom späten Mittelalter bis zur Neuzeit*, edited by Barbara Vogel and Ulrike Weckel, 7–26. Hamburg, 1991.

de Vries, Simon Ph. *Jüdische Riten und Symbole.* Hamburg, 1990. Originally published in Dutch, Amsterdam, 1927.

Wachstein, Bernhard. "Das Statut der jüdischen Bevölkerung der Grafschaft Wied Runkel (Pinkas Runkel)." *Zeitschrift für die Geschichte der Juden in Deutschland* 4 (1932): 129–149.

Walz, Rainer. "Der nahe Fremde. Die Beziehungen zwischen Christen und Juden in der Frühen Neuzeit." In *Fremdsein—Historische Erfahrungen,* edited by Paul Münch, 54–63. Essen, 1995.

Weber, Marianne. *Ehefrau und Mutter in der Rechtsentwicklung. Eine Einführung.* Tübingen, 1907 (reprint, Aaalen, 1989).

Wehler, Hans-Ulrich. *Deutsche Gesellschaftsgeschichte, Bd, 1: Vom Feudalismus des alten Reiches bis zur defensiven Modernisierung der Reformära: 1700–1815.* Munich, 1987.

———. "Alltagsgeschichte: Königsweg zu neuen Ufern oder Irrgarten der Illusionen?." In *Aus der Geschichte lernen?,* edited by Hans-Ulrich Wehler, 130–151. Munich, 1988.

———. "Was ist Gesellschaftsgeschichte?" In Hans-Ulrich Wehler, *Aus der Geschichte lernen?,* 115–129. Munich, 1988.

Weigel, Sigrid. "Frauen und Juden in Konstellationen der Modernisierung— Vorstellungen und Verkörperungen des 'internen Anderen.' Ein Forschungsprogramm." In *Jüdische Kultur und Weiblichkeit in der Moderne,* edited by Inge Stephan, Sabine Schilling, and Sigrid Weigel, 333–351. Cologne, 1994.

Weisgerber, Gerd. "Widerspenstige Untertanen." *Quellen und Beiträge zur Geschichte des Dorfes und der Herrschaft Saarwellingen* 17 (1970): 1–4; 18 (1970): 1–4.

Weissler, Chava. "The Religion of Traditional Ashkenazic Women. Some Methodological Issues." *Association for Jewish Studies Review* 12 (1987): 73–94.

———. "Mitzvot Built into the Body: Tkhines for Niddah, Pregnancy, and Childbirth." In *People of the Body. Jews and Judaism from an Embodied Perspective,* edited by Howard Eilberg-Schwartz, 101–115. Albany, 1992.

Weitzel, Jürgen. *Der Kampf um die Appellation am Reichskammergericht. Zur politischen Geschichte der Rechtsmittel in Deutschland.* Cologne, 1976.

Welsch, Wolfgang. *Unsere postmoderne Moderne,* 3rd ed. Weinheim, 1991.

Werner, G. "Prozeßparteien." *HRG,* vol. 4: 62–66. Berlin, 1990.

West, Candace and Don H. Zimmerman. "Doing Gender." In *The Social Construction of Gender,* edited by Judith Lorber and Susan A. Farell, 13–37. Newbury Park, Calif., 1991.

Westphalen, R. de. *Petit Dictionnaire des traditions populaires messines.* Metz, 1934.

Wiegelmann, Günter. "Bäuerliche Arbeitsteilung in Mittel- und Nordeuropa." *Ethnologia Scandinavica* 1 (1975): 5–22.

Wiesemann, Falk, ed. *Genizah–Hidden Legacies of the German Village Jews. Genisa–Verborgenes Erbe der deutschen Landjuden. Ausstellungskatalog.* Munich, 1992.

Wiesner, Merry E. *Women and Gender in Early Modern Europe.* Cambridge, 1993.

———. "The Midwives of South Germany and the Public/Private Dichotomy." In *The Art of Midwifery. Early Modern Midwives in Europe,* edited by Hilary Marland, 77–94. London, 1993.

Wilmin, Henri. *Forbach. La ville et le canton pendant le Révolution française. 1789–1799.* Forbach, 1980.

Wohlhaupter, Eugen. *Die Kerze im Recht.* Forschungen zum deutschen Recht 4.1. Weimar, 1940.

Wolff, Siegfried. "Parnass." *Jüdisches Lexikon* IV/1: 821. Berlin, 1928.

Wrightson, Keith. *English Society, 1580–1680.* London, 1982.

Wülfing, Wulf. "Die heilige Luise von Preußen. Zur Mythisierung einer Figur der Geschichte in der deutschen Literatur des 19. Jahrhunderts." In *Bewegung und Stillstand in Metaphern und Mythen. Fallstudien zum Verhältnis von elementarem Wissen und*

Literatur im 19. Jahrhundert, edited by Jürgen Link and Wulf Wülfing, 233–275. Stuttgart, 1984.

Wunder, Heide. "Zur Stellung der Frau im Arbeitsleben und in der Gesellschaft des 15.–18. Jahrhunderts. Eine Skizze." *Geschichtsdidaktik* 3 (1981): 239–251.

———. "Einleitung." In *Wandel der Geschlechterbeziehungen zu Beginn der Neuzeit*, edited by Heide Wunder and Christina Vanja, 7–11. Frankfurt am Main, 1991.

———. "'Jede Arbeit ist ihres Lohnes wert.' Zur geschlechtsspezifischen Teilung und Bewertung von Arbeit in der Frühen Neuzeit." In *Geschlechterhierarchie und Arbeitsteilung. Zur Geschichte ungleicher Erwerbschancen von Männern und Frauen*, edited by Karin Hausen, 19–39. Göttingen, 1993.

———. "*He is the Sun, She is the Moon.*" *Women in Early Modern Germany*. Translated by Thomas Dunlap. Cambridge, Mass., 1998.

——— and Christina Vanja, eds. *Weiber, Menscher, Frauenzimmer. Frauen in der ländlichen Gesellschaft, 1500–1800*. Göttingen, 1996.

———. "Herrschaft und öffentliches Handeln von Frauen in der Gesellschaft der Frühen Neuzeit." In *Frauen in der Geschichte des Rechts. Von der Frühen Neuzeit bis zur Gegenwart*, edited by Ute Gerhard, 27–54. Munich, 1997.

Zedler, Johann Heinrich. *Universallexikon*, 64 vols. Halle, 1739–1750, reprint (Graz, 1961–1969).

Zeller, Gaston, "Note sur le rôle ancien de la Sarre comme frontière." *Bulletin de la société des amis des pays de la Sarre* (1928): 257–260.

Zimmermann, Clemens. *Reformen in der bäuerlichen Gesellschaft. Studien zum aufgeklärten Absolutismus in der Markgrafschaft Baden 1750–1790*. Ostfildern, 1983.

Zink, Anne. "L'indifférence à la différence: les forains dans la France du Sud-Ouest." *Annales* 43, no. 1 (1988): 149–172.

———. *L'Héritier de la maison. Géographie coutumière du Sud-Ouest de la France sous l'Ancien Régime*. Civilisations et Sociétés 87. Paris, 1993.

Zolty, Shoshona Pantel. "*And All Your Children Shall Be Learned.*" *Women and the Study of Torah in Jewish Law and History*. Northvale, 1993.

Zunkel, Friedrich. "Ehre, Reputation." In *Geschichtliche Grundbegriffe*, vol. 2: 1–64. Stuttgart, 1975.

INDEX OF SUBJECTS

INDEX OF AUTHORS